SOMETHING ABOUT THE AUTHOR®

Something about
the Author *was named
an "Outstanding
Reference Source,"*
*the highest honor given
by the American
Library Association
Reference and Adult
Services Division.*

ISSN 0276-816X

something
ABOUT THE
AUThOR®

Facts and Pictures about Authors
and Illustrators of Books for Young People

volume 167

THOMSON

GALE

Detroit • New York • San Francisco • San Diego • New Haven, Conn. • Waterville, Maine • London • Munich

Something About the Author, Volume 167

Project Editor
Lisa Kumar

Editorial
Michelle Kazensky, Joshua Kondek, Tracey Matthews, Julie Mellors, Mary Ruby, Mark Rzeszutek

Permissions
Ronald D. Montgomery, Shalice Shah-Caldwell, Andrew Specht

Imaging and Multimedia
Leitha Etheridge-Sims, Lezlie Light

Composition and Electronic Capture
Carolyn Roney

Manufacturing
Drew Kalasky

Product Manager
Chris Nasso

LIBRARY OF CONGRESS CATALOG CARD NUMBER 62-52046

ISBN 0-7876-8791-X
ISSN 0276-816X

This title is also available as an e-book.
ISBN 1-4144-1068-9
Contact your Thomson Gale sales representative for ordering information.

Printed in the United States of America
10 9 8 7 6 5 4 3 2 1

Contents

Authors in Forthcoming Volumes

Below are some of the authors and illustrators that will be featured in upcoming volumes of SATA. These include new entries on the swiftly rising stars of the field, as well as completely revised and updated entries (indicated with *) on some of the most notable and best-loved creators of books for children.

Patricia Bow ▮ Beginning her career as a librarian, Bow started a second career as a writer while raising her son, and her mystery and fantasy novels are now published in both North America and Germany. Her nonfiction work for younger readers includes *Chimpanzee Rescue,* which describes chimps and their struggle as an endangered species. More imaginative fare is served up in *The Bone Flute,* a dark fantasy that recalls the folk tales of Old Europe due to its primitive woodland setting.

*Joanna Cole ▮ Best known for her "Magic School Bus" books, Cole is also the author of a variety of other works for children, including beginning readers, humorous chapter books, adaptations of folk tales and myths, and science-based nonfiction. The winner of numerous awards, Cole inspires readers to share her diverse interests, which range from the life cycles of animals and insects to favorite playground games. Under the guidance of her fictional alter-ego, the equally curious Miss Frizzle, in her popular series Cole invites readers to board her Magic School Bus, an amazing vehicle through which she introduces them to the fascinating world of science while also spinning an engaging story.

Sylviane A. Diouf ▮ Diouf has lived in France, Senegal, Gabon, Italy, and the United States, and she has worked as a journalist as well as a writer. While much of her writing is scholarly in nature, in her books for children she reveals how the culture and history of Africa are relevant to today's young students. In addition to her other nonfiction books such as *Growing up in Crawfish Country: A Cajun Childhood,* Diouf's picture book *Bintou's Braids* focuses on a young girl living in an African village and shows that children around the world share the same desire to grow up quickly.

*Virginia Kroll ▮ With dozens of picture books and hundreds of articles to her credit, Kroll is a versatile and prolific writer; in fact, she is so prolific that she adopted two pen names to differentiate her work. Often broaching inconventional subjects, books such as *Masai and I, Woodhoopoe Willie,* and *Faraway Drums* focus on the lives of African-American children, while in *A Carp for Kimiko* Kroll introduces readers to a Japanese girl who longs to have the advantages of her older brother on a special children's holiday. Writing under the pseudonym Melrose Cooper, Kroll has also penned inspirational stories of family life and overcoming the effects of illness.

Meghan McCarthy ▮ A graduate of the Rhode Island School of Design, Meghan McCarthy has made her mark on children's literature via her fanciful stories and her unique cartoon-style artwork.

The picture books *George Upside Down* and *The Adventures of Patty and the Big Red Bus* focus on the power of a child's imagination, while in other books McCarthy brings to light lesser-known aspects of American cultural history through an entertaining text and her characteristic google-eyed characters.

Takayo Noda ▮ Born in Japan, Noda moved to New York City in the late 1980s, and her intricate, colored-paper collage art has since found a perfect home in the picture-book medium. Praised for their multidimensional effect, Noda's illustrations are balanced by her simple evocative poems, and the two elements combine in books that have been praised for their sensitivity and sense of joy. Her best-known work, *Dear World,* explores the beauty and joy of a child's world, while lush collage gardens spill off the pages of *Song of the Flowers,* which also features lullabies composed of Noda's short, thoughtful verse.

*Marjorie Priceman ▮ While she has created art for the texts of numerous other writers since the late 1980s, Priceman is quick to admit that illustrating someone else's story is not nearly as fun as illustrating one's own. Many readers have become fans of her self-authored picture books, which include the cat-authored *My Nine Lives: by Clio* and *Princess Picky.* Combining an intelligent, sometimes dry, but always contagious humor with an energetic drawing style, Priceman consistently wins over critics, parents, and readers alike.

*Darren Shan ▮ Shan is the pseudonymous author of the popular "Saga of Darren Shan," a series of young-adult horror novels. Including *The Vampire's Assistant, Tunnels of Blood,* and *Allies of the Night,* the twelve-volume series follows the fictional Shan as he unwittingly becomes a vampire's assistant forced to constantly seek out and battle the most unwholesome among the undead. The imaginative Irish writer is also responsible for the "Demonata" books, which feature Grubbs Grady and his ongoing battle with demonic entities. Armed with a book by Shan, such as *Lord Loss,* in which Grubbs discovers that his parents have met an unpleasant end at the hands of demons, the most mild-mannered teachers or librarians are sure to win over reluctant readers.

EdNah New Rider Weber ▮ Weber, a member of the Pawnee Nation, recalls her experiences growing up as a Native American during the early 1900s in her autobiographical *Rattlesnake Mesa: Stories from a Native American Childhood.* Featuring photographs of modern-day reservation life by Richela Renkun, the memoir follows seven-year-old Weber as she has a blissful summer at the Crown Point Indian Reservation in New Mexico before encountering the harsh environment of a government-run Indian boarding school. Despite strict discipline and a measure of adversity, Weber's optimism makes her story a compelling one for modern readers.

Dar Williams ▮ Since releasing her first album, *The Honesty Room,* in 1993, Williams has become well known as a singer/songwriter and acoustic performer. In 2004, the musician found a new outlet for her storytelling skill, publishing the well-received middle-grade novel *Amalee*. A sixth grader living with her single dad, Amalee learns about friendship and character when her dad falls ill and the ragtag friends the girl has often found annoying step in to care for the family. In addition to her writing, which includes more books about Amalee, Williams has shared the musical stage with such artists as Sara McLachlan, Pete Seeger, and the Indigo Girls.

Introduction

Something about the Author (*SATA*) is an ongoing reference series that examines the lives and works of authors and illustrators of books for children. *SATA* includes not only well-known writers and artists but also less prominent individuals whose works are just coming to be recognized. This series is often the only readily available information source on emerging authors and illustrators. You'll find *SATA* informative and entertaining, whether you are a student, a librarian, an English teacher, a parent, or simply an adult who enjoys children's literature.

What's Inside *SATA*

SATA provides detailed information about authors and illustrators who span the full time range of children's literature, from early figures like John Newbery and L. Frank Baum to contemporary figures like Judy Blume and Richard Peck. Authors in the series represent primarily English-speaking countries, particularly the United States, Canada, and the United Kingdom. Also included, however, are authors from around the world whose works are available in English translation. The writings represented in *SATA* include those created intentionally for children and young adults as well as those written for a general audience and known to interest younger readers. These writings cover the entire spectrum of children's literature, including picture books, humor, folk and fairy tales, animal stories, mystery and adventure, science fiction and fantasy, historical fiction, poetry and nonsense verse, drama, biography, and nonfiction. Obituaries are also included in *SATA* and are intended not only as death notices but also as concise overviews of people's lives and work. Additionally, each edition features newly revised and updated entries for a selection of *SATA* listees who remain of interest to today's readers and who have been active enough to require extensive revisions of their earlier biographies.

Autobiography Feature

Beginning with Volume 103, many volumes of *SATA* feature one or more specially commissioned autobiographical essays in each volume. These unique essays, averaging about ten thousand words in length and illustrated with an abundance of personal photos, present an entertaining and informative first-person perspective on the lives and careers of prominent authors and illustrators profiled in *SATA*.

Two Convenient Indexes

In response to suggestions from librarians, *SATA* indexes no longer appear in every volume but are included in alternate (odd-numbered) volumes of the series, beginning with Volume 57.

SATA continues to include two indexes that cumulate with each alternate volume: the Illustrations Index, arranged by the name of the illustrator, gives the number of the volume and page where the illustrator's work appears in the current volume as well as all preceding volumes in the series; the Author Index gives the number of the volume in which a person's biographical sketch, autobiographical essay, or obituary appears in the current volume as well as all preceding volumes in the series.

These indexes also include references to authors and illustrators who appear in *Gale's Yesterday's Authors of Books for Children*, *Children's Literature Review*, and *Something about the Author Autobiography Series*.

Easy-to-Use Entry Format

Whether you're already familiar with the *SATA* series or just getting acquainted, you will want to be aware of the kind of information that an entry provides. In every *SATA* entry the editors attempt to give as complete a picture of the person's life and work as possible. A typical entry in *SATA* includes the following clearly labeled information sections:

PERSONAL: date and place of birth and death, parents' names and occupations, name of spouse, date of marriage, names of children, educational institutions attended, degrees received, religious and political affiliations, hobbies and other interests.

ADDRESSES: complete home, office, electronic mail, and agent addresses, whenever available.

CAREER: name of employer, position, and dates for each career post; art exhibitions; military service; memberships and offices held in professional and civic organizations.

MEMBER: professional, civic, and other association memberships and any official posts held.

AWARDS, HONORS: literary and professional awards received.

WRITINGS: title-by-title chronological bibliography of books written and/or illustrated, listed by genre when known; lists of other notable publications, such as plays, screenplays, and periodical contributions.

ADAPTATIONS: a list of films, television programs, plays, CD-ROMs, recordings, and other media presentations that have been adapted from the author's work.

WORK IN PROGRESS: description of projects in progress.

SIDELIGHTS: a biographical portrait of the author or illustrator's development, either directly from the biographee—and often written specifically for the *SATA* entry—or gathered from diaries, letters, interviews, or other published sources.

BIOGRAPHICAL AND CRITICAL SOURCES: cites sources quoted in "Sidelights" along with references for further reading.

EXTENSIVE ILLUSTRATIONS: photographs, movie stills, book illustrations, and other interesting visual materials supplement the text.

How a *SATA* Entry Is Compiled

A *SATA* entry progresses through a series of steps. If the biographee is living, the *SATA* editors try to secure information directly from him or her through a questionnaire. From the information that the biographee supplies, the editors prepare an entry, filling in any essential missing details with research and/or telephone interviews. If possible, the author or illustrator is sent a copy of the entry to check for accuracy and completeness.

If the biographee is deceased or cannot be reached by questionnaire, the *SATA* editors examine a wide variety of published sources to gather information for an entry. Biographical and bibliographic sources are consulted, as are book reviews, feature articles, published interviews, and material sometimes obtained from the biographee's family, publishers, agent, or other associates.

Entries that have not been verified by the biographees or their representatives are marked with an asterisk (*).

Contact the Editor

We encourage our readers to examine the entire *SATA* series. Please write and tell us if we can make *SATA* even more helpful to you. Give your comments and suggestions to the editor:

Editor
Something about the Author
Thomson Gale
27500 Drake Rd.
Farmington Hills MI 48331-3535

Toll-free: 800-877-GALE
Fax: 248-699-8070

Something about the Author Product Advisory Board

The editors of *Something about the Author* are dedicated to maintaining a high standard of excellence by publishing comprehensive, accurate, and highly readable entries on a wide array of writers for children and young adults. In addition to the quality of the content, the editors take pride in the graphic design of the series, which is intended to be orderly yet inviting, allowing readers to utilize the pages of *SATA* easily and with efficiency. Despite the longevity of the *SATA* print series, and the success of its format, we are mindful that the vitality of a literary reference product is dependent on its ability to serve its users over time. As literature, and attitudes about literature, constantly evolve, so do the reference needs of students, teachers, scholars, journalists, researchers, and book club members. To be certain that we continue to keep pace with the expectations of our customers, the editors of *SATA* listen carefully to their comments regarding the value, utility, and quality of the series. Librarians, who have firsthand knowledge of the needs of library users, are a valuable resource for us. The *Something about the Author* Product Advisory Board, made up of school, public, and academic librarians, is a forum to promote focused feedback about *SATA* on a regular basis. The nine-member advisory board includes the following individuals, whom the editors wish to thank for sharing their expertise:

Eva M. Davis
Youth Department Manager,
Ann Arbor District Library,
Ann Arbor, Michigan

Joan B. Eisenberg
Lower School Librarian,
Milton Academy,
Milton, Massachusetts

Francisca Goldsmith
Teen Services Librarian,
Berkeley Public Library,
Berkeley, California

Susan Dove Lempke
Children's Services Supervisor,
Niles Public Library District,
Niles, Illinois

Robyn Lupa
Head of Children's Services,
Jefferson County Public Library,
Lakewood, Colorado

Victor L. Schill
Assistant Branch Librarian/Children's Librarian,
Harris County Public Library/Fairbanks Branch,
Houston, Texas

Caryn Sipos
Community Librarian,
Three Creeks Community Library,
Vancouver, Washington

Steven Weiner
Director,
Maynard Public Library,
Maynard, Massachusetts

Acknowledgments

Grateful acknowledgment is made to the following publishers, authors, and artists whose works appear in this volume.

ALLABY, MICHAEL ▮ Allaby, Michael, photograph. Photo courtesy of Michael Allaby.

ANDREWS, JAN ▮ Wallace, Ian, illustrator. From an illustration in *Very Last First Time,* by Jan Andrews. Illustrations copyright © 1985 by Ian Wallace. Groundwood Books Ltd., 1985. Reproduced by permission. / Young, Cybele, illustrator. From an illustration in *Pa's Harvest,* by Jan Andrews. Groundwood Books Ltd., 2000. Illustrations copyright © 2000 by Cybele Young. Reproduced by permission. / Ng, Simon, illustrator. From an illustration in *Out of the Everywhere: Tales for a New World,* by Jan Andrews. Groundwood Books Ltd., 2000. Illustrations copyright © 2000 by Simon Ng. Reproduced by permission. / Andrews, Jan, photograph. Photo courtesy of Jan Andrews.

BALDRY, CHERITH ▮ Wyatt, David, illustrator. From an illustration in *The Lake of Darkness,* by Cherith Baldry. Mondo Publishing, 2001. Illustrations copyright © 2001 by David Wyatt. Reproduced by permission, courtesy of Sarah Brown Agency.

BAUER, MICHAEL GERARD ▮ Bauer, Michael Gerard, photograph. Photo courtesy of Michael Gerard Bauer.

BLEDSOE, KAREN ▮ From an illustration in *The World's Fastest Dragsters,* by Karen Bledsoe. Capstone High-Interest Books, 2003. Photo copyright © Corbis/AFP.

BROWNE, N.M. ▮ LaRuse, Jenna, cover designer. From a cover of *Warriors of Alavna,* by N.M. Browne. Bloomsbury USA Children's Books, 2002. Reproduced by permission. / Browne, N.M., photograph. Photo by Paul Tennant. Courtesy of N.M. Browne.

BURGAN, MICHAEL ▮ Schulz, Barbara, illustrator. From a cover of *The Curse of King Tut's Tomb,* by Michael Burgan. Capstone Press, 2005. Reproduced by permission.

EATON, ANTHONY ▮ Danalis, Johnny, illustrator. From a cover of *The Girl in the Cave,* by Anthony Eaton. University of Queensland Press, 2004. Reproduced by permission.

FARRER, VASHTI ▮ Curtis, Neil, illustrator. From an illustration in *Mr Noah and the Cats,* by Vashti Farrer. Thomas C. Lothian Pty Ltd, 2004. Illustration copyright © Neil Curtis 2004. Reproduced by permission. / Farrer, Vashti, photograph. Photo courtesy of Vashti Farrer.

FELL, DEREK ▮ From an illustration in *Cézanne's Garden,* by Derek Fell. Simon & Schuster, 2003. Copyright © 2003 by Derek Fell. Reprinted with the permission of Simon & Schuster Adult Publishing Group. / Fell, Derek, photograph. Photo courtesy of Derek Fell.

FOX, PAULA ▮ Waldman, Neil, illustrator. From a jacket of *One-Eyed Cat,* by Paula Fox. Jacket painting copyright © 1984 Simon & Schuster, Inc. Reprinted with the permission of Atheneum Books for Young Readers, an imprint of Simon & Schuster Children's Publishing Division. / Hamanaka, Sheila, illustrator. From a jacket of *The Village by the Sea,* by Paula Fox. Orchard Books, 1988. Jacket painting © 1988 by Sheila Hamanaka. Reprinted by permission of Orchard books, an imprint of Scholastic Inc. / Popp, Wendy, illustrator. From a cover of *The Slave Dancer,* by Paula Fox. Yearling Books, 1991. Used by permission of Dell Publishing, a division of Random House, Inc. / From a cover of *Borrowed Finery,* by Paula Fox. © 2002 by Henry Holt and Company. Reprinted by permission of Henry Holt and Company, LLC.

GRANSTRÖM, BRITA ▮ Granström, Brita, illustrator. From an illustration in *A Chick Called Saturday,* by Brita Granström. Eerdmans Books for Young Readers, 2003. Illustrations copyright © Brita Granström 2003. Reproduced by permission.

GUEVARA, SUSAN ▮ Guevara, Susan, illustrator. From an illustration in *Chato and the Party Animals,* by Gary Sota. G. P. Putnam's Sons, 2000. Illustrations copyright © Susan Guevara, 2000. All rights reserved. Used by permission of G. P. Putnam's Sons, a division of Penguin Young Readers Group, a member of Penguin Group (USA) Inc., 345 Hudson Street, New York, NY 10014. / Guevara, Susan, illustrator. From a book illustration in *Tiger, Tiger,* by Dee Lillegard. G. P. Putnam's Sons, 2002. Illustrations copyright © 2002 by Susan Guevara. All rights reserved. Used by permission of G. P. Putnam's Sons, a division of Penguin Young Readers Group, a member of Penguin Group (USA) Inc., 345 Hudson Street, New York, NY 10014.

HAND, ELIZABETH ▮ From a jacket of *Mortal Love,* by Elizabeth Hand. William Morrow, 2004. Copyright © 2004 by Elizabeth Hand. Cover painting © by Erich Lessing/Art Resource, NY. Reproduced by permission of HarperCollins Publishers, and Art Resource, NY.

HEUSTON, KIMBERLEY ▮ Botticelli, Sandro, "Dante". From a jacket of *Dante's Daughter,* by Kimberley Heuston. Photograph by Eric Baden. Front Street, 2003. Cover photograph copyright © 2000 by Eric Baden. Reprinted with the permission of Boyds Mills Press, Inc.

HODGES, MARGARET MOORE ▮ Hyman, Trina Schart, illustrator. From an illustration in *Saint George and the Dragon,* by Margaret Hodges. Little, Brown, and Company, 1984. Text copyright © 1984 by Margaret Hodges. Illustrations copyright © 1984 by Trina Schart Hyman. By permission of Little, Brown and Company, Inc. All rights reserved. To purchase copies of this book, please call 1.800.759.0190 / Rayevsky, Robert, illustrator. From an illustration in *Joan of Arc: The Lily Maid,* by Margaret Hodges. Holiday House, 1999. Illustrations copyright © 1999 by Robert Rayevsky. Reproduced by permission. / Sogabe, Ari, illustrator. From an illustration in *The Boy Who Drew Cats,* by Margaret Hodges. Holiday House, 2002. Illustrations copyright © 2002 by Aki Sogabe. Reproduced by permission. / Hyman, Trina Schart, illustrator. From an illustration in *Merlin and the Making of the King,* by Margaret Hodges. Holiday Menus, 2004. Illustrations copyright © 2004 by Trina Schart Hyman. Reproduced by permission.

HORNIMAN, JOANNE ▮ From a cover of *A Charm of Powerful Trouble,* by Joanne Horniman. Allen & Unwin, 2002. Cover photograph by The Photo Library. Reproduced by permission of Allen & Unwin, www.allenandunwin.com.au., and Photo Researchers, Inc. / O'Rourke, Ericka, cover artist. From a book cover of *Mahalia,* by Joanne Horniman. Alfred A. Knopf, 2003. Cover illustration copyright © 2003 by Ericka O'Rourke. Used by permission of Random House Children's Books, a division of Random House, Inc.

HRDLITSCHKA, SHELLEY ▮ From a cover of *Dancing Naked,* by Shelley Hrdlitschka. Orca Book Publishers, 2001. Cover photograph by Digital Vision. Image copyright © Digital Vision. Reproduced by permission. / Robertson, Christy, illustrator. From a cover of *Kat's Fall,* by Shelley Hrdlitschka. Orca Book Publishers, 2004. Reproduced by permission. / From a cover of *Sun Signs,* by Shelley Hrdlitschka. Orca Book Publishers, 2005. Reproduced by permission. / Hrdlitschka, Shelley, photograph. Photo courtesy of Shelley Hrdlitschka.

INGRAM, SCOTT ▮ From an illustration in *The Song Dynasty,* by Scott Ingram. Blackbirch Press, 2003. Photograph copyright © The Art Archive/Freer Gallery of Art. Reproduced by permission. / From an illustration in *Nicolaus Copernicus,* by Scott Ingram. Blackbirch Press, 2004. Photograph copyright © Erich Lessing/ Art Resource, NY. Reproduced by permission.

JACKSON, ELLEN B. ▮ Faulkner, Matt, illustrator. From an illustration in *Scatterbrain Sam,* by Ellen Jackson. Whispering Coyote, 2001. Text copyright © 2001 by Ellen Jackson. Illustrations copyright © 2001 by Matt Faulkner. All rights reserved. Used by permission of Charlesbridge Publishing, Inc. / Dillon, Leo & Diane, illustrators. From a book illustration in *Earth Mother,* by Ellen Jackson. Walker Publishing Company, 2005. Illustrations copyright © 2005 by Leo and Diane Dillon. Reproduced by permission.

KAY, GUY GAVRIEL ▮ Odem, Mel, illustrator. From a cover of *The Lions of Al-Rassan,* by Guy Gavriel Kay. EOS, an imprint of HarperCollins Publishers, 2000. Copyright © 1995 by Guy Gavriel Kay. Reprinted by permission of HarperCollins Publishers. / Birdsong, Keith, illustrator. From a cover of *Sailing to Sarantium,* by Guy Gavriel Kay. EOS, an imprint of HarperCollins Publishers, 2000. Copyright © 1998 by Guy Gavriel Kay. Illustration copyright © 1998 by Keith Birdsong. Reprinted by permission of HarperCollins Publishers. / From a cover of *Lord of Emperors,* by Guy Gavriel Kay. EOS, an imprint of HarperCollins Publishers, 2000. Copyright © 2000 by Guy Gavriel Kay. Reprinted by permission of HarperCollins Publishers. / Odem, Mel, illustrator. From a cover of *The Last Light of the Sun,* by Guy Gavriel Kay. Copyright © 2004 by Guy Gavriel Kay. ROC, New American Library, a division of Penguin Group (USA), 2004. Used by permission of Dutton Signet, a division of Penguin Group (USA) Inc.

KETTEMAN, HELEN ▮ Shed, Greg, illustrator. From an illustration in *I Remember Papa,* by Helen Ketteman. Dial Books for Young Readers, a division of Penguin Putnam Inc., 1998. Illustrations copyright © 1998 by Greg Shed. All rights reserved. Used by permission of Dial Books for Young Readers, a division of Penguin Young Readers Group, a member of Penguin Group (USA) Inc., 345 Hudson Street, New York, NY 10014. / Graves, Keith, illustrator. From an illustration in *Armadillo Tattletale,* by Helen Ketteman. Scholastic Press, 2000. Illustration copyright © 2000 by Keith Graves. Reprinted by permission of Scholastic Inc. / Col-

lins, Matt, illustrator. From an illustration in *The Great Cake Bake,* by Helen Ketteman. Walker & Company, 2005. Illustrations copyright © 2005 by Matt Collins. Reproduced by permission.

KINSEY-WARNOCK, NATALIE ▮ Yamasaki, James, illustrator. From a cover of *If Wishes Were Horses,* by Natalie Kinsey-Warnock. Dutton Children's Books, 2000. Copyright © 2000 by Natalie Kinsey-Warnock. All rights reserved. Used by permission of Dutton Children's Books, a division of Penguin Young Readers Group, a member of Penguin Group (USA) Inc., 345 Hudson Street, New York, NY 10014. / Bernardin, James, illustrator. From an illustration in *Lumber Camp Library,* by Natalie Kinsey-Warnock. Harper Trophy, an imprint of HarperCollins Publishers, 2003. Illustrations copyright © 2002 by James Bernardin. Used by permission of HarperCollins Publishers. / Azarian, Mary, illustrator. From an illustration in *From Dawn till Dusk,* by Natalie Kinsey-Warnock. Houghton Mifflin Company, 2002. Illustration copyright © 2002 by Mary Azarian. Reproduced by permission. / McCully, Emily Arnold, illustrator. From an illustration in *Nora's Ark,* by Natalie Kinsey-Warnock. HarperCollins Children's Books, 2005. Illustrations copyright © 2005 by Emily Arnold McCully. Used by permission of HarperCollins Publishers. / Kinsey-Warnock, Natalie, photograph. Photo courtesy of Natalie Kinsey-Warnock.

KIRK, CONNIE ANN ▮ Rossiter, Richard, cover designer. Rafael Fuchs/Corbis Outline, cover image photographer. From a cover of *J. K. Rowling: A Biography,* by Connie Ann Kirk. Greenwood Press, 2003. Cover image copyright © Rafael Fuchs/Corbis Outline. / Hale, Christy, illustrator. From an illustration in *Sky Dancers,* by Connie Ann Kirk. Lee & Low Books, Inc., 2004. Illustrations copyright © 2004 by Christy Hale. Reproduced by permission.

KORMAN, GORDON ▮ From a cover of *On The Run: Chasing the Falconers,* by Gordon Korman. Scholastic, Inc. 2005. Reprinted by permission of Scholastic Inc.

LLOYD, DAVID T. ▮ Lloyd-Bolland, Catrin, cover photographer. From a cover of *Boys,* by David T. Lloyd. Syracuse University Press, 2004. Reproduced by permission. / Lloyd, David T., photograph. Photo by Hopeton F. Smalling. Courtesy of David T. Lloyd.

LUCKETT, DAVE ▮ Andreasen, Dan, illustrator. From a book cover of *The Girl, the Dragon, and the Wild Magic,* by Dave Luckett. Scholastic Inc., 2003. Cover copyright © 2003 by Scholastic Inc. Reprinted by permission of Scholastic Inc. / Andreasen, Dan, illustrator. From a cover of *The Girl, the Apprentice, and the Dogs of Iron,* by Dave Luckett. Scholastic Inc. 2004. Cover copyright © 2004 by Scholastic Inc. Reprinted by permission of Scholastic Inc.

MANZANO, SONIA ▮ Muth, Jon J., illustrator. From an illustration in *No Dogs Allowed!* by Sonia Manzano. Atheneum Books for Young Readers, 2004. Illustrations copyright © 2004 by Jon J. Muth. Reprinted with the permission of Atheneum Books for Young Readers, an imprint of Simon & Schuster Children's Publishing Division.

MARCIANO, JOHN BEMELMANS ▮ From an illustration in *There's a Dolphin in the Grand Canal!* by John Bemelmans Marciano. Viking Children's Books, a division of Penguin Young Readers Group. All rights reserved. Used by permission of Viking Children's Books, a division of Penguin Young Readers Group, a member of Penguin Group (USA) Inc., 345 Hudson Street, New York, NY 10014. / From an illustration in *Delilah,* by John Bemelmans Marciano. Viking Children's Books, a division of Penguin Putnam Books for Young Readers, 2002. Copyright © 2002 by John Bemelmans Marciano. All rights reserved. Used by permission of Viking Children's Books, a division of Penguin Young Readers Group, a member of Penguin Group (USA) Inc., 345

Hudson Street, New York, NY 10014. / From an illustration in *Harold's Tail,* by John Bemelmans Marciano. Viking Children's Books, a division of Penguin Young Readers Group, 2003. Copyright © 2003 by John Bemelmans Marciano. All rights reserved. Used by permission of Viking Children's Books, a division of Penguin Young Readers Group, a member of Penguin Group (USA) Inc., 345 Hudson Street, New York, NY 10014.

MARSZALEK, JOHN F. ∎ Marszalek, John F., photograph by Fred Y. Faulk. Courtesy of Mississippi State University.

MARTINEZ, AGNES ∎ Tauss, Marc, jacket photographer. From a jacket of *Poe Park,* by Agnes Martinez. Holiday House, 2004. Reproduced by permission.

MAZER, HARRY ∎ Freeman, Tom, illustrator. From a cover of *The Last Mission,* by Harry Mazer. Dell Laurel-Leaf, an imprint of Random House Children's Books, 1981. Used by permission of Dell Publishing, a division of Random House, Inc. / Elwell, Tristan, illustrator. From a cover of *A Boy at War,* by Harry Mazer. Aladdin Paperbacks, an imprint of Simon & Schuster Children's Publishing Division, 2002. Cover illustration copyright © 2002 by Tristan Elwell. Reprinted with the permission of Aladdin Paperbacks, an imprint of Simon & Schuster Children's Publishing Division, and by permission of the illustrator. / Elwell, Tristan, illustrator. From a jacket of *A Boy No More,* by Harry Mazer. Simon & Schuster Books for Young Readers, 2004. Jacket illustration copyright © 2004 by Tristan Elwell. Reprinted with the permission of Simon & Schuster Books for Young Readers, an imprint of Simon & Schuster Children's Publishing Division, and by permission of the illustrator. / Elwell, Tristan, illustrator. From a book jacket of *Heroes Don't Run,* by Harry Mazer. Simon & Schuster Books for Young Readers, 2005. Jacket illustration copyright © 2005 by Tristan Elwell. Reprinted with the permission of Simon & Schuster Books for Young Readers, an imprint of Simon & Schuster Children's Publishing Division, and by permission of the illustrator.

MEDINA, JANE ∎ Martinez, Edward, illustrator. From an illustration in *Tomás Rivera,* by Jane Medina. Green Light Readers, a division of Harcourt, Inc., 2003. Copyright © 2003 by Harcourt, Inc. Reprinted by permission of the publisher. / Casilla, Robert, illustrator. From an illustration in *The Dream on Blanca's Wall,* by Jane Medina. Wordsong, Boyds Mills Press, 2004. Illustrations copyright © 2004 by Robert Casilla. Reproduced by permission. / Medina, Jane, photograph. Photo courtesy of Jane Medina.

MORROW, BARBARA OLENYIK ∎ Jenkins, Leonard, illustrator. From an illustration in *A Good Night for Freedom,* by Barbara Olenyik Marrow. Holiday House, 2004. Illustrations copyright © 2004 by Leonard Jenkins. Reproduced by permission. / Morrow, Barbara Olenyik, photograph. Photo courtesy of Pictures Plus/Michael Watson.

NICKELL, JOE ∎ Nickell, Joe, photographer. From an illustration in *The Mystery Chronicles: More Real-Life X Files,* by Joe Nickell. The University Press of Kentucky, 2004. Reproduced by permission. / Nickell, Joe, photograph by Andrew A. Skolnick. Copyright © 2005 Andrew A. Skolnick. Reproduced by permission.

RAPPAPORT, KEN ∎ From an illustration in *Sheryl Swoopes: Star Forward,* by Ken Rappaport. Enslow Publishers, Inc. 2002. AP Images. / From a jacket of *Ladies First: Women Athletes Who Made a Difference,* by Ken Rappoport. Photographs by Al Brodsky/Associated Press/World Wide Sports. Peachtree Publishers, 2005. Reproduced by permission.

RAYBAN, CHLOË ∎ Gosney, Joy, illustrator. From a book cover of *Drama Queen,* by Chloë Rayban. Bloomsbury Children's Books, 2004. Reproduced by permission. / Rayban, Chloë, photograph. Photo courtesy of Chloë Rayban.

ROOP, PETER ∎ Kubinyi, Laszio, illustrator. From an illustration in *The Diary of David R. Leeper: Rushing for Gold,* by Peter and Connie Roop. Benchmark Books, Marshall Cavendish Corporation, 2001. Illustrations copyright © 2001 by Marshall Cavendish Corp. Reproduced by permission.

SMEE, NICOLA ∎ From an illustration in *No Bed Without Ted,* by Nicola Smee. Bloomsbury Publishing, 2005. Reproduced by permission.

STAUNTON, TED ∎ Lafontaine, Roger, illustrator. From a cover of *Two False Moves,* by Ted Staunton. Red Deer Press, 2000. Reproduced by permission. / From a cover of *Sounding Off,* by Ted Staunton. Cover photograph by Super Stock. Northern Lights Young Novels, Red Deer Press, 2004. Reproduced by permission.

STEWART, MELISSA ∎ From an illustration in *Maggots, Grubs, and More: The Secret Lives of Young Insects,* by Melissa Stewart. The Millbrook Press, 2003. Image copyright © M. H. Sharp/Photo Researchers. Reproduced by permission. / From an illustration in *Air Is Everywhere,* by Melissa Stewart. Compass Point Books, 2005. Image copyright © Kevin R. Morris/Corbis.

STRACHAN, LINDA ∎ Wojtowycz, David, illustrator. From an illustration in *What Color is Love?* by Linda Strachan. Bloomsbury Children's Books, 2003. Illustrations copyright © 2003 by David Wojtowycz. Reproduced by permission. / Strachan, Linda, photograph. Photo courtesy of Linda Strachan.

SWANSON, WAYNE ∎ From an illustration in *Why the West was Wild,* by Wayne Swanson. Annick Press, 2004. Reproduced by permission.

SWEENEY, JOYCE ∎ Sweeney, Joyce. From a cover of *Players,* by Joyce Sweeney. Marshall Cavendish, 2000. Reproduced by permission. / Wattenberg, Jane, illustrator. From a jacket of *Waiting for June,* by Joyce Sweeney. Marshall Cavendish, 2003. Jacket art copyright © 2003 by Jane Wattenberg. Reproduced by permission. / From a jacket of *Take Down,* by Joyce Sweeney. Marshall Cavendish, 2004. Jacket illustration copyright © 2004 by Joyce Sweeney. Reproduced by permission.

WEILL, CYNTHIA ∎ Trang, To Ngoc, illustrator. From an illustration in *Ten Mice for Tet!* by Cynthia Weill. Chronicle Books, 2003. © 1999 by To Ngoc Trang. Used with permission of Chronicle Books LLC, San Francisco. Visit ChronicleBooks.com

WISE, LEONARD ∎ From a cover of *The Way Cool License Plate Book,* by Leonard Wise. Firefly Books, Ltd., 2002. Reproduced by permission. / Wise, Leonard, photograph. Photo courtesy of Leonard Wise.

WOLFER, DIANNE ∎ From a cover of *Border Line,* by Dianne Wolfer. Fremantle Arts Centre Press, 1998. Reproduced by permission. / From a cover of *Choices,* by Dianne Wolfer. Fremantle Arts Centre Press, 2001. Reproduced by permission.

something ABOUT the AUThOR

ALLABY, John Michael
   See ALLABY, Michael

*   *   *

ALLABY, Michael 1933-
  (John Michael Allaby)

Personal

Born September 18, 1933, in Belper, Derbyshire, England; son of Albert Theodore (a chiropodist) and Jessie May (King) Allaby; married Ailsa Marthe McGregor (a homemaker), January 3, 1957; children: Vivien Gail, Robin Graham. *Politics:* "Left of center." *Hobbies and other interests:* "Reading (for pleasure as well as work), watching movies, listening to music, gardening, walking (gently!)."

Addresses

Home—Braehead Cottage, Tighnabruaich, Argyll PA21 2ED, Scotland. *E-mail*—mike_allaby@compuserve. com.

Career

Variously employed as police cadet, 1949-51, and actor, 1954-64; Soil Association, Suffolk, England, member of editorial department, 1964-72, editor of *Span,* 1967-72;

Michael Allaby

Ecosystems Ltd., Wadebridge, Cornwall, England, member of board of directors, associate editor of *Ecologist,* 1970-72, managing editor, 1972-73; freelance writer, 1973—. *Military service:* Royal Air Force, 1951-54, served as pilot; became pilot officer.

Member

Society for the History of Natural History, Planetary Society, American Association for the Advancement of Science, Institute of Biology (affiliate member), New York Academy of Sciences, British Society of Authors, Association of British Science Writers, National Association of Writers in Education.

Awards, Honors

Runner-up, *Times Educational Supplement* Information Book Award, 1984, for *The Food Chain; Hurricanes* selected among New York Public Library's 1998 Books for the Teen Age; Aventis Junior Prize for Science Books, 2001, *for How the Weather Works; Encyclopedia of Weather and Climate* listed among *Booklist* Top-Ten Science Reference Sources, 2002; Society of School Librarians honor book selection, science 7-12 category, 2002.

Writings

NONFICTION

The Eco-Activists, Knight (London, England), 1971.

Who Will Eat? The World Food Problem, Stacey (London, England), 1972.

(With others) *A Blueprint for Survival,* Houghton Mifflin (Boston, MA), 1972.

(With Colin Blythe and Colin Hines) *Losing Ground: The First of Three Discussion Papers on United Kingdom Food Prospects,* Friends of the Earth (London, England), 1974.

(With Floyd Allen) *Robots behind the Plow: Modern Farming and the Need for an Organic Alternative,* Rodale Press (Emmaus, PA), 1974.

Ecology, Hamlyn (New York, NY), 1975.

(With Marika Hanbury-Tenison, Hugh Sharman, and John Seymour) *The Survival Handbook: Self-Sufficiency for Everyone,* Macmillan (London, England), 1975.

Inventing Tomorrow: How to Live in a Changing World, Hodder & Stoughton (London, England), 1976.

World Food Resources: Actual and Potential, Applied Science Publishers (London, England), 1977.

(With Colin Tudge) *Home Farm: Complete Food Self-Sufficiency,* Macmillan (London, England), 1977.

Animals That Hunt, Hamlyn (New York, NY), 1979.

Wildlife of North America, Hamlyn (New York, NY), 1979.

Making and Managing a Smallholding, David & Charles (North Pomfret, VT), 1980.

(With Peter Bunyard) *The Politics of Self-Sufficiency,* Oxford University Press (New York, NY), 1980.

A Year in the Life of a Field, David & Charles (North Pomfret, VT), 1981.

Le foreste tropicale, Instituto Geografico de Agostini (Italy), 1981.

Animal Artisans, Knopf (New York, NY), 1982.

(With Peter Crawford) *The Curious Cat,* M. Joseph (London, England), 1982.

(With James Lovelock) *The Great Extinction: The Solution to One of the Great Mysteries of Science, the Disappearance of the Dinosaurs,* Doubleday (Garden City, NY), 1983.

(With James Lovelock) *The Greening of Mars,* St. Martin's Press (New York, NY), 1984.

2040: Our World in the Future, Gollancz (London, England), 1985.

Your Child and the Computer, Methuen (London, England), 1985.

(With Jane Burton) *Your Cat's First Year,* photographs by Burton and Kim Taylor, Simon & Schuster (New York, NY), 1985.

(With Jane Burton) *Nine Lives: A Year in the Life of a Cat Family,* photographs by Burton and Kim Taylor, Ebury Press (London, England), 1985.

The Woodland Trust Book of British Woodlands, David & Charles (North Pomfret, VT), 1986.

Ecology Facts, Hamlyn (New York, NY), 1986, 2nd revised edition published as *Green Facts,* 1986.

(With Jane Burton) *A Dog's Life,* photographs by Burton and Kim Taylor, Howell Book (New York, NY), 1986.

(With Jane Burton) *A Pony's Tale: A Year in the Life of a Foal,* photographs by Burton and Kim Taylor, Half Halt Press (Gaithersburg, MD), 1987.

A Guide to Gaia, Macdonald-Optima (London, England), 1989, published as *A Guide to Gaia: A Survey of the News Science of Our Living Earth,* Dutton (New York, NY), 1990.

Into Harmony with the Planet: The Delicate Balance between Industry and the Environment, Bloomsbury Publishing (London, England), 1990.

(With Neil Curtis) *Planet Earth,* Kingfisher (New York, NY), 1993.

How the Weather Works, Reader's Digest (Pleasantville, NY), 1995.

Facing the Future, Bloomsbury Publishing (London, England), 1995.

Basics of Environmental Science, Routledge (New York, NY), 1996, 2nd edition, 2000.

DK Guide to the Weather, Dorling Kindersley (New York, NY), 2000.

The Environment, illustrated by Mike Saunders and others, Gareth Stevens (Milwaukee, WI), 2000.

Tornadoes and Other Dramatic Weather Systems, Dorling Kindersley (New York, NY), 2001.

(With Robert Anderson and Ian Crofton) *Deserts and Semideserts,* Raintree Steck-Vaughn (Austin, TX), 2002.

The Facts on File Weather and Climate Handbook, Facts on File (New York, NY), 2002.

Encyclopedia of Weather and Climate, two volumes, Facts on File (New York, NY), 2002.

The World's Weather, Gareth Stevens (Milwaukee, WI), 2002.

(With Derek Gjertsen) *Makers of Science,* five volumes, Oxford University Press (New York, NY), 2002.

India ("Countries of the World" series), Chelsea House (New York, NY), 2005.

Also author of *The Changing Uplands,* Countryside Commission, 1983; *The Food Chain,* Andre Deutsch, 1984; *The Ordnance Survey Outdoor Handbook,* Macmillan/Ordnance Survey, 1987; *Conservation at Home: A Practical Handbook,* Unwin-Hyman, 1988; and *Living in the Greenhouse,* Thorsons, 1990. Contributor to books, including *The Environmental Handbook,* edited by John Barr, Ballantine, 1971; *Can Britain Survive?,* edited by Edward Goldsmith, Stacey, 1971; *Teach-in for Survival: A Record of the Teach-in on a Blueprint for Survival,* edited by Michael Schwab,

Robinson & Watkins, 1972; *Ecology,* edited by Jonathan Benthall, Longmans, Green, 1973; *Nightwatch,* edited by Linda Gamlin, M. Joseph, 1983; and *Ecology 2000: The Changing Face of the Earth,* edited by Edmund Hillary, Beaufort Books, 1984. Also contributor to *Encyclopaedia Britannica,* to CD-ROMs *Encarta '98* and *Eyewitness Encyclopedia of Science,* and to magazines, journals, and newspapers, including *New Scientist.*

Allaby's works have been translated into foreign languages, including Chinese, French, German, Italian, Norwegian, Swedish, and Finnish.

"ELEMENTS" SERIES

Air: The Nature of Atmosphere and the Climate, Facts on File (New York, NY), 1992.
Water: Its Global Nature, Facts on File (New York, NY), 1992.
Earth: Our Planet and Its Resources, Facts on File (New York, NY), 1993.
Fire: The Vital Source of Energy, Facts on File (New York, NY), 1993.

"DANGEROUS WEATHER" SERIES

Hurricanes, Facts on File (New York, NY), 1997, 2nd edition, 2003.
Tornadoes, Facts on File (New York, NY), 1997, 2nd edition, illustrated by Richard Garratt, 2004.
Blizzards, illustrated by Richard Garratt, Facts on File (New York, NY), 1997, 2nd edition, 2004.
Droughts, Facts on File (New York, NY), 1998, 2nd edition, 2003.
Floods, Facts on File (New York, NY), 1998, 2nd edition, illustrated by Richard Garratt, 2003.
A Chronology of Weather, Facts on File (New York, NY), 1998, 2nd edition, illustrated by Richard Garratt, 2004.
Fog, Smoke, and Poisoned Rain, illustrated by Richard Garratt, Facts on File (New York, NY), 2003.
A Change in the Weather, illustrated by Richard Garratt, Facts on File (New York, NY), 2004.

"BIOMES OF THE EARTH" SERIES

Polar Regions, Grolier Educational (Danbury, CT), 1999.
Deserts, illustrated by Richard Garratt, Grolier Educational (Danbury, CT), 1999.
Oceans, Grolier Educational (Danbury, CT), 1999.
Wetlands, Grolier Educational (Danbury, CT), 1999.
Mountains, Grolier Educational (Danbury, CT), 1999.
Temperate Forests, illustrated by Richard Garratt, Grolier Educational (Danbury, CT), 1999.
Tropical Forests, illustrated by Richard Garratt, Grolier Educational (Danbury, CT), 1999.
Grasslands, illustrated by Richard Garratt, Grolier Educational (Danbury, CT), 1999.

"PLANTS AND PLANT LIFE" SERIES

Plant Ecology, Grolier Educational (Danbury, CT), 2001.
Plants Used by People, Grolier Educational (Danbury, CT), 2001.
Conifers, Grolier Educational (Danbury, CT), 2001.
Flowering Plants: The Monocotyledons, Grolier Educational (Danbury, CT), 2001.
Flowering Plants: The Dicotyledons, Grolier Educational (Danbury, CT), 2001.

"ECOSYSTEM" SERIES

Temperate Forests, Facts on File (New York, NY), 1999.
Deserts, Facts on File (New York, NY), 2001.

EDITOR

A Dictionary of the Environment, Macmillan (New York, NY), 1977, 4th edition published as *Macmillan Dictionary of the Environment,* Macmillan (London, England), 1994.
The Oxford Dictionary of Natural History, Oxford University Press (New York, NY), 1985.
(With wife, Ailsa Allaby) *The Concise Oxford Dictionary of Earth Sciences,* Oxford University Press (New York, NY), 1990, 3rd edition, 2003.
The Concise Oxford Dictionary of Zoology, Oxford University Press (New York, NY), 1991, 3rd edition, 2003.
The Concise Oxford Dictionary of Botany, Oxford University Press (New York, NY), 1992, 2nd edition published as *Oxford Dictionary of Plant Sciences,* Oxford University Press (New York, NY), 1998.
The Concise Oxford Dictionary of Ecology, Oxford University Press (New York, NY), 1994, 3rd edition, 2004.

Editor of *Thinking Green: An Anthology of Essential Ecological Writing,* Barrie & Jenkins, 1989. Advisory editor of *Illustrated Dictionary of Science,* Facts on File (New York, NY), 1995. Editorial consultant to Dorling Kindersley and Monkey Puzzle Media.

Work in Progress

A third edition of the *Dictionary of Plant Sciences,* for Oxford University Press; revising *Deserts* and *Temperate Forests* for a second edition of the "Ecosystems" series; revising the *Encyclopedia of Weather and Climate;* a brochure for the World Meteorological Organization titled "Preventing and Mitigating Natural Disasters"; seven volumes in the "Discovering the Earth" series.

Sidelights

British writer Michael Allaby specializes in nonfiction, and has produced numerous books that focus primarily on scientific topics such as ecology and weather. In addition to contributing to multi-volume series such as "Plants and Plant Life" and "Ecosystems," he has produced many stand-alone works and has written and edited encyclopedias and dictionaries for prominent publishers such as Facts on File, Macmillan, and Oxford University Press. As the author/editor wrote on his home page, "In my books you'll find simply written explanations of what really goes on in the world around us. Over the years I've written about ecology, animal behaviour, farming, and the countryside. . . . Many of my books are for young readers, but I like to think I'm talking to anyone who'll listen."

Born in Belper, Derbyshire, England, in 1933, Allaby first trained as a police cadet, then worked in a morgue, acted in children's repertory theater, piloted planes for the Royal Air Force, and worked on the staff of an environmentalist magazine in England. Becoming a freelance writer in 1973, he first ranged widely in focus, producing titles that included *Your Child and the Computer, The Ordnance Survey Outdoor Handbook, The Woodland Trust Book of British Woodlands,* and *Into Harmony with the Planets.*

A major focus of Allaby's works has been weather and climate. He has written encyclopedias, dictionaries, and handbooks on weather and climate, and has penned an entire book series on dangerous weather conditions. As Allaby once explained, his interest in climate and the weather was inspired by a "shift away from scientific, indeed rational, thought in popular culture" that he maintains is the result of "the exaggerated propaganda of the populist environmental movement and by wide, but uninformed concern over ethical issues raised by potential scientific or technological developments." "I believe these views must be challenged in the strongest possible terms," he added, "lest their gloomy forebodings become self-fulfilling prophecies."

Allaby's "Dangerous Weather" series includes volumes on severe weather conditions such as droughts, blizzards, floods, hurricanes, tornadoes, and even fog. *Booklist* reviewer Mary Romano Marks observed that the examples in *Droughts* "vividly bring to life the reality of extreme forms of weather." Shauna Yusko, writing in *School Library Journal,* commented that while the chapters in *Fog, Smog, and Poisoned Rain* are "somewhat dense," the "well-written" book will "provide enough material for students researching meteorology, climatology, and the environment." In the *DK Guide to the Weather,* he presents information on each type of weather phenomenon on a two-page spread featuring color photographs. *Booklist* contributor Carolyn Phelan called the photographs "clear, colorful, and dramatic" and noted that "students researching specific topics will find themselves browsing widely through this impressive volume."

In his two-volume *Encyclopedia of Weather and Climate* Allaby provides a comprehensive overview of weather-related terms and offers biographical informa-

tion on those men and women who have contributed to the study of weather. Included in the book are a bibliography; references to helpful books, Web sites, and other resources; and five appendices with titles such as "Chronology of Disasters," "Chronology of Discoveries," and "Tornadoes of the Past." In *School Library Journal* Dana McDougald labeled the *Encyclopedia of Weather and Climate* "a much-needed resource that does not disappoint." Similarly, as Mary Ellen Quinn wrote in *Booklist,* Allaby's work "stands out" due to its "easy-to-understand, well-put-together text." The *Facts on File Weather and Climate Handbook* also received good reviews from critics, Robin N. Sinn, writing in the *Reference and User Services Quarterly,* calling Allaby's "a nice reference work covering the basic terms in climate and weather."

Moving to broader environmental issues, in *Basics of Environmental Science,* according to Jonathan Horner in the *Geographical Journal,* "Allaby considers a very wide range of topical environmental concerns including global warming, eutrophication, soil erosion, overfishing, and pollution." Horner praised the author, writing that "Allaby is to be commended for producing a very readable up-to-date introduction to the major disciplines comprising environmental science." In *The Environment* Allaby writes about nutrient cycles, biomes, the ozone layer, and other topics. Kathleen Isaacs commented in *School Library Journal* that the book "presents a broad, browsable introduction . . . [to] the make-up and natural systems of our planet." Among Allaby's other science writings are the eight "Biomes of the World" books, which describe polar regions, oceans, wetlands, and other ecosystems throughout the world; his five contributions to the "Plants and Plant Life" series; the "Elements" series, which explains earth, fire, water, and air; and the "Ecosystem" series, which includes the volumes *Deserts* and *Temperate Forests,* the former which discusses the geography, geology, biology, history, economics, health, and management of deserts. Claudia Moore, writing in *School Library Journal,* called *Deserts* "a wonderful, reader-friendly work" and praised its "outstanding color photographs and clear diagrams."

A collaboration with Derek Gjertsen, the five-volume *Makers of Science* reference work takes "a slightly different approach to ordinary biographical information on scientists," according to a *Booklist* contributor. The series "incorporates the political and social setting as well as the scientific achievements" of forty-one important scientists, from Aristotle to Stephen Hawking, while also including information regarding 300 other important men and women. "Scientific principles are clearly explained," added the *Booklist* reviewer, noting that "intriguing personal stories are woven in" to Allaby's text. *School Library Journal* contributor John Peters wrote that, "For scope, ease of use, and clarity of presentation, this set . . . is likely to become the first choice of middle graders on research missions," while the *Booklist* critic concluded: "Science teachers will love the connections made between different inventors' works and how science is relevant to our life today."

Allaby told *SATA:* "I've been writing ever since they taught me to read and write as a small boy. Starting with straightforward plagiarism from stories I'd read and movies I'd seen, I advanced (?) to short stories, poems, plays—the usual stuff.

"My dream was to be either an actor or a writer—ideally, both, declaiming my own lines to an audience of millions. So they sent me to work in an office (hated it), then as a police cadet (great fun). At age eighteen I joined the Royal Air Force as a pilot because they told me that when I left they'd pay me a gratuity I could use to go to drama college—and that's what happened.

"While was an out-of-work actor I had a temporary job for an organisation where I was encouraged to write short articles. Then one thing led to another and eventually I was commissioned to write my first book.

"I've written on many subjects, but especially on weather and climate; an interest in that began in my flying days.

"Now I'm getting on a bit, but still at it, working full time. I live in the West Highlands of Scotland, where EVERYONE is interested in the weather!"

Biographical and Critical Sources

PERIODICALS

American Reference Books Annual, 1996, review of *The Concise Oxford Dictionary of Ecology,* p. 777, and *Illustrated Dictionary of Science,* p. 639; 1999, review of *Blizzards, A Chronology of Weather, Droughts, Floods, Hurricanes,* and *Tornadoes,* pp. 634-235.

American Scientist, November, 1995, review of *Illustrated Dictionary of Science,* p. 563.

Appraisal, Volume 29, 1996, review of *Illustrated Dictionary of Science,* p. 6.

Booklist, January 15, 1995, review of *The Concise Oxford Dictionary of Ecology,* p. 950, review of *A Dictionary of the Environment,* p. 950; October 1, 1995, review of *Illustrated Dictionary of Science,* p. 350; December 1, 1997, Mary Romano Marks, review of *Droughts,* p. 621; December 1, 2000, Carolyn Phelan, review of *DK Guide to Weather,* p. 729; May 1,2002, Mary Ellen Quinn, review of *Encyclopedia of Weather and Climate,* p. 1542; June 1, 2002, review of *Makers of Science,* p. 1776.

Book Report, January-February, 1998, James Gross, review of *Blizzards, Hurricanes,* and *Tornadoes,* p. 53; September, 1998, review of *Floods,* p. 72; September-October, 1999, Sandra J. Morton, review of *Temperate Forests,* p. 70; November, 1999, review of *Biomes of the World,* p. 85; March, 2002, review of *Makers of Science,* p. 57.

Books for Keeps, May, 2001, review of *DK Guide to Weather,* p. 25.

Children's Bookwatch, March, 1998, review of *Droughts,* p. 2.

Choice, January, 1995, N. Chipman-Shlaes, review of *The Concise Oxford Dictionary of Ecology,* p. 744; June, 2002, J.C. Stachacz, review of *Encyclopedia of Weather and Climate,* p. 1740.

Christian Science Monitor, August 31, 1983.

Geographical Journal, November, 1997, Jonathan Horner, review of *Basics of Environmental Science,* pp. 310-311.

Kirkus Reviews, September 1, 1997, review of *Tornadoes,* p. 1384; November 1, 1997, review of *Droughts,* p. 1640.

Library Journal, October 15, 1995, Laura Lipton, review of *Illustrated Dictionary of Science,* p. 54; November 1, 2002, Nancy R. Curtis, review of *Encyclopedia of Weather and Climate,* p. 76.

Nature, June 2, 1994, John Lawton, review of *The Concise Oxford Dictionary of Ecology,* p. 368; February 1, 1996, review of *Facing the Future,* p. 412; February 29, 1996, review of *The Concise Oxford Dictionary of Ecology,* p. 784.

New Scientist, April 8, 1995, review of *How the Weather Works,* p. 41; June 10, 1995, review of *Facing the Future,* p. 43; October 11, 1997, review of *Basics of Environmental Science,* p. 48.

New Technical Books, May, 1994, review of *The Concise Oxford Dictionary of Ecology,* p. 575.

New York Times Book Review, January 6, 1985.

Personal Computer World, May, 1996, Jessica Hodgson, review of *Facing the Future,* p. 228.

Population Studies, November, 1995, Richard Sandbrook, review of *Macmillan Dictionary of the Environment,* 4th edition, p. 537.

Publishers Weekly, August 28, 2000, "A Wonderful World," review of *DK Guide to Weather,* p. 85.

Reference and Research Book News, March, 1994, review of *Fire: The Vital Source of Energy,* p. 52; December, 1994, review of *The Concise Oxford Dictionary of Ecology,* p. 41; September, 1995, review of *Illustrated Dictionary of Science,* p. 57.

Reference and User Services Quarterly, spring, 2003, Robin N. Sinn, review of *The Facts on File Weather and Climate Handbook,* p. 265.

Reference Reviews, May, 2001, review of *Deserts;* March, 2002, review of *Encyclopedia of Weather and Climate.*

School Librarian, winter, 1999, review of *Temperate Forests,* p. 219.

School Library Journal, February, 1994, John Peters, review of *Planet Earth,* p. 108; September, 1995, review of *Illustrated Dictionary of Science,* p. 237; April, 1998, Jeffrey A. French, review of *Hurricanes,* p. 140, review of *Tornadoes,* p. 140; November, 1999, review of *Biomes of the World,* p. 75; March, 2001, Kathleen Isaacs, review of *The Environment,* p. 259; August, 2001, Claudia Moore, review of *Deserts,* p. 211; May, 2002, Dana McDougald, review of *Encyclopedia of Weather and Climate,* p. 91; February, 2002, John Peters, review of *Makers of Science,* p. 84;

May, 2003, John Peters, review of *Makers of Science,*
p. 101; October, 2003, review of *Makers of Science,*
p. 46, Shauna Yusko, review of *Fog, Smog, and Poisoned Rain,* p. 103.

Science Books and Films, October, 1995, review of *Illustrated Dictionary of Science,* p. 206; November, 1999,
review of *Biomes of the World,* p. 274.

SciTech Book News, December, 1994, review of *The Concise Oxford Dictionary of Ecology,* p. 17; July, 1995,
review of *The Illustrated Dictionary of Science,* p. 4;
June, 1999, review of *Temperate Forests,* p. 70;
March, 2001, review of *Deserts,* p. 61; September,
2001, review of *Basics of Environmental Science,* 2nd
edition, p. 10.

Times (London, England), January 23, 1986.

Times Educational Supplement, July 7, 1995, Dennis Ashton, review of *How the Weather Works,* p. R4.

Times Literary Supplement, July 29, 1986.

Voice of Youth Advocates, December, 1995, review of *How
the Weather Works,* p. 319; June, 2001, review of
Deserts, p. 149.

ONLINE

Michael Allaby Home Page, http://www.michaelallaby.
com (June 30, 2004).*

*   *   *

ANDREWS, Jan 1942-

Personal

Born June 6, 1942, in Shoreham-by-the-Sea, Sussex,
England; immigrated to Canada, 1963; became Canadian citizen, 1971; daughter of Sydney Frederick (an
accountant) and Georgina (a dog breeder; maiden name,
Welsman) Ellins; divorced; children: Miriam, Kieran.
Education: University of Reading, B.A. (with honors),
1963; University of Saskatchewan, M.A. (English),
1969; attended Carson Grove Language Centre, 1975.
Hobbies and other interests: Canoeing, kayaking, cross-
country skiing, gardening, rock climbing.

Addresses

Home—R.R. 2, Lanark, Ontario K0G 1K0, Canada.
E-mail—jandrews@magma.ca.

Career

Writer, storyteller, and editor. CFQC-Radio, Saskatoon,
Saskatchewan, Canada, copywriter, 1963; Murray Memorial Library, Saskatoon, library clerk, 1965; Office of
the Secretary of State, Ottawa, Ontario, Canada, grants
officer in citizenship branch, 1972, program officer with
native citizens program, 1973, literary projects officer,
then writing and publications officer and acting head of
academic and cultural resources in Multicultural Direc-
torate, 1976, 1978, 1984; freelance writer, editor, story-

Jan Andrews

teller, educator, and organizer and presenter of children's literature workshops, beginning 1977.
Counterpoint School (parent-run cooperative), Ottawa,
coordinator, 1981, 1984-85; developer of oral history
program "Out of Everywhere," Expo '86, 1985-86;
Andrews-Cayley Enterprises, Ottawa, founder and partner, beginning 1987. Writer and coordinator for recording *A Band of Storytellers,* Ottawa, 1985; National Library of Canada, researcher for exhibitions "The Chance
to Give," 1986-87, and "The Secret Self," 1988. Programmer for National Gallery of Canada and for Cultures Canada Festival, Ottawa, 1988; MASC (arts education organization), Ottawa, co-founder, 1990; Stories
from the Ages, artistic director, 1995—writer-in-
residence, Ottawa Public Library, 2000-01; Ottawa Storytellers at the National Arts Centre Fourth Stage, artistic director, 2000—visiting fellow to Jane Franklin Hall,
Hobart, Tasmania, 2005. Reader, workshop presenter,
and performer at schools and at storytelling festivals
across Canada.

Member

Writers' Union of Canada, Canadian Society of Children's Authors, Illustrators, and Performers, Storytellers
of Canada/Conteurs du Canada (founding member; national coordinator, 1996, 1997).

Awards, Honors

Canada Council grants, 1983, 1987, 1991; Bologna In-
ternational Children's Book Fair entry, 1985, Best
Books for Young Adults designation, *School Library
Journal,* Notable Books selection, American Library
Association (ALA), Ruth Schwartz Award shortlist,
Canada Council Children's Literature Prize, and On-
tario Arts Council honor, all 1986, and Washington
State Children's Choice Picture Book Award, 1989, all
for *Very Last First Time;* Ontario Arts Council writers-
in-schools grants, 1990, 1993, 1994, 1996; Regional

Municipality of Ottawa-Carleton grant, 1991; Governor General's Literary Award shortlist, and Ruth Schwartz Children's Literature Award, both 1990, both for *The Auction;* Governor General's Literary Award shortlist, 1996, for *Keri; Alice Kane Storytelling Award, 2002.*

Writings

PICTURE BOOKS

Fresh Fish . . . and Chips, illustrated by Linda Donnelly, Canadian Women's Educational Press (Toronto, Ontario, Canada), 1973.

Ella, an Elephant/ Ella, un elephant, illustrated by Pat Bonn, Tundra Books (Montreal, Quebec, Canada), 1976.

Very Last First Time, illustrated by Ian Wallace, Groundwood Books (Vancouver, British Columbia, Canada), 1985, Atheneum (New York, NY), 1986, published as *Eva's Ice Adventure,* Methuen (London, England), 1986.

Pumpkin Time, illustrated by Kim LaFave, Groundwood Books (Toronto, Ontario, Canada), 1990.

The Auction, illustrated by Karen Reczuch, Groundwood Books (Toronto, Ontario, Canada), 1990.

Pa's Harvest: A True Story Told by Ephrem Carrier, illustrated by Cybéle Young, Groundwood Books (Toronto, Ontario, Canada), 2000.

Out of the Everywhere: Tales for a New World, illustrated by Simon Ng, Douglas & McIntyre (Toronto, Ontario, Canada), 2000.

The Twelve Days of Summer, illustrated by Susan Rennick Jolliffe, Orca Book (Custer, WA), 2005.

OTHER

(Editor) *The Dancing Sun: Stories and Poems Celebrating Canadian Children,* illustrated by Renée Mansfield, Press Porcepic (Victoria, British Columbia, Canada), 1981.

Coming of Age (dramatic montage), produced at National Library of Canada, 1985.

Keri (young-adult novel), Groundwood Books (Toronto, Ontario, Canada), 1996.

Winter of Peril: The Newfoundland Diary of Sophie Loveridge ("Dear Canada" series), Scholastic Canada (Markham, Ontario, Canada), 2001.

Contributor to periodicals, including *Canadian Children's Annual, Cricket, Ahoy,* and language arts publications in Canada and the United States. Contributor, *The Canadian Family Tree,* Don Mills, 1979.

Sidelights

A British-born author and storyteller who now makes her home in rural eastern Canada, Jan Andrews draws much of her inspiration from the natural world around her. "Most of my writing seems to be very firmly rooted

Sharing their universal relevance with young readers, Andrews retells traditional stories from India, Russia, Greece, Finland, and China in her anthology **Out of the Everywhere: Tales for a New World.** *(Illustration by Simon Ng.)*

in some place or another," Andrews once explained to *SATA.* "I often wonder whether, if I had not come to North America, I would ever have started writing at all. There is something about the way of the land—its vastness and strength, the space of it—that speaks to me very deeply." The way of the land is an element that runs throughout such picture books as *The Auction, Very Last First Time,* and *The Twelve Days of Summer,* as well as in her 1996 young-adult novel *Keri* and in her "Dear Canada" series installment *Winter of Peril: The Newfoundland Diary of Sophie Loveridge.* In addition, she addresses the desire of Canadian children for stories that build on regional traditions with the ten-story anthology *Out of the Everywhere: Tales for a New World,* which melds folk stories from around the world with "the climate and physical features of Canada," according to *School Library Journal* contributor Wendy Lukehart. Dubbing Andrews' theme of featuring immigrant protagonists a "masterstroke," *Horn Book* reviewer Nell D. Beram also praised the collection, writing that these immigrant-told tales are "swift and taut" in the telling and "occasionally wink playfully at the reader."

Born in Shoreham-by-Sea, England, in 1942, Andrews earned her bachelor's degree in Great Britain before marrying and moving to Saskatchewan, Canada, in 1963. At first awed by the vast prairies that dominate the landscape of central Canada, she became inspired by the stories she created for her own children to begin writing and researching. Andrews' first children's book, *Fresh Fish . . . and Chips,* was published in 1973, followed by the bilingual *Ella, an Elephant/Ella, un elephant.* Beginning in the mid-1970s, she began working independently as a writer and has also taught and organized workshops focusing on children's literature. Her career as a storyteller with a particular focus on traditional folk material and epic began in 1986.

Andrews' 1985 picture book *Very Last First Time*—published in England as *Eva's Ice Adventure*—focuses on Eva Padlyat, a young Inuit girl, as she makes her first solo trip under the ice that covers Canada's Ungava Bay during the winter months, there to collect mussels that scatter across the ocean floor during low tide. As taught by her family, she lowers herself through a hole cut through the thick ice into the bone-chilling darkness below, a method of food-gathering that, while a tradition of the Inuit of the region, is also dangerous. The mussel-gatherer must carry a candle at all times in order to see beneath the thick crust of ice; he or she also has to be cautious enough to be prepared to quickly exit back through the hole to the ice's surface before the frigid waters return.

Lucy Young Clem, in her review for *School Library Journal,* called *Very First Last Time* "well developed, with just the right amount of suspense" and "an intriguing view of a little-known way of life." Clem's praise was echoed by other reviewers, including Mary Ellen Binder. "Children find it easy to identify with Eva's changing emotions as she moves from excited anticipation, through happiness and satisfaction as she completes her task, the terror of being alone in the darkness under the ice, and finally to the relief of finding herself back with her mother again," noted Binder in her review for *Canadian Children's Literature. New York Times Book Review* contributor Selma G. Lanes lauded Andrews' work as "the very model of what a factual picture book can be." As Lanes added: "How lean the prose, like that of a fable, and how artfully its well-chosen words hold the reader in thrall."

The Auction concerns a young boy's apprehension upon discovering that his grandfather is selling the family's farm. Gran has died and the farm is too much for one

A young Eskimo girl learns the skills involved in the dangerous traditions of fishing below the ice at low tide in the picture book **Very Last First Time**. *(Illustration by Ian Wallace.)*

person to keep up. Coming to terms with the loss of the beloved property, Todd spends the night before the auction with Gramps, indulging in happy memories, good-bye tears, and a few of the remaining homemade pickles Gran had put up the year before. By the end of the evening the pair has filled the auction site with scarecrows, a playful activity that transforms a sad occasion into a new memory that both will be able to recall with happiness. While *Quill & Quire* contributor Christtine Fondse noted that the "slow pace" of *The Auction* might discourage some young solo readers, she added that most "will enjoy sharing its nostalgic look at the past with a discerning adult."

Another boy growing up during a family's hard times is the focus of *Pa's Harvest: A True Story Told by Ephrem Carrier.* In this story, based on the recollections of co-author Ephrem Carrier, a boy describes growing up in a farm family during the Great Depression of the 1930s, when money was tight but food was fortunately plentiful. In *School Library Journal* Lee Bock praised the book as "a metaphor of the sustaining love" that helps close-knit families survive "in good times and bad," while also noting that Cybéle Young's illustrations enhance "the nostalgic tone of the story and its simple truth."

Andrews addresses an older readership with *Keri,* a "spare, powerful story of a single weekend in the life of an adolescent Newfoundland girl," according to *Horn Book* critic Sarah Ellis. The daughter of a fisherman who has been forced to take a job away from his boats after the region's fish supply is depleted due to generations of overfishing, Keri fears the impending loss of her family's stability. The thirteen year old's worries are quickly compounded by the death of her beloved Gran. Keri's growing insecurity, anger, and resentment find a focus in her mother, and soon the girl has alienated herself from everyone in her family except her younger brother, Grae. Ultimately, a beached whale discovered during a morning walk draws Keri out of her self and prompts her to heroism in her efforts to save the animal from death. Andrews draws her young-adult novel to a conclusion in a somewhat un-conventional manner, but despite a tragic ending the protagonist is redeemed by story's end.

"*Keri* is not about saving a whale," noted Ellis. "It is about an encounter with grandeur, an encounter from which one cannot emerge unchanged." Julie Bergwerff agreed in *Books in Canada,* adding praise for the author's spare style and the novel's realistic outcome, an outcome reflected by nature. "There is a true sense of "wordscaping" in all of Jan Andrews's books," explained Bergwerff, "words and language reflect and grow out of the landscape in her work. . . . *Keri*'s landscape is harsh, spare, and tough, and the novel's prose echoes this ruggedness."

"I write for young people because I can't seem to help it," Andrews once told *SATA.* Although admitting to a "passionate interest in adult life," stories about young

In Pa's Harvest a young boy raised on a potato farm during the Great Depression learns how to deal with both survival and setbacks through the example of his hard-working father. (Illustration by Cybéle Young.)

people and nature continue to dominate her imagination. As a co-founder of Storytellers of Canada/Conteurs du Canada, Andrews also performs before audiences. "I find that, as a storyteller, it is the old traditional folk and fairy tales that interest me the most," she explained. "They seem to carry the age-old wisdoms within them and yet speak very directly to us as we struggle with our problems today. Both storytelling and writing have brought travel to distant locations and that has meant new friends. Storytellers particulary like to gather Perhaps that's part of the reason I organized twenty tellers and fifteen listeners to get together and tell Homer's *Odyssey* from beginning to end at my home one summer weekend. The telling took fourteen hours, but nobody wanted to miss a word.

"The *Odyssey* was followed by The *Iliad* and the great Indian epic *The Mahabharata* in other years. My organizational work has become another lifetime constant. I am the artistic director for two storytelling series and I

find choosing material and tellers wonderfully stimulating. I am less enthusiastic about fundraising and promotion, but see the necessity for those as well. I am also director of Storytellers of Canada's StorySave project for recording the voices of elders from the Canadian storytelling community for audio Web site and on CDs. Some of the results of this work can be found at WWW.StorySave.com.

"I cannot imagine not telling stories, not writing, not giving workshops and organizing events to help others who want to do the same," Andrews once admitted to *SATA*. But she also makes an effort to balance her intellectual pursuits with those of a more athletic nature. "I . . . know . . . that I need physical as well as mental activity. Apart from anything else, moving my body helps to move the writing along whenever it gets stuck. Perhaps that's why I've recently added rock climbing to my hobbies. I love the challenge of it. In 2005 I spent three months in Tasmania. I was working on a novel but I made sure I got in lots of bushwalking.

"Do I like being a storyteller and a writer? I love it, but not every day. All jobs have their frustrations and mine is no exception. Each book is a voyage of discovery; each has its times of struggle. Maybe that's why I like it. Maybe it's the hardest thing I know how to do."

Biographical and Critical Sources

BOOKS

Sixth Book of Junior Authors and Illustrators, edited by Sally Holmes Holtze, H.W. Wilson (New York, NY), 1989.

PERIODICALS

Booklist, June 15, 1986, p. 1537.
Books in Canada, October, 1997, Julie Bergwerff, review of *Keri.*
Bulletin of the Center for Children's Books, February, 1991, p. 135.
Canadian Children's Literature, number 45, 1987, Mary Ellen Binder, review of *Very Last First Time,* pp. 82-86; number 64, 1991, p. 92; winter, 1997, pp. 74-76.
Canadian Review of Materials, May, 1986, review of *Very Last First Time,* p. 134; January, 1991, p. 25; March, 1991, Kay Kerman, review of *The Auction.*
Children's Literature in Education, September, 1993, pp. 226-227.
Growing Point, July, 1986, p. 4657.
Horn Book, September-October, 1996, Sarah Ellis, review of *Keri,* pp. 662-663; September, 2001, Nell D. Beram, review of *Out of the Everywhere: Tales for a New World,* p. 599.
Junior Bookshelf, August, 1986, p. 137.
Kirkus Reviews, April 15, 1991, p. 542.

New York Times Book Review, June 15, 1986, Selma G. Lanes, review of *Very Last First Time,* p. 38.

Quill & Quire, December, 1985, p. 24; November, 1990, p. 12; December, 1990, Christtine Fondse, review of *The Auction,* p. 18; May, 1996, p. 33.

School Library Journal, May, 1986, Lucy Young Clem, review of *Very Last First Time,* p. 67; May, 1991, p. 74; February, 2001, Lee Bock, review of *Pa's Harvest: A True Story Told by Ephrem Carrier,* p. 109; September, 2001, Wendy Lukehart, review of *Out of the Everywhere,* p. 237; June, 2004, Rosalyn Pierini, review of *The Twelve Days of Summer,* p. 102.

ONLINE

Canadian Society of Children's Authors, Illustrators, and Performers Web site, http://www.canscaip.org/ (January 2, 2006), "Jan Andrews."

Storytellers of Canada/Conteurs du Canada Web site, http://www.sc-cc.com/ (March 26, 2006), "Jan Andrews."

Storytellers School of Toronto Web site, http://www.storytellingtoronto.org/ (March 26, 2006), "Jan Andrews."

B-C

BALDRY, Cherith 1947-

Personal

Born April 3, 1947, in Lancaster, Lancastershire, England; daughter of William (a factory foreman) and Evelyn Annie (a homemaker; maiden name, Dixon) Baker; married Peter James Baldry (a scientist), September 3, 1971 (deceased); children: William, Adam. *Education:* University of Manchester, B.A. (with honors), 1969; St. Anne's College, Oxford, B.Litt, 1973; Aberdeen Teacher Training College, teaching certificate, 1974. *Religion:* Church of England (Anglican). *Hobbies and other interests:* Early music.

Addresses

Home—12 Wraylands Dr., Reigate, Surrey RH2 OLG, England.

Career

Novelist and educator. Jewish High School for Girls, Manchester, England, teacher of English, 1971-73; St. Margaret's School for Girls, Aberdeen, Scotland, teacher of English, speech, and drama, 1975; Fourah Bay College, Freetown, Sierra Leone, lecturer in English literature, 1976-79; Tandridge School District, Surrey, England, teacher of adult-education English, 1980-81; Associated Examining Board of Guilford, Surrey, England, assistant examiner, 1980—; moderator of General Certificate of Secondary Education English literature, 1987—; Stowford College, Sutton, Surrey, teacher of English literature, 1986-88; Priory School, Banstead, Surrey, teacher of English and librarian, 1988—; Cambridge Board, Cambridge, England, assistant examiner of English, 1989—.

Member

Fellowship of Christian Writers (committee member, 1991—), British Science Fiction Association.

Awards, Honors

First prize, *London Calling* magazine competition, 1988, for short story "Happiness Inc."; Nottingham and Notts Drama Association Award, 1991, for *Achilles His Armour.*

Writings

FICTION

Drew's Talents (for children), illustrated by Deirdre Counihan, Palm Tree (Bury St. Edmunds, England), 1997.
Mutiny in Space (for children), illustrated by Mark Edwards, Puffin (London, England), 1997.
Exiled from Camelot, Green Knight, 2001.
The Reliquary Ring, Macmillan (London, England), 2003.
The Roses of Roazon, Macmillan (London, England), 2004.

Also author of *The Other Side of the Mountains,* Kingsway (Eastborne, England). Stories included in anthologies, including *Fantasy Stories,* 1996; *Royal Whodunnits,* 1999; and *Vector 163.* Contributor of short stories to periodicals, including *Surrey Mirror, Vector, Marion Zimmer Bradley's Fantasy Magazine, Interzone,* and *Xenos.*

"SAGA OF THE SIX WORLDS" SERIES; FOR CHILDREN

The Book and the Phoenix, illustrated by Vic Mitchell, Kingsway (Eastborne, England), 1989, published as *A Rush of Golden Wings,* Crossway (Wheaton, IL), 1991, revised as *Cradoc's Quest,* Chariot Books (Elgin, IL), 1994.
Hostage of the Sea, illustrated by Vic Mitchell, Kingsway, 1990, published as *Rite of Brotherhood,* Chariot Books (Elgin, IL), 1994.
The Carpenter's Apprentice, illustrated by Vic Mitchell, Kingsway (Eastborne, England), 1992.
Storm Wind, illustrated by Vic Mitchell, Chariot Books (Elgin, IL), 1994.

"EAGLESMOUNT MYSTERIES" SERIES; FOR CHILDREN

The Silver Horn, illustrated by David Wyatt, Macmillan Children's (London, England), 2001, Mondo (New York, NY), 2002.

The Emerald Throne, illustrated by David Wyatt, Macmillan Children's (London, England), 2001, Mondo (New York, NY), 2003.

The Lake of Darkness, illustrated by David Wyatt, Macmillan Children's (London, England), 2001, Mondo (New York, NY), 2004.

"ABBY MYSTERIES" SERIES; FOR CHILDREN

The Buried Cross, Oxford University Press (Oxford, England), 2004.

The Silent Man, Oxford University Press (Oxford, England), 2004.

The Scarlet Spring, Oxford University Press (Oxford, England), 2004.

The Drowned Sword, Oxford University Press (Oxford, England), 2005.

PLAYS

Where Late the Sweet Birds Sang (one-act; produced in Surrey, England), published in *Triad 74: A Fine Selection of One-Act Plays,* New Playwrights' Network, 1989.

Achilles His Armour (one-act; produced in Nottinghamshire, England), Nottingham and Notts Drama Association (Nottinghamshire, England), 1991.

Also author of plays *Out of Darkness* and *House Arrest.*

OTHER

A Students' Guide to "The Silver Box" by John Galsworthy, Graham Brash (Singapore), 1989.

Questions and Answers on "The Merchant of Venice", Tynron (Lutterworth, England), 1992.

The Merchant of Venice: A Study Guide, First and Best in Education (Peterborough, England), 1996.

Sidelights

Cherith Baldry is a British writer who has combined her interest in fantasy and science fiction with her Christian beliefs and her interest in Arthurian legend to create novels such as *The Roses of Roazon* and *Exiled from Camelot,* as well as several fiction series for young-adult readers. She moves to science fiction in *The Reliquary Ring,* a futuristic novel set in an alternate Venice in which humans rule over a genetically manufactured humanoid underclass. Amid palace scandals, masked costume balls, and assorted intrigues, Baldry weaves a multilayered tale that features an evil villain, a plucky young heroine, and a Christian message that does not overwhelm the plot. Praising *The Reliquary Ring, Infinity Plus* online reviewer Stephen Palmer

wrote that "readers who yearn for well-written, literate, atmospheric fantasy that doesn't feature massed battles and orcs will find much here to enjoy," while Victoria Strauss commented for *SFSite.com* that in "crafting a delightfully absorbing narrative," the author "richly evokes her nameless city, its exquisite surfaces roiled by dark undercurrents of corruption and cruelty that invest even the most perfect places with the whiff of decay."

The first volume of her "Saga of the Six Worlds" series, *A Rush of Golden Wings* (published in England as *The Book and the Phoenix* and revised as *Cradoc's Quest*), introduces a barren world whose dispirited human population gains a growing awareness of the value of freedom, commitment, and an afterlife after a young boy distributes copies of a forbidden book containing an inspiring text—the Bible. The power of God is also the theme of *Rite of Brotherhood* (published in England as *Hostage of the Sea*), which finds fifteen-year-old Aurion held captive by a warlike king. As her captor prepares to make war on his enemies and conquer the planet, Aurion draws on her knowledge of the Christian faith to win the king to God's love and change his plans.

Baldry's "Eaglesmount" series focuses on more mainstream fantasy, as Vair, a young pine marten, confronts a challenge and discovers his destiny after his father's death in *The Silver Horn.* Vair's story continues in *The Emerald Throne,* as he joins several friends on a journey that will take him to Eaglesmount, his task to preserve the throne of the Eagle Kings against the efforts of the Lord Owl from ruling the kingdom of Riverbourne. In *The Lake of Darkness* Vair and the other creatures of Riverbourne confront a greater threat to their peace when the throne of the kingdom remains empty.

Baldry once told *SATA:* "I can't remember a time when I didn't write; certainly, I have memories of doing so as a very small child. My grandfather was a wonderful storyteller, and so making up stories always seemed a natural thing to do. It's only quite recently that I realized not everyone has characters walking around in their head.

"I also became interested in science fiction from a very early age, mainly through sneaking a look at my father's library books. I didn't understand them—they were aimed at adults anyway—but I'll never forget the sensation of something excitingly unusual. Although I started reading children's science fiction as well, in those days it was mostly adventure stories in space suits, and, with a few exceptions, it didn't capture the imagination in the same way.

"When I started writing seriously for publication, I wrote some science fiction, and an Arthurian novel, and quite a lot of detective fiction, all unpublished. I still have an ambition to publish a detective story of the classic puzzle type.

Baldry's "Eaglesmount" trilogy concludes in The Lake of Darkness, *which finds the heroic Vair leading the animals of Riverbourne against a long-hidden evil. (Illustration by David Wyatt.)*

"In all this early material, I never thought of myself as a Christian writer. Although I've always been a Christian, writing a novel about my faith seemed far too difficult an undertaking. Then I began a science-fiction novel about a group of people living in a very restricted society, who were gradually going to wake up to the possibilities of freedom and personal commitment. I realized that if I was going to write this book honestly, they had to wake up spiritually as well, and so, terrified, I introduced a Christian theme.

"This book was rejected by a couple of publishers, and then I went with my husband to Sierra Leone, where we worked for four years, and though I continued to write, difficulties with postage meant that I submitted very little work for publication.

"Back in England I dusted off the Christian book and tried it again, this time with specifically Christian publishers, and once again it was rejected, for perfectly valid reasons, but enough interest was shown to make me realize that I had to write another Christian book. I also began to realize that I could write for older children.

"I had no ideas whatsoever, except that I wanted the book to be science fiction and that I felt more comfort-

able dealing with Christian themes in a symbolic way. Then I had the idea—while standing outside Foyle's book shop at the top of the Charing Cross Road in London—of using one of the medieval symbols of Christ: what about a phoenix? Going home on the train I was simmering away, and by the time I reached home I had the outline of the plot and the main characters of what eventually became *The Book and the Phoenix,* published in the United States as *A Rush of Golden Wings.*

"Even before *The Book and the Phoenix* was accepted for publication, I wanted to write another book using the same basic background of the 'Six Worlds' series. For a long time I had had the idea of writing a book about the developing friendship between two very different young men, but although I had ideas for incidents that would build up the relationship, the story had no basic direction; it was impossible to write it. Seeing it as another 'Six Worlds' book gave that direction, and *Hostage of the Sea* came into being. After Kingsway accepted these books, they asked for another in the series, [with led to] *The Carpenter's Apprentice.*"

Biographical and Critical Sources

PERIODICALS

Extrapolation, summer, 2002, Ann F. Howey, "A Churlish Hero: Contemporary Fantasies Rewrite Sir Kay," p. 115.

Guardian (London, England), January 15, 2005, Jon Courtenay Grimwood, review of *The Roses of Roazon.*

School Librarian, autumn, 2004, Angela Lepper, review of *The Buried Cross,* p. 135; spring, 2005, Peter Andrews, review of *The Silent Man,* p. 24; summer, 2004, Andrea Rayner, review of "The Drowned Sword," p. 79.

School Library Journal, July, 2004, Mara Alpert, review of *The Lake of Darkness,* p. 66.

ONLINE

Infinity Plus Web site, http://www.infinityplus.co.uk/ (January 1, 2006), Stephen Palmer, review of *The Reliquary Ring.*

SFSite.com, http://www.sfsite.com/ (January 2, 2006, Victoria Strauss, review of *The Reliquary Ring* and *The Roses of Roazon.**

*   *   *

BAUER, Michael Gerard 1955-

Personal

Born August 10, 1955, in Brisbane, Queensland, Australia; married; children: Meg, Joseph. *Education:* University of Queensland, B.A. and Dip.Ed., 1977.

Michael Gerard Bauer

Addresses

Home—Brisbane, Queensland, Australia. *Agent*—c/o Author Mail, Omnibus Books/Scholastic Australia, 335 Unley Rd., Malvern, South Australia 5061, Australia.

Career

Writer and educator. Teacher of economics and English teacher in Brisbane and Ipswich, Queensland, Australia.

Awards, Honors

Brisbane Writers Festival WriteSmall Competition winner, 2003; New South Wales Premier's Literary Award shortlist, Children's Book Council of Australia Book of the Year for Older Readers award, *Courier Mail* People's Choice Award for Younger Readers, and Victorian Premier's Award shortlist, all 2005, all for *The Running Man.*

Writings

The Running Man, Omnibus Books (Malvern, South Australia, Australia), 2004.
Don't Call Me Ishmael!, Omnibus Books (Malvern, South Australia, Australia), 2006.

Sidelights

Australian-born author and educator Michael Gerard Bauer's debut novel *The Running Man* was met with much praise upon its publication in 2004, and has also

earned recognition by several of the country's top awards. The novel's main character is a fourteen-year-old boy named Joseph. A talented artist, Joseph is asked by the woman who lives next door to paint a portrait of her brother Tom, a withdrawn, unsociable man who is known around town primarily because of his status as a Vietnam War veteran. Behind Tom's constant scowl and dark moods is an even darker history that Joseph must unlock in order to clearly capture the man's image on canvas. Joseph's quest to make sense of his older neighbor despite his own shyness also helps the teen deal with his own childhood turmoil and help him avoid the scars that have so clearly damaged Tom.

Bauer studied English at the University of Queensland, and now teaches English and economics at the secondary-school level in the city of Brisbane, where he was born and now lives with his wife and two children. Discussing his second career as a writer on the *Scholastic Australia* Web site, he noted: "I have always been interested in writing and over the years have dabbled in song lyrics, short stories and poetry with no real thought of ever being published. For quite a few years I kept diaries where I would write about my experiences and innermost feelings in verse heavily disguised by symbols and images. Looking back I think this was probably a good way of developing and improving writing skills without realizing it."

Biographical and Critical Sources

PERIODICALS

Magpies, November, 2004, Jo Goodman, review of *The Running Man,* p. 39.
Viewpoint, autumn, 2005, Nicky Lo Bianco, review of *The Running Man,* p. 26.

ONLINE

AustLit Web site, http://www.austlit.edu.au/ (September 26, 2005).
Booked Out Speakers Agency Web site, http://www. bookedout.com.au/queensland (March 26, 2006), "Michael Gerard Bauer."
Curriculum Materials Information Services Web site, http://www.amlib.eddept.wa.edu.au/ (December 19, 2005), Les Strong, review of *Running Man.*
Scholastic Australia Web site, http://www.scholastic.com. au/ (November 26, 2005), "Michael Gerard Bauer."

*   *   *

BEAR, Carolyn
See RAYBAN, Chloë

*   *   *

BELL, Jadrien
See GOLDEN, Christie

BENATAR, Raquel 1955-

Personal

Born October 21, 1955, in Morocco; daughter of Isaac Benatar and Reina Macias; married Sam Laredo (a publisher) November 20, 1994. *Education:* University of Toulouse, degree (psychology).

Addresses

Home—9400 Lloydcrest Dr., Beverly Hills, CA 90210.

Career

Psychologist and writer. Child psychologist in private practice, Madrid, Spain, 1978-94; consultant in human resources, Madrid, 1988-94; Laredo Publishing/ Renaissance House, Beverly Hills, CA, editorial director, 1995-2005; author.

Writings

Caperucita roja y el lobo goloso (translation of "Little Red Riding Hood"), illustrations by Pablo Torrecilla, Laredo Publishing (Beverly Hills, CA), 2000.

Gabriel García Márquez and His Magical Universe, illustrated by Pablo Torrecilla, Piñata Books (Houston, TX), 2002.

Isabel Allende: recuerdos para un cuento/Isabel Illende: Memories for a Story (bilingual biography), illustrations by Fernando Molinari, Piñata Books (Houston, TX), 2003.

Also author of bilingual books in McGraw-Hill's "Stories of America" series, including *La Madremonte; Los genios de la montaña; Los gigantes de Sumpa; El galipote y los caminanates; El nacimiento de Irupé; La isla encantada; El joven Ollac; Chirumá;* and *Talé y el secreto de la laguna.* Author of biography *Mario Moreno, Cantinflas,* for Piñata Books. Author of bilingual books in NTC's "Journals for Children" series, including *My Family; Me, Myself, and I; All of Us; My Friends; I Like to Write;* and *I Like to Read.* Author of Spanish-language biographies *Ellen Ochoa, la astronauta; Lucila imagina a Gabriela; Mario Moreno Cantinflas;* and *Salvadore Dali,* all for SRA/McGraw-Hill. Author of *Yo,* for Houghton Mifflin.

Biographical and Critical Sources

PERIODICALS

Kirkus Reviews, April 15, 2004, review of *Isabel Allende: recuerdos para un cuento/ Isabel Allende: Memories for a Story,* p. 390.

School Library Journal, September, 2004, Ann Welton, review of *Isabel Allende: recuerdos para un cuento,* p. 195.

ONLINE

Arte Público Press Web site, http://www.arte.uh.edu/ (December 19, 2005).

*   *   *

BLEDSOE, Karen E. 1962-

Personal

Born April 15, 1962, in Salem, OR; daughter of Don James (an accountant and Christmas tree farmer) and Harriet Elizabeth (a medical technologist and Christmas tree farmer; maiden name, Hiday) Lytle; married Glen Leonard Bledsoe (a teacher and writer), June 28, 1992; children: Gabriel Scott (stepson), James Wesley Solonika. *Education:* Willamette University, B.S., 1985, M.A.T., 1991; Oregon State University, M.S., 1988; doctoral study in science and mathematics education. *Hobbies and other interests:* Gardening, shin-shin toitsu aikido.

Addresses

Home—Salem, OR. *Office*—Department of Biology, Linn-Benton Community College, 6500 Pacific Blvd. SW, Albany, OR 97321. *E-mail*—bledsok@linnbenton. edu.

Career

Educator and author. Temporary and substitute teacher at public schools in Salem, OR, 1991-95; Western Oregon University, Monmouth, instructor in biology, beginning 1995; Linn-Benton Community College, Albany, OR, currently instructor in biology. Oregon Academy of Science, science education co-chairperson and Web page designer, 1996—; Oregon Collaborative for Excellence in the Preparation of Teachers, faculty fellow, 1997—; Oregon Public Education Network, team coach for Master WEBster Web page design contest, 1998-99. U.S. Forest Service, seasonal biological technician, 1985; City of Salem, seasonal recreational leader and environmental educator, 1989-94; *School Science and Mathematics Journal,* managing editor; Science and Math Investigative Learning Experiences (SMILE), Oregon State University, curriculum coordinator.

Member

Society of Children's Book Writers and Illustrators, National Biology Teachers Association, Oregon Science Teachers Association, Phi Delta Kappa.

Awards, Honors

Oregon Writing Project, Willamette University, fellow.

Writings

FOR YOUNG PEOPLE; WITH HUSBAND, GLEN BLEDSOE

Classic Ghost Stories II, Lowell House (Los Angeles, CA), 1998.

Classic Sea Stories, Lowell House (Los Angeles, CA), 1999.

Creepy Classics III: More Hair-Raising Horror from the Masters of the Macabre, Lowell House (Los Angeles, CA), 1999.

Classic Mysteries II, Lowell House (Los Angeles, CA), 1999.

Classic Adventures, Lowell House (Los Angeles, CA), 2000.

OTHER

(With Candyce Norvall) *365 Nature Crafts,* Publications International (Lincolnwood, IL), 1997.

Best Friends, Publications International (Lincolnwood, IL), 1997.

School Memories Album, Publications International (Lincolnwood, IL), 1998.

Millennium Album, Publications International (Lincolnwood, IL), 1998.

(With Maria Birmingham and Kelly Milner Halls) *365 Outdoor Activities,* illustrated by Anne Kennedy, Publications International (Lincolnwood, IL), 2000.

(With Glen Bledsoe) *Ballooning Adventures,* Capstone Books (Mankato, MN), 2001.

(With Glen Bledsoe) *The Blue Angels: The U.S. Navy Flight Demonstration Squadron,* Capstone High-Interest Books (Mankato, MN), 2001.

(With Glen Bledsoe) *The World's Fastest Helicopters,* Capstone High-Interest Books (Mankato, MN), 2002.

(With Glen Bledsoe) *The World's Fastest Trucks,* Capstone High-Interest Books (Mankato, MN), 2002.

(With Glen Bledsoe) *Airplane Adventures,* Capstone High-Interest Books (Mankato, MN), 2002.

(With Glen Bledsoe) *Bicycling Adventures,* Capstone High-Interest Books (Mankato, MN), 2002.

(With Glen Bledsoe) *The World's Fastest Dragsters,* Capstone High-Interest Books (Mankato, MN), 2003.

(With Glen Bledsoe) *The World's Fastest Indy Cars,* Capstone High-Interest Books (Mankato, MN), 2003.

Daredevils of the Air: Thrilling Tales of Pioneer Aviators, Avisson Press (Greensboro, NC), 2003.

Hanukkah Crafts, Enslow Publishers (Berkeley Heights, NJ), 2004.

Chinese New Year Crafts, Enslow Publishers (Berkeley Heights, NJ), 2005.

Genetically Engineered Foods, Blackbirch Press (San Diego, CA), 2005.

Work in Progress

A series of five short books on the human body; two books on military vehicles with husband and coauthor Glen Bledsoe.

Sidelights

In addition to focusing on her writing, both independently and with husband and coauthor Glen Bledsoe, Karen E. Bledsoe is also a biology instructor as well as the managing editor of the School Science and Mathematics Journal. Having loved writing since she was a young girl, Bledsoe openly admits to having had a long-time love affair with literature. The husband-and-wife team have coauthored a number of informational children's books, including *The World's Fastest Dragsters* and *Bicycling Adventures.* While she continues to work with her husband, Bledsoe has also begun publishing on her own, and has produced books such as *Daredevils of the Air: Thrilling Tales of Pioneer Aviators* and *Hanukkah Crafts.*

Daredevils of the Air begins with Orville and Wilbur Wright's invention of the airplane in 1903 and works its way forward through history. Bledsoe also provides readers with background on famous aviators such as Eddie Rickenbacker, Glenn Curtiss, and Charles Kingsford-Smith, who often risked their lives while advancing man's mastery of the skies, as safety was often not a top priority in early aviation history. Vicki Re-

Among the many books written by Bledsoe and husband, Glen Bledsoe, is The World's Fastest Dragsters, *which contains photographs from Florida's Museum of Drag Racing.*

utter, writing in *School Library Journal,* commented that the book provides readers with "a solid introduction to a group of courageous individuals."

Bledsoe once commented: "Writing and teaching are natural careers for me. I've always liked telling what I know to a captive audience.

"Words have been my toys since I first taught myself to read at the age of three. I spent many hours manufacturing little books, hand-illustrated and bound with a stapler. Inventions were a favorite theme, followed closely by mysteries, code books, and adventure stories. When I wasn't writing, I was gobbling up books as fast as I could get my hands on them. Books were my best friends during my school years when we moved every year—sometimes twice a year. I was a wallflower and had difficulty making friends.

"In junior high and high school, when the family was more settled and I finally had friends again, I turned to more challenging themes in both my reading and writing: high fantasy, supernatural adventure, lengthy sagas. I churned out the usual dreary, self-pitying poetry characteristic of angst-ridden teen writers, wrote for the school yearbook, and got a fair start on a lengthy fantasy novel that I may yet finish. My best subjects were English and science, and I chose the life sciences as my college path.

"College and a disastrous marriage occupied the next eight years of my life. Though I had little energy to spare for it, I still dabbled at writing. With a sister-in-law, I completed my first novel, a cliché-ridden romantic spoof that will never see the light of print (nor was it meant to) but which taught me much about what it takes to finish a book. Earning my bachelor's degree and a master of arts in botany during this period taught me plenty about perseverance in adverse circumstances.

"Finding that teaching was more to my liking than scientific research, I enrolled in the master of arts in teaching program at Willamette University, where I earned my teaching certificate and met my current husband. The two events marked a new era in my life. In the mutually supportive environment we've nurtured in our home, we have both blossomed creatively. We always have projects going: novels in progress, Web pages going up, art work, music, gardening, while the television slowly gathers dust. When we write, it is often literally together, with two keyboards plugged in series into the back of a Macintosh. Our publishing successes have been modest so far, but we intend to persevere until we can retire from teaching and earn our living as writers."

Biographical and Critical Sources

PERIODICALS

School Library Journal, March, 2002, Diane Olivo-Posner, review of *Bicycling Adventures,* p. 208; November, 2003, Jeffrey A. French, review of *The World's Fast-* est Dragsters, p. 153; June, 2005, Tanaz Sutaria, review of *Chinese New Year Crafts,* p. 133; January, 2004, Vicki Reutter, review of *Daredevils of the Air: Thrilling Tales of Pioneer Aviators,* p. 140.

ONLINE

Glen and Karen Bledsoe Home Page, http://www.gkbledsoe.com (December 19, 2005).*

*   *   *

BOLLINGER, Max 1929-

Personal

Born April 23, 1929, in Glarus, Switzerland; son of Jacques and Maria Regula (Durst) Bolliger. *Education:* Studied in Switzerland at progymnasium, 1943-46, Seminar Wettingen, 1946-51, and University of Zurich, 1958-61; also studied in London, England, 1956.

Addresses

Home—Zurich, Switzerland. *Agent*—c/o Author Mail, Henry Holt & Co. Children's Books, 115 W. 18th St., New York, NY 10011.

Career

Educator and writer. Teacher in Kallern, Switzerland, 1951-54, Meisterschwanden, Switzerland, 1954-56, and in Luxembourg, 1957; worked as school psychologist in Adliswil, Zurich, Switzerland, beginning 1961.

Awards, Honors

National German Children's Book Award for *David,* 1966; *Noah and the Rainbow* was a Children's Book Showcase title, 1973.

Writings

Verwundbare Kindheit (stories), Tschudy, 1957.
Ausgeschichte Taube (poems), Eirene Verlag, 1958.
Knirps (picture books), Comenius (Lucerne, Switzerland), 1963.
David, ein Hirtenjunge wird König (juvenile), illustrated by Edith Schindler, Otto Maier Verlag (Ravensburg, Germany), 1965, English translation by Marion Koenig, Delacorte (New York, NY), 1967, published as *Giant-Slayer: The Story of David,* Lion (Oxford, England), 1989.
Joseph, illustrated by Edith Schindler, Otto Maier Verlag (Ravensburg, Germany), 1967, English translation by Marion Koenig, Delacorte (New York, NY), 1969, translation published as *Dream-Teller: The Story of Joseph,* Lion (Oxford, England), 1989.

Mose, illustrated by Edith Schindler, Otto Maier Verlag (Ravensburg, Germany), 1967, translated by Christine Blackmore as *Freedom-Fighter: The Story of Moses,* Lion (Oxford, England), 1989.

Daniel und ein Volk in Gefangenschaft (juvenile), illustrated by Edith Schindler, Otto Maier Verlag (Ravensburg, Germany), 1968, translated by Marion Koenig as *Daniel,* Dell (New York, NY), 1970, published as *King's Captive: The Story of Daniel,* Lion (Batavia, IL), 1989.

Marios Trompete, Otto Maier Verlag (Ravensburg, Germany), 1968.

The Golden Apple, translated from the German by Roseanna Hoover, illustrated by Celestino Piatti, Atheneum (New York, NY), 1970.

The Fireflies (juvenile), translated from the German by Roseanna Hoover, illustrated by Jiri Trnka, Atheneum (New York, NY), 1970.

Der Regenbogen, Artemis, 1972, translated by Clyde Robert Bulla as *Noah and the Rainbow,* Crowell (New York, NY), 1973.

Der Mann aus Holz, illustrated by Fred Bauer, Atemis (Zurich, Switzerland), 1974, translated as *The Wooden Man,* Seabury Press (New York, NY), 1974.

Das Riesenfest: eine Geschichte, illustrated by Monika Laimgruber, Artemis (Zurich, Switzerland), 1975, translated by Barbara Willard as *The Giants' Feast,* Addison-Wesley (Reading, MA), 1976.

Was soll nur aus dir warden? 6 Lebensbilder, Frauenfeld (Stuttgart, Germany), 1977.

Das Schönste lied, illustrated by Jindra Capek, [Switzerland], 1979, translated as *The Most Beautiful Song,* Little, Brown (Boston, MA), 1980.

(With others) *Eine Rolle für Anna: Sechs Weihnachtsgeschichten,* F. Reinhardt (Basel, Switzerland), 1982.

The Lonely Prince, illustrated by Jürg Obrist, Atheneum (New York, NY), 1982.

Eine Zwergengeschichte, illustrated by Peter Sis, Bohem Press (Zurich, Switzerland), 1983, translated by Nina Ignatowicz as *The Happy Troll,* Henry Holt (New York, NY), 2005.

Der goldene Fisch: zehn Märchen, illustrated by Stepán Zavrel, Bohem Press (Zurich, Switzerland), 1984.

Die Riesenberge: eine Geschichte, illustrated by Stepán Zavrel, Bohem Press (Zurich, Switzerland), 1985.

Der Bunte vogel, [Switzerland], 1985, translated by Anthea Bell as *The Magic Bird,* illustrated by Jan Lenica, Anderson Press (London, England), 1986.

Ein Stern am Himmel: Niklaus von Flüe, Comenius (Lucerne, Switzerland), 1987, illustrated by Ulrich Stückelberger, NZN Buchverlag (Zurich, Switzerland), 2000.

Der Bärenberg, illustrated by Józef Wildón, [Switzerland], 1987, translated by Gabriella Modan as *Three Little Bears,* Adama Books (New York, NY), 1987.

An einem schönen Sommertag, illustrated by Jindra Capek, Bohem Press (Zurich, Switzerland), 1988, translated by Joel Agee as *Tales of a Long Afternoon: Five Fables and One Other,* E.P. Dutton (New York, NY), 1989.

Stummel unterwegs: Gutenachtgeschichten für Kinder und ihre Eltern, illustrations by Sita Jucker, AT Verlag (Aarau, Switzerland), 1988.

The Rabbit with the Sky Blue Ears, Canongate Pub. (Edinburgh, Scotland), 1987.

Author of scripts for Swiss television; author of notes for musical recordings.

Bollinger's books have been translated into several languages, including French and Spanish.

Biographical and Critical Sources

PERIODICALS

Economist, December 26, 1981, review of *The Lonely Prince,* p. 106.

Horn Book, February, 1971; February, 1973; March, 1988, review of *Joseph,* p. 236.

Kirkus Reviews, June 1, 2005, review of *The Happy Troll,* p. 633.

Publishers Weekly, January 15, 1982, review of *The Lonely Prince,* p. 98; January 13, 1989, review of *The Rabbit with the Sky Blue Ears,* p. 87.

Reading Teacher, October, 1990, review of *Tales of a Long Afternoon,* p. 150.

School Librarian, May, 1989, review of *The Rabbit with the Sky Blue Ears,* p. 53; August, 1989, review of *One Fine Day in Summertime,* p. 98.

School Library Journal, February, 1982, Patricia Dooley, review of *The Most Beautiful Song,* p. 64; April, 1982, review of *The Lonely Prince,* p. 56; January, 1990, Denise Anton Wright, review of *Tales of a Long Afternoon,* p. 94.

Wilson Library Bulletin, May, 1982, review of *The Most Beautiful Song,* p. 688.*

*   *   *

BROWNE, N.M. 1960-
(Nicola Matthews, Nicky Matthews Browne)

Personal

Born November 21, 1960, in Burnley, Lancashire, England; daughter of Donald (a teacher and painter) and Shirley Smith (a teacher) Matthews; married Paul Browne (a strategy implementation program director) July 18, 1987; children: William, Morgan, Owen, Christa. *Education:* New College, Oxford, B.A. (philosophy and theology; with honors), 1983; Kings College, Cambridge, P.G.C.E.; Manchester Business School, M.B.A., 1987. *Politics:* "Liberal/Left." *Religion:* Church of England (Anglican). *Hobbies and other interests:* "Singing (badly), walking, rowing a Thames skiff, socialising."

N.M. Browne

Addresses

Agent—Mic Cheetham, 11/12 Dover St., London W1S 4LJ, England. *E-mail*—nicky.matthews@btinternet.com.

Career

Writer and business executive. Worked as a teacher in Kettering, Northamptonshire, England, 1984-85; Shell International, London, England, marketing executive, 1987-89; Shell UK, marketing executive, 1989-91; writer and "full-time mum," beginning 1991.

Member

British Society of Authors, Scattered Authors Society.

Awards, Honors

Lancashire Book Award runner-up, 2000, for *Warriors of Alavna;* Carnegie Medal nomination, 2004, for *Basilisk.*

Writings

YOUNG-ADULT FANTASY NOVELS

Warriors of Alavna, Bloomsbury (London, England), 2000, Bloomsbury (New York, NY), 2002.

Hunted, Bloomsbury Children's Books (New York, NY), 2002.

Warriors of Camlann (sequel to *Warriors of Alavna*), Bloomsbury (New York, NY), 2003.

Basilisk, Bloomsbury (New York, NY), 2004.

The Story of Stone, Bloomsbury (New York, NY), 2005.

UNDER NAME NICOLA MATTHEWS

The Extraordinary Lightening Conductor, illustrated by Rachel Pearce, Bloomsbury (London, England), 1995.

The Extraordinary Adventures of Joe Sloop, Bloomsbury (London, England), 1995.

"I Don't Like Space Glop!" ("Crazy Gang" reader series), illustrated by Eleanor Taylor, Bloomsbury (London, England), 1998.

"Og Fo," Says the Space Bug ("Crazy Gang" reader series), illustrated by Eleanor Taylor, Bloomsbury (London, England), 1998.

Pets Just Want to Have Fun! ("Crazy Gang" reader series), illustrated by Eleanor Taylor, Bloomsbury (London, England), 1998.

This Is Yum! ("Crazy Gang" reader series), illustrated by Eleanor Taylor, Bloomsbury (London, England), 1998.

"Is That a Dog in the Sky?" ("Crazy Gang" reader series), illustrated by Eleanor Taylor, Bloomsbury (London, England), 1999.

Work in Progress

The Spellgrinder's Apprentice; Googol.

Sidelights

Beginning her writing career authoring simple but humorous stories for fledgling readers under the name Nicola Matthews, British author N.M. Browne has gained a following among young-adult fans of her fantasy novels. *Warriors of Alavna* and its sequel, *Warriors of Camlann,* follow two modern-day teens who pass through a phenomenon called the Veil and find themselves transported back in time. Shifts in time also figure in *Hunted,* in which a teen named Karen lies in a coma as the result of a vicious attack. While her body is comatose, her spirit has morphed into an "arl": moving to another realm of being, it has taken the shape of a fox. Now confronting a host of new dangers in her fox shape, Karen befriends a shepherd and slowly begins to understand and deal with her new reality. In *Publishers Weekly* a contributor praised *Hunted* for its "fight scenes, escapes and revelations," adding that Browne "cleverly mixes fantasy and action." Noting that the author brings to life her alternative world "with subtlety and style," a *Kirkus Reviews* critic added that the book mixes "shapeshifting with a complexly realized fantasy world in a fast-paced plot."

Basilisk is the story of a fantasy world where outcasts live below the once-beautiful city of Lunnzia, a place where people's station in life is predetermined and assigned and society above-ground has disintegrated into

Two modern fifteen year olds find themselves in first-century Britain, where they must help defend the Celts against Roman invaders in Browne's entertaining 2000 fantasy novel. (Cover illustration by Jenna LaRue.)

chaos. Rej, a Comber who lives in the subterranean world of Below, and Donna, one of the Abovers, come together as a result of their shared dreams of dragons and basilisks. Confronted with a murder Rej knows he must solve, the pair soon discover a plot that threatens to destroy the gentle Combers. Reviewing *Basilisk*, Hillias J. Martin commented in *School Library Journal* that, "once hooked, . . . patient readers will enjoy the spooky atmosphere [and] . . . intriguing and often untrustworthy characters," found in Browne's tale. A *Kirkus Reviews* critic called the novel "suspenseful and rather original," while in the London *Times* Amanda Craig compared Browne's story to H.G. Wells's *The Time Machine*, writing that in *Basilisk* the author draws readers into "an entirely different world whose strangeness and detail exert a hypnotic pull on the reader."

Browne told *SATA:* "I wanted to be a writer as a child, but did not really do anything about it until I was on a career break after having given birth to my second child. My father, a painter, had died not long before and with a lot of encouragement from my sister, who is also a painter, I realized that if I was ever going to fulfill that ambition I should 'seize the day.'

"In the first place I write to entertain both myself and, I hope, my readers. I want to give readers the strong sense of having been elsewhere, to a real but different place for the duration of my novels.

"I would love to say I get up at 6:00 am every day and, after a work out and a small cup of lemon tea, work for eight hours straight, but it wouldn't be true. I work my writing round my kids' school day and fit in a little socializing and coffee drinking as often as possible. I am nowhere near as disciplined as I'd like to be.

"I loved C.S. Lewis, Rosemary Sutcliffe, and Alan Garner as a child but also enjoyed Biggles and 'Just William' and all the science fiction I could get my hands on. In general I enjoy anything with a powerful atmosphere and a certain weirdness. I have probably been influenced by every book I've ever read and every film I've ever seen. I think this is a perfect time to be a book-loving child, even if it is a depressing time to be an author: there is just so much brilliant writing around at the moment—far too much competition.

"I think there is only one piece of advice I'd give to an aspiring writer or illustrator: 'Just do it!' That's it."

Biographical and Critical Sources

PERIODICALS

Booklist, April 15, 2004, Jennifer Mattson, review of *Basilisk,* p. 1450.

Bulletin of the Center for Children's Books, October, 2002, review of *Warriors of Alavna,* p. 50; July-August, 2004, Timnah Card, review of *Basilisk,* p. 457.

Kirkus Reviews, May 15, 2003, review of *Warriors of Camlann,* p. 746; June 1, 2002, review of *Hunted,* p. 801; September 1, 2002, review of *Warriors of Alavna,* p. 1305; April 15, 2004, review of *Basilisk,* p. 391.

Kliatt, July, 2002, Paula Rohrlick, review of *Hunted,* p. 7.

Library Media Connection, February, 2005, Stephanie L. Dobson, review of *Basilisk,* p. 74.

Locus, May, 2004, Carolyn Cushman, review of *Basilisk.*

Publishers Weekly, July 1, 2002, review of *Hunted,* p. 80; April 14, 2003, review of *Warriors of Camlann,* p. 72; April 19, 2004, review of *Basilisk,* p. 62.

School Librarian, winter, 2000, review of *Warriors of Alavna,* p. 211; summer, 2002, review of *Hunted,* p. 99; winter, 2003, review of *Warriors of Camlann,* p. 207; autumn, 2004, Susan Elkin, review of *Basilisk,* p. 155.

School Library Journal, August, 2002, Beth Wright, review of *Hunted,* p. 182; January, 2003, review of *Warriors of Alavna,* p. 133; July, 2003, Patricia A. Dollish, review of *Warriors of Camlann,* p. 124; June, 2004, Hillias J. Martin, review of *Basilisk,* p. 135.

Times (London, England), April 3, 2004, Amanda Craig, review of *Basilisk*.

Voice of Youth Advocates, February, 2003, review of *Warriors of Alavna,* p. 485; June, 2003, review of *Warriors of Camlann,* p. 146; August, 2004, review of *Basilisk,* p. 227.

*   *   *

BROWNE, Nicky Matthews
See BROWNE, N.M.

*   *   *

BURGAN, Michael 1960-

Personal

Born March 15, 1960, in Hartford, CT; son of Bernard and Irene (Zeppa) Burgan; married Samantha Strauss, May 6, 2000. *Education:* University of Connecticut, B.A., 1983; attended Emerson College, 1987-88. *Politics:* Democrat. *Religion:* Unitarian-Universalist. *Hobbies and other interests:* Playwriting, films, music, travel, cooking, sports.

Addresses

Home—Chicago, IL. *Agent*—c/o Author Mail, Compass Point Books, Compass Point Books, 3109 W. 50th St., No. 115, Minneapolis, MN 55410. *E-mail*—Mburgan@aol.com.

Career

Weekly Reader Corp., Middletown, CT, editor, 1988-94; freelance writer, 1994—. Hartford Food System, member of board of directors, 1997—.

Member

Dramatists Guild of America, Phi Beta Kappa, Phi Kappa Phi.

Writings

Boris Bigfoot's Big Feat, HarperCollins (New York, NY), 1995.

The Curse of Cleo Patrick's Mummy, HarperCollins (New York, NY), 1996.

Zelda's Zombie Dance, HarperCollins (New York, NY), 1996.

(Reteller) Stephen Crane, *The Red Badge of Courage,* illustrated by Kathryn Yingling and Ed Parker, HarperCollins (New York, NY), 1996.

(Reteller) Mary Wollstonecraft Shelley, *Frankenstein,* illustrated by Kathryn Yingling and Ed Parker, HarperCollins (New York, NY), 1996.

(Reteller) Miguel de Cervantes, *Don Quixote,* illustrated by Kathryn Yingling, Lars Hokanson, and Frances Cichetti, HarperCollins (New York, NY), 1996.

Tiki Doll of Doom, HarperCollins (New York, NY), 1997.

Chocolate Cake, Huckleberry Press (South Glastonbury, CT), 1997.

The Prize, Huckleberry Press (South Glastonbury, CT), 1997.

The Pro Sports Halls of Fame: Basketball, two volumes, Grolier, 1997.

The Associated Press Library of Disasters, four volumes, Grolier, 1998.

American Immigration, two volumes, Grolier, 1998.

Madeleine Albright, Millbrook Press (Brookfield, CT), 1998.

Dominik Hasek, Chelsea House (Philadelphia, PA), 1999.

Maryland, Children's Press (New York, NY), 1999.

Argentina, Children's Press (New York, NY), 1999.

England, Children's Press (New York, NY), 1999.

The Pontiac Firebird, RiverFront Books (New York, NY), 1999.

The Porsche 911, RiverFront Books (New York, NY), 1999.

The Toyota Land Cruiser, RiverFront Books (New York, NY), 1999.

Belgium, Children's Press (New York, NY), 2000.

Travel Agent, Capstone Books (Mankato, MN), 2000.

Veterinarian, Capstone Books (Mankato, MN), 2000.

U.S. Army Special Forces: Airborne Rangers, RiverFront Books (New York, NY), 2000.

U.S. Navy Special Forces: SEAL Teams, RiverFront Books (New York, NY), 2000.

U.S. Navy Special Forces: Special Boat Units, RiverFront Books (New York, NY), 2000.

Dino-Might! (includes games), illustrated by Bernard Adnante, Innovative KIDS (Norwalk, CT), 2000.

The World's Fastest Military Airplanes Capstone Books (Mankato, MN), 2001.

Supercarriers, Capston High Interest (Mankato, MN), 2001.

Sheryl Swoopes, Chelsea House (Philadelphia, PA), 2001.

Nuclear Submarines, Capstone High Interest (Mankato, MN), 2001.

John F. Kennedy, World Almanac Library (Milwaukee, WI), 2001.

John Adams: Second U.S. President, Chelsea House (Philadelphia, PA), 2001.

Henry Ford, Industrialist, Ferguson Publishing (Chicago, IL), 2001.

The World's Wildest Roller Coasters, Capston Books (Mankato, MN), 2001.

Leif Eriksson, Heinmann Library (Chicago, IL), 2002.

Henry Ford, World Almanac Library (Milwaukee, WI), 2002.

Great Moments in the Olympics ("Great Moments in Sports" series), World Almanac Library (Milwaukee, WI), 2002.

Great Moments in Basketball ("Great Moments in Sports" series), World Almanac Library (Milwaukee, WI), 2002.

Great Moments in Baseball ("Great Moments in Sports" series), World Almanac Library (Milwaukee, WI), 2002.

George Rogers Clark: American General, Chelsea House (Philadelphia, PA), 2002.

The Beatles, World Almanac Library (Milwaukee, WI), 2002.

William Henry Seward: Senator and Statesman, Chelsea House (Philadelphia, PA), 2002.

The Story of Levi's, illustrated by Ronald Himler, Scholastic (New York, NY), 2002.

Marco Polo: Marco Polo and the Silk Road to China, Compass Point (Minneapolis, MN), 2002.

Magellan: Ferdinand Magellan and the First Trip around the World, Compass Point (Minneapolis, MN), 2002.

Puerto Rico, Children's Press (New York, NY), 2003.

Puerto Rico and Outlying Territories, World Almanac Library (Milwaukee, WI), 2003.

New Mexico, Land of Enchantment, World Almanac Library (Milwaukee, WI), 2003.

The Korean War, Heinemann Library (Chicago, IL), 2003.

Connecticut, Benchmark Books (New York, NY), 2003.

The Connecticut Colony, Child's World (Chanhassen, MN), 2003.

Colonial and Revolutionary Times: A Watts Guide, Franklin Watts (New York, NY), 2003.

California, Benchmark Books (New York, NY), 2003.

Buddhist Faith in America, Facts on File (New York, NY), 2003.

Maryland, Children's Press (New York, NY), 2004.

John Paul Jones: Naval Hero, Child's World (Chanhassen, MN), 2004.

Henry Clay: The Great Compromiser, Child's World (Chanhassen, MN), 2004.

Christopher Columbus: Opening the Americas to European Exploration, Child's World (Chanhassen, MN), 2004.

African Americans ("Our Cultural Heritage" series), Child's World (Chanhassen, MN), 2004.

The Vietnam War, Heinemann Library (Chicago, IL), 2004.

Inuit, Gareth Stevens (Milwaukee, WI), 2005.

George W. Bush: Our Forty-third President, Child's World (Chanhassen, MN), 2005.

Empire of the Mongols ("Great Empires of the Past" series), Facts on File (New York, NY), 2004.

Empire of Ancient Rome, Facts on File (New York, NY), 2005.

Bigfoot, Edge Books (Mankato, MN), 2005.

The Automobile, World Almanac Library (Milwaukee, WI), 2005.

Voices from Colonial America: Massachusetts, 1620-1776, National Geographic Society (Washington, DC), 2005.

The Valley of the Kings: Egypt's Greatest Mummies, Capstone Press (Mankato, MN), 2005.

Thomas Paine: Great Writer of the Revolution ("Signature Lives" series), Compass Point Books (Minneapolis, MN), 2005.

Samuel Adams: Patriot and Statesman ("Signature Lives" series), Compass Point Books (Minneapolis, MN), 2005.

King Tut's Tomb: Ancient Treasures Uncovered, Capstone Press (Mankato, MN), 2005.

Jim Morrision, Capstone Press (Mankato, MN), 2005.

Japan, Capstone Press (Mankato, MN), 2005.

Italian Immigrants ("Immigration to the United States" series), Facts on File (New York, NY), 2005.

John Winthrop: First Governor of Massachusetts ("Signature Lives" series), Compass Point Books (Minneapolis, MN), 2006.

Hillary Rodham Clinton: First Lady and Senator, Compass Point Books (Minneapolis, MN), 2006.

Escaping to Freedom: The Underground Railroad, Facts on File (New York, NY), 2006.

Elizabeth Cady Stanton: Social Reformer ("Signature Lives" series), Compass Point Books (Minneapolis, MN), 2006.

Voiced from Colonial America: New York, 1609-1776, National Geographic Society (Washington, DC), 2006.

Spying and the Cold War, Raintree (Chicago, IL), 2006.

Roger Williams: Founder of Rhode Island ("Signature Lives" series), Compass Point Books (Minneapolis, MN), 2006.

Thomas Alva Edison: Great American Inventor ("Signature Lives" series), Compass Point Books (Minneapolis, MN), 2006.

Miranda v. Arizona: The Rights of the Accused ("Snapshots in History" series), Compass Point Books (Minneapolis, MN) 2007.

J. Pierpont Morgan: Industrialist and Financier ("Signature Lives" series), Compass Point Books (Minneapolis, MN), 2007.

Alexander the Great: World Conqueror ("Signature Lives" series), Compass Point Books (Minneapolis, MN), 2007.

Contributor to books, including *Leading American Businesses: Profiles of Major American Companies and the People Who Made Them Important,* UXL (Farmington Hills, MI), 2003.

Burgan's books have been translated into Spanish.

"COLD WAR" SERIES

The Threats, Raintree Steck-Vaughn (Austin, TX), 2001.

Hot Conflicts, Raintree Steck-Vaughn (Austin, TX), 2001.

The Separation, Raintree Steck-Vaughn (Austin, TX), 2001.

The Collapse, Raintree Steck-Vaughn (Austin, TX), 2001.

"PRO-WRESTLER" SERIES

Goldberg: Pro Wrestler Bill Goldberg, Capston High Interest (Mankato, MN), 2002.

Stone Cold: Pro Wrestler Steve Austin, Capston High-Interest (Mankato, MN), 2002.

The Rock: Pro Wrestler Rocky Maivia, Capston Press (Mankato, MN), 2002.

"WE THE PEOPLE" SERIES

The Boston Tea Party, Compass Point Books (Minneapolis, MN), 2000.

The Trail of Tears, Compass Point Books (Minneapolis, MN), 2001.

The Declaration of Independence, Compass Point Books (Minneapolis, MN), 2001.

The Battle of Gettysburg, Compass Point Books (Minneapolis, MN), 2001.

The Alamo, Compass Point Books (Minneapolis, MN), 2001.

The Great Depression, Compass Point Books (Minneapolis, MN), 2002.

The Bill of Rights, Compass Point Books (Minneapolis, MN), 2002.

The Louisiana Purchase, Compass Point Books (Minneapolis, MN), 2002.

Valley Forge, Compass Point Books (Minneapolis, MN), 2004.

The Titanic, Compass Point Books (Minneapolis, MN), 2004.

Monticello, Compass Point Books (Minneapolis, MN), 2004.

Great Women of the American Revolution, Compass Point Books (Minneapolis, MN), 2005.

The Boston Massacre, Compass Point Books (Minneapolis, MN), 2005.

The Assassination of Abraham Lincoln, Compass Point Books (Minneapolis, MN), 2005.

The Nineteenth Amendment, Compass Point Books (Minneapolis, MN), 2005.

The Stamp Act of 1765, Compass Point Books (Minneapolis, MN), 2005.

The Salem Witch Trials, Compass Point Books (Minneapolis, MN), 2005.

The Lincoln-Douglas Debates, Compass Point Books (Minneapolis, MN), 2006.

The Haymarket Square Tragedy, Compass Point Books (Minneapolis, MN), 2006.

The Gettysburg Address, Compass Point Books (Minneapolis, MN), 2006.

Fort Sumter, Compass Point Books (Minneapolis, MN), 2006.

The Battle of the Ironclads, Compass Point Books (New York, NY), 2006.

The Reconstruction Amendments, Compass Point Books (Minneapolis, MN), 2006.

The Missouri Compromise, Compass Point Books (Minneapolis, MN), 2006.

"PROFILES OF THE PRESIDENTS" SERIES

George Washington, Compass Point Books (Minneapolis, MN), 2002.

Franklin D. Roosevelt, Compass Point Books (Minneapolis, MN), 2002.

John Quincy Adams, Compass Point Books (Minneapolis, MN), 2003.

Andrew Johnson, Compass Points Books (Minneapolis, MN), 2003.

Lyndon Baines Johnson, Compass Point Books (Minneapolis, MN), 2004.

George W. Bush, Compass Point Books (Minneapolis, MN), 2004.

William Howard Taft, Compass Point Books (Minneapolis, MN), 2004.

"GRAPHIC LIBRARY" SERIES

The Curse of King Tut's Tomb, illustrated by Barbara Schulz, Capstone Press (Mankato, MN), 2005.

The Boston Massacre, illustrated by Keith Williams, Capstone Press (Mankato, MN), 2005.

The Battle of Gettysburg, illustrated by Steve Erwin, Keith Williams, and Charles Barnett III, Capstone Press (Mankato, MN), 2006.

Nat Turner's Slave Rebellion, illustrated by Richard Dominguez, Bib Wiacek, and Charles Barnett III, Capstone Press (Mankato, MN), 2006.

Sidelights

A prolific writer of nonfiction for younger readers, Michael Burgan has contributed to numerous book series since beginning his publishing career in the mid-1990s. Although he has produced fiction and adaptations of several literary works, Burgan focuses for the most part on American history and on writing biographies of notable men and women from history. In addition to conventional histories such as *The Trail of Tears*, which was dubbed "concise" and objective by *School Library Journal* contributor Ann Welton, he has also helped encourage reluctant readers by penning boy-centered books such as *The World's Fastest Military Airplanes, Great Moments in Basketball,* biographies of professional wrestlers "Stone Cold" Steve Austin and The Rock, and several titles in Capstone Press's "Graphic History" series. Presenting factual topics in a fully illustrated graphic-novel format, book such as Burgan's *The Curse of King Tut's Tomb* were praised by *School Library Journal* contributor Peg Glisson as "historically accurate" as well as "fun and interesting reads" capable of inspiring further research into their "high-interest subject matter."

Burgan once told *SATA:* "I had originally hoped to be a teacher, but one semester of student-teaching during graduate school convinced me that I should stick to my first love, writing—if I could make a living at it. Thankfully I took a job at *Weekly Reader* and found my niche: writing social studies for children. I was able to pursue my interest in history and current events while feeling I was making a contribution as an educator (of a sort). Freelancing has enabled me to pursue a wide range of topics and also try some children's fiction. With the fiction, I get to use some of my skills as a would-be playwright and, I hope, make kids laugh."

Biographical and Critical Sources

PERIODICALS

Booklist, May 1, 2002, Heather Hepler, review of *Henry Ford,* p. 1519; May, 1, 2004, Jennifer Mattson, review of *The Titanic,* p. 1556.

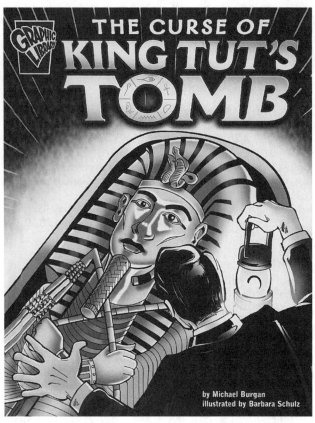

Burgan recounts the adventures of British archaeologist Howard Carter who, in 1922, discovered the first intact tomb of an Egyptian pharaoh to survive antiquity. (Cover illustration by Barbara Schulz.)

National Geographic World, January, 1999; May, 1999; October, 1999; December, 1999; April, 2000.

Publishers Weekly, September 11, 2000, review of *Dino-Might!,* p. 93.

School Library Journal, June, 1999, p. 140; June, 2001, Ann Welton, review of *The Trail of Tears,* p. 134, and Steve Clancy, review of *The World's Fastest Military Airplanes,* p. 164; August, 2001, John Sigwald, review of *The Alamo,* p. 167; October, 2001, Elizabeth Talbot, review of *The Collapse,* p. 179; December, 2001, David M. Alperstein, review of *The Separation,* p. 153; January, 2002, Pamela K. Bomboy, review of *Magellan: Ferdinand Magellan and the First Trip around the World,* p. 146, and Janie Schomberg, review of *The Great Depression* and *The Bill of Rights,* p. 148; June, 2002, Tim Wadham, review of *The Beatles,* p. 154; July, 2002, Dona J. Helmer, review of *The Louisiana Purchase,* p. 131; August, 2002, Mary Mueller, review of *Marco Polo: Marco Polo and the Silk Road to China,* p. 202; March, 2003, Kate Kohlbeck, review of *Great Moments in Basketball,* p. 247; July, 2003, Jeffrey A. French, review of *Colonial and Revolutionary Times: A Watts Guide,* p. 138; March, 2004, Andrew Medlar, review of *Great Moments in the Olympics,* p. 69; February, 2005, Kathleen Kelly MacMillan, review of *Maryland,* p. 114; April, 2005, Linda Greengrass, review of *Italian Immigrants,* p. 81; June, 2005, Janet Gillen, review of *Great Women of the American Revolution,* p. 175; July, 2005, Peg Glis-

son, review of *The Curse of King Tut's Tomb,* p. 124; September, 2005, Heather Ver Voort, review of *George W. Bush,* p. 219; December, 2005, Anne L. Tormohlen, review of *Spying and the Cold War,* p. 150.

*　　*　　*

CANNON, Curt
See HUNTER, Evan

*　　*　　*

CASTILLO, Edmund L. 1924-2005

OBITUARY NOTICE—See index for *SATA* sketch: Born November 13, 1924, in Toledo, OH; died of congestive heart failure, August 24, 2005, in Washington, DC. Naval officer, government official, and author. Castillo was a retired U.S. Navy captain, where he served as a public affairs officer, and later worked as spokesman for Fairfax County in Virginia. After graduating from Northwestern University in 1945, he was commissioned as an officer in the Naval Reserve just in time to see action in the Pacific theater during the last months of World War II. In 1949 he was commissioned in the regular navy and became a public affairs specialist. Castillo served until 1968, rising to the rank of captain. During this time, he held several posts, including press officer for the Department of Navy, officer-in-charge of the Navy Journalist School, and press officer of the Department of Defense. During his time in the navy, Castillo also wrote several nonfiction books for children, including *All about the United States Navy* (1961), *The Seabees of World War II* (1963), and *Flat-Tops— The Story of Aircraft Carriers* (1969). Castillo continued his education in the 1950s, earning a master's degree in communication from Boston University in 1954. After retiring from the U.S. Navy, he put his public relations experience to good use by becoming the spokesman for Fairfax County. Castillo also earned a Ph.D. in public administration from George Washington University in 1978. He left his job as spokesman in 1984 to become executive assistant to the county executive, retiring from public service in 1990.

OBITUARIES AND OTHER SOURCES:

PERIODICALS

Washington Post, September 13, 2005, p. B6.
Washington Times, September 9, 2005, p. B2.

*　　*　　*

COLLINS, Hunt
See HUNTER, Evan

D-E

DUNBAR, Fiona 1961-

Personal

Born July 3, 1961, in Hemel Hempstead, England; daughter of William Dunbar (a salesman) and Christine Partridge (an actress and writer); married Pano Pliotis (a tax attorney) February 3, 1993; children: Helena Christine, George Frederick. *Education:* Attended Buckinghamshire College of Further Education. *Politics:* "Liberal Democrat." *Religion:* "Spiritual, not religious." *Hobbies and other interests:* "My work IS my hobby! But I also love cooking and anything creative."

Addresses

Agent—Hilary Delamere, The Agency, 24 Pottery Lane, London W11 4LZ, England. *E-mail*—fidunbar@yahoo.co.uk.

Career

Illustrator, writer, and artist. Square One Studios, London, England, commercial artist, 1979-87; freelance illustrator, beginning 1987; writer.

Member

British Society of Authors.

Writings

FOR YOUNG READERS; SELF-ILLUSTRATED

You'll Never Guess!, Dial Books for Young Readers (New York, NY), 1991.
My Secret Brother, Hutchinson (London, England), 1992.
Under the Stairs, Red Fox (London, England), 1993.
Cupid Cakes, Orchard (London, England), 2005.
Toon-Head, Orchard (New York, NY), 2006.

"LULU BAKER" SERIES; NOVELS

The Truth Cookie, Orchard Books (London, England), 2004, Orchard Books (New York, NY), 2005.
Chocolate Wishes, Orchard (New York, NY), 2005.

ILLUSTRATOR

Betsy Duffey, *Camp Knock Knock,* Delacorte Press (New York, NY), 1996.
Shelley Harwayne, *What's Cooking?,* Mondo (Greenvale, NY), 1996.
Betsy Duffey, *The Camp Knock Knock Mystery,* Doubleday Book for Young Readers (New York, NY), 1997.
Stuart J. Murphy, *Every Buddy Counts,* HarperCollins (New York, NY), 1997.
Mary Hoffman and Rhiannon Lassiter, editors, *Lines in the Sand,* Frances Lincoln (London, England), 2003.
Anna Wilson, editor, *Princess Stories,* Macmillan (London, England), 2005.

Sidelights

Graphic artist and illustrator Fiona Dunbar contributed her artistic talents to a number of picture books by other writers before making her own writing debut with *You'll Never Guess!* In this 1991 picture book, which features Dunbar's engaging artwork, readers are treated to a clever guessing game as misleading silhouettes are displayed on the edges of a family portrait picture frame. Readers attempt to guess what has created these shadows, but a turn of the page reveals that the silhouette is usually of something completely unexpected; in one case what appears to be a little girl is actually a rather silly-looking dog! In a review for *Publishers Weekly,* a critic enjoyed Dunbar's work, calling *You'll Never Guess!* "a dashing debut for a promising author-illustrator" in which "readers will . . . be especially entertained by Dunbar's unexpected ending."

Dunbar has more recently shifted her attention to an older audience with a series of books that include *The Truth Cookie, Cupid Cakes,* and *Chocolate Wishes.* The quick-reading novels feature Lulu Baker, a teen whose goal, in addition to surviving adolescence, is to rescue her widowed father from an unhealthy romantic entanglement with the maniacal temptress and evil stepmother-wannabe Varaminta le Bone. Fortunately, Lulu has help from a powerful source: a magical recipe book titled *The Apple Star,* which literally falls into her hands, perhaps a gift from her deceased mother. Also for older readers, *Toon-Head* focuses on a boy named Pablo who can predict the future by drawing cartoons. While his talent at first seems like a good thing, when his special gift is discovered by some unsavory characters, Pablo must find a way to focus his cartooning to keep himself safe.

Dunbar told *SATA:* "I am self-taught, both in illustration and in writing; the latter is something I fell into sideways. I had always assumed I was most suited to the visual arts, so no one was more surprised then I was when the writing started to take off. Yet when it did, it felt like a tremendous release. When you are illustrating, your job is to interpret other people's ideas most of the time; being allowed to lose myself so completely in my own imagination was a revelation! Although I had written and illustrated some picture books, catering to such a young readership can be confining. Now it's as if I'm directing a movie in my head, only I don't have to get the funding first—fantastic!

"One of the most exciting moments ever was when I read the Greek myths for the first time; I think I was about nine. I find those stories—as well as myths from other parts of the world—an inexhaustible source of fascination. Hans Christian Andersen's stories also had a powerful effect on me, especially *The Snow Queen.* Still, my influences come from very disparate sources and, unsurprisingly for a former illustrator, the visual arts have an influence too, such as Saul Steinberg's drawings or Tim Burton's films. As an adult I am strongly drawn to the absurd and the satirical, from Lewis Carroll to Douglas Adams. I love the wicked playfulness of Roald Dahl. I enjoy the kind of fantasy that is rooted in reality, and that is the sort of story I tend to write."

Biographical and Critical Sources

PERIODICALS

Booklist, February 1, 1997, Hazel Rochman, review of *Every Buddy Counts,* p. 943.

Publishers Weekly, December 14, 1990, review of *You'll Never Guess!,* p. 65.

School Librarian, February, 1993, review of *My Secret Brother,* p. 14; November, 1993, review of *Under the Stairs,* p. 148; autumn, 2004, Lucinda Fox, review of *The Truth Cookie,* p. 145.

School Library Journal, August, 1991, Marianne L. Pilla, review of *You'll Never Guess!,* p. 144.

ONLINE

Fiona Dunbar Home Page, http://www.fionadunbar.com (December 19, 2005).

Watts Publishing Group Web site, http://www.wattspub.co.uk/ (December 19, 2005), "Fiona Dunbar."

EATON, Anthony 1971-

Personal

Born 1971, in New Guinea; married; wife's name Imogen. *Education:* University of Western Australia, doctoral studies (creative writing). *Hobbies and other interests:* Water activities, traveling, skiing, cycling, hiking, fishing, reading, writing.

Addresses

Home—Western Australia. *Agent*—c/o Author Mail, University of Queensland Press, P.O. Box 6042, St. Lucia, Queensland 4067, Australia. *E-mail*—Anthony_Eaton@dodo.com.au.

Career

Educator and writer. Worked variously as a security guard, car park attendant, sailing instructor, and rowing coach; Trinity College, Perth, Western Australia, Australia, teacher of English until 2002; writer, 1997—, and lecturer.

Awards, Honors

West Australian Premier's award for young-adult fiction, and Aureolis Award for Best Adult Fantasy shortlist, both 2000, both for *The Darkness;* Children's Book Council of Australia Award (CBCA) notable book designation, International Youth Library Notable Book selection, Western Australian Premier's Award shortlist and Vision Australia Young Adult Audio Book of the Year award, all 2002, all for *A New Kind of Dreaming;* Western Australian Premier's Award shortlist, 2003, for *Nathan Nuttboard Hits the Beach;* Western Australian Premier's Award, 2004, and CBCA Award honor book, 2005, both for *Fireshadow;* Australian Antarctic Division Antarctic arts fellow, 2005-06; Aureolis Award shortlist for best adult fantasy and for best young-adult fantasy, both 2006, both for *Nightpeople.*

Writings

The Darkness, University of Queensland Press (St. Lucia, Queensland, Australia), 2000.

A New Kind of Dreaming, University of Queensland Press (St. Lucia, Queensland, Australia), 2001.

Nathan Nuttboard Hits the Beach, University of Queensland Press (St. Lucia, Queensland, Australia), 2002.

Fireshadow, University of Queensland Press (St. Lucia, Queensland, Australia), 2004.

The Girl in the Cave, illustrated by Johnny Danalis, University of Queensland Press (St. Lucia, Queensland, Australia), 2004.

Nightpeople (first novel in "The Darklands" trilogy), University of Queensland Press (St. Lucia, Queensland, Australia), 2005.

Work in Progress

Nathan Nuttboard: Family Matters; Skypeople, the second novel in "The Darklands" trilogy.

Sidelights

Anthony Eaton took up writing professionally in 1997 after meeting well-known Australian author Gary Crew at a writer's workshop held in Eaton's native West Australia. Eaton made his publishing debut in 2000 with the award-winning young-adult novel *The Darkness,* about two young people who find themselves caught up in the paranoid mind-set overshadowing their isolated community. Two years later, Eaton resigned from his full-time teaching position at Perth's Trinity College in order to pursue the full-time writing career that has earned him fans in a range of ages. He introduces middle-grade readers to a quirky young protagonist in his semi-autobiographical *Nathan Nuttboard Hits the Beach,* opens up a new fantasy world in *Nightpeople,* and shares his passion for history with older readers in 2004's *Fireshadow.* Reviewing Eaton's humorous elementary-grade reader, titled *The Girl in the Cave,*

Although Kate finds it strange that she is forced to live in a cave behind her aunt and uncle's home, a surprise visit from a stranger soon makes life even stranger in Eaton's quirky novel for younger readers. (Cover illustration by Johnny Danalis.)

Aussie Reviews Online contributor Sally Murphy noted that the book's "twists and turns are zany and unbelievable—which is just what kids like."

Taking place during World War II, *Fireshadow* follows two seventeen-year-old boys. Erich Pieters joins the German Wehrmacht to fight for Chancellor Adolf Hitler in 1941, and winds up in an Australian Prisoner of War camp after fighting in North Africa. Half a century later, Vinnie Santiani flees into the remote Australian Bush in an effort to cope with the tragic death of his sister. Despite the fact that they live in different epochs, the boys' lives intertwine in the novel with haunting results. A reviewer for *Magpies* commented that the award-winning book's "language is exceptional throughout . . . while the author's insights into the emotional lives of the young people are sensitively conveyed."

On his home page, Eaton commented that, "for me, a story begins with a character—and it is the process of exploring that character's experiences that reveals the story." In planning the three-part series that begins with the futuristic novel *Nightpeople,* Eaton explained that he "wanted to explore a society turned in upon itself, which has been struggling to survive, and which is reaching the end of its history. I was also keen to write something with a strong female protagonist—so far my main characters have all been male, and I thought it would be fun to try something from another point of view."

Biographical and Critical Sources

PERIODICALS

Magpies, September, 2000, James Moloney, interview with Eaton, p. 14, review of *The Darkness,* p. 38; September, 2001, review of *A New Kind of Dreaming,* p. 38; November, 2002, review of *Nathan Nuttboard Hits the Beach,* p. 33; May, 2004, review of *Fireshadow,* p. 41; July, 2004, review of *The Girl in the Cave,* p. 34; September, 2005, Rayma Turton, review of *Nightpeople,* p. 42.

School Library Journal, January, 2003, review of *A New Kind of Dreaming,* p. 138.

ONLINE

Anthony Eaton Home Page, http://members.dodo.net.au/%7Eeatont (September 26, 2005).

Aussie Reviews Online, http://www.aussiereviews.com/ (February 4, 2006), Sally Murphy, review of *The Girl in the Cave.*

Booked Out Speakers Agency Web site, http://www.booked out.com.au/ (September 26, 2005), "Anthony Eaton."*

EVAN, Frances Y. 1951-

Personal

Born May 10, 1951, in Walthamstow, Stow, England; daughter of Maurice W. and Vera G. Middleton Brown; married Joseph G. Evan (a controller) June 2, 1972; children: Peter, Thomas. *Education:* Attended Central Connecticut State College; Kree Institute of Electrolysis, diploma, 1986. *Politics:* "Independent." *Religion:* Protestant.

Addresses

Home—44 Marcroft St., Stratford, CT 06614. *E-mail*—frany51@aol.com.

Career

Church school teacher, 1977-93; freelance electrologist; Norwalk Seaport Association, Norwalk, CT, education coordinator, 1989-2004; Staples High School, Westport, CT, social studies and math department paraprofessional, 2003—; writer.

Writings

The Forgotten Flag: Revolutionary Struggle in Connecticut, White Mane Kids (Shippensburg, PA), 2003.

Work in Progress

St. Katharine's Dock; Curse of the Shark's Tooth; The Brass Bell.

Sidelights

Frances Y. Evan told *SATA:* "My writing career began more than fifteen years ago when I worked as an education coordinator for a nonprofit seaport association in Norwalk, Connecticut. The association offered field trips at its facility for pre-school and elementary school children and introduced the nautical topic of the day with a story told in an entertaining and creative manner. My associate and I often found it difficult to find stories suitable for our needs and so I began to write them myself. My original stories were well received and highly praised by students, teachers, and parents attending our program. I became more and more comfortable, confident, and excited about writing.

"My love of history and the mysterious find of a vintage American flag stuffed in the attic rafters of our pre-Revolutionary War farmhouse inspired me to write a story of historical fiction for older children. I wanted to explain the reason the flag was hidden in the attic and began researching the records, documents, and written accounts of Fairfield, Connecticut during the Revolutionary War. I wove my fictitious story into the town's history, keeping the historical characters, dates, and events as accurate as possible. *The Forgotten Flag: Revolutionary Struggle in Connecticut* is my first published work.

"History is the telling of true stories. Historical fiction is a tool that can be used to enhance actual personalities and events of the past. It can create a deeper understanding of the passions of the time period and a better explanation for decisions and behaviors of individuals living at the time. I find myself drawn to this genre. I have recently completed a work of historical fiction for young adults and am currently writing my first novel of adult fiction.

"One of my favorite authors is Anya Seton. I had the privilege of meeting her in her home in Old Greenwich, Connecticut toward the end of her career. My favorite novel remains one of hers, *Katherine,* a work of historical fiction that takes place in fourteenth-century England."

Biographical and Critical Sources

PERIODICALS

School Library Journal, February, 2004, Karen T. Bilton, review of *The Forgotten Flag: Revolutionary Struggle in Connecticut,* p. 146.

F

FARRER, Vashti

Personal
Married; children: three. *Education:* M.A. (English literature). *Hobbies and other interests:* Acting, watching plays and films, attending concerts, reading. Has lived with assorted pets, including a rat, possums, and axolotls.

Addresses
Agent—c/o Author Mail, Scholastic Australia, P.O. Box 579, Gosford, New South Wales 2250, Australia. *E-mail*—info@vashtifarrer.com.

Career
Writer. Has worked as an advertising copywriter, book reviewer and film extra; Mitchell Library, Sydney, New South Wales, Australia, research librarian; teacher of creative writing.

Member
New South Wales Military Historical Society (vice president).

Awards, Honors
Children's Book Council of Australia Book of the Year: Early Childhood shortlist, 2005, for *Mr Noah and the Cats.*

Writings

All in Together, illustrated by Patricia Mullins, Angus & Robertson (Sydney, New South Wales, Australia), 1974.

Tales of the Dreamtime, illustrated by Walter Cunningham, Angus & Robertson (Sydney, New South Wales, Australia), 1975.

Vashti Farrer

Escape to Eaglehawk, Millennium Books (Newtown, New South Wales, Australia), 1991.

Eureka Gold, Millennium Books (Newtown, New South Wales, Australia), 1993.

Ned's Kang-U-Roo, illustrations by John Nicholson, Lothian Books (Port Melbourne, Victoria, Australia), 1997.

Princess Euphorbia (also see below), illustrated by Nan Bodsworth, Addison Wesley Longman (South Melbourne, Victoria, Australia), 1997, Sundance (Littleton, MA), 1999, adapted as a play, illustrated by Betina Ogden, Pearson Education (South Melbourne, Victoria, Australia), 2001.

Molly O'Malley and the Magpies, illustrated by Margaret Power, Macmillan Educational (South Yarra, Victoria, Australia), 1998.

Plagues and Federation; The Diary of Kitty Barnes, the Rocks, Sydney, 1901, Scholastic Australia (Sydney, New South Wales, Australia), 2000.

Walers Go to War, illustrated by Sue O'Loughlin, ANZAC Day Commemoration Committee (Aspley, Queensland, Australia), 2001.

Letters Back Home (play), illustrated by Penel Gamble, Pearson Education (South Melbourne, Victoria, Australia), 2002.

Fearsome Creatures, illustrated by Melissa Web, Pearson Education (South Melbourne, Victoria, Australia), 2002.

Lulubelle and Her Bones, illustrated by David Cox, Scholastic Press (Sydney, New South Wales, Australia), 2003.

Mr Noah and the Cats, illustrated by Neil Curtis, Lothian (South Melbourne, Victoria, Australia), 2004.

Atlanta: The Fastest Runner in the World, Pearson Education (South Melbourne, Victoria, Australia), 2004.

Breakfast with Buddha, illustrated by Gaye Chapman, Scholastic Press (Gosford, New South Wales, Australia), 2005.

(With Mary Small) *Feathered Soldiers,* illustrated by Elizabeth Alger, ANZAC Day Commemoration Committee (Aspley, Queensland, Australia), 2005.

Big Feet, Very Sweet, illustrated by Neil Curtis, Lothian (South Melbourne, Victoria, Australia), 2006.

Sidelights

Australian writer Vashti Farrer writes for both children and older readers. In addition to short fiction for adults, she draws on her interest in Australian history in books such as *Escape to Eaglehawk, Plagues and Federation: The Diary of Kitty Barnes,* and *Feathered Soldiers,* the last a tribute to the messenger pigeons that aided the Australian forces during World War II that was coauthored with Mary Small. A former librarian who has also studied ancient history, English literature, and archeology, Farrer is an active member of the New South Wales Military Historical Society.

In *Breakfast with Buddha* Farrer presents young readers with a worthwhile lesson about patience, and uses her favorite animal to teach it. When Sati the cat suddenly finds herself homeless after a giant flood, she makes her way to a nearby monastery, hoping to find shelter. While Sati is happily taken in by the monks, she suddenly realizes that her life as top cat has ended; in the monastery she is only one among many cats that have been adopted. With the guidance and patience of a caring monk, Sati learns to overcome her natural pride. Farrer's picture book, with its ties to Buddhism, presents readers with a "window into a culture rarely shown" and provides a positive "model of conflict resolution," according to Robin Morrow in *Australian Bookseller and Publisher.*

Farrer retells the biblical tale of Noah and the ark with a pro-feline spin in the 2004 picture book **Mr Noah and the Cats.** *(Illustration by Neil Curtis.)*

Cats also star in Farrer's *Mr Noah and the Cats,* an updated rendition of the Biblical story about Noah and the Ark. In her interpretation of the traditional story, Farrer focuses on desert cats Urshanabi and Nishaba, who stow away on the Ark. When their meowing gives them away, the two felines become favored seafaring companions.

Biographical and Critical Sources

PERIODICALS

Australian Bookseller and Publisher, August, 2005, Robin Morrow, review of *Breakfast with Buddha.*

Magpies, September, 1997, review of *Ned's Kang-U-Roo,* p. 37; September, 2000, review of *Plagues and Federation,* p. 34; September, 2003, review of *Lulubelle and Her Bones,* p. 34; September, 2005, Russ Merrin, review of *Big Feet, Very Sweet,* p. 31.

ONLINE

Aussie Reviews Online, http://www.aussiereviews.com/ (September 26, 2005), Sally Murphy, review of *Lulubelle and Her Bones.*

Lateral Learning Speakers' Agency Web site, http://www.laterallearning.com/ (September 26, 2005), "Vashti Farrer."

Vashti Farrer Home Page, http://www.vashtifarrer.com (December 19, 2005).

*   *   *

FELL, Derek 1939-
(Derek John Fell)

Personal

Born September 28, 1939, in Morecambe, England; immigrated to United States, 1966; naturalized citizen, 1971; son of Albert John (a restaurateur) and Mary (a restaurateur; maiden name, McCafferty) Fell; married Maria Braksal, August 20, 1964 (divorced October, 1981); married Rosemary Wilkens, February 26, 1984 (divorced July, 1987); married Elizabeth Murray, October 10, 1987 (divorced November, 1988); married Carolyn Kreider (a landscape designer), January, 1995; children: (first marriage) Christina Mary, Derek John, Jr.; (second marriage) Victoria Rose. *Ethnicity:* "Englishman." *Education:* Attended British military school in Wilhemshaven, West Germany (now Germany). *Politics:* Republican. *Religion:* Christian. *Hobbies and other interests:* Gardening, swimming, adventure travel.

Addresses

Home—53 Iron Bridge Rd., Pipersville, PA 18947. *Agent*—Albert Zuckerman, Writers House, 21 W. 26th St., New York, NY 10010. *E-mail*—fellpix@comcat.com.

Career

Writer, photographer, and horticulturalist. Reporter for *Newport Advertiser,* Newport, England, and *Shrewsbury Chronicle,* c. 1957-59; O.D. Gallagher Ltd. (public relations agency), London, England, copywriter and account executive, 1958-64; W. Atlee Burpee Co., Philadelphia, PA, catalog manager and horticulturalist, 1964-72; All-America Selections, Gardenville, PA, executive secretary, 1972-74; freelance photographer and garden writer, 1974—. Host of television program *Step-by-Step Gardening,* QVC, 1994-2000, and CD-ROMs *Complete Gardening,* Microsoft, 1996, and *The Garden Companion.* Director of National Garden Bureau; horticultural consultant to the White House and various periodicals; lecturer. *Exhibitions:* Photographs exhibited at Pennsylvania Horticultural Society, 1970, 1994; Bucks County Garden Fair, Doylestown, PA, 1994; Lambertville House, Lambertville, NJ, 1997; Delaware Valley College, Doylestown, PA, 2001; and Haas-Muth Gallery, New Hope, PA, 2005.

Member

Garden Writers Association of America (fellow; past member of board of directors), Society of American Travel Writers.

Derek Fell

Awards, Honors

Over twelve awards from Garden Writers Association of America, beginning 1982, including three for best book, six for best photography, and three for best magazine article; Lifestyle Landscape Design Contest First Prize for best interpretation of an impressionist garden, 1991; Pennsylvania Horticultural Society Landscape Design Contest awards for Best Flower Garden Design, Best Water Garden Design, and Best of Show for Garden Design, all 1994; Quill & Trowel Award for Best Photography, 2001, for *Van Gogh's Gardens.*

Writings

How to Plant a Vegetable Garden, Countryside Books (Milwaukee, WI), 1975.

New Ideas in Flower Gardening, Countryside Books (Milwaukee, WI), 1976.

How I Planned to Plant the White House Vegetable Garden, Exposition Banner, 1976.

House Plants and Crafts for Fun and Profit, Bookworm, 1978.

How to Photograph Flowers, Plants, and Landscapes, H.P. Books (Tucson, AZ), 1980.

(Editor) Alan Bloom, *Perennials for Your Garden,* Floraprint U.S.A., 1981.

The Vegetable Spaghetti Cookbook, Pine Row (Washington Crossing, PA), 1982.

Vegetables: How to Select, Grow, and Enjoy, H.P. Books (Tucson, AZ), 1982.

Annuals: How to Select, Grow, and Enjoy, H.P. Books (Tucson, AZ), 1983.

Trees and Shrubs, H.P. Books (Tucson, AZ), 1986.

Deerfield: An American Garden through Four Seasons, Pidcock Press, 1986.

(Co-author) *Hillside Gardening: Evaluating the Site, Designing Views, Planting Slopes,* Simon & Schuster (New York, NY), 1986.

Garden Accents: The Complete Guide to Special Features for Creative Landscaping, Holt (New York, NY), 1987.

(Co-author) *The Complete Book of Gardening: All You Need to Know about Lawns,* Oracle Books, 1987.

The Inspired Garden: Imaginative Ideas and Features in Full Colour, Friedman (New York, NY), 1987.

Garden Accents, Holt (New York, NY), 1987.

The One-Minute Gardener, Running Press (Philadelphia, PA), 1988.

Great Gardens (calendar), Portal (Novato, CA), 1988.

(Co-author) *Home Landscaping: Ideas, Styles, and Designs for Creative Outdoor Spaces,* Simon & Schuster (New York, NY), 1988.

(Photographer) *The Three Year Garden Journal: With Regional Gardening Guides,* Starwood, 1989.

A Kid's First Book of Gardening: Growing Plants Indoors and Out, Running Press (Philadelphia, PA), 1989.

(Editor and Photographer) *The Complete Garden Planning Manual,* HP Books (Tucson, AZ), 1989.

(Photographer) *Essential Annuals: The 100 Best for Design and Cultivation,* Crescent Books (Avenel, NJ), 1989.

Essential Bulbs: The 100 Best for Design and Cultivation, Crescent Books (Avenel, NJ), 1989.

Essential Perennials: The 100 Best for Design and Cultivation, Crescent Books (Avenel, NJ), 1989.

Essential Herbs: The 100 Best for Design and Cultivation, Crescent Books (Avenel, NJ), 1990.

Essential Roses: The 100 Best for Design and Cultivation, Crescent Books (Avenel, NJ), 1990.

The Easiest Flowers to Grow, Ortho Books, 1990.

Renoir's Garden, Frances Lincoln (London, England), 1991.

550 Home Landscaping Ideas, Simon & Schuster (New York, NY), 1991.

The Encyclopedia of Flowers, Smithmark, 1992.

The Impressionist Garden, Frances Lincoln (London, England), 1994.

550 Perennial Garden Ideas, Simon & Schuster (New York, NY), 1994.

The Pennsylvania Gardener, Camino Press (Philadelphia, PA), 1995.

(Photographer) *Flowering Shrubs and Small Trees,* Friedman/Fairfax (New York, NY), 1995.

(Photographer) *Ornamental Grass Gardening: Design Ideas, Functions, and Effects,* Friedman/Fairfax (New York, NY), 1995.

(Photographer) *The Practical Gardener: An A-to-Z Guide to Techniques and Tips,* Friedman/Fairfax (New York, NY), 1995.

In the Garden with Derek, Camino Books (Philadelphia, PA), 1995.

(Photographer) *Gardens of Philadelphia and the Delaware Valley,* Temple University Press (Philadelphia, PA), 1995.

(Co-author) *All about Azaleas, Camellias, and Rhododendrons,* Ortho Books, 1995.

Creative Landscaping: Ideas, Designs, and Blueprints, Friedman/Fairfax (New York, NY), 1995.

(Co-author) *The Garden Planning Kit: An Interactive Guide to Designing, Planning, and Planting the Garden of Your Dreams,* HarperCollins (New York, NY), 1996.

Roses: Growing and Design Tips for 200 Favorite Flowers, Friedman/Fairfax (New York, NY), 1996.

Bulbs: Growing and Design Tips for 200 Favorite Flowers, Friedman/Fairfax (New York, NY), 1996.

Perennials: Growing and Design Tips for 200 Favorite Flowers, Friedman/Fairfax (New York, NY), 1996.

Annuals: Growing and Design Tips for 200 Favorite Flowers, Friedman/Fairfax (New York, NY), 1996.

(Co-author) *Glorious Flowers: Arranging for Every Occasion,* Friedman/Fairfax (New York, NY), 1996.

Derek Fell's Perennial Gardening, Friedman/Fairfax (New York, NY), 1996.

Derek Fell's Vegetable Gardening, Friedman/Fairfax (New York, NY), 1996.

Derek Fell's Herb Gardening, Friedman/Fairfax (New York, NY), 1997.

Secrets of Monet's Garden: Bringing the Beauty of Monet's Style to Your Own Garden, Friedman/Fairfax (New York, NY), 1997.

Derek Fell's Bulb Gardening, Friedman/Fairfax (New York, NY), 1997.

Derek Fell's Shade Gardening, Friedman/Fairfax (New York, NY), 1998.

(Co-author) *Impressionist Bouquets: 24 Exquisite Arrangements Inspired by the Impressionist Masters,* Friedman/Fairfax (New York, NY), 1998.

Impressionist Roses: Bringing The Romance of the Impressionist Style to Your Garden, Friedman/Fairfax (New York, NY), 1999.

Flower and Garden Photography, Silver Pixel Press, 2000.

Water Gardening for Beginners, Friedman/Fairfax (New York, NY), 2000.

Herb Gardening for Beginners, Friedman/Fairfax (New York, NY), 2000.

Van Gogh's Gardens, Simon & Schuster (New York, NY), 2001.

Campbell Island: Land of the Blue Sunflower, David Bateman (Auckland, New Zealand), 2003.

(And photographer) *Great Gardens of New Zealand,* David Bateman (Auckland, New Zealand), 2003.

Cézanne's Garden, Simon & Schuster (New York, NY), 2004.

Van Gogh's Women: His Love Affair and His Journey into Madness, Carroll & Graf (New York, NY), 2004.

The Encyclopedia of Garden Design and Structure, Bateman (Auckland, New Zealand), 2006.

Contributor to *Encyclopaedia Britannica.* Contributor of articles and photographs to magazines and newspapers, including *Architectural Digest, Woman's Day,*

Connoisseur, and *New York Times Magazine.* Past editor of *Garden Writers Bulletin.* Photographs reproduced in numerous calendars published by Portal, Cambridge-Pacific, and Starwood, beginning 1988.

"LET'S INVESTIGATE" SERIES

Cacti, Creative Education (Mankato, MN), 1999.
Herbs, Creative Education (Mankato, MN), 1999.
Orchids, Creative Education (Mankato, MN), 1999.
Wildflowers, Creative Education (Mankato, MN), 1999.

Work in Progress

A romantic mystery novel set in the 1820s; a second book about Monet's garden, titled *The Magic of Monetapos;s Garden; The Encyclopedia of Hardy Plants;* and *The Encyclopedia of Tropical Plants for Temperate Climates.*

Sidelights

Derek Fell is a writer and photographer who specializes in writing about gardening topics and travel. In addition to his many books, which include *Van Gogh's Gardens, Essential Perennials,* and *Impressionist Bouquets,* Fell has amassed a stock photo library containing over 150,000 images. Appearing on greeting cards, calendars, and posters, Fell's photographs have also served as illustrations for his books and works by other garden writers. While most of Fell's books are geared for adults ranging from budding to well-established gardeners, his *A Kid's First Book of Gardening: Growing Plants Indoors and Out* is geared for beginning green thumbs and includes gardening projects and interesting plant-related facts. Fell's "Let's Investigate" series, published by educational publisher Creative Education, is also designed for younger readers; the books present information specific to herbs and cacti, as well as to plants ranging from the most common wild flower to the most exotic orchid.

Fell has credited several individuals with inspiring him in a career that has spanned many decades. As he once told *SATA,* "The writer who most influenced my work, was E. O'Dowd Gallagher, a British war correspondent whose best work appeared in the *Daily Express.* After retiring from newspapers, Gallagher started the public relations agency where I worked as a copywriter and account executive.

"At this time, I also became influenced by the work of Harry Smith, a British plant photographer. I emulated his style of horticultural photography and, as a result, I have become the world's most widely published plant photographer and owner of the Derek Fell Horticultural Color Picture Library.

"The third most important influence was meeting and working with David Burpee, president of W. Atlee Burpee Co., mail order seedsman. Before his death in 1980 I worked six years with him, learning how to communicate gardening."

Fell's love of both fine art and gardening has combined in such photographic studies as Cézanne's Garden, *which focuses on nineteenth-century painter Paul Cézanne's garden in Aix-en-Provence, France.*

Born and raised in England, Fell now lives on a farm in Bucks County, Pennsylvania, where he has established areas for horticultural trials and an outdoor photography studio. In addition to writing and photography, he has served as a horticultural consultant to the White House, and was host of the QVC television program *Step-by-Step Gardening.*

Biographical and Critical Sources

BOOKS

Wuthnow, Robert, *Creative Spirituality,* University of California Press (Los Angeles, CA), 2001.

PERIODICALS

American Artist, July, 2004, review of *Cézanne's Garden,* p. 74.
Architectural Digest, December, 1980.
Art Matters, June, 1995.

Beautiful Gardens, November-December, 1994.

Booklist, August, 2000, p. 2094; January 1, 2004, Alice Joyce, review of *Cézanne's Garden,* p. 893; January 1, 2005, Donna Seaman, review of *Van Gogh's Women: His Love Affair and Journey into Madness,* p. 798.

Christian Science Monitor, December 17, 1982.

Garden Design, winter, 1986; winter, 1994.

Green Scene, November-December, 1987.

Hemispheres, June, 1995.

Mother Earth News, November, 1976.

New Hope Gazette, June 10, 1982.

New York Times, May 10, 1976.

Publishers Weekly, November 15, 2004, review of *Van Gogh's Women,* p. 49.

School Library Journal, September, 2004, John Kiefman, review of *Cézanne's Garden,* p. 236.

ONLINE

Derek Fell Home Page, http://www.derekfell.net (January 15, 2006).

OTHER

Gardening Diary (television series), Home & Garden Network, 2001.

Nature's Best Photography (television series), Outdoor Life Network, 1999.

*   *   *

FELL, Derek John
See FELL, Derek

*   *   *

FOX, Paula 1923-

Personal

Born April 22, 1923, in New York, NY; daughter of Paul Hervey (a writer) and Elsie (de Sola) Fox; married Howard Bird (a merchant seaman), c. 1940 (divorced, c. 1940); married Richard Sigerson (a public relations agent), 1948 (divorced, 1954); married Martin Greenberg (an editor and translator), June 9, 1962; children: Linda; (second marriage) Adam, Gabriel. *Education:* Attended Columbia University, 1955-58.

Addresses

Home—49 E. 19th St., New York, NY 10003. *Agent*—Robert Lescher, 155 E. 71st St., New York, NY 10021.

Career

Novelist. Worked variously as a model; saleswoman; public-relations worker and machinist; Victor Gollancz (publisher), London, England, former staff member; reader for a film studio; reporter in Paris, France, and Warsaw, Poland, for British wire service Telepress; English-as-a-second-language instructor, and teacher at Ethical Culture School, New York, NY, and for emotionally disturbed children in Dobbs Ferry, NY; University of Pennsylvania, Philadelphia, professor of English literature, beginning 1963.

Member

PEN, Authors League of America, Authors Guild.

Awards, Honors

National Book Award finalist in children's book category, 1971, for *Blowfish Live in the Sea;* National Institute of Arts and Letters Award, 1972; Guggenheim fellowship, 1972; National Endowment for the Arts grant, 1974; Newbery Medal, American Library Association, 1974, for *The Slave Dancer;* Hans Christian Andersen Medal, 1978; National Book Award nomination, 1979, for *The Little Swineherd and Other Tales;* *New York Times* Outstanding Books listee, 1980, and American Book Award for Children's Fiction Paperback, 1983, both for *A Place Apart;* Child Study Association (CSA) Children's Book Award, Bank Street College of Education, and *New York Times* Notable Books designation, both 1984, Christopher Award, and Newbery Honor Book selection, both 1985, and International Board on Books for Young People Honor List for Writing, 1986, all for *One-Eyed Cat;* Brandeis fiction citation, 1984; Rockefeller Foundation grant, 1984; *The Moonlight Man* selected among *New York Times* Notable Books, 1986, and CSA Children's Books of the Year, 1987; Silver Medallion, University of Southern Mississippi, 1987; *Boston Globe/Horn Book* Award for fiction, and Newbery Honor Book, 1989, for *The Village by the Sea;* Empire State Award for children's literature, 1994; O. Henry Prize, 2005, for short story "Grace."

Writings

FOR JUVENILES

Maurice's Room, illustrated by Ingrid Fetz, Macmillan (New York, NY), 1966.

A Likely Place, illustrated by Edward Ardizzone, Macmillan (New York, NY), 1967.

How Many Miles to Babylon?, illustrated by Paul Giovanopoulos, David White, 1967.

The Stone-Faced Boy, illustrated by Donald A. Mackay, Bradbury Press (New York, NY), 1968, reprinted, Front Street Books (Asheville, NC), 2005.

Dear Prosper, illustrated by Steve McLachlin, David White, 1968.

Portrait of Ivan, illustrated by Saul Lambert, Bradbury Press (New York, NY), 1969, reprinted, Front Street Books (Asheville, NC), 2004.

The King's Falcon, illustrated by Eros Keith, Bradbury Press (New York, NY), 1969.

Hungry Fred, illustrated by Rosemary Wells, Bradbury Press (New York, NY), 1969.

Blowfish Live in the Sea, Bradbury Press (New York, NY), 1970.

Good Ethan, illustrated by Arnold Lobel, Bradbury Press (New York, NY), 1973.

The Slave Dancer, illustrated by Eros Keith, Bradbury Press (New York, NY), 1973.

The Little Swineherd and Other Tales, Dutton (New York, NY), 1978, new edition illustrated by Robert Byrd, 1996.

A Place Apart, Farrar, Straus (New York, NY), 1980.

One-Eyed Cat, Bradbury Press (New York, NY), 1984.

(Author of introduction) Marjorie Kellogg, *Tell Me That You Love Me, Junie Moon,* Farrar, Straus (New York, NY), 1984.

The Moonlight Man, Bradbury Press (New York, NY), 1986, reprinted, Aladdin (New York, NY), 2003.

Lily and the Lost Boy, Orchard Books, 1987, published as *The Lost Boy,* Dent (London, England), 1988.

The Village by the Sea, Orchard Books (New York, NY), 1988, published as *In a Place of Danger,* 1989.

Monkey Island, Orchard Books (New York, NY), 1991.

(With Floriano Vecchi) *Amzat and His Brothers: Three Italian Tales,* illustrated by Emily Arnold McCully, Orchard Books (New York, NY), 1993.

Western Wind, Orchard Books (New York, NY), 1993.

The Eagle Kite, Orchard Books (New York, NY), 1995.

Radiance Descending, D.K. Ink (New York, NY), 1997.

FOR ADULTS

Poor George, Harcourt (New York, NY), 1967, with an introduction by Jonathan Lethem, Norton (New York, NY), 2001.

Desperate Characters, Harcourt (New York, NY), 1970, with an afterword by Irving Howe, Nonpareil, 1980.

The Western Coast, Harcourt (New York, NY), 1972, with an introduction by Frederick Busch, Norton (New York, NY), 2001.

The Widow's Children, Dutton (New York, NY), 1976.

A Servant's Tale, North Point Press, 1984, with an introduction by Melanie Rehack, Norton (New York, NY), 2001.

The God of Nightmares, North Point Press (San Francisco, CA), 1990, with an introduction by Rosellen Brown, Norton (New York, NY), 2002.

OTHER

Borrowed Finery: A Memoir, Henry Holt (New York, NY), 2001.

The Coldest Winter: A Stringer in Liberated Europe (memoir), Henry Holt (New York, NY), 2005.

Also author of television scripts. Contributor to periodicals, including *Paris Review.*

Adaptations

Desperate Characters was adapted as a motion picture starring Shirley Maclaine, Paramount, 1970; a cassette and a film strip accompanied by cassette have been produced of *One-eyed Cat* by Random House.

Sidelights

Paula Fox is best known for her children's books, which have won numerous awards, including the prestigious Hans Christian Andersen Medal, the Newbery Medal, and an American Book Award. She is also the author of novels for adults, and has been described by *Nation* contributor Blair T. Birmelin as "one of our most intelligent (and least appreciated) contemporary novelists." Fox, however, does not feel the need to distinguish between these two types of writing. She commented in John Rowe Townsend's *A Sense of Story: Essays on Contemporary Writers for Children,* "I never think I'm writing for children, when I work. A story does not start for anyone, nor an idea, nor a feeling of an idea; but starts more for oneself." "At the core of everything I write," she explained to *Publishers Weekly* interviewer Sybil S. Steinberg, "is the feeling that the denial of the truth imprisons us even further in ourselves. Of course there's no one 'truth.' The great things, the insights that happen to you, come to you in some internal way."

Fox spent her childhood moving from place to place and school to school. She later recalled her alcoholic father in the *New York Times* as "an itinerant writer." Working in New York City, he earned a living by rewriting plays by other authors, as well as writing several of his own, and later he went to Hollywood and England to work for film studios. While her self-absorbed parents were traveling about, Fox was sent to live with Elwood Corning, a Congregational minister who took the baby girl into the home he shared with his invalid mother in New York's Hudson Valley. An avid reader, poet, and history buff, her beloved "Uncle Elwood" had a profound influence on Fox. The Reverend Corning taught her to read and to appreciate the works of authors like Rudyard Kipling, Eugene Field, Mark Twain, Washington Irving, and Walt Whitman; he also told her tales of the Revolutionary War and other events in history. All these stories inevitably rubbed off on the young Fox. "When I was five, I had my first experience of being a ghost writer—of sorts," she once related, recalling how the minister once accepted her suggestion to write a sermon about a waterfall. For "an instant," she added, "I grasped consciously what had been implicit in every aspect of my life with the minister—that everything could count, that a word, spoken as meant, contained in itself an energy capable of awakening imagination, thought, emotion." It was this experience that first inspired Fox to become a writer.

When Fox was six years old, her parents returned to reclaim her, and she moved to California where she was passed from her too-busy parents to a succession of family friends, institutions, and foster situations. In

1931 she relocated another great distance, this time to live with her grandmother on a sugar plantation in Cuba. Here, Fox quickly picked up Spanish from her fellow students while attending classes in a one-room schoolhouse. Three years after her arrival, the revolution led by Batista y Zaldivar forced Fox to return to New York City. By this time, she had attended nine schools and had hardly ever seen her parents. Fortunately, she found some solace and stability in her life by visiting public libraries. "Reading was everything to me," Fox revealed to Steinberg. "Wherever I went—except in Cuba—there was a library. Even though my schools changed, I'd always find a library."

Fox worked several different jobs after finishing high school, ranging from machinist to publishing company employee. Her desire to travel led her to a position as a stringer for a leftist British news service which assigned her to cover postwar Poland, Spain, Czechoslovakia, and France. Later, she returned to the United States, married, and had children, but the marriage ended in divorce. Afterwards, Fox resolved to finish her education, and attended Columbia University for four years, until she could no longer afford the expense and had to leave

When eleven-year-old Ned accidentally shoots a stray cat with his uncle's air rifle he must share his secret with an elderly neighbor in order to help the wounded creature survive the coming harsh winter.

before receiving her degree. Fox's knowledge of Spanish now helped her find a job as an English teacher for Spanish-speaking children. She also found other teaching positions, including one as a teacher for the emotionally disturbed. In 1962, Fox married an English professor and moved to Greece for six months while her husband wrote on a Guggenheim fellowship.

It was during her trip to Greece that Fox finally began to realize her dream of becoming a writer. "I remember when I was finally able to quit my teaching job and devote myself full-time to writing. People asked me, 'But what will you do?' 'I'm going to write books,' I would say. And they would reply, 'Yes, but what will you DO?' People have this idea that a life spent writing is essentially a life of leisure. Writing is tremendously hard work. There is nothing more satisfying, but it is work all the same." For Fox, the same reason for reading books applies to her desire to write them: books help both reader and writer to experience and understand—if not necessarily sympathize with—the lives of other people. In her acceptance speech for the Newbery award, reprinted in *Newbery and Caldecott Medal Winners, 1966-1975,* she declared that writing helps us "to connect ourselves with the reality of our own lives. It is painful; but if we are to become human, we cannot abandon it." In time, the reality of Fox's own life expanded to include five new grandchildren in 1991, when Linda, the daughter she had given up for adoption, sought her birth mother out. One of those grandchildren is rock musician Courtney Love.

Fox's juvenile novels have a complexity and sincerity that make them popular with readers and critics alike. These books cover a wide range of subjects, including parental conflict, alcoholism, and death. Frequently, her young protagonists are emotionally withdrawn children who undertake a journey that is symbolic of their emotional development. In *Blowfish Live in the Sea,* for example, nineteen-year-old Ben travels from New York to Boston to see his estranged, alcoholic father after a twelve-year absence. Because of a past trauma involving a lie his father told him, Ben has withdrawn into himself to the point where he no longer speaks to anyone. His sister Carrie is the only family member who tries to reach out to Ben. The importance of Ben and Carrie's journey to Boston, explained a *Horn Book* reviewer, is that "each step . . . relays something further in their tenuous gropings towards an understanding of themselves and of others."

Other award-winning children's novels by Fox, such as *A Place Apart, One-Eyed Cat,* and *The Village by the Sea,* are similarly concerned with relationships, strong characterization, and emotionally troubled protagonists. *New Statesman* contributor Patricia Craig remarked that *A Place Apart* "depends on subtleties of characterisation . . . rather than on an arresting plot." The novel concerns Victoria Finch, a thirteen year old whose comfort and security are shaken when her father dies suddenly. Victoria's grief, wrote *Washington Post Book*

Rooming with an alcoholic aunt while her father recovers from heart surgery, ten-year-old Bea learns the woman's secret and gains a measure of compassion in Fox's sensitive 1990 novel.

World contributor Katherine Paterson, "is the bass accompaniment to the story. Sometimes it swells, taking over the narrative, the rest of the time it subsides into a dark, rhythmic background against which the main story is played." Victoria must also come to terms with her infatuation with Hugh, a manipulative boy who "exerts . . . a power over her spirit," according to Paterson. This relationship compels Victoria "to explore the difficult terrain between the desire for closeness and the tendency to 'make ourselves a place apart,'" observed Jean Strouse in *Newsweek*.

One-Eyed Cat, according to *Dictionary of Literary Biography* contributor Anita Moss, "is one of Fox's finest literary achievements." The title refers to a stray cat which the main character Ned accidentally injures with an air rifle. The guilt Ned feels afterward plagues him through most of the rest of the book, even making him physically ill at one point. At last he confesses his thoughtless act to his mother, who in turn confesses that she once deserted Ned and his father when he was younger. Recognizing that all people have flaws leads Ned to a reconciliation with his parents and himself.

A typical Fox device is to put a main character in an unfamiliar and hostile setting. In *The Village by the Sea*, for example, Emma is sent to live with her uncle and her neurotic, alcoholic aunt for two weeks when her father has to go to the hospital for heart surgery. Unable to cope with her hateful aunt and troubled about her father's health, Emma finds some solace in creating a make-believe village on the beach. But, as Rosellen Brown related in the *New York Times Book Review*, "Emma's miniature haven is ultimately beyond her protection. She can only cherish the building of it, and then the memory."

Of all her books, Fox is most often associated with her controversial yet highly acclaimed work *The Slave Dancer*, which won the 1974 Newbery Medal. It is the story of a New Orleans boy who is kidnapped and placed on a slave ship bound for West Africa. The boy, Jessie Bollier, is chosen for his ability to play the fife; his task aboard ship is to "dance" the slaves so they can exercise their cramped limbs. Eventually, Jessie escapes when the ship's crew is drowned in a storm, but he is forever scarred by his experience. Despite the praise the novel received, a number of critics complained that Fox's portrayal of slaves made them akin to merely dispirited cattle, and that she appeared to excuse the slave drivers as being victims of circumstance. Binnie Tate, for one, commented in *Interracial Books for Children*: "Through the characters' words, [Fox] . . . excuses the captors and places the blame for the slaves' captivity on Africans themselves. The author slowly and systematically excuses almost all the whites in the story for their participation in the slave venture and by innuendo places the blame elsewhere."

Other reviewers, however, viewed *The Slave Dancer* as a fair and humane treatment of a sensitive subject. In *Horn Book*, Alice Bach called the novel "one of the finest examples of a writer's control over her material. . . . With an underplayed but implicit sense of rage, Paula Fox exposes the men who dealt in selling human beings." *The Slave Dancer*, concluded Kevin Crossley-Holland in the *New Statesman*, is "a novel of great moral integrity. . . . From start to finish Miss Fox tells her story quietly and economically; she is candid but she never wallows."

Continuing her practice of placing her young protagonists in difficult circumstances, Fox, in *Monkey Island*, examines the issue of homelessness and explores the more general childhood fear of abandonment. The story concerns an eleven-year-old, middle-class boy named Clay Garrity, whose father loses his job as a magazine art director and abandons his family. Because his mother is eight months' pregnant and cannot work, Clay fears the social services department will take him away and put him in a foster home. "The novel individualizes the problems of homeless people and puts faces on those whom society has made faceless," remarked Ellen Fader in a *Horn Book* review. Fader felt "readers' perceptions will be changed after reading the masterfully crafted

Monkey Island." Writing in the *New York Times Book Review,* Dinitia Smith called the novel "delicate and moving," and a "relentless story that succeeds in conveying the bitter facts" of homelessness.

In *Western Wind* Fox takes a rather well-worn premise in children's literature—a lonely young girl is sent by her parents to live with an elderly relative who proves to be quite wise—and making it original and interesting. This is achieved mainly by Fox's depiction of the young heroine's grandmother, an eccentric painter who lives on a remote island off the coast of Maine in a house without indoor plumbing. Though *Booklist* reviewer Ilene Cooper found Fox's "delicate craftsmanship" overdone, others praised the author's descriptive skills and emotional insights. Patricia J. Wagner, writing in the *Bloomsbury Review,* concluded that both "adult and junior fiction writers should study her work with care," and Betsy Hearne, in the *Bulletin of the Center for Children's Books,* observed that "Fox's style especially suits this taut narrative."

Homosexuality and AIDS are the issues Liam Cormac and his family must confront in *The Eagle Kite,* a novel

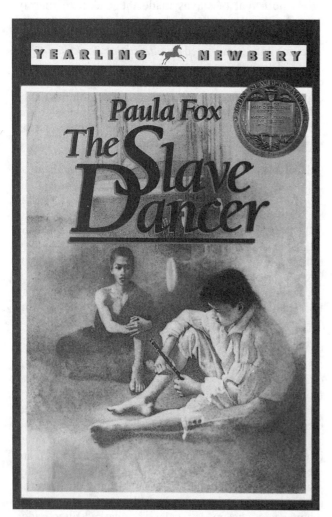

Fox's 1973 novel follows a young teen who, kidnaped and taken aboard a slave ship docked in New Orleans, must "dance" the slaves with music to keep them working.

that *Horn Book* writer Nancy Vasilakis hailed for its "painstaking honesty." Young Liam's father is dying from AIDS. The man's imminent death and the circumstances under which he contracted the disease cause the family almost unbearable grief; they also provide the narrative struggles through which some memorable characters are defined. In *Voice of Youth Advocates,* W. Keith McCoy described the book as "a brief, but intense, portion of one young boy's life," and further noted that "Fox's spare prose enhances the emotions that are buffeting the Cormacs."

Such emotional honesty is also displayed in *Radiance Descending,* the story of an adolescent boy struggling with his resentment toward a younger brother who has Down's syndrome. Having just moved to Long Island from New York City, Paul is eager to avoid Jacob, who nevertheless idealizes him. Paul is also frustrated at how Jacob monopolizes all their parents' attention. Slowly, however, Paul comes to realize that the mere fact of avoiding Jacob is still focusing on him, and that there may be a middle ground. "Older readers will find many layers of meaning in this novel," noted a reviewer for *Publishers Weekly.* "Younger readers may be put off by a few esoteric allusions . . . but will still be able to recognize the gradual blossoming of Paul's compassion." Edward Sullivan, writing in *Voice of Youth Advocates,* considered *Radiance Descending* "a quiet, introspective novel told with great eloquence."

Although Fox has not received as much recognition for her adult novels as she has for her children's books, she has nevertheless been widely praised for *Desperate Characters* and *The Widow's Children,* as well as for the memoirs *Borrowed Finery* and *The Coldest Winter: A Stringer in Liberated Europe.* Her adult novels are "concerned with the cataclysmic moments of private lives, and the quiet desperation of ordinary people," wrote Linda Simon in *Commonweal. Desperate Characters* explores the lives of Sophie and Otto Bentwood, a childless couple in their mid-forties who are "facing the abstract menace of a world perhaps they helped through inadvertence to create," wrote John Leonard in the *New York Times.* The Bentwoods live in a renovated Brooklyn townhouse amid the squalor of a slum. While their marriage was described by *New York Times Book Review* contributor Peter Rowley as, "if not dead, at best warring," they are content with their orderly, comfortable lives. As the novel progresses, however, their security is gradually encroached upon. "Sophie and Otto . . . are slowly revealed to be menaced by forces . . . giving off a growl of danger all the more ominous for being so essentially nameless and faceless and vague," observed Pearl K. Bell in the *New Leader.* Bell concluded that *Desperate Characters* "is a small masterpiece, a revelation of contemporary New York middle-class life that grasps the mind of the reader with the subtle clarity of metaphor and the alarmed tenacity of nightmare."

In both Fox's children's and adult novels, her characters suffer through tragic situations for which there are

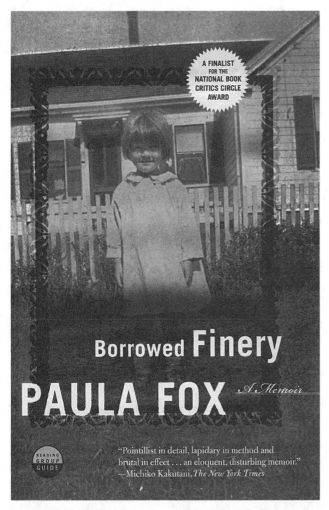

A FINALIST
FOR THE
NATIONAL BOOK
CRITICS CIRCLE
AWARD

Borrowed **Finery**

PAULA FOX *A Memoir*

READING
GROUP
GUIDE

"Pointillist in detail, lapidary in method and
brutal in effect . . . an eloquent, disturbing memoir."
—Michiko Kakutani, *The New York Times*

Fox shares the childhood experiences that, while difficult, taught her much about human character and the importance of stability and a sense of belonging. (Cover design by Linda Fyfe.)

no simple solutions, and this has led some critics to categorize her as an author of serious and depressing works. Fox has at times been frustrated by this label. "People are always saying my work is 'depressing,'" she told Feitlowitz. "But what does that mean? They said *Desperate Characters* was depressing too, and it's been reissued twice. I'm so used to having the word 'depressing' tied to me I feel like a dog accustomed to the tin can around its neck. The charge can still make me angry, not because of how it might reflect on my work, but because of what it tells me about reading in this country. Is *Anna Karenina* depressing? Is *Madame Bovary*? 'Depressing,' when applied to a literary work is so narrow, so confining, so impoverished and impoverishing. This yearning for the proverbial 'happy ending' is little more than a desire for oblivion."

A number of critics have defended Fox's approach to fiction, and have praised her ability to address her younger audience frankly. "What sets [Fox] above the gaudy blooms—the social workers and fortunetellers—who are knocking out books as fast as kids can swallow them," wrote *Horn Book* contributor Alice Bach, "is her uncompromising integrity. Fox is nobody's mouthpiece.

Her unique vision admits to the child what he already suspects: Life is part grit, part disappointment, part nonsense, and occasionally victory. . . . And by offering children no more than the humanness we all share— child, adult, reader, writer—she acknowledges them as equals."

For Fox, writing for children is, except for a few considerations, not that different from writing for adults. "Children have everything adults have," the author told Feitlowitz, "with the exception of judgment, which comes only over the course of time." While she avoids writing detailed scenes for children involving sex, extreme violence, or subjects outside their experience like teenage pregnancy, Fox maintains that "children know about pain and fear and unhappiness and betrayal. And we do them a disservice by trying to sugarcoat dark truths. There is an odd kind of debauchery I've noticed, particularly in societies that consider themselves 'democratic' or 'liberal': they display the gory details but hide meaning, especially if it is ambiguous or disturbing." And so, above all else, Fox strives for honesty and integrity in her writing. She concluded, "We must never, ever try to pull the wool over children's eyes by 'watering down' powerful stories."

As Cathryn M. Mercier noted in an essay on Fox in the *St. James Guide to Young-Adult Writers:* "In every novel, Fox attributes significant capabilities to her readers. She pays tribute to their emotional, intellectual, and psychological abilities with layered, probing narratives, identifiable characters who achieve genuine illumination, and lucid, striking prose." As the acclaimed writer told London-based *Guardian Unlimited* online contributor Aida Edemariam, her approach reflects her experience of life. "I think what my growing up gave me was that I didn't just swim like a goldfish, unaware of anything—water, my environment," Fox told Edemariam. "I had leapt out of the bowl, so I could see in a certain way that is given to some people and not to others. I write mostly about children who, like me, are out of the bowl."

Biographical and Critical Sources

BOOKS

A Sounding of Storytellers: New and Revised Essays on Contemporary Writers for Children, Lippincott (Philadelphia, PA), 1979.

Authors and Artists for Young Adults, Thomson Gale (Detroit, MI), Volume 3, 1990, Volume 37, 2001.

Beacham's Guide to Literature for Young Adults, Beacham Publishing (Osprey, FL), Volume 3, 1990, Volume 8, 1994.

Benbow-Pfalzgraf, Taryn, editor, *American Women Writers,* 2nd edition, St. James Press (Detroit, MI), 2000.

Carpenter, Humphrey, and Mari Prichard, *The Oxford Companion to Children's Literature,* Oxford University Press (Oxford, England), 1984.

Children's Literature Review, Thomson Gale (Detroit, MI), Volume 1, 1976, Volume 44, 1997.

Contemporary Literary Criticism, Thomson Gale (Detroit, MI), Volume 2, 1974, Volume 8, 1978, Volume 121, 2000.

Dictionary of Literary Biography, Volume 52: *American Writers for Children since 1960: Fiction,* Thomson Gale (Detroit, MI), 1986.

Drew, Bernard A., *The One Hundred Most Popular Young-Adult Authors,* Libraries Unlimited (Englewood, CO), 1996.

Kingman, Lee, editor, *Newbery and Caldecott Medal Winners, 1966-1975,* Horn Book, 1975.

Ousby, Ian, editor, *The Cambridge Guide to Literature in English,* Cambridge University Press (London, England), 1988.

Pendergast, Tom, and Sara Pendergast, editors, *St. James Guide to Young-Adult Writers,* 2nd edition, St. James Press (Detroit, MI), 1999.

Silvey, Anita, editor, *Children's Books and Their Creators,* Houghton Mifflin (Boston, MA), 1995.

Townsend, John Rowe, *A Sense of Story: Essays on Contemporary Writers for Children,* Lippincott (Philadelphia, PA), 1971.

Ward, Martha E., and others, editors, *Authors of Books for Young People,* 3rd edition, Scarecrow Press (Metuchen, NJ), 1990.

PERIODICALS

Bloomsbury Review, March-April, 1994, Patricia J. Wagner, review of *Western Wind.*

Book, September, 2001, James Schiff, review of *Borrowed Finery,* p. 77.

Bookbird, December 13, 1978, Paula Fox, "Acceptance Speech—1978 H.C. Andersen Author's Medal," pp. 2-3.

Booklist, March 15, 1993, p. 64; October 15, 1993, Ilene Cooper, review of *Western Wind,* p. 432; February 1, 1995, p. 1003; September 1, 1997, p. 124; September 1, 2001, Hazel Rochman, review of *Borrowed Finery,* p. 43.

Bulletin of the Center for Children's Books, November, 1980, Zena Sutherland, review of *A Place Apart,* p. 52; September, 1993, Betsy Hearne, review of *Western Wind,* pp. 9-10.

Chicago Tribune, April 9, 1995, p. 7.

Children's Book Review, December, 1972; winter, 1974-75, C.S. Hannabuss, review of *The Slave Dancer.*

Commonweal, January 11, 1985, Linda Simon, review of *A Servant's Tale.*

English Journal, November, 1996, p. 132.

Entertainment Weekly, September 6, 2002, review of *Borrowed Finery,* p. 77.

Globe and Mail (Toronto, Ontario, Canada), February 6, 1988.

Horn Book, September-October, 1967, Ruth Hill Viguers, review of *How Many Miles to Babylon?;* August, 1969; April, 1970; November-December, 1970, review of *Blowfish Live in the Sea;* August, 1974; September-October, 1977, Alice Bach, "Cracking Open the Geode: The Fiction of Paula Fox," pp. 514-521; October,

1978; April, 1984; January-February, 1985, Ethel L. Heins, review of *One-Eyed Cat,* pp. 57-58; September-October 1991, Ellen Fader, review of *Monkey Island,* pp. 596-597; July-August, 1993, p. 468; March-April, 1994, p. 198; September-October, 1995, Nancy Vasilakis, review of *The Eagle Kite,* pp. 608-609; September-October, 1997, p. 569.

Hudson Review, winter, 1972-73.

Interracial Books for Children, Volume 5, number 5, 1974, Albert V. Schwartz and Binnie Tate, review of *The Slave Dancer.*

Kirkus Reviews, April 1, 1968, review of *Dear Prosper,* p. 393; September 1, 1997, review of *Radiance Descending,* p. 1389.

Library Journal, September 1, 2001, Stephanie Maher, review of *Borrowed Finery,* p. 177.

Los Angeles Times, November 21, 1987.

Los Angeles Times Book Review, September 25, 1988; July 16, 1995, p. 27.

Miami Herald, October 19, 2001, Connie Ogle, review of *Borrowed Finery.*

Ms., October, 1984.

Nation, November 3, 1984, Blair T. Birmelin, review of *A Servant's Tale.*

New Leader, July 3, 1967; February 2, 1970.

New Republic, March 18, 1967; January 15, 1977.

New Statesman, November 8, 1974; December 4, 1981.

Newsweek, March 16, 1970; September 27, 1976; December 1, 1980.

New Yorker, February 7, 1970; November 1, 1976.

New York Review of Books, June 1, 1967; October 5, 1972; October 28, 1976; June 27, 1985; April 25, 2002, Jennifer Schuessler, review of *Borrowed Finery,* p. 47.

New York Times, February 10, 1970, p. 41; September 22, 1972; September 16, 1976; September 25, 2001, Michiko Kakutani, review of *Borrowed Finery,* p. E6.

New York Times Book Review, July 21, 1968, Margaret F. O'Connell, review of *Dear Prosper,* p. 22; February 1, 1970, p. 47; October 8, 1972; January 20, 1974, Julius Lester, review of *The Slave Dancer;* October 3, 1976; November 9, 1980, Anne Tyler, "Staking out Her Own Territory," p. 55; July 12, 1981; November 11, 1984, Anne Tyler, "Trying to Be Perfect," p. 48; November 18, 1984; February 5, 1989, Rosellen Brown, review of *The Village by the Sea,* p. 37; July 8, 1990, p. 18; November 10, 1991, Dinitia Smith, "No Place to Call Home," p. 52; November 10, 1993, p. 52; April 10, 1994, p. 35; December 2, 2001, review of *Borrowed Finery,* p. 12; August 25, 2002, review of *The God of Nightmares,* p. 24; December 8, 2002, review of *Borrowed Finery,* p. 80.

Publishers Weekly, April 6, 1990, Sybil S. Steinberg, interview with Fox, pp. 99-100; April 12, 1993, p. 64; August 23, 1993, p. 73; April 10, 1994, p. 35; February 20, 1995, p. 207; January 13, 1997, p. 36; July 27, 1997, review of *Radiance Descending,* p. 202; July 9, 2001, review of *Borrowed Finery,* p. 54; September 5, 2005, Jenny Brown, interview with Fox, p. 44, and review of *The Coldest Winter: A Stringer in Liberated Europe,* p. 45.

Saturday Review, October 22, 1966; July 19, 1969; January 23, 1971; October 16, 1976.

School Library Journal, February, 1979, Linda Silver, "From Baldwin to Singer: Authors for Kids and Adults," pp. 27-29; August, 1988, Amy Kellerman, review of *The Village by the Sea,* p. 93; August, 1991, p. 164; April, 1992, p. 42; July, 1993, p. 90; December, 1993, p. 111; February, 1995, p. 63; April, 1995, p. 150; September, 1997, p. 216; December, 2001, Barbara A. Genco, review of *Borrowed Finery,* p. 57.

Time, October 4, 1976.

Times Literary Supplement, June 6, 1968; February 21, 1986; November 28, 1986; January 15, 1988; December 6, 2002, review of *Borrowed Finery,* p. 13.

Tribune Books (Chicago, IL), September 1, 2002, review of *Borrowed Finery,* p. 6.

Voice of Youth Advocates, December, 1993, p. 290; June, 1995, W. Keith McCoy, review of *The Eagle Kite,* pp. 93-94; October, 1995, p. 210; February, 1998, Edward Sullivan, review of *Radiance Descending,* p. 383.

Washington Post, June 7, 1990; October 28, 2001, Chris Lehmann, review of *Child of Misfortune,* p. T5.

Washington Post Book World, September 24, 1972; October 31, 1976; February 8, 1981, Katherine Paterson, review of *A Place Apart;* September 23, 1984; March 24, 1991; May 7, 1995, Elizabeth Hand, review of *The Eagle Kite,* p. 14.

ONLINE

Guardian Unlimited, http://books.guardian.co.uk/ (June 21, 2003), Aida Edemariam, "A Qualified Optimist."

OTHER

A Talk with Paula Fox (video), Good Conversations, 1992.*

G

GOLDEN, Christie 1963-
(Jadrien Bell)

Personal
Born November 21, 1963, in Atlanta, GA; married Michael Georges (an artist). *Education:* University of Virginia, B.A. (English), 1985. *Hobbies and other interests:* Herbalism, making soap.

Addresses
Home—Loveland, CO. *Agent*—c/o Author Mail, Ace Books, Putnam Berkley Group, Inc., 200 Madison Ave., New York, NY 10016. *E-mail*—christie@christiegolden. com.

Career
Novelist.

Member
Science Fiction Writers of America, Horror Writers of America, Society for Creative Anachronism.

Writings

Instrument of Fate, Ace (New York, NY), 1996.
Star Trek Voyager: The Murdered Sun, Pocket Books (New York, NY), 1996.
Star Trek Voyager: Marooned, Pocket Books (New York, NY), 1997.
King's Man and Thief, Ace (New York, NY), 1997.
Star Trek Voyager: Seven of Nine, Pocket Books (New York, NY), 1998.
Invasion America (based on *Invasion America* television series), ROC (New York, NY), 1998.
Invasion America: On the Run (based on *Invasion America* television series), ROC (New York, NY), 1998.
(With Michael Jan Friedman) *Star Trek: The Next Generation: Double Helix: The First Virtue* (sixth book in a series), Pocket Books (New York, NY), 1999.

(Under pseudonym Jadrien Bell) *A.D. 999,* Ace (New York, NY), 1999.
Shadow of Heaven ("Star Trek: Voyager: Dark Matters Trilogy"), Pocket Books (New York, NY), 2000.
Ghost Dance ("Star Trek: Voyager: Dark Matters Trilogy"), Pocket Books (New York, NY), 2000.
Cloak and Dagger ("Star Trek: Voyager: Dark Matters Trilogy"), Pocket Books (New York, NY), 2000.
No Man's Land ("Star Trek: Voyager" series), Pocket Books (New York, NY), 2001.
Lord of the Clans ("Warcraft" series), Pocket Books (New York, NY), 2001.
The Last Round-up ("Star Trek" series), Pocket Books (New York, NY), 2002.
Star Trek: Homecoming, Pocket Books (New York, NY), 2003.
The Farther Shore (sequel to *Star Trek: Homecoming*), Pocket Books (New York, NY), 2004.
Enemy of My Enemy ("Star Trek: Voyager: Spirit Walk" series), Pocket Books (New York, NY), 2004.
Old Wounds ("Star Trek: Voyager: Spirit Walk" series), Pocket Books (New York, NY), 2004.

Contributor to anthologies, including *Realms of Valor,* TSR (Geneva, WI), 1993; *Realms of Infamy,* TSR, 1994; *Realms of Magic,* TSR, 1995; *Blood Muse,* Fine, 1995; *Lammas Night,* Baen (New York, NY), 1996; *OtherWere,* Ace (New York, NY), 1996; *Urban Nightmares,* Baen, 1997; *Highwaymen: Robbers and Rogues,* DAW (New York, NY), 1997; and *Star Trek: Starfleet Corps of Engineers,* Pocket Books (New York, NY), 2002.

"RAVENLOFT" SERIES

Vampire of the Mists, TSR (Geneva, WI), 1991.
Dance of the Dead, TSR (Geneva, WI), 1992.
The Enemy Within, TSR (Geneva, WI), 1994.

"FINAL DANCE" SERIES

On Fire's Wings, Luna (New York, NY), 2004.
In Stone's Clasp, Luna (New York, NY), 2005.

Work in Progress

Under Sea's Shadow, By Wind's Tempest, and *Through Soul's Desire,* further novels in the "Final Dance" series; more novels in the "Star Trek: Voyager" relaunch series.

Sidelights

Christie Golden combines elements of Gothic horror, fantasy, and science fiction in her work. In addition to her "Ravenloft" novel trilogy, she has produced both novels and short stories that contain fantasy elements, often drawing readers into worlds wherein mythic creatures and humans interact. A fan of the *Star Trek: Voyager* television series, she has also penned a number of novels set in that well-known universe, and has contributed *Lord of the Clans* to the series based on the *Warcraft* computer game.

"When I was old enough to clutch a crayon between my little fingers I was scribbling 'books,'" Golden recalled in an interview with Desiree Gentle for the *Para-Normal Romance* Web site. "I remember in seventh grade asking my English teacher if I could write the first chapter of a novel instead of the required short story," the novelist continued, "and she said yes. That first chapter launched me into my first original fantasy series." Golden saw her first novel, *Vampire of the Mists,* published in 1991.

Vampire of the Mists is set in the horror-laden realm of Ravenloft, a land rife with ghosts and werewolves and ruled by Count Strahd Von Zarovich. The plot revolves around a vampire elf who is forced out of the Forgotten Realm and into Ravenloft, where he must confront von Zarovich. Golden continues her "Ravenloft" saga in two further novels: *Dance of the Dead* and *The Enemy Within. Dance of the Dead* is the story of a young dancer named Larisa Snowmane who travels by ship through Ravenloft, seemingly unaware of the sinister threats that exist there. Unknown to Larisa, an evil captain with a chilling secret directs the ship she has boarded. When her ship arrives at a Ravenloft island full of zombies, Larisa must enlist the help of the island's more compassionate residents and perform the magic Dance of the Dead in order to save herself from the evil the ship's captain represents. Praising both the "exciting, well-developed story" and the book's "excellent character development," *Kliatt* reviewer Amos C. Patterson predicted that *Dance of the Dead* will keep readers' attention through "to the completion of the story."

Golden mixes aspects of romantic literature, fantasy, and history in *King's Man and Thief.* The main character, Deveran, has two disparate identities. Publicly he is a man of wealth and a great benefactor of the arts. However, since his wife's brutal murder eight years earlier, he also rules the city's thieves in secret. While attempting to lead the thieves away from a life of crime and into a more honorable line of work, Deveran must fight factions within his group who oppose him. Led by Marrika, the evil forces launch a plan to make every inhabitant of the city capable of new levels of evil and darkness. In a romantic twist, Deveran encounters the goddess Health, who holds for him the key to saving the city. Calling the intricate, seven-layered religion depicted in *King's Man and Thief* "the novel's most distinctive feature," *Voice of Youth Advocate* critic Margaret Miles suggested that readers of fantasy, horror, and romance continue to look for Golden's work in the future.

With *On Fire's Wings* Golden begins her second fantasy series, this one titled "Final Dance." Set in the country of Aruka, the novel follows Kevla Bai-sha, a young woman whose birthright as the daughter of a prostitute promises her little in life. Eventually "bought" by the powerful Tahmu-kha Rakyn—who, unknown to Kevla is her father—she becomes a servant to Tahmu's wife Yeshi. When her true identity is revealed, Kevla is viewed as a threat by Yeshi; meanwhile, the young woman begins to realize that she holds inside her a power that may allow her to defend the forces that threaten not only her family but Arukan as well.

Praising *On Fire's Wings* as "a definite gem in the world of sci-fi fantasy," *Best Reviews* online contributor Anne Barringer added that Golden "weaves a splendiferous tale of exotic magic and the courage of the human heart." In her *SFSite* online review, Victoria Strauss dubbed the novel "a treat for fans of romantic fantasy," writing that *On Fire's Wings* presents readers with "an interestingly detailed, Eastern-influenced world, filled with appealing characters, complex relationships, and plenty of action."

As Golden explained to Gentle of the projected five-volume "Final Dance" series: "I'm really enjoying [writing] these books; they start off with such a narrow focus in *On Fire's Wings* and expand, as Kevla's knowledge of her world expands. By the end of the series, I think 'epic fantasy' will be an accurate term." Further titles in the series include *In Stone's Clasp, By Wind's Tempest,* and *Under Sea's Shadow.*

Biographical and Critical Sources

BOOKS

Reginald, Robert, *Science Fiction and Fantasy Literature, 1975-1991,* Thomson Gale (Detroit, MI), 1992.

PERIODICALS

Kliatt, November, 1992, Amos C. Patterson, review of *Dance of the Dead,* p. 14; July, 2002, Hugh M. Flick, Jr., review of *Star Trek: Starfleet Corps of Engineers,* p. 32; November, 2003, Hugh M. Flick, Jr., review of *The Farther Shore,* p. 241; May, 2005, Hugh M. Flick, Jr., review of *Old Wounds,* p. 34.

Locus, October, 1991, p. 46; November, 1991, p. 35.
Rapport, April, 1992, p. 21.
Voice of Youth Advocates, August, 1997, Margaret Miles, review of *King's Man and Thief,* pp. 192-193.

ONLINE

Best Reviews Online, http://thebestreviews.com/ (September 26, 2005), Anne Barringer, review of *On Fire's Wings.*
Christie Golden Home Page, http://www.christiegolden. com (September 26, 2005).
ParaNormal Romance Web site, http://writerspace.com/ ParanormalRomance/ (September 26, 2005), Desiree Gentle, interview with Golden.
SFSite.com, http://www.sfsite.com/ (September 26, 2005), Victoria Strauss, review of *On Fire's Wings.*
Wizards Web site, http://www.wizards.com/ (September 26, 2005), "Christie Golden."*

*   *   *

GRANSTRÖM, Brita 1969-

Personal

Born July 23, 1969, in Eskilstuna, Sweden; married Mick Manning (a writer and illustrator); children: Max, Björn. *Education:* Attended Örebro Konstskola; Konstfack (national college of art, craft, and design), Stockholm, Sweden, M.F.A.

Addresses

Home—North England. *Agent*—c/o Candlewick Press, 2067 Massachusetts Ave., Cambridge, MA 02140. *E-mail*—brita@mickandbrita.com.

Career

Artist and illustrator of children's books. Has worked as a medical illustrator for AMREF. *Exhibitions:* Paintings exhibited at University Gallery, Newcastle, England; for Society of American Illustrators, New York, NY; and elsewhere.

Member

Society of Authors.

Awards, Honors

Smarties Silver Award, 1996, for *The World's Full of Babies!; Times Educational Supplement* Award, 1997, for *What's under the Bed?;* shortlisted for Rhone Poulenc science prize, 1998, for *Yum-Yum!,* and *How Did I Begin?,* and 1999, for *Science School;* Key Stage 1 Nonfiction Award, English Association, 2000, for *Wash, Scrub, Brush!,* and 2005, for *Voices of the Rainforest;* shortlisted for Key Stage 2 Award, English Association, 2005, for *Fly on the Wall: Roman Fort;* Oppenheim Toy Portfolio Gold Award, and Book of the Year citation, *Parenting* magazine, both for *Eyes, Nose, Fingers, Toes;* Oppenheim Toy Portfolio Platinum Award, for *Does a Cow Say Boo?;* Blue Peter Awards shortlist, 2005, for *What's My Family Tree?*

Writings

SELF-ILLUSTRATED

Ten in the Bed, Candlewick Press (Cambridge, MA), 1996.
Many Hands Counting Book, edited by Gale Pryor, Candlewick Press (Cambridge, MA), 1999.
My First Words and Pictures, Walker (London, England), 2004.

Other books include *Wof Här Kommer Jag!* and *Fina och Telefonen,* published by Raben & Sjögren.

ILLUSTRATOR

Mick Manning, *The World Is Full of Babies!,* Delacorte (New York, NY), 1996.
Mick Manning, *Art School,* Kingfisher (New York, NY), 1996.
Christine Morley and Carole Orbell, *Me and My Pet Dog,* World Book/Two-Can (Chicago, IL), 1996.
Christine Morley and Carole Orbell, *Me and My Pet Cat,* World Book/Two-Can (Chicago, IL), 1996.
Christine Morley and Carole Orbell, *Me and My Pet Rabbit,* World Book/Two-Can (Chicago, IL), 1997.
Mick Manning, *What's Up?,* F. Watts (London, England), 1997.
Christine Morley and Carole Orbell, *Me and My Pet Fish,* World Book/Two-Can (Chicago, IL), 1997.
Pippa Goodhart, *Bed Time,* F. Watts (London, England), 1997, published as *My Bed Time,* 2002.
Pippa Goodhart, *Morning Time,* F. Watts (London, England), 1997, published as *My Morning Time,* 2002.
Pippa Goodhart, *Play Time,* F. Watts (London, England), 1997.
Pippa Goodhart, *Shopping Time,* F. Watts (London, England), 1997.
Mick Manning, *How Did I Begin?,* F. Watts (London, England), 1997.
Mick Manning, *Rainy Day,* F. Watts (London, England), 1997.
Mick Manning, *Snowy Day,* F. Watts (London, England), 1997.
Mick Manning, *Sunny Day,* F. Watts (London, England), 1997.
Mick Manning, *Windy Day,* F. Watts (London, England), 1997.
Mick Manning, *Science School,* Kingfisher (New York, NY), 1998.
Mick Manning, *Collect-o-Mania,* F. Watts (London, England), 1998.
Judy Hindley, *Eyes, Nose, Fingers, and Toes: A First Book about You,* Candlewick Press (Cambridge, MA), 1999.

Sam McBratney, *Bert's Wonderful News,* Walker & Co.(London, England), 1999.

Mick Manning, *Drama School,* Kingfisher (New York, NY), 1999.

Mick Manning, *Let's Build a House!,* F. Watts (London, England), 1999.

Mick Manning, *Let's Party!,* Big Fish (London, England), 2000.

Mick Manning, *Wheels Keep Turning,* F. Watts (London, England), 2000.

Maddie Stewart, *Clever Daddy,* Early Learning Centre (Swindon, England), 2000.

Pippa Goodhart, *Molly and the Beanstalk,* Walker & Co. (London, England), 2001.

Kathy Henderson, *Baby Knows Best,* Little, Brown (Boston, MA), 2001.

Mick Manning, *What's My Family Tree?,* F. Watts (London, England), 2001.

Mick Manning, *How Should I Behave?,* F. Watts (London, England), 2002.

Mick Manning, *The Power Cut,* F. Watts (London, England), 2002.

Mick Manning, *Watch Out! Builders About!,* F. Watts (London, England), 2002.

Judy Hindley, *Does a Cow Say Boo?,* Candlewick Press (Cambridge, MA), 2002.

Joyce Dunbar, *A Chick Called Saturday,* Eerdmans (Grand Rapids, MI), 2003.

Mick Manning, *Make Your Own Museum,* F. Watts (London, England), 2003.

Kathy Henderson, *Dog Story,* Bloomsbury (London, England), 2004.

Paeony Lewis, *No More Cookies!,* Chicken House (New York, NY), 2005.

Judy Hindley, *Baby Talk,* Candlewick Press (Cambridge, MA), 2006.

Illustrator of *Ben's Bring Your Bear Party,* by Martin Waddell, Walker & Co.; and *Kisses Are Little, Smiles Are Wide,* Candlewick Press.

ILLUSTRATOR WITH PARTNER, MICK MANNING

Mick Manning, *Nature Watch,* Kingfisher (New York, NY), 1997.

Mick Manning, *Honk! Honk! A Story of Migration,* Kingfisher (New York, NY), 1997.

Mick Manning, *Yum-Yum!,* F. Watts (London, England), 1997.

Mick Manning, *My Body, Your Body,* F. Watts (London, England), 1997.

Mick Manning, *Splish, Splash, Splosh!,* F. Watts (London, England), 1997.

Mick Manning, *What's under the Bed?,* F. Watts (London, England), 1997.

Mick Manning, *Nature School,* Kingfisher (New York, NY), 1997.

Mick Manning, *Out There Somewhere,* F. Watts (London, England), 1998.

Mick Manning, *What If? A Book about Recycling,* F. Watts (London, England), 1998.

Mick Manning, *Wild and Free,* F. Watts (London, England), 1998.

Mick Manning, *Sael Ungen,* Raben & Sjögren (Stockholm, Sweden), 1998.

Mick Manning, *Super School,* Kingfisher (New York, NY), 1999.

Mick Manning, *Super Mum,* F. Watts (London, England), 1999, published as *Supermom,* Albert Whitman (Morton Grove, IL), 2001.

Mick Manning, *Wash, Scrub, Brush!,* F. Watts (London, England), 1999, Albert Whitman (Morton Grove, IL), 2001.

Mick Manning, *Stone Age, Bone Age,* F. Watts (London, England), 2000.

Mick Manning, *What a Viking!,* Raben & Sjögren (New York, NY), 2000.

Mick Manning, *Dinomania,* F. Watts (London, England), 2001, Holiday House (New York, NY), 2002.

Mick Manning, *The Story of a Storm,* F. Watts (London, England), 2001.

Mick Manning, *High Tide, Low Tide,* F. Watts (London, England), 2001.

Mick Manning, *Seasons Turning,* F. Watts (London, England), 2001.

Mick Manning, *When the Sun Goes Down,* F. Watts (London, England), 2001.

Mick Manning, *How Will I Grow?,* F. Watts (London, England), 2002.

Mick Manning, *Voices of the Rainforest,* F. Watts (London, England), 2004.

Mick Manning, *Seaside Scientist,* F. Watts (London, England), 2004.

Mick Manning, *Fly on the Wall: Roman Fort,* Frances Lincoln (London, England), 2004.

Mick Manning, *Yuck!,* Frances Lincoln (London, England), 2005.

Mick Manning, *Fly on the Wall: Viking Longship,* Frances Lincoln (London, England), 2006.

Mick Manning, *Snap!,* Frances Lincoln (London, England), 2006.

Also illustrator, with Manning, of *Fly on the Wall: Pharaoh's Egypt,* and *Dino Dinners!,* both by Manning and Granström, for Frances Lincoln (London, England). Collaborator, with Manning, on "Max and Kate" series for *Ladybug* magazine, beginning 1999.

Books have been translated into Welsh, Japanese, Korean, German, Serbo-Croat, Chinese, Dutch, Portugese, Swedish, Spanish, and Brazilian.

Sidelights

Swedish-born artist Brita Granström is well known for her work as an illustrator, many of which are done in collaboration with her husband, writer and illustrator Mick Manning. A prolific team, Manning and Granström have produced picture books for young readers as well as nonfiction titles. Because both studied art and design, they work together on both the writing and illustration stages of the book, although Granström explains that her input in the writing process is "collaborative" and

A curious little chick is determined to fly the coop and see the world in Joyce Dunbar's engaging picture book A Chick Called Saturday, *featuring illustrations by Granström.*

credits her husband as author. "We try to stay flexible," the couple explained in an interview with Pam Kelt that was posted on their home page. In their illustrations, Granström typically focuses on human characters while Manning draws the animals. "In some books, one of us might draw and the other might colour the same artwork," the author/illustrators explained to Kelt. "Then we enjoy it when people say they can't see the join!" Along with their many books, Manning and Granström have also written and illustrated a five-page feature for *Ladybug* magazine called "Max and Kate," which features the amusing adventures of two preschool neighbors.

Manning and Granström's *Wash, Scrub, Brush!,* a book of instruction about personal hygiene, is one of several collaborations that has won an award. The title teaches basic behaviors in washing and grooming through a story of children preparing for a party. "The authors skillfully cover basic grooming and hygiene within a story framework," complimented Marilyn Ackerman in *School Library Journal. Booklist* contributor Connie Fletcher praised the pair's use of art, commenting that "the illustrations, crowded with happy kids sprucing up, are bright and lively."

Other titles by the pair focus on the science of daily life or on science topics that appeal to young readers. Their book *Supermom* shows similarities between human mothers and their animal counterparts as they care for their young ones. "The watercolor, graphite, and crayon artwork reflects the light approach to scientific facts," according to Carolyn Janssen in a *School Library Journal* review. *Dinomania* focuses on modern paleontology, and provides hands-on activities for young people

who want to learn more about dinosaurs. Augusta R. Malvagno, writing for *School Library Journal,* commented on the book's "kid-friendly text, expressive and colorful illustrations, and creative activities and crafts." Ellen Mandel, writing in *Booklist,* commented that the crafts included are "fun activities for hands-on learning." The picture books *Yuck!* and *Snap!* discuss the food chain; *Yuck!* shows slimy, gross, and disgusting meals eaten by various animal babies. *Snap!* follows along the food chain as a frog is eaten by a duckling, which is eaten by a large fish, which is eaten by a fisherman. However, something lurks in the pictures that prompts readers to realize that the fisherman is not the end of the food chain after all.

Along with her work with Manning, Granström is also the illustrator of several children's books by well-known authors including Pippa Goodhart, Sam McBratney, and Judy Hindley. A *Kirkus Reviews* contributor labeled her work for Hindley's *Does a Cow Say Boo?* as "delightful pencil, watercolor, and crayon illustrations." A *Publishers Weekly* critic commented on the "vibrantly colored farm scenes" in the same title, while Diane Foote, writing in *Booklist,* considered them "bright, energetic illustrations." Of her work in Joyce Dunbar's *A Chick Called Saturday,* a *Kirkus Reviews* contributor commented that Granström's "loose watercolor-and-pencil pictures and a touch of appropriately 'scratchy' calligraphy put readers in the right farm—uh, frame—of mind." A *Publishers Weekly* critic called the title a "sunnyhued picture book," while Ilene Cooper noted in *Booklist* that the small spot art and large illustrations together make "a dynamic combination that will keep kids' interest." Granström was honored when the Society of American

Illustrators invited her to exhibit an image from *A Chick Called Saturday* at their annual show.

Granström once told *SATA:* "I love my job. It's a dream come true. When I'm not illustrating children's books, I go out painting. I fill the baby's pram with acrylic paints and go painting on the spot." Granström lives in northern England with her husband and children.

Biographical and Critical Sources

PERIODICALS

Booklist, January 1, 2000, review of *Eyes, Nose, Fingers, and Toes,* p. 824; March 15, 2001, Ellen Mandel, review of *Supermom,* p. 1404; May 1, 2001, Connie Fletcher, review of *Wash, Scrub, Brush!,* p. 1686; June 1, 2002, Ellen Mandel, review of *Dinomania,* p. 1717, and Diane Foote, review of *Does a Cow Say Boo?,* p. 1738; August, 2003, Ilene Cooper, review of *A Chick Called Saturday,* p. 1988.

Kirkus Reviews, May 1, 2002, review of *Does a Cow Say Boo?* p. 656; July 1, 2003, review of *A Chick Called Saturday,* p. 909.

Publishers Weekly, June 21, 1999, review of *Eyes, Nose, Fingers, and Toes,* p. 66; May 13, 2002, review of *Does a Cow Say Boo?,* p. 69; June 2, 2003, review of *A Chick Called Saturday,* p. 50.

School Librarian, winter, 2004, Don Brothwell, review of *Fly on the Wall: Roman Fort,* p. 209.

School Library Journal, July, 1999, Olga R. Barnes, review of *Eyes, Nose, Fingers, and Toes,* p. 73; September, 1999, Cris Riedel, review of *Drama School,* p. 214; April, 2001, Marilyn Ackerman, review of *Wash, Scrub, Brush!,* and Carolyn Janssen, review of *Supermom,* p. 133; April, 2002, Jean Pollock, review of *Let's Party!: Celebrate with Children All around the World,* and Augusta R. Malvagno, review of *Dinomania,* p. 137; August, 2003, Bina Williams, review of *A Chick Called Saturday,* p. 126; July, 2005, Lynda S. Poling, review of *Fly on the Wall: Roman Fort,* p. 91.

ONLINE

Brita Granström and Mick Manning's Home Page, http://www.mickandbrita.com (January 16, 2006).

*   *   *

GUEVARA, Susan

Personal

Born in Walnut Creek, CA; married; husband's name Blair. *Education:* San Francisco Art Academy, B.F.A.; studied painting at Belgium's Royal Academy of Fine Art.

Addresses

Home—San Francisco, CA. *Agent*—c/o Author Mail, G.P. Putnam, 375 Hudson St., New York, NY 10014. *E-mail*—susanguevara@jps.net.

Career

Illustrator.

Awards, Honors

Pura Belpre award for illustration, Association for Library Services to Children/National Association to Promote Library Services to the Spanish-Speaking, 1995, for *Chato's Kitchen,* and 2002, for *Chato and the Party Animals.*

Illustrator

Ned Miller, *Emmett's Snowball,* Holt (New York, NY), 1990.

Dian Curtis Regan, *The Class with the Summer Birthdays,* Holt (New York, NY), 1991.

Kathryn Lasky, *I Have an Aunt on Marlborough Street,* Macmillan (New York, NY), 1992.

Arthur A. Levine, *The Boardwalk Princess,* Morrow (New York, NY), 1993.

(With others) Margarita Robleda Moguel, *El carrito de monchito,* Houghton (Boston, MA), 1993.

Aileen Friedman, *The King's Commissioners,* Scholastic (New York, NY), 1994.

Virginia Haviland, reteller, *Favorite Fairy Tales Told in Italy,* Morrow (New York, NY), 1995.

Gary Soto, *Chato's Kitchen,* Putnam (New York, NY), 1995.

Marion Dane Bauer, *Jason's Bears,* Bridgewater Books (Mahwah, NJ), 1996.

Tony Johnston, *Isabel's House of Butterflies,* Sierra Club Books for Children (San Francisco, CA), 1997.

Ana Castillo, *My Daughter, My Son, the Eagle, the Dove,* Dutton (New York, NY), 2000.

Gary Soto, *Chato and the Party Animals,* Putnam (New York, NY), 2000.

Jane Yolen, reteller, *Not One Damsel in Distress: World Folktales for Strong Girls,* Silver Whistle Books (New York, NY), 2000.

Dee Lillegard, *Tiger, Tiger,* Putnam (New York, NY), 2002.

Judith Head, *Mud Soup,* Random House (New York, NY), 2003.

Gary Soto, *Chato Goes Cruisin',* Putnam (New York, NY), 2004.

Alex and Arthur Dorros, *The Winner,* Harry N. Abrams (New York, NY), 2006.

Several books illustrated by Guevara have been published in Spanish.

Adaptations

Chato's Kitchen was adapted as a video recording, 1999.

Sidelights

Latina artist Susan Guevara has created illustrations for a wide variety of books for young readers, from traditional European fairy tales to stories set in the modern

Los Angeles barrio. In books ranging from Virginia Haviland's anthology *Favorite Fairy Tales Told in Italy* to works by award-winning Chicano writer Gary Soto, Guevara reflects and enhances the vision of the writers she works with. Training at both the San Francisco Art Academy and Belgium's Royal Academy of Fine Art, Guevara developed technical skills and creative interpretations that have been praised by reviewers and readers alike.

Guevara's first published illustration project was the 1990 picture book *Emmett's Snowball,* written by Ned Miller. In this story, a young boy begins to make a snowball and with the help of friends and neighbors his efforts eventually result in the largest snowball in the world. Guevara's watercolor and charcoal drawings, which use contrasting warm and cool colors to depict the warmth of friends and neighbors amid the chill of winter, were cited as an "ideal complement to [Miller's] slightly offbeat story" by Denise Anton Wright in *School Library Journal.* In the equally offbeat *The Boardwalk Princess,* Arthur A. Levine's lighthearted fairy tale about an evil witch, a magic potion, and a clever young girl is interspersed with "humorously illustrated . . . watercolors loaded with [Guevara's] period detail," according to *Booklist* contributor Janice Del Negro. In the opinion of Kay Weisman in her review for *Booklist,* Guevara's "brightly colored acrylic paintings add humor" to Aileen Friedman's *The King's Commissioners,* an upbeat story about a king's frustration with simple mathematics. Another highly praised picture book featuring Guevara's artwork, Dee Lillegard's *Tiger, Tiger,* prompted a *Kirkus Reviews* contributor to cite the book's "stunning, jewel-toned illustrations in gouache and chalk pastel," while *School Library Journal* Jody

McCoy wrote that the book's pictures "conjure up all the magic needed for a tantalizing flight of fancy."

Chato's Kitchen, written by acclaimed poet and children's author Soto, introduces a wily cat and his feline friends. Chato decides to lure the small *ratoncitos* (mice) of his barrio home to an untimely end by preparing a bounty of good food. Soon the scent of everything from enchiladas to frijoles fills the air, and the hungry cat and his cat cohorts extend an invitation to their intended main course, only to be outsmarted in return. Guevara's illustrations for this highly praised though controversial work, which earned her the first Pura Belpre award for illustration, features what a *Publishers Weekly* critic termed "wickedly funny, urban paints" and felines that the critic called "delicious send-ups of *barrio* characters."

Guevara has re-teamed with Soto for the storybook sequels *Chato and the Party Animals* and *Chato Goes Cruisin',* the first which earned her a second Pura Belpre award. In *Chato and the Party Animals* the cat throws a birthday party for his friend Novio, but when party time comes the birthday cat is nowhere to be found. Novio re-pals with Chato in *Chato Goes Cruisin',* which finds the two friends winning a free cruise, only to discover that the entire cruise ship is full of seasick dogs. Praising *Chato and the Party Animals,* Ann Welton wrote in *School Library Journal* that the "lively acrylic-on-scratch-board" artwork created by Guevara "have a verve and style that will make readers long to join the fun."

In her acceptance speech for her first Pura Belpre award, published in the *Journal of Youth Services in Libraries,* Guevara described the process of illustrating a chil-

A young boy creates a tiger with the help of a magic feather, then worries that his magic will not be enough to help his village when the beast grows hungry in Dee Lilegard's **Tiger, Tiger.** *(Illustration by Susan Guevara.)*

Guevara's illustrations for Gary Soto's **Chato and the Party Animals** *bring to life the anticipation of planning a surprise birthday party for a best friend.*

dren's book. "A good story gives me wings," the illustrator explained. "Wings to zoom me in, out, over the character's world. . . . Wings to carry me someplace worth going, someplace readers might wish to go." She cited as her main task "communicating the ideas and beliefs of a specific world" created by the author, her tools for communicating being "technique, palette, viewpoint, and subject matter." Immersing herself in the world of her characters, Guevara researches movies, books, settings, and other illustrations of the period or place where the story takes place. In the case of *Chato's*

Kitchen, her immersion in the culture of the barrio even resulted in a vision: "Tijuana black velvet paintings" were the inspiration for much of Guevara's work for the book.

Biographical and Critical Sources

PERIODICALS

Booklist, January 15, 1993, p. 921; April 15, 1993, Janice Del Negro, review of *The Boardwalk Princess,* p. 1519; February 15, 1995, Kay Weisman, review of *The King's Commissioners,* p. 1092; November 15, 1998, Isabel Schon, review of *Chato's Kitchen,* p. 599; August, 2003, Hazel Rochman, review of *Mud Soup,* p. 1989.

Horn Book, September-October, 1995, pp. 591-592.

Journal of Youth Services in Libraries, spring, 1997, Susan Guevara, "Pura Belpre Award Acceptance Speech for Illustration 1995," pp. 273-275.

Kirkus Reviews, October 1, 2002, review of *Tiger, Tiger,* p. 1474.

Publishers Weekly, May 3, 1993, p. 308; February 6, 1995, review of *Chato's Kitchen,* pp. 84-85; March 6, 1995, p. 70.

School Library Journal, February, 1991, Denise Anton Wright, review of *Emmett's Snowball,* p. 73; March, 1993, p. 189; June, 1993, p. 98; July, 2000, Ann Welton, review of *Chato and the Party Animals,* p. 88; April, 2002, Luann Toth, "Pura Belpre Awards Announced in New Orleans," p. 10; December, 2002, Jody McCoy, review of *Tiger, Tiger,* p. 100.

ONLINE

Susan Guevara Home Page, http://www.susanguevara.com (January 3, 2006).*

H-I

HAND, Elizabeth 1957-

Personal

Born March 29, 1957, in San Diego, CA; daughter of Edward (an attorney) and Alice Ann (a social worker; maiden name, Silverthorn) Hand; children: Callie Anne Silverthorn. *Education:* Catholic University of America, B.A., 1984. *Religion:* Roman Catholic.

Addresses

Home—P.O. Box 133, Lincolnville, ME 04849. *Agent*—Martha Millard Literary Agency, 204 Park Ave., Madison, NJ 07940. *E-mail*—iotar@hotmail.com.

Career

National Air and Space Museum, Smithsonian Institution, Washington, DC, archival researcher, 1979-86, and co-founder of archival videodisc program; writer.

Awards, Honors

Philip K. Dick Award finalist, for *Winterlong, Aestival Tide,* and *Icarus Descending;* James Tiptree, Jr. Award, 1995, and Mythopoeic Society Fantasy Award for Adult Literature, 1996, both for *Walking the Moon;* Nebula Award for best novella, Science Fiction and Fantasy Writers of America, and World Fantasy Award, World Fantasy Convention, both 1995, both for "Last Summer at Mars Hill"; Battersea Arts Center award finalist, Fringe Theater Festival (London, England), 1997, for one-act play, *The Have-Nots;* International Horror Guild Award, for novella "Cleopatra Brimstone" and short story "Pavane for a Prince of the Air"; World Fantasy Award, World Fantasy Convention, 2004, for *Bibliomancy.*

Writings

FICTION

Winterlong, Bantam (New York, NY), 1990.
Aestival Tide, Bantam (New York, NY), 1991.
Icarus Descending, Bantam (New York, NY), 1993.
Walking the Moon, HarperPrism (New York, NY), 1995.
Glimmering, HarperPrism (New York, NY), 1997.
Last Summer at Mars Hill (short stories), HarperPrism (New York, NY), 1998.
Black Light, HarperCollins (New York, NY), 1999.
Bibliomancy (includes "Cleopatra Brimstone," "Chip Crockett's Christmas Carol," "The Last Trumps," and "Pavane for a Prince of the Air"; also see below) P.S. Publishing (Hornsea, East Yorkshire, England), 2003.
Mortal Love, Ballantine (New York, NY), 2004.
Saffron and Brimstone (includes "Cleopatra Brimstone," "Chip Crockett's Christmas Carol," and "Pavane for a Prince of the Air"; also see below), M. Press (New York, NY), 2006.
Chip Crockett's Christmas Carol, Beccon Press (London, England), 2006.
Generation Loss, in press.
The Bride of Frankenstein, DH Press, 2006.

MEDIA TIE-INS

12 Monkeys (film novelization), HarperCollins (New York, NY) 1995.
Anna and the King (based on the screenplay by Steve Meerson and others), HarperCollins (New York, NY), 1999.
The Affair of the Necklace (film novelization), HarperEntertainment (New York, NY) 2001.
Maze of Deception: A Clone Wars Novel ("Star Wars: Boba Fett" series), Scholastic (New York, NY), 2003.
Hunted: A Clone Wars Novel ("Star Wars: Boba Fett" series), Scholastic (New York, NY), 2003.
Fight to Survive: A Clone Wars Novel ("Star Wars: Boba Fett" series), Scholastic (New York, NY), 2003.
Pursuit: A Clone Wars Novel ("Star Wars: Boba Fett" series), Scholastic (New York, NY), 2004.
A New Threat: A Clone Wars Novel ("Star Wars: Boba Fett" series), Scholastic (New York, NY), 2004.
Catwoman (based on a screenplay by John Rogers, Mike Ferris, and John Brancato), Ballantine (New York, NY), 2004.

Also author or coauthor audiobook scripts, including *Anna and the King,* 2001; author of *The Frenchman* (television pilot). Contributor to "X-Files" and "Millennium" fiction series, based on television shows.

OTHER

Also author of one-act play *The Have-Nots.* Critic for *Washington Post, Detroit Metro Times,* and *San Francisco Eye.* Regular reviewer for *Magazine of Fantasy & Science Fiction, Washington Post Book World,* and *Voice Literary Supplement.* Co-creator of DC Comics comic-book series *Anima.*

Contributor of stories to books, including *Year's Best Horror Stories XVII,* edited by Karl E. Wagner, DAW (New York, NY), 1989, *Full Spectrum 2,* Doubleday (New York, NY), 1989, and *Year's Best Horror 2,* edited by Ramsey Campbell, Carroll & Graf (New York, NY), 1991.

Work in Progress

A "gritty mainstream" novel.

Sidelights

Elizabeth Hand emerged on the science-fiction scene after publishing only three short works. While her novels and short stories are geared toward an adult audience, several of her books have appeal for young-adult readers. Several of her movie tie-ins and novelisations also appeal to younger readers, including her contributions to the "Star Wars" novel series. She has also worked on comic books as a co-creator, with Paul Witcover, of the DC Comics series *Anima,* and Hand's novels such as *Black Light* feature young-adult narrators. In a review of her short-story collection *Last Summer at Mars Hill,* a *Publishers Weekly* critic noted that Hand produces "beautiful writing" that is tempered with "healthy doses of skepticism." Noting the author's lyrical style, *Science Fiction Weekly Online* contributor Nick Gevers called Hand "one of American literature's finest prose poets of the fantastic."

Hand's first published short story, "Prince of Flowers," appeared in *Twilight Zone,* and is a fantasy story about a woman, Helen, who works in a museum in Washington, DC. Helen's job is to open new crates and inventory the strange objects and papers received by the museum. Among the items she takes home to liven up her apartment is a "spirit puppet," an Indonesian item that had been packed away in storage for nearly a century. "On the Town Route," which first appeared in *Pulphouse,* concerns a woman who travels with an ice-cream-truck vendor through an impoverished area of Virginia, where they distribute ice cream to the poor people of the region until an accident disrupts their charitable efforts. "The Boy in the Tree," which was published shortly before Hand's first novel, *Winterlong,* is noticeably more akin to science fiction due to its futuristic setting: a research facility that treats psychopaths.

Published in 1990, *Winterlong* describes a future Earth where biological weapons have destroyed much of the planet's population. Wendy and Raphael, twins who have been separated since birth, travel across the nightmarish landscape, facing danger from mutated cannibalistic children and deadly exotic plants. As the twins reunite, they enact the legend of the Final Ascension, which will decide the future of humankind. As D. Douglas Fratz wrote in *Twentieth-Century Science-Fiction Writers,* "There are some marvelous characters here, but none seems to act on his or her own volition; all feel driven by unseen forces." Sherry Hoy, reviewing *Winterlong* in *Voice of Youth Advocates,* stated that Hand "weaves a tale that is achingly haunting and disquieting, surreal yet compelling." The novels *Aestival Tide* and *Icarus Descending* continue the topics and themes Hand first develops in *Winterlong,* and many reviewers have viewed the three as a series. Themes in these novels also appear in Hand's award-winning *Walking the Moon* and *Black Light.*

In the novel *Black Light* Hand tells the story of high-school senior Charlotte Moylan and Charlotte's godfather, filmmaker Axel Kern. The notorious Kern arrives in Charlotte's hometown of Kamensic to host a Halloween party replete with drugs and dark and perverse characters, including various members of the Benandanti and the Malandanti, who are, as a critic for *Kirkus Reviews* explained, "two opposing groups of magicians . . . [that] struggle to control human destiny." After experiencing unsettling visions and meeting the strange Professor Warnick, Charlotte learns that her godfather is deeply involved in a dangerous conspiracy. Jackie Cassada praised Hand's "lucid style" in *Library Journal,* and a reviewer for *Publishers Weekly* declared that the book "should strongly appeal to aficionados of sophisticated horror."

Four of Hand's novellas, one of which was previously published online, appeared together in print in *Bibliomancy,* published in England. (Three of these stories also appear in *Saffron and Brimstone,* published in the United States.) Her novella "Cleopatra Brimstone" gives the story of a young woman's recovery from rape a horrific twist as the injured protagonist channels her rage and lust for vengeance and morphs into an insectile serial killer. "Pavane for a Prince of the Air" is a semi-autobiographical story about the death of a friend. Both of these novellas were nominated for an International Horror Guild award. "The Least Trumps" deals with tattooing and tarot, while "Chip Crockett's Christmas Carol" features the character Tony Maroni and an old-time children's television program. Hand told Nick Gevers in *Science Fiction Weekly Online* that the story is a tribute to Charles Dickens's *A Christmas Carol:* "I just love Dickens, and Christmas, and I've always wanted to write a Christmas story." Reviewing this collected short fiction, Paul di Filippo, in a review for the *Washington Post Book World,* noted that "Hand's close attention to the cherished dailiness of life is matched only by the subtlety of her fantastical conceits."

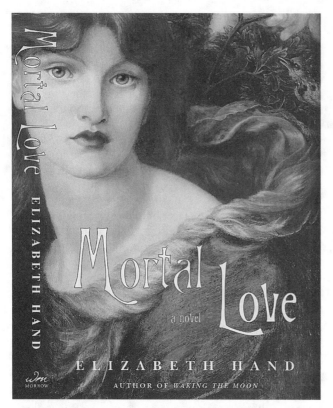

With its start in Victorian London, Hand's 2004 novel links Romantic poet Algernon Swinburne, Edwardian artist Radborne Comstock, and modern-day journalist Daniel Rowlands in a mystery that transcends time. (Cover illustration by Erich Lessing.)

Mortal Love delves into artistic inspiration: essentially, what drives artists to create art. Hand pictures the inspiration of various male artists as a beautiful woman whose name changes depending on the artist to whom she appears; she eventually drives at least one of these men into madness. "On one level I think *Mortal Love* served as a way of examining the source of my own creative activity, by looking at that of other writers or visual artists," Hand explained to Gevers in *Science Fiction Weekly Online*. *Washington Post Book World* reviewer Lawrence Norfolk summed up the novel, writing that "*Mortal Love* is at once a painting in prose, an investigation into artistic obsession and a re-evaluation." Noting that the book was marketed to mainstream audiences as well as science-fiction and fantasy readers, a *Publishers Weekly* critic commented that Hand's "timeless tale of desire and passion should reach many readers beyond [the author's] usual fantasy base."

While Hand continues to work on novelisations of media events as well as original science-fiction and fantasy works, she has also moved into more mainstream fiction. Discussing the novel *Generation Loss,* she described the story as more gritty than her previous works. Hand lives with her two children in a home located on the coast of Maine, "within shouting distance of her cottage studio," according to an essay on her home page.

Biographical and Critical Sources

BOOKS

Twentieth-Century Science-Fiction Writers, 3rd edition, St. James Press (Detroit, MI), 1991.

PERIODICALS

Analog, February, 1991, p. 176; April, 1993, p. 160; February, 1994, p. 159; December, 1995, p. 181.
Booklist, February 15, 1998, Nancy Spillman, review of *The Frenchman,* p. 1026; June 1, 2004, Mary Ellen Quinn, review of *Mortal Love,* p. 1700.
Kirkus Reviews, March 15, 1999, review of *Black Light,* p. 418; May 15, 2004, review of *Mortal Love,* p. 459.
Library Journal, March 15, 1997, Susan Hamburger, review of *Glimmering,* p. 93; April 15, 1999, Jackie Cassada, review of *Black Light,* p. 148; April 1, 2004, Jennifer Baker, review of *Mortal Love,* p. 122.
Locus, October, 1992, p. 35; February, 1995, p. 17; July, 2002, interview with Hand.
Magazine of Fantasy and Science Fiction, October, 1995, p. 43; April, 1999, review of *Last Summer at Mars Hill,* p. 41.
Mythprint, April, 1997, review of *Walking the Moon* and *Glimmering.*
New York Times Book Review, December 9, 1990, p. 32; September 12, 1993, p. 36; September 10, 1995, p. 46.
Publishers Weekly, February 3, 1997, review of *Glimmering,* p. 99; August 10, 1998, review of *Last Summer at Mars Hill,* March 8, 1999, review of *Black Light,* p. 51; May 3, 2004, review of *Mortal Love,* p. 169.
Voice of Youth Advocates, April, 1991, Sherry Hoy, review of *Winterlong,* p. 43; April, 2000, review of *Black Light,* p. 11.
Washington Post Book World, October 28, 1990, p. 10; October 25, 1992, p. 9; September 26, 1993, p. 11; August 13, 1995, p. 9; June 8, 1997, p. 7; December 14, 2003, Paul di Filippo, review of *Bibliomancy,* p. 14; June 27, 2004, Lawrence Norfolk, review of *Mortal Love,* p. 6.

ONLINE

Agony Column Online, http://www.trashotron.com/ (January 1, 2004), Rick Kleffel, review of *Bibliomancy.*
Elizabeth Hand Home Page, http://www.elizabethhand.com (January 14, 2006).
Science Fiction Weekly Online, http://www.scifi.com/sfw/ (November 22, 2004), Nick Gevers, interview with Hand.
Strange Horizons Web site, http://www.strangehorizons.com/ (November 29, 2004), Cheryl Morgan, interview with Hand.*

*   *   *

HANNON, Ezra
See HUNTER, Evan

HEAD, Tom 1978-

Personal
Born July 14, 1978, in Jackson, MS; son of John (a salesman) and Carol (a nurse; maiden name Carwile) Head. *Ethnicity:* "Caucasian" *Education:* Regents College, B.A. (liberal arts), 1996; California State University, Dominguez Hills, M.A. (humanities), 2000; doctoral study at Edith Cowan University. *Politics:* "Independent." *Religion:* Unitarian Universalist/Episcopalian. *Hobbies and other interests:* Reading, meditation, cooking, conversation, volunteer work; avid Macintosh user.

Addresses
Office—c/o Que Publishing, 800 E. 96th St., Indianapolis, IN 46240. *E-mail*—tom@nwujackson.org.

Career
Editor and writer. Bookstore assistant, Choctaw Books, Jackson, MS, 1998-2000; freelance writer, 2000—.

Member
National Writers Union, Authors Guild, Publishers Marketing Association.

Writings

NONFICTION

(With Mariah Bear and John Bear) *Get Your IT Degree and Get Ahead,* Osborne/McGraw-Hill, 2000.
(With John Bear and Mariah Bear) *Bears' Guide to Earning Degrees by Distance Learning,* 14th edition, Ten Speed Press (Berkeley, CA), 2001.
(With John Bear, and Mariah Bear, and Larry McQueary) *Bears' Guide to the Best Computer Degrees by Distance Learning,* Ten Speed Press (Berkeley, CA), 2001.
(With John Bear, Mariah Bear, and Thomas Nixon) *Bears' Guide to the Best Education Degrees by Distance Learning,* Ten Speed Press (Berkeley, CA), 2001.
Freedom of Religion, Facts on File (New York, NY), 2005.
Absolute Beginner's Guide to the Bible, Que Publishing (Indianapolis, IN), 2005.

EDITOR

Confederate Generals, Blackbirch Press (San Diego, CA), 2003.
Mikhail Gorbachev, Greenhaven Press (San Diego, CA), 2003.
Slaves, Blackbirch Press (San Diego, CA), 2003.
Union Generals, Blackbirch Press (San Diego, CA), 2003.
Women and Families, Blackbirch Press (San Diego, CA), 2003.

The Bill of Rights, Greenhaven Press (San Diego, CA), 2004.
(With mother, Carol Carwile Head) *1966,* Greenhaven Press (San Diego, CA), 2004.
The Future of the Internet, Greenhaven Press (San Diego, CA), 2004.
Mysterious Places, Greenhaven Press (San Diego, CA), 2004.
Possessions and Exorcisms, Greenhaven Press (San Diego, CA), 2004.
Religion and Education, Greenhaven Press (San Diego, CA), 2005.
Conversations with Carl Sagan, University Press of Mississippi (Jackson, MS), 2006.
What Is the State of Human Rights?, Greenhaven Press (San Diego, CA), 2006.
Is Torture Ever Justified?, Greenhaven Press (San Diego, CA), 2006.

Work in Progress
A lengthy documentary history of American criminal justice with Miami University crime historian David Wolcott, for Facts on File.

Biographical and Critical Sources

PERIODICALS

School Library Journal, November, 2003, Elizabeth Talbot, review of *Mikhail Gorbachev,* p. 160.*

                    *   *   *

HEUSTON, Kimberley 1960-
(Kimberley Burton Heuston)

Personal
Born October 20, 1960, in Provo, UT; daughter of Dustin (an educator) and Nancy (an educator; maiden name, Moebus) Heuston; married Kerry Sorenson, May 29, 1980 (divorced, 1992); children: Mark Edward, Jennifer Lynn, Alexander Genial, Andrew Burton. *Ethnicity:* "Caucasian." *Education:* Harvard University, A.B., 1981; Vermont College, M.F.A., 2000. *Politics:* "Independent." *Religion:* Church of Latter-Day Saints (Mormon).

Addresses
Home—9277 Sterling Dr., Sandy, UT 84093. *Office*—Waterford School, 1480 E. 9400 S., Sandy, UT 84093. *E-mail*—kimheuston@aol.com.

Career
Waterford School, Sandy, UT, teacher, 1984—.

Member

Utah Children's Writers and Illustrators.

Awards, Honors

Association for Mormon Letters Award for Young-Adult Literature, honorable mention, 2002, for *The Shakeress;* Association for Mormon Letters Award for Young-Adult Literature, 2003, and Children's Book Award Notable Book designation, International Reading Association, Books for the Teen Age designation, New York Public Library, and Canadian Children's Book Centre Choice designation, all 2004, all for *Dante's Daughter.*

Writings

FOR CHILDREN AND YOUNG ADULTS

The Shakeress, Front Street (Asheville, NC), 2002.
Dante's Daughter, Front Street (Asheville, NC), 2003.
(With Jonathan M. Kenoyer) *The Ancient South Asian World* (juvenile nonfiction), Oxford University Press (New York, NY), 2005.

OTHER

Single Parenting: Help for Latter-Day Saint Families, Deseret Book (Salt Lake City, UT), 1998.

Work in Progress

The Velvet Years, an historical fiction novel about the 1989 Velvet Revolution in Czechoslovakia; books on Mesoamerica and the Spanish-American War; a young-adult novel about seventeenth-century Dutch and English history.

Sidelights

Kimberley Heuston worked as an English and history teacher for several years before she decided to start writing books; although she had always loved books while growing up, writing one seemed too daunting. In an author interview for the Utah Writers and Illustrators Web site, Heuston explained: "I taught English and history, and after a while, writing wasn't scary anymore. I finally figured out that if you spend enough time on something, eventually you will figure out what it is you really want to say and then all you have to do is say it."

Much of Heuston's writing focuses on young people in history who are in the process of finding out who they are. In her first novel, *The Shakeress,* set in the 1820s, Naomi and her siblings are orphaned. Instead of staying with their stern aunt, Naomi takes the children to live in a Shaker community where they are taken in and cared for. After a few years among the Shakers, Naomi realizes that she is hungry to experience more of life, and

With her father, Italian poet Dante Alighieri, Antonia shares the life of a pilgrim while also nurturing her own artistic muse. *(Cover design by Helen Robinson.)*

that she does not share the Shakers' beliefs. Leaving her siblings, she goes on a journey both to find who she is meant to be and to discover her relationship with God—a relationship she eventually finds in the Mormon faith. While some critics, including a reviewer for *Publishers Weekly,* felt that "character development takes a backseat to protestations of faith and to cultural history," other reviewers cited Heuston's treatment of religion as well-handled. "What is noteworthy about this story is the intensity with which it treats spiritual questions," commented a critic for *Kirkus Reviews. Kliatt* reviewer Claire Rosser felt that "since Naomi is such a strong heroine, with skills and common sense, and with a great love of live, most YAs will enjoy reading her story."

Another strong young woman is at the center of Heuston's second novel, *Dante's Daughter.* The writer Dante Alighieri, who lived in fourteenth-century Italy and wrote *The Divine Comedy,* had a young daughter named Antonia; very little is known about her life except that she eventually became a nun. Heuston imagines what Antonia's life was like as the daughter of the famous storyteller. Noting the details of the setting and the historical events the story encompasses, a *Publishers Weekly* reviewer considered *Dante's Daughter* "rich in its setting and ambitious in its scope, if less than fully successful as fiction." Hazel Rochman, writing in *Booklist,* also noted that the historical detail "overwhelms the story," but added that "Heuston has clearly done her research." Gerry Larson, writing for *School Library Journal,* did not feel that history overwhelms Heuston's tale; instead, the critic wrote, "This well-researched, imaginative story unfolds steadily with factual information smoothly interwoven into it."

Heuston told *SATA:* "About ten years ago, I heard Lois Lowry give a speech about her road to becoming a writer at an English teacher's convention and thought, 'I could do that!' On my way home, I bought a copy of the *Horn Book,* saw that Vermont College was beginning a low-residency program in writing for children, and signed up. I was incredibly fortunate in the instruction and inspiration I received in that wonderful place.

"I was raised in New York City, where my father was the headmaster of the Spence School. We spent our summers in Waterford Springs, Vermont, in a house my father built bit by bit. Later, this would be the setting for my first novel, *The Shakeress.* (Its wonderful cover was painted by my daughter Jennifer.)

"Today I am an English and history teacher during the school year and a writer during the summers, although the two jobs are really impossible to divide neatly. I hope my novels are deepened by both my teaching and by my experience as a mother to four very distinct and wonderful personalities. I also hope that they are informed and shaped by the realities of the historical period that they seek to describe; that they treat the lives of those who have gone before with honesty, sympathy, and dignity."

Biographical and Critical Sources

PERIODICALS

Booklist, January 1, 2004, Hazel Rochman, review of *Dante's Daughter,* p. 844; June 1, 2002, Frances Bradburn, review of *The Shakeress,* p. 1706.
Bulletin of the Center for Children's Books, March, 2004, Karen Coats, review of *Dante's Daughter,* p. 278; June, 2002, review of *The Shakeress,* p. 366.
Kirkus Reviews, April 1, 2002, review of *The Shakeress,* p. 492; November 1, 2003, review of *Dante's Daughter,* p. 1311.
Kliatt, May, 2002, Claire Rosser, review of *The Shakeress,* p. 10.
Library Media Connection, March, 2004, review of *Dante's Daughter,* p. 67.
Publishers Weekly, April 1, 2002, review of *The Shakeress,* p. 84; December 15, 2003, review of *Dante's Daughter,* p. 74.
School Library Journal, July, 2002, Renee Steinberg, review of *The Shakeress,* p. 120; February, 2004, Gerry Larson, review of *Dante's Daughter,* p. 148.
Voice of Youth Advocates, April, 2004, Rebecca Barnhouse, review of *Dante's Daughter,* p. 46; August, 2002, review of *The Shakeress,* p. 192.

ONLINE

Utah Children's Writers and Illustrators Web site, http://www.ucwi.org/ (January 16, 2006), "Kimberley Heuston."

*   *   *

HEUSTON, Kimberley Burton
See HEUSTON, Kimberley

*   *   *

HODGES, Margaret 1911-2005
(Margaret Moore Hodges)

Personal

Born Sarah Margaret Moore, July 26, 1911, in Indianapolis, IN; died December 13, 2005, in Verona, PA; daughter of Arthur Carlisle (in business) and Anna Marie (Mason) Moore; married Fletcher Hodges, Jr. (a museum curator), September 10, 1932; children: Fletcher III, Arthur Carlisle, John Andrews. *Education:* Vassar College, A.B. (with honors), 1932; Carnegie Institute of Technology (now Carnegie-Mellon University), M.L.S., 1958. *Politics:* Republican. *Religion:* Episcopalian. *Hobbies and other interests:* Traveling, reading, folklore, gardening.

Career

Carnegie Library of Pittsburgh, Pittsburgh, PA, special assistant and children's librarian, 1953-64; Pittsburgh Public Schools, story specialist in compensatory education department, 1964-68; University of Pittsburgh, Graduate School of Library and Information Science, lecturer, 1964-68, assistant professor, 1968-72, associate professor, 1972-75, professor 1975-77, professor emeritus, beginning 1978. Storyteller on program *Tell Me a Story,* WQED-TV, 1965-76.

Member

Zonta International, American Library Association (member of Newbery-Caldecott committee, 1960), Pennsylvania Library Association, Distinguished Daughters of Pennsylvania, Pittsburgh Bibliophiles, Pittsburgh Vassar Club.

Awards, Honors

Carnegie Library staff scholarship, 1956-58; American Library Association (ALA) Notable Book citation, *New York Times* Ten Best Picture Books of the Year citation, both 1964, and Silver Medal, Biennal (Brazil), 1965, all for *The Wave; Lady Queen Anne* selected a Best Book for Young Adults by an Indiana Author, 1970; *The Making of Joshua Cobb* selected a *New York Times* Outstanding Juvenile Book, 1971; ALA Notable Book citation, 1972, for *The Fire Bringer;* John G. Bowman Memorial grant, 1974; named Distinguished Alumna, Carnegie Library School and Graduate School of Library and Information Science, 1976; Outstanding Pennsylvania Children's Author award, Pennsylvania School Librarians Association, 1977; Daughter of Mark Twain Award, 1980; *New York Times* Best Illustrated Children's Book Award, 1984, Carolyn W. Field Award for best children's book by a Pennsylvania author, *Horn Book* Honor Book designation, and Caldecott Award for illustrations by Trina Schart Hyman, all 1985, all for *Saint George and the Dragon;* Margaret Hodges Day citation from University of Pittsburgh School of Library and Information Science, 1985; Keystone State Reading Award, 1985; Margaret Hodges scholarship established, 1989; ALA Best Books for Young Adults citation, 1989, for *Making a Difference;* Notable Children's Trade Book citation, National Council for Social Studies/ Children's Book Council (CBC), 1989, for *The Arrow and the Lamp;* Parents' Choice Honor for Story Books, and CBC award, both 1990, both for *Buried Moon;* ALA Notable Book designation, 1991, for *St. Jerome and the Lion;* Park Tudor (Tudor Hall) Distinguished Alumna Award, 1992; Parents' Choice Recommendation, 1999, for *Joan of Arc.*

Writings

FICTION

One Little Drum, illustrated by Paul Galdone, Follett, 1958.

What's for Lunch, Charley?, illustrated by Aliki, Dial (New York, NY), 1961.

A Club against Keats, illustrated by Rick Schreiter, Dial (New York, NY), 1962.

The Secret in the Woods, illustrated by Judith Brown, Dial (New York, NY), 1963.

The Hatching of Joshua Cobb, illustrated by W.T. Mars, Farrar, Straus (New York, NY), 1968.

Sing Out, Charley!, illustrated by Velma Ilsley, Farrar, Straus (New York, NY), 1968.

The Making of Joshua Cobb, illustrated by W.T. Mars, Farrar, Straus (New York, NY), 1971.

The Freewheeling of Joshua Cobb, illustrated by Pamela Johnson, Farrar, Straus (New York, NY), 1974.

The High Riders, Scribner (New York, NY), 1980.

The Avenger, Scribner (New York, NY), 1982.

NONFICTION

Lady Queen Anne: A Biography of Queen Anne of England, illustrated with photographs, Farrar, Straus (New York, NY), 1968.

Hopkins of the Mayflower: Portrait of a Dissenter, Farrar, Straus (New York, NY), 1972.

Knight Prisoner: The Tale of Sir Thomas Malory and His King Arthur, decorations by Don Bolognese and Elaine Raphael, Farrar, Straus (New York, NY), 1976.

Making a Difference: The Story of an American Family, illustrated with photographs, Scribner (New York, NY), 1989.

Silent Night: The Song and Its Story, illustrated by Tim Ladwig, Eerdmans (Grand Rapids, MI), 1997.

The True Tale of Johnny Appleseed, illustrated by Kimberly Bulcken Root, Holiday House (New York, NY), 1997.

Joan of Arc: The Lily Maid, illustrated by Robert Rayevsky, Holiday House (New York, NY), 1999.

RETELLINGS

The Wave (adapted from Lafcadio Hearn's *Gleanings in Buddha Fields*), illustrated by Blair Lent, Houghton (Boston, MA), 1964.

The Gorgon's Head: A Myth from the Isles of Greece, illustrated by Charles Mikolaycak, Little, Brown (Boston, MA), 1972.

The Fire Bringer: A Paiute Indian Legend, illustrated by Peter Parnall, Little, Brown (Boston, MA), 1972.

Persephone and the Springtime: A Greek Myth, illustrated by Arvis Stewart, Little, Brown (Boston, MA), 1973.

The Other World: Myths of the Celts, illustrated by Eros Keith, Farrar, Straus (New York, NY), 1973.

Baldur and the Mistletoe: A Myth of the Vikings, illustrated by Gerry Hoover, Little, Brown (Boston, MA), 1974.

The Little Humpbacked Horse: A Russian Tale (adapted from a translation by Gina Kovarsky of a poem by Peter Pavlovich Yershov), illustrated by Chris Conover, Farrar, Straus (New York, NY), 1980.

Saint George and the Dragon: A Golden Legend (adapted from Edmund Spenser's *Faerie Queen*), illustrated by Trina Schart Hyman, Little, Brown (Boston, MA), 1984.

If You Had a Horse: Steeds of Myth and Legend, illustrated by D. Benjamin Van Steenburgh, Scribner (New York, NY), 1984.

The Voice of the Great Bell (adapted from Lafcadio Hearn's *Some Chinese Ghosts*), illustrated by Ed Young, Little, Brown (Boston, MA), 1989.

The Arrow and the Lamp: The Story of Psyche, illustrated by Donna Diamond, Little, Brown (Boston, MA), 1989.

Buried Moon, illustrated by Jamichael Henterly, Little, Brown (Boston, MA), 1990.

The Kitchen Knight: A Tale of King Arthur, illustrated by Trina Schart Hyman, Holiday House (New York, NY), 1990.

St. Jerome and the Lion, illustrated by Barry Moser, Orchard Books (New York, NY), 1991.

Hauntings: Ghosts and Ghouls from around the World, illustrated by David Wenzel, Little, Brown (Boston, MA), 1991.

Brother Francis and the Friendly Beasts, illustrated by Ted Lewin, Scribner (New York, NY), 1991.

The Golden Deer, illustrated by Daniel San Souci, Scribner (New York, NY), 1992.

Don Quixote and Sancho Panza, illustrated by Stephen Marchesi, Scribner (New York, NY), 1992.

(With Margery Evernden) *Of Swords and Sorcerers: The Adventures of King Arthur and His Knights,* illustrated by David Frampton, Scribner (New York, NY), 1992.

Saint Patrick and the Peddler, illustrated by Paul Brett Johnson, Orchard (New York, NY), 1993.

The Hero of Bremen, illustrated by Charles Mikolaycak, Holiday House (New York, NY), 1993.

Hidden in Sand, illustrated by Paul Birling, Scribner (New York, NY), 1994.

Gulliver in Lilliput, illustrated by Kimberly Bulcken Root, Holiday House (New York, NY), 1995.

Comus (adapted from John Milton's *A Masque at Ludlow Castle*), illustrated by Trina Schart Hyman, Holiday House (New York, NY), 1996.

Molly Limbo, illustrated by Elizabeth J. Miles, Atheneum (New York, NY), 1996.

Up the Chimney, illustrated by Amanda Harvey, Holiday House (New York, NY), 1998.

The Boy Who Drew Cats (adapted from Lafcadio Hearn's *Japanese Fairy Tales*), illustrated by Aki Sogabe, Holiday House (New York, NY), 2002.

The Legend of Saint Christopher: From the Golden Legend Englished by William Caxton, 1483, illustrated by Richard Jesse Watson, Eerdmans (Grand Rapids, MI), 2002.

Merlin and the Making of the King (based on Thomas Malory's *Le morte d'Arthur*), illustrated by Trina Schart Hyman, Holiday House (New York, NY), 2004.

The Wee Christmas Cabin (adapted from Ruth Sawyer's *The Long Christmas*), illustrated by Kimberly Bulcken Root, Holiday House (New York, NY), 2005.

Moses, illustrated by Barry Moser, Harcourt (San Diego, CA), 2006.

Dick Whittington and His Cat, illustrated by Mélisand Potter, Holiday House (New York, NY), 2006.

EDITOR

Kathleen Monypenny, *The Young Traveler in Australia,* Dutton (New York, NY), 1954.

H.M. Harrop, *The Young Traveler in New Zealand,* Dutton (New York, NY), 1954.

Lucile Iremonger, *The Young Traveler in the West Indies,* Dutton (New York, NY), 1955.

Geoffrey Trease, *The Young Traveler in Greece,* Dutton (New York, NY), 1956.

(With others) *Stories to Tell to Children,* Carnegie Library of Pittsburgh (Pittsburgh, PA), 1960.

Tell It Again: Great Tales from around the World, illustrated by Joan Berg, Dial (New York, NY), 1963.

Constellation: A Shakespeare Anthology, Farrar, Straus (New York, NY), 1968.

(With Susan Steinfirst) Elva S. Smith, *The History of Children's Literature: A Syllabus with Selected Bibliographies,* second edition, American Library Association, 1980.

OTHER

Also author of radio scripts; contributor to journals.

Collections of Hodges's works are housed in the Kerlan Collection, University of Minnesota; de Grummond Collection, University of Southern Mississippi; and Elizabeth Nesbitt Room, University of Pittsburgh.

Sidelights

Beginning her working life as a children's librarian, Margaret Hodges ultimately established a distinguished career in children's books that lasted over half a century. Her first book, *One Little Drum,* was published in 1958, when Hodges was forty-seven years old; she went on to author over fifty other books for young readers prior to her death in 2005. Producing stand-alone fiction based on the antics of her own three boys as well as biographies, Hodges was best known for her retellings of myths and folk tales presented in a picture-book format. Her award-winning adaptations include *Saint George and the Dragon: A Golden Legend, The Arrow and the Lamp: The Story of Psyche, St. Jerome and the Lion,* and *The Hero of Bremen.* Throughout her career, Hodges viewed herself not as a creator, "but rather as a sort of midwife, simply bringing out life that already existed in itself," as she once remarked in an essay for the *Something about the Author Autobiography Series* (*SAAS*). Praising one of the author's final works, a story about fifteenth-century Japanese artist Sesshu Toyo titled *The Boy Who Drew Cats, School Library Journal* contributor Margaret A. Chang cited Hodges for her "direct, clear adaptation" of a story first penned by Lafcadio Hearn, deeming the book a "shivery page-turner celebrating the power of art."

Hodges' mother died six months after the author's birth, leaving her father to bring an older cousin, Margaret

Based on a story by Lafcadio Hearn, Hodges' **The Boy Who Drew Cats** *introduces a young artist whose obsession with cats is powerful enough to change his life. (Illustration by Ari Sogabe.)*

Hodges' adaptation of Edmund Spenser's Faerie Queene *is paired with illustrations by Trina Schart Hyman in the 1984 picture book* Saint George and the Dragon.

Carlisle, into the household to take care of the family, which also included a brother and Hodges' paternal grandfather. Hodges heard "superb storytelling" at Sunday school, and both her cousin Margaret and her father provided her with many books. Robert Louis Stevenson's poems, Beatrix Potter's *Tale of Peter Rabbit*, and George Macdonald's *The Princess and the Goblin* and its sequel, *The Princess and Curdie*, were early loves, followed by books by Lewis Carroll, Rudyard Kipling, and Charles Dickens. Long poems such as Kipling's "The Ballad of East and West" and Browning's "The Pied Piper of Hamelin," once memorized, would become useful for Hodges in her later career as a storyteller.

Hodges began writing at an early age, and her first work, "Miss Matty's Library," was published in the

magazine for Indianapolis's Public School Number 60. She also submitted a poem to *St. Nicholas*, a children's magazine that encouraged contributions from its readers and awarded silver and gold badges. Later, at Vassar College, Hodges majored in English, and received training in the Stanislavsky method of acting—another useful tool for a budding storyteller.

After graduating from Vassar, Hodges married Fletcher Hodges, Jr., in 1932 and moved with her family to Pittsburgh in 1937. While raising her three sons, she penned scripts for a radio program called *The Children's Bookshelf*. In 1953, she became a storyteller for the Carnegie Library of Pittsburgh's Boys and Girls Department, her sessions broadcast as the radio program *Let's Tell a Story*—this later became the television program *Tell Me a Story*. Working in the Boys and Girls Room inspired

Hodges' first book: *One Little Drum* is based on the real-life adventures of her energetic sons, as were several of the books that followed, including a trilogy focusing on a young boy named Joshua Cobb. *The Hatching of Joshua Cobb* follows the adventures of Hodges' ten-year-old protagonist as he spends time away from home for the first time at summer camp. *The Making of Joshua Cobb* follows Joshua to boarding school, while *The Freewheeling of Joshua Cobb* takes Josh on a summer vacation bike trip with a group that includes his former camp counselor, Dusty, and a girl named Cassandra who initially proves difficult to like. A reviewer in *Horn Book* noted the "fresh background" of the final volume in the "Joshua Cobb" trilogy, and praised Hodges for portraying the "personality changes" of her characters. In the *Bulletin of the Center for Children's Books,* a writer commented that "the writing style has vitality, the characters individuality."

With her own children grown, Hodges moved into biography and retellings, producing such life histories as *Knight Prisoner: The Tale of Sir Thomas Malory and His King Arthur* and *Joan of Arc: The Lily Maid,* as well as folk-tale-based *The Hero of Bremen* and *Up the Chimney.* In *Knight Prisoner* she focuses on the widely known fifteenth-century English translator of *Le morte d'Arthur,* the legend of King Arthur. While there is little information actually available about Thomas Malory, Hodges "makes the most of the ascertainable facts and speculations," noted a reviewer in *Horn Book.* In the book Malory recalls episodes of his life and his experiences with some of the most famous people of his time, including Joan of Arc, King Henry V, and King Edward IV. A reviewer for the *Bulletin of the Center for Children's Books* remarked that while the multitude of historical and literary details might overwhelm some readers, *Knight Prisoner* "has both biographical and historical interest." Ruth M. McConnell concluded in *School Library Journal* that Hodges produces "a most readable political and social history."

In *Joan of Arc* Hodges tells the story of the French peasant girl who, raised on stories of the Catholic saints, witnessed a vision of St. Michael the Archangel at age thirteen and was told she would save France. In a *Booklist* review, Ilene Cooper noted that "Hodges tells Joan's story with simplicity, distilling the myriad events of bravery and betrayal down to their essence." Cooper further commented that the book's artwork gives the whole a feel of a "medieval work," but one with "lots of child appeal."

Works of literature also were retold for younger readers, among them the Don Quixote story, a well-known Elizabethan poem, and the Arthurian legend. *Don Quixote and Sancho Panza* "capture[s] famous incidents from [Miguel] Cervantes' novel," explained to Betsy Hearne writing in the *Bulletin of the Center for Children's Books.* Hearne went on to comment on the "pathetic-to-bitter range of humor" in the original which Hodges's "adaptation has captured so well."

Drawing on Malory's *Le morte d'Arthur, The Kitchen Knight: A Tale of King Arthur, Of Swords and Sorcerers: The Adventures of King Arthur and His Knights,* and *Merlin and the Making of the King* retell stories of the knights of Arthur's round table. With compelling art by illustrators Hyman and David Frampton, the books bring to life such well-known characters as Queen Guinevere, Sir Lancelot, the sword Excalibur, Merlin the magician, and the treacherous Morgan Le Fay, whose stories intersect in the magical land of Camelot. *Of Swords and Sorcerers* was described by a writer for *Publishers Weekly* as a "carefully considered" retelling of the Arthurian legend divide into nine tales that "sparkle with the rich language of professional storytellers." In *Kirkus Reviews* a writer noted of the three stories included in *Merlin and the Making of the King* that Hodges' "language is simple and lucid enough for young children without diluting the power of the telling." In *Booklist* Carolyn Phelan praised Hyman's "dramatic" medieval-styled illustrations and noted that the book "gives meaning and context to the . . . tales of knightly deeds."

Awarded a Caldecott award for its illustrations by Trina Schart Hyman, *Saint George and the Dragon* is based on the first book of Edmund Spenser's epic poem *The Faerie Queen.* In the story, Saint George rescues a maiden and slays a dragon to save the young woman's family; eventually the hero and his love wed and live

The life of the peasant girl destined to lead France to war against England is brought to life in **Joan of Arc: The Lily Maid.** *(Illustration by Robert Rayevsky.)*

In **Merlin and the Making of the King** *Hodges brings to life the legend of King Arthur in three stories of Camelot lushly illustrated by Trina Schart Hyman.*

happily ever after. In the main portion of Hodges' retelling, which follows George's three-day battle with the dragon, the serpent "virtually bursts off the page," proclaimed Rosalie Byard in a review for the *New York Times Book Review,* adding that Hodges "offers a faithful translation of Spenser's detailed account" of the battle. A reviewer for the *Bulletin of the Center for Children's Books* called the adaptation "capable," highlighting the author's judicious use of Spenser's complex and archaic language. *School Library Journal* contributor Janice M. Del Negro noted that the action is "fast-paced and immediate," adding that Hodges transforms Spenser's classic poem into "a coherent, palatable story suitable for a wide range of ages."

Further literary retellings include *Gulliver in Lilliput,* an adaptation of Jonathan Swift's *Gulliver's Travels,* and *Comus,* from English writer John Milton's long poem *A Masque at Ludlow Castle.* Reviewing Hodges' adaptation of the Swift satire, *Horn Book* contributor Ann A. Flowers praised the book as a "masterful retelling" that "emphasizes the adventures of Gulliver which are most appealing to children." *Booklist* contributor Del Negro

felt that Hodges retells Milton's tale of good versus evil in "accessible, beautiful language."

Hodges served up folktales and tall tales from around the world for her youngest fans in books such as *The Hero of Bremen, The True Tale of Johnny Appleseed,* and *Up the Chimney.* The medieval German city of Bremen is the scene for *The Hero of Bremen,* in which a shoemaker who is unable to walk helps out his hometown with the aid of the hero, Roland. "Hodges quickens her retelling with the assurance of a master storyteller," remarked Kate McClelland in a *School Library Journal* review of the book. In *The True Tale of Johnny Appleseed* Hodges relates a "well-shaped, anecdotal account of the legendary Johnny Chapman," according to Margaret A. Bush, describing the book in *School Library Journal.* Chapman traveled into America's unsettled west, planting apple seeds along the way in an effort to make the region a more hospitable place for new settlers. "A bit of tongue-in-cheek and a suggestion of tall tale spark the felicitous blend of biography and folklore," Bush further noted of the book. With *Up the Chimney,* a retelling of an English folktale about two sisters who seek their fortune and receive very different fates, *Booklist* reviewer Cooper concluded that Hodges presents youngsters with a "pleasant version of the Jacobs' 'The Old Witch.'"

In *The Arrow and the Lamp: The Story of Psyche* Hodges returns to the rich world of myth and legend, this time retelling the ancient Greek myth of Psyche, a mortal whose love for a god changes her existence. A critic for the *Bulletin of the Center for Children's Books* called Hodges' work "a haunting myth well adapted by an experienced storyteller." *School Library Journal* contributor Connie C. Rockman judged *The Arrow and the Lamp* to be a "smooth, straightforward retelling."

The stories of the Catholic saints are the focus of several books by Hodges. *St. Jerome and the Lion* recounts the story of how Saint Jerome pulled a thorn from a lion's paw and formed a strong bond with the ferocious creature as a result, while in *The Legend of Saint Christopher: From the Golden Legend Englished by William Caxton, 1483* she relates the story of Offero, a man whose kindness to Jesus was repaid when he became the patron saint of travelers. Shirley Wilton, writing in *School Library Journal,* labeled *St. Jerome and the Lion* a "moral tale" and a "gentle story," while a reviewer for *Publishers Weekly* called the book a "sensitive adaptation" with "language and rhythms sensitively attuned to contemporary readers." Noting that "Hodges does a fine job of adapting and retelling" in *The Legend of Saint Christopher,* *School Library Journal* critic Jane G. Connor added that the writing is "fluid and has the cadence and rhythm of an experienced storyteller."

The story of Saint Francis of Assisi appears in *Brother Francis and the Friendly Beasts,* which a reviewer for the *Bulletin of the Center for Children's Books* called a "graceful and smooth" retelling. *Saint Patrick and the Peddler,* an adaptation from Irish sources, deals with yet another saint, who appears in the dreams of a peddler during the Irish potato famine and encourages the man to go to Dublin. There the peddler meets another man who has had the same dream, and this meeting leads to the discovery of buried gold. "Ever the story-teller," Judith Gloyer wrote in a *School Library Journal* review, "Hodges includes a two-page condensation of St. Patrick's life, as well as notes on how her version of the story came about."

In *Hauntings: Ghosts and Ghouls from around the World,* Hodges retells sixteen ghost stories drawn from cultures the world over, including Europe, Asia, America, and India. The tales are "more mysterious than they are scary," noted Maeve Visser Knoth in *Horn Book,* calling *Hauntings* "one fresh, readable volume." "Hodges's polished retellings retain the flavor of the originals," declared Margaret A. Chang in *School Library Journal,* while the "meaty retellings" also won praise from Denia Hester in her *Booklist* review. Another "spooky" tale, according to Del Negro in *Bulletin of the Center for Children's Books,* Hodges' *Molly Limbo* is an adaptation of a ghostly folktale. Molly, a pirate's wife, haunts Mr. Means's house and also lends a helping hand to the harried housekeeper. Dubbing the book "an entertaining tale," *Horn Book* contributor Mary M. Burns added that *Molly Limbo* "reflects the touch of a true storyteller with its lilting phrases and narrative pace."

"The art of storytelling thrilled me because I saw it as the best way to lead children to good literature, to leap the boundaries between literacy and illiteracy, and to bring marvelous old tales to listeners of all ages," Hodges once explained in her *SAAS* essay. With the timelessness of a good folktale, her retellings of classic legends and myths from around the world ensure her a place on the children's literature bookshelf and also ensure that those legends, myths, and other works resonate with new generations of young readers.

Biographical and Critical Sources

BOOKS

Authors of Books for Young People, 3rd edition, Scarecrow Press (Metuchen, NJ), 1990.
Silvey, Anita, editor, *Children's Books and Their Creators,* Houghton (Boston, MA), 1995.
Something about the Author Autobiography Series, Volume 9, Thomson Gale (Detroit, MI), 1990.

PERIODICALS

Booklist, November 15, 1991, Denia Hester, review of *Hauntings: Ghosts and Ghouls from around the World,*

p. 624; February, 1993, Betsy Hearne, review of *Don Quixote and Sancho Panza,* p. 171; September 1, 1993, p. 64; April 15, 1995, Hazel Rochman, review of *Gulliver in Lilliput: From Gulliver's Travels by Jonathan Swift,* p. 1500; March 1, 1996, Janice M. Del Negro, review of *Comus,* p. 1182; September 15, 1996, p. 243; November 15, 1998, Ilene Cooper, review of *Up the Chimney,* p. 593; November 1, 1999, Ilene Cooper, review of *Joan of Arc: The Lily Maid,* p. 524; June, 2002, Gillian Engberg, review of *The Boy Who Drew Cats,* p. 1726; October, 1, 2002, Ilene Cooper, review of *The Legend of Saint Christopher,* p. 342; September 15, 2004, Carolyn Phelan, review of *Merlin and the Making of the King,* p. 241.

Bulletin of the Center for Children's Books, November, 1967, review of *The Hatching of Joshua Cobb,* p. 43; March, 1975, review of *The Freewheeling of Joshua Cobb;* April, 1977, review of *Knight Prisoner: The Tale of Sir Thomas Malory and His King Arthur,* p. 126; October, 1984, review of *Saint George and the Dragon: A Golden Legend,* p. 27; January, 1985, review of *If You Had a Horse: Steeds of Myth and Legend,* p. 87; February, 1990, review of *The Arrow and the Lamp: The Story of Psyche,* pp. 138-139; September, 1991, review of *St. Jerome and the Lion,* p. 12; November, 1991, review of *Brother Francis and the Friendly Beasts,* p. 64; October, 1993, p. 47; January, 1994, p. 156; January, 1995, pp. 12-13; April, 1996, pp. 266-267; October, 1996, Janice M. Del Negro, review of *Molly Limbo,* p. 64; December, 1997, p. 129; December, 1998, p. 133; April, 2002, review of *The Boy Who Drew Cats,* p. 282.

Childhood Education, spring, 2000, Irene A. Allen, review of *Joan of Arc,* p. 173.

Horn Book, June, 1971, review of *The Making of Joshua Cobb,* p. 287; October, 1974, review of *The Freewheeling of Joshua Cobb,* p. 137; December, 1976, review of *Knight Prisoner,* pp. 632-633; February, 1981, review of *The Little Humpbacked Horse: A Russian Tale,* p. 61; September, 1989, review of *Making a Difference: The Story of an American Family,* pp. 636-637; September-October, 1991, review of *Brother Francis and the Friendly Beasts,* p. 611; November-December, 1991, Maeve Visser Knoth, review of *Hauntings,* pp. 747-748; November-December, 1993, pp. 748-749; July-August, 1995, Ann A. Flowers, review of *Gulliver in Lilliput,* p. 450; November-December, 1996, Mary M. Burns, review of *Molly Limbo,* p. 749; May-June, 2002, Joanna Rudge Long, review of *The Boy Who Drew Cats,* p. 339.

Kirkus Reviews, February 1, 2002, review of *The Boy Who Drew Cats,* p. 182; August 1, 2004, review of *Merlin and the Making of the King,* p. 742.

Library Journal, September 15, 1969, Nathan Berkowitz, review of *Lady Queen Anne: A Biography of Queen Anne of England,* p. 3218; September 15, 1967, Jean C. Thomson, review of *The Hatching of Joshua Cobb,* p. 118; April 15, 1971, Sandra Scheraga, review of *The Making of Joshua Cobb,* p. 1504.

New York Times Book Review, November 4, 1984, Rosalie Byard, review of *Saint George and the Dragon,* p. 22;

July 23, 1989, Jean Fritz, review of *Making a Difference,* p. 28; December 20, 1998, p. 24.

Publishers Weekly, May 19, 1969, review of *Lady Queen Anne,* p. 71; March 22, 1971, review of *The Making of Joshua Cobb,* p. 53; November 14, 1980, review of *The Little Humpbacked Horse,* p. 55; November 23, 1984, p. 75; November 30, 1984, review of *If You Had a Horse,* p. 89; April 28, 1989, review of *Making a Difference,* p. 80; July 5, 1991, review of *St. Jerome and the Lion,* p. 64; May 3, 1993, review of *Of Swords and Sorcerers,* p. 310; August 23, 1993, review of *St. Patrick and the Peddler,* p. 70; September 13, 1993, review of *The Hero of Bremen,* p. 128; March 6, 1995, review of *Gulliver in Lilliput,* p. 69; February 19, 1996, review of *Comus,* p. 215; November 23, 1998, review of *Up the Chimney,* p. 66; February 1, 1999, p. 87; October 18, 1999, review of *Joan of Arc,* p. 82; January 28, 2002, review of *The Boy Who Drew Cats,* p. 290; September 30, 2002, review of *The Legend of Saint Christopher,* p. 69; August 9, 2004, review of *Merlin and the Making of the King,* p. 251.

School Library Journal, December, 1976, Ruth M. McConnell, review of *Knight Prisoner,* p. 60; January, 1985, Janice M. Del Negro, review of *Saint George and the Dragon,* p. 76; May, 1989, pp. 129-130; December, 1989, Connie C. Rockman, review of *The Arrow and the Lamp: The Story of Psyche,* p. 108; September, 1991, Shirley Wilton, review of *St. Jerome and the Lion,* p. 246; November, 1991, Margaret A. Chang, review of *Hauntings,* p. 129; August, 1993, p. 174; October, 1993, Kate McClelland, review of *The Hero of Bremen,* p. 118; November, 1993, Judith Gloyer, review of *Saint Patrick and the Peddler,* p. 99; June, 1995, Nancy Menaldi-Scanlon, review of *Gulliver in Lilliput,* p. 114; September, 1996, p. 197; September, 1997, Margaret A. Bush, review of *The True Tale of Johnny Appleseed,* p. 203; January, 1999, Susan Scheps, review of *Up the Chimney,* p. 116; March, 2002, Margaret A. Chang, review of *The Boy Who Drew Cats,* p. 214; November, 2002, Jane G. Connor, review of *The Legend of Saint Christopher,* p. 144; September, 2004, Lynda Ritterman, review of *Merlin and the Making of the King,* p. 188.

OBITUARIES

ONLINE

Los Angeles Times Online, http://www.latimes.com/ (December 28, 2005).

New York Times Online, http://www.nytimes.com/ (December 20, 2005).

School Library Journal Web site, http://www.schoollibrary journal.com/ (December 15, 2005).*

*   *   *

HODGES, Margaret Moore
See HODGES, Margaret

HORNIMAN, Joanne 1951-

Personal

Born November 2, 1951, in Murwillumbah, New South Wales, Australia; daughter of J.W.R. (an overseer of works) and J.A. (a chef; maiden name, Tunsted) Horniman; married Tony Chinnery (a potter), 1978; children: Ry, Kay (sons). *Education:* Macquarie University, B.A. (English), 1973; Armidale College of Advanced Education, graduate diploma (infants/primary education), 1988. *Hobbies and other interests:* Collecting and planting seeds from rainforest plants, drinking coffee, talking with friends, reading.

Addresses

Home—602 Cawongla Rd., Via Lismore, New South Wales 2480, Australia.

Career

New South Wales Department of Education's *School Magazine,* Sydney, New South Wales, Australia, assistant editor, 1973-77; writer. Part-time lecturer in children's literature at Southern Cross University; adult literacy teacher at New South Wales department of technical and further education.

Member

Australian Society of Authors.

Awards, Honors

Children's Book Council of Australia (CBCA) Notable Book designation, for *Sand Monkeys, Jasmine, Bad Behaviour,* and *Billygoat Goes Wild;* New South Wales Premier's Award shortlist, 1994, and Australian Multicultural Children's Literature Award shortlist, 1995, both for *The Serpentine Belt;* Literature Board of the Australia Council fellowship, 1995; Children's Peace Literature Award recommendation, 2001, and CBCA Honor Book designation, New South Wales Premier's Literary Award shortlist, and Ethel Turner Prize for Books for Young Adults, all 2002, all for *Mahalia;* Victorian Premier's Award for Young-Adult Fiction shortlist, New South Wales Premier's Award shortlist, and Queensland Premier's Award shortlist, all 2003, all for *A Charm of Powerful Trouble;* CBCA Book of the Year shortlist, New South Wales Premier's Award shortlist, Victorian Premier's Prize for Young-Adult Literature shortlist, Queensland Premier's Award for Young-Adult Literature, and Courier Mail Book of the Year shortlist, all 2005, all for *Secret Scribbled Notebooks.*

Writings

The End of the World Girl, Collins Dove (Melbourne, Victoria, Australia), 1988.

The Ghost Lasagna, illustrated by Margie Chellew, Omnibus (Norwood, South Australia, Australia), 1992.

Sand Monkeys, Omnibus (Norwood, South Australia, Australia), 1992.

The Serpentine Belt, Omnibus (Norwood, South Australia, Australia), 1994.

Furry-Back and the Lizard-Thing, illustrated by Samone Turnbull, Omnibus (Norwood, South Australia, Australia), 1995.

Jasmine, illustrated by Margaret Power, Omnibus (Norwood, South Australia, Australia), 1995.

(With Jacqueline Kent) *Bad Behaviour* (stories), Omnibus (Norwood, South Australia, Australia), 1996.

Billygoat Goes Wild, illustrated by Robert Roennfeldt, Omnibus (Norwood, South Australia, Australia), 1996.

Loving Athena, Omnibus (Norwood, South Australia, Australia), 1997.

Sunflower!, Omnibus (Norwood, South Australia, Australia), 1999.

Mahalia, Allen & Unwin (Crows Nest, New South Wales, Australia), 2001, Knopf (New York, NY), 2003.

A Charm of Powerful Trouble, Allen & Unwin (Crows Nest, New South Wales, Australia), 2002, Allen & Unwin/Independent Publishers Group (Chicago, IL), 2005.

Secret Scribbled Notebooks, Allen & Unwin (Crows Nest, New South Wales, Australia), 2004.

Little Wing, Allen & Unwin (Crows Nest, New South Wales, Australia), 2006.

Contributor to periodicals, including *Viewpoints.*

Horniman's works have been translated into Dutch.

Sidelights

Australian writer Joanne Horniman has written novels and short stories for young adults centering on the realistic portrayal of unusual relationships, as well as picture books and easy readers for children. Many of her books take place in the rural Australian rainforest where she grew up. Her novels *Sand Monkeys, The Serpentine Belt,* and *Loving Athena* involve the search for a lost parent, as well as the establishment of strong bonds between characters who are not blood relations, while in *A Charm of Powerful Trouble* teen sisters Laura and Lizzie are absorbed in learning about their family history although their bohemian mother refuses to discuss her own past. As the novel unfolds, a visit from old friends fragments the family and exposes the past, creating an intricately woven storyline that a *Kirkus Reviews* critic deemed "atmospheric and exotic."

Horniman was born in Murwillumbah, New South Wales, and spent her childhood riding her bicycle near her rural home as well as reading and developing a puppet theatre to entertain her friends and fellow students. In college she studied English, history, and philosophy, then moved to Sydney where she worked as a magazine editor. Moving back to northern Australia several years later, she became involved in creating poster art, several examples of which were exhibited at Australia's National Gallery of art in Canberra. In addition to beginning her writing career in the late 1980s, Horniman works as a teacher and is involved in preserving the native plants of her rainforest region. Her first novel for children, *The End of the World Girl,* was published in 1988.

Horniman's imagination takes hold in her second novel, *The Ghost Lasagna,* about a mysterious invisible lasagna that replenishes itself after each bite. Antonella and Dip discover the ghost lasagna in a deserted restaurant and enjoy it daily, until the owner of the place catches them there. The ending emphasizes the importance of friendship and community. *Magpies* commentator Nola Cavallaro called the novel "appealing and accessible for newly independent readers."

Describing another of her books for younger children, Horniman once told *SATA* that *Billygoat Goes Wild* "was written for my son Kay about his pet hen (what we call in Australia a 'chook'). It was only afterwards that I considered I might offer it for publication. At the heart of it is the idea of what goes on outside at night when we are normally asleep, through the eyes of a do-

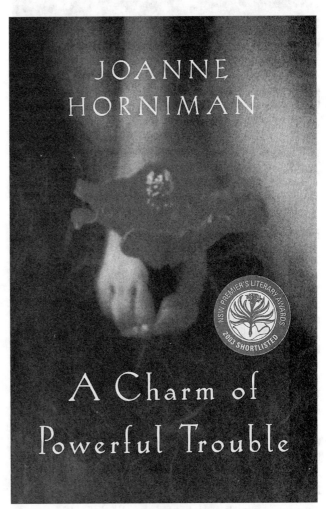

Horniman explores the complex and evolving relationship between two sisters as the young women gain the maturity needed to understand her mother's past. (Cover design by Jo Hunt.)

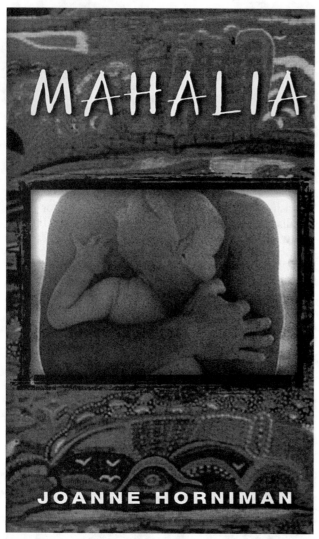

Teen parenthood is shown from a new perspective in Horniman's novel of a doting father who struggles to do the right thing by his infant daughter. (Cover illustration by Ericka O'Rourke.)

mestic hen. It is really a much more difficult and dangerous other world."

Geared for older readers, *The Serpentine Belt* also deals with friendship. In this case, long-time friends Emily and Kat, who are both sixteen, find themselves growing apart as each learns more about her own unique background. While Kat becomes interested in her Koori heritage, Emily discovers that her own past may in fact be different from what she has been told. In the end, both girls learn to take a broader view of friendship. Horniman employs an unusual structural device in the novel, which is told as a series of interconnecting stories. *The Serpentine Belt* has "strongly-drawn characters and lots of ideas for the reader to chew on," according to *Magpies* contributor Moira Robinson, the critic adding that the book is "leisurely, reflective and highly enjoyable."

Jasmine is a realistic tale of one girl's difficulties growing up. In particular, Jazz has trouble making friends, especially with the new boy at school. Then she discov-

ers an enchanting, magical new shop and its equally fascinating owner, Rosie. Jazz wonders if Rosie might be able to help her solve her problem. Writing in *Magpies,* Alan Horsfield commented that the children's and adults' "fears, anxieties, confusion and their pleasures all contribute to the portrayal of characters with which the reader can empathise."

Mahalia, an award-winning novel in Horniman's native Australia, was the first of the author's books to be released in the United States. Praised by a *Kirkus Reviews* contributor as "refreshingly honest," the novel focuses on Matt, a seventeen year old who, after his girlfriend abandons their newborn daughter, Mahalia, struggles to take care of the five-month-old infant by himself. Moving near his mother's home, he takes on full responsibility as a parent, and when his girlfriend returns to take custody of Mahalia, Matt has grown to a point where he can deal with the situation maturely. In *School Library Journal* Jane Halsall praised Mahalia and Matt as "winning, engaging, and genuine" characters and the novel as "a poignant and memorable love story" about a father and daughter. Noting the novel's lack of sentimentality, *Kliatt* reviewer Claire Rosser wrote that Horniman's text includes "vivid details of the realities of everyday life," while in *Horn Book* Kitty Flynn described *Mahalia* as "a starkly candid and sensitive portrait of teenage parenthood."

"I've been writing now for twenty-one years," Horniman explained to *SATA.* "Where once my books were for a range of ages and genres, since *Mahalia* in 2001, I've been working exclusively in young-adult literature, particularly for the older end of the market. My particular interest now is in portraying the lives of young women. Place, particularly the far north coast of New South Wales where I was born and still live, has always been an important element in my writing. A former Labour Prime Minister of Australia, Paul Keating, once insultingly commented that if you weren't living in Sydney you were 'camping out.' I hope my works portray the richness, in both their interior and exterior lives, of young people living in rural areas."

Biographical and Critical Sources

BOOKS

Niewenhuizen, Agnes, *More Good Books for Teenagers,* Reed (Australia), 1996.

PERIODICALS

Australian Book Review, April, 2005, Mike Shuttleworth, review of *Secret Scribbled Notebooks,* pp. 57-58.
Booklist, July, 2003, Gillian Engberg, review of *Mahalia,* p. 1881.
Bulletin of the Center for Children's Books, June, 2003, review of *Mahalia,* p. 405.

Five Owls (annual), 2003, review of *Mahalia,* p. 30.

Horn Book, July-August, 2003, Kitty Flynn, review of *Mahalia,* p. 458.

Kirkus Reviews, March 1, 2003, review of *Mahalia,* p. 388; February 1, 2005, review of *A Charm of Powerful Trouble,* p. 138.

Kliatt, March, 2003, Claire Rosser, review of *Mahalia,* p. 12.

Magpies, November, 1992, Nola Cavallaro, review of *The Ghost Lasagna,* p. 30; March, 1995, Moira Robinson, review of *The Serpentine Belt,* p. 32; September, 1995, Alan Horsfield, review of *Jasmine,* pp. 31-32; July, 1996; March, 2001, review of *Mahalia,* p. 39; November, 2002, review of *A Charm of Powerful Trouble,* p. 38.

School Library Journal, April, 2003, Jane Halsall, review of *Mahalia,* p. 164.

Viewpoint, winter, 1997; spring, 2004, Judith Ridge, review of *Secret Scribbled Notebooks,* p. 33.

Voice of Youth Advocates, June, 2003, review of *Mahalia,* p. 134.

ONLINE

Allen & Unwin Web site, http://www.allenandunwin.com/ (December 12, 2005), "Joanne Horniman."

Aussie Reviews Online, http://www.ausiereviews.com/ (September 26, 2005), Sally Murphy, review of *A Charm of Powerful Trouble.*

Blurb.com, http://www.theblurb.com.au/ (September 26, 2005), Michele Perry, review of *A Charm of Powerful Trouble.*

Compulsive Readers Online, http://www.compusivereader.com/ (September 26, 2005), Bob Williams, review of *A Charm of Powerful Trouble.*

*   *   *

HRDLITSCHKA, Shelley 1956-
(Shelley Joanne Hrdlitschka)

Personal

Surname pronounced Herd-*litch*-ka; born July 22, 1956, in Vancouver, British Columbia, Canada; daughter of Robert and Vivienne (Lyon) Frampton; married Peter Hrdlitschka (vice president of a construction company), 1977; children: Danielle, Cara, Kyla. *Education:* Simon Fraser University, teaching certificate. *Religion:* Unitarian-Universalist. *Hobbies and other interests:* Music, browsing at bookstores and libraries, theatre, hiking, traveling to warm places, watching her daughters participate in sports, music, and dance.

Addresses

Home and office—905 Roslyn Blvd., North Vancouver, British Columbia V7G 1PG, Canada. *E-mail*—shelley.hrdlitschka@shaw.ca.

Shelley Hrdlitschka

Career

Elementary schoolteacher in Delta, British Columbia, Canada, 1979-86; currently, writer and teacher of creative writing classes.

Member

Writers Union of Canada, Canadian Society of Children's Authors, Illustrators, and Performers, Vancouver Children's Literature Roundtable, Children's Writers and Illustrators of British Columbia.

Awards, Honors

Our Choice Award, Canadian Children's Book Centre; BC2000 Book Award, 2000, for *Tangled Web;* Canadian Library Association Young-Adult Honor Book citation, White Pine Award, and CCBC Our Choice Award, all 2002, Best Book nomination and Quick Pick for Reluctant Readers, both American Library Association (ALA), both 2003, Popular Paperback citation, ALA, 2005, and Choice for Young Adults citation, International Reading Association, all for *Dancing Naked;* New York Public Library Books for the Teen Age selection, White Pines Honor Book designation, and Arthur Ellis Award nomination, Crime Writers of Canada, all 2005, all for *Kat's Fall.*

Writings

Beans on Toast, illustrated by Ljuba Levstek, Orca (Victoria, British Columbia, Canada), 1998.

Disconnected, Orca (Victoria, British Columbia, Canada), 1998.

Tangled Web (sequel to *Disconnected*), Orca (Custer, WA), 2000.

Dancing Naked, Orca (Victoria, British Columbia, Canada), 2001, Orca (Custer, WA), 2002.

Kat's Fall, Orca (Custer, WA), 2004.

Sun Signs, Orca (Custer, WA), 2005.

Newspaper columnist. Contributor of articles and reviews to magazines.

Sidelights

Canadian author Shelley Hrdlitschka began her writing career while she was still a teacher. As she once told *SATA:* "I discovered my love of children's literature while teaching elementary school, so, while on a parenting leave, I decided to try writing children's stories myself. It took ten long years before I landed my first book contract, but the wait made it that much more rewarding. The second book contract came six months af-

In this award-winning novel a pregnant teen realizes that she must make some of the crucial choices in her life on her own.

ter the first! I've written and published many parenting articles, book reviews, and newspaper columns, but I focus solely on teen fiction now. I never did get back to teaching, but I now enjoy visiting schools and libraries and talking to students about the writing process and about the value of perseverance—setting goals and sticking to them."

Hrdlitschka's three daughters provided their mother with source material during their teen years. As she wrote on her home page, "Although I try not to write about them specifically, they do influence my writing in many ways." "Although my story ideas usually come from my own experiences, my three daughters help me with the details," Hrdlitschka also explained to *SATA,* "reminding me that fourteen-year-old boys don't usually drink coffee, and they don't say things like 'cute' any more." Her daughters have not been the sole source of subject material, however; Hrdlitschka also gets ideas from her own life, as well as from stories she hears on the news, and the protagonists of her novels deal with a wide variety of issues, from teen pregnancy, loneliness, and extremely disfunctional families.

Beans on Toast, Hrdlitschka's first novel, is geared for younger readers. It tells the story of Madison, who feels like an outsider during her first experience at Band Camp. Her parents have just divorced, and Madison feels like something of an ugly duckling. Over the two-week camp session, however, she begins to realize some of her strengths and starts to gain confidence in herself.

In her first two novels for an older, teen readership, Hrdlitschka introduces Alex and Tanner, twins who were separated at birth. In *Disconnected* the twins begin dreaming of each other's lives, unable to figure out where the strange dreams are coming from. Alex cannot wait to leave the small coastal town he lives in and move to the city, while city-boy Tanner hopes to find peace by visiting the coast and the sea that figures in his strange dreams. In the sequel, *Tangled Web,* the boys have been reunited and are now learning to become brothers when a savage crime rocks their summer vacation. Roger Leslie, writing in *Booklist,* commented on the "nice light suspense, and the short, dialogue-driven chapters" in the two novels, while *School Library Journal* reviewer Elizabeth A. Kaminetz commented that the books' "exciting and fast moving . . . action will keep readers engaged."

Hrdlitschka takes on the serious issue of teen pregnancy and adoption in *Dancing Naked.* After having sex with her boyfriend Derek, Kia discovers she is pregnant. Rather than having an abortion—as her father and Derek both advise—Kia decides to have the baby and give the infant up for adoption. She finds support for her decision from the members of a youth group at a local church, especially from the group's leader, Justin, who is gay. Nicole M. Marcuccilli, writing in *School Library*

Although forgiveness is hard for Darcy to feel when his mother is released from prison, things change when the teen faces a similar burden of proof after being is accused of an act he did not commit in Hrdlitschka's 2004 novel.

Journal, called the novel "thought-provoking and competently done," while *Booklist* contributor Francisca Goldsmith noted that Hrdlitschka's "subject matter, plus strong writing and plotting, invites recreational reading."

In *Kat's Fall* Darcy Frasier is not looking forward to his mother's release from prison; she was convicted of dropping Darcy's younger sister, Kat, from a balcony ten years ago. His mother wants them to be a family again, but the boy finds it impossible to trust her—that is, until he, too, is accused of a horrible crime. "This powerful novel is both heart wrenching and shocking," wrote Leigh Ann Morlock in *School Library Journal.*

The characters in *Sun Signs,* while not dealing with convicted parents or teen pregnancy, nonetheless have troubling complications in their lives. Told through

e-mails, diary entries, and other correspondence, *Sun Signs* reveals the results of a project that Kaleigh and several of her online classmates must complete for school. By studying astrology, they begin to reveal things about each other's lives that brings them closer together. Cancer, the Internet, juvenile delinquency, and other topics "are explored in a sensitive manner," according to *Resource Links* critic Myra Junyk.

On her home page, Hrdlitschka talked about what she enjoys about her job. "I LOVE being a writer," she confessed. "I can set my own hours, I can wear anything I want to work, I can use my imagination, and I am my own boss. Sometimes I think writing is a compulsion or an obsession as much as anything else." She also enjoys receiving correspondence from her fans. As Hrdlitschka once told *SATA,* "If a young person writes to me and gives me feedback on my books, I keep their name to use in a future story. That's the little prize they get for going to the trouble of letting me know how they liked my story!"

Formatted as a series of e-mails, this 2004 novel introduces a trusting teen who learns that, because they avoid providing visual clues as to their character, online "friends" are not always who they claim to be. (Cover design by Lynn O'Rourke.)

Biographical and Critical Sources

PERIODICALS

Booklist, October 15, 2000, Roger Leslie, review of *Tangle Web,* p. 431; March 15, 2002, Francisca Goldsmith, review of *Dancing Naked,* p. 1251; March 15, 2003, review of *Dancing Naked,* p. 1311.
Canadian Book Review Annual, 2001, review of *Dancing Naked,* p. 494.
Canadian Children's Literature, summer, 2000, review of *Beans on Toast,* pp. 75-76.
Canadian Review of Materials, December 15, 2000, review of *Tangled Web;* November 16, 2001, review of *Dancing Naked.*
Kliatt, July, 2002, Deborah Kaplan, review of *Dancing Naked,* p. 21; July, 2004, Ann Hart, review of *Kat's Fall,* p. 20.
Resource Links, February, 2002, Gail De Vos, review of *Dancing Naked,* p. 27; April, 2005, Myra Junyk, review of *Sun Signs,* p. 34.
School Library Journal, October, 2000, Elizabeth A. Kaminetz, review of *Tangled Web,* p. 161; March, 2002, Nicole M. Marcuccilli, review of *Dancing Naked,* p. 232; August, 2004, Leigh Ann Morlock, review of *Kat's Fall,* p. 124.
Voice of Youth Advocates, December, 2000, review of *Tangled Web,* p. 350; April, 2002, review of *Dancing Naked,* p. 44; December, 2004, review of *Kat's Fall,* p. 382; June, 2005, Diane Emge and Billy Palmer, review of *Sun Signs,* p. 131.

ONLINE

Shelley Hrdlitschka Home Page, http://members.shaw.ca/shelleyhrdlitschka (May 4, 2005).

*   *   *

HRDLITSCHKA, Shelley Joanne
See HRDLITSCHKA, Shelley

*   *   *

HUMPHREY, Carol Sue 1956-

Personal

Born 1956, in NC. *Education:* University of North Carolina, Wilmington, B.A. (history), 1978; Wake Forest University, M.A. (American history), 1979; University of North Carolina, Chapel Hill, Ph.D. (American history), 1985.

Addresses

Home—OK. *Office*—Oklahoma Baptist University, Owens Hall 312, University, Shawnee, OK 74804. *E-mail*—carol_humphrey@mail.okbu.edu.

Career

Writer and educator.

Writings

This Popular Engine: New England Newspapers during the American Revolution, 1775-1789, University of Delaware Press (Newark, DE), 1992.
The Press of the Young Republic, 1783-1833, Greenwood Press (Westport, CT), 1996.
The Revolutionary Era: Primary Documents on Events from 1776 to 1800 ("Debating Historical Issues in the Media of the Time" series), Greenwood Press (Westport, CT), 2003.
(With David Copeland) *The Greenwood Library of American War Reporting: The War of 1812,* Greenwood Press (Westport, CT), 2005.
The Greenwood Library of American War Reporting: The Revolutionary War, Greenwood Press (Westport, CT), 2005.

Contributor to books, including *History of the Mass Media in the United States: An Encyclopedia,* edited by Margaret A. Blanchard, Garland Publishing, 1998; *The Media and Religion in American History,* edited by William David Sloan, Vision Press, 1999; *George Washington and the Origins of the American Presidency,* edited by Mark J. Rozell and others, Praeger, 2000; and *Fair and Balanced: A History of Journalistic Objectivity,* edited by Steven Knowlton and Karen L. Freeman, Vision Press, 2005. Contributor of articles and reviews to periodicals, including *American Journalism, Media History Digest, Journalist History, Georgia Historical Quarterly, Historian, Pennsylvania Magazine of History and Biography, Southern Historian, Journal of American History,* and *Social Science Perspectives Journal.*

Biographical and Critical Sources

PERIODICALS

Choice, September, 1992, R. Halverson, review of *This Popular Engine: New England Newspapers during the American Revolution, 1775-1789,* p. 106; April, 1997, review of *The Press of the Young Republic, 1783-1833,* p. 34.
Food Technology, winter, 1992, review of *This Popular Engine,* p. 1056.
Historian, spring, 1998, Andrew Cayton, review of *The Press of the Young Republic, 1783-1833,* p. 634.
History: The Journal of the Historical Association, October, 1993, Roger Thompson, review of *This Popular Engine,* p. 454.
Journalism and Mass Communication Educator, spring, 1997, Brian Thornton, review of *The Press of the Young Republic, 1783-1833,* p. 83.

Journalism and Mass Communication Quarterly, spring, 1997, Ross F. Collins, review of *The Press of the Young Republic, 1783-1833,* p. 218.

Journalism History, autumn, 1977, Ralph Frasca, review of *The Press of the Young Republic, 1783-1833,* p. 141.

Journalism Quarterly, winter, 1992, Kathryn M. Burton, review of *This Popular Engine,* p. 1056.

Journal of American Studies, August, 1993, Richard Middleton, review of *This Popular Engine,* p. 264.

Journal of the Early Republic, summer, 1997, Catherine C. Mitchell, review of *The Press of the Young Republic, 1783-1833,* p. 322.

New England Quarterly, September, 1992, Richard D. Brown, review of *This Popular Engine,* p. 503.

Reference & Research Book News, February, 1997, review of *The Press of the Young Republic, 1783-1833,* p. 82; Nay, 2004, review of *The Revolutionary Era: Primary Documents on Events from 1776 to 1800,* p. 59.

School Library Journal, August, 2004, Ann W. Moore, review of *The Revolutionary Era,* p. 56.

William and Mary Quarterly, January, 1998, John K. Alexander, review of *The Press of the Young Republic, 1783-1833,* p. 167.

ONLINE

Oklahoma Baptist University Web site, http://www2.okbu.edu/ (December 19, 2005), "Carol Sue Humphrey."*

*   *   *

HUNTER, Evan 1926-2005
(Curt Cannon, Hunt Collins, Ezra Hannon, Richard Marsten, Ed McBain)

OBITUARY NOTICE—See index for *SATA* sketch: Born October 15, 1926, in New York, NY; died of larynx cancer, July 6, 2005, in Weston, CT. Writer. Hunter was a bestselling novelist famous for his "87th Precinct" series written under the pen name Ed McBain, as well as for such novels as *The Blackboard Jungle.* Born Salvatore Lombino to a family of Italian immigrants, Hunter later changed his name because he felt there was too much prejudice against Italian writers in America. After serving in the U.S. Navy during the last two years of World War II, he graduated from Hunter College in 1950 and found a job as a New York City high school vocational teacher. It was this experience that he drew on to write his first bestseller, *The Blackboard Jungle* (1954), under the name Hunter. He had already published five novels before this one, but the gritty story of a teacher struggling to educate tough, streetwise kids hit a chord with readers and was adapted as an acclaimed 1955 film. Hunter would go on to write many novels and short stories with great success, but he broke new ground with the police series "87th Precinct" under his McBain pseudonym. Beginning with 1956's *Cop Hater,* these books are highly realistic stories about ide-alistic cops trying to control crime in a decaying urban setting; not only are they considered original for steering away from the classic mystery style of erudite detectives focusing on complex murder mysteries, but they are also unique in that the author combines several parallel storylines featuring various cops in the precinct. Although the attempt to adapt the idea to a television series in the early 1960s failed, some critics, including Hunter, felt that his books inspired the *Hill Street Blues* television series of the 1980s. In addition to his novels, many of which were adapted to film, Hunter also wrote dozens of movie screenplays, with his most acclaimed being *The Birds* (1963), a classic horror tale directed by Alfred Hitchcock. The winner of the 1986 Grand Master Award for lifetime achievement from the Mystery Writers of America, as well as other honors such as the Cartier Diamond Dagger award in 1998 from the Crime Writers Association of Great Britain, Hunter spent his career refusing to be pigeonholed into a particular genre. He thought of himself as a serious writer of realistic fiction, and not as an author of police procedurals or mysteries. Though he fell ill in the years before his death, he continued to publish. Among his final projects were a final "87th Precinct" novel titled *Fiddlers* (2005); a short story collection titled *Learning to Kill* (2006); and an unfinished collaboration on a musical comedy based on the movie *The Night They Raided Minsky's.*

OBITUARIES AND OTHER SOURCES:

PERIODICALS

Chicago Tribune, July 7, 2005, section 3, p. 10.
Los Angeles Times, July 8, 2005, p. B9.
New York Times, July 7, 2005, p. A24; July 8, 2005, p. A2.
Times (London, England), July 8, 2005, p. 70.

*   *   *

INGRAM, Scott 1948-
(W. Scott Ingram)

Personal

Born September 27, 1948, in Schenectady, NY; son of William Ingram (a consultant) and Winifred Sellick (a realtor); married, 1976; wife's name Carol (an artist); children: Miles, Abby. *Education:* University of Connecticut, B.A.; Wesleyan University, M.A. *Hobbies and other interests:* Bicycling, guitar.

Addresses

Home—101 Culver Lane, Portland, CT 06480. *Office*—245 Long Hill Rd., Middletown, CT 06457. *E-mail*—singram@weeklyreader.com.

Career

Weekly Reader Corp., Middletown, CT, managing editor, 1979—. Member of Board of Education, Portland, CT.

Awards, Honors

Educational Press Awards, 1985, 1988, 1994, 1995.

Writings

JUVENILE NONFICTION

Bloody Waters: Terrorizing Shark Tales, illustrated by Ron Rundo, Lowell House, 1995.

Beast: Hair-Raising Horror Stories, illustrated by Brian W. Dow, Lowell House (Los Angeles, CA), 1996.

More Scary Stories for Stormy Nights, illustrated by Eric Angeloch, Lowell House (Los Angeles, CA), 1996.

Scary Shark Stories, illustrated by Eric Angeloch, Lowell House (Los Angeles, CA), 1997.

Maggot Madness!, illustrated by Ginny Pruitt, Random House (New York, NY), 1997.

(As W. Scott Ingram) *Oregon,* Children's Press (New York, NY), 2000.

The Battle of Yorktown ("Triangle Histories of the Revolutionary War" series), Blackbirch Press (San Diego, CA), 2002.

(As W. Scott Ingram) *The Battle of Fredericksburg* ("Triangle Histories of the Revolutionary War" series), Blackbirch Press (San Diego, CA), 2002.

(As W. Scott Ingram) *Aaron Burr and the Young Nation* ("Notorious Americans and Their Times" series), Blackbirch Press (Woodbridge, CT), 2002.

John Paul Jones, Blackbirch Press (San Diego, CA), 2002.

(As W. Scott Ingram) *Jefferson Davis,* Blackbirch Press (Woodbridge, CT), 2002.

George Washington, Blackbirch Press (San Diego, CA), 2002.

Kansas ("From Sea to Shining Sea" series), Children's Press (New York, NY), 2003.

Frank Lloyd Wright, Raintree (Chicago, IL), 2003.

(With Christina M. Girod) *The Indian Americans* ("Immigrants in America" series), Lucent Books (San Diego, CA), 2004.

The Battle of Valcour Bay ("Triangle Histories of the Revolutionary War" series), Blackbirch Press (San Diego, CA), 2004.

The Battle of Long Island ("Triangle Histories of the Revolutionary War" series), Blackbirch Press (San Diego, CA), 2004.

The Battle of Bunker Hill ("Triangle Histories of the Revolutionary War" series), Blackbirch Press (San Diego, CA), 2004.

Paul Revere, Blackbirch Press (San Diego, CA), 2004.

The Panama Canal ("Building World Landmarks" series), Blackbirch Press (San Diego, CA), 2004.

Nicolaus Copernicus: Father of Modern Astronomy ("Giants of Science" series), Blackbirch Press (San Diego, CA), 2004.

King George III, Blackbirch Press (San Diego, CA), 2004.

The Writing of "The Star-Spangled Banner," World Almanac Library (Milwaukee, WI), 2004.

The Song Dynasty ("Life during the Great Civilizations" series), Blackbirch Press (San Diego, CA), 2004.

The Chernobyl Nuclear Disaster ("Environmental Disasters" series), Facts on File (New York, NY), 2005.

A Basketball All-Star, Heinemann Library (Chicago, IL), 2005.

The 1963 Civil Rights March ("Landmark Events in American History" series), World Almanac Library (Milwaukee, WI), 2005.

Tsunami!: The 1946 Hilo Wave of Terror ("X-treme Disasters That Changed America" series), Bearport Pub. (New York, NY), 2005.

The Stock Market Crash of 1929 ("Landmark Events in American History" series), World Almanac Library (Milwaukee, WI), 2005.

(As W. Scott Ingram) *Polish Immigrants* ("Immigration to the United States" series), Facts on File (New York, NY) 2005.

(As W. Scott Ingram) *Japanese Immigrants* ("Immigration to the United States" series), Facts on File (New York, NY) 2005.

(As W. Scott Ingram) *Greek Immigrants* ("Immigration to the United States" series), Facts on File (New York, NY) 2005.

A Football All-Pro ("Making of a Champion" series), Heinemann Library (Chicago, IL), 2005.

Want Fries with That?: Obesity and the Supersizing of America, Franklin Watts (New York, NY), 2006.

Dolphins ("Smart Animals!" series), Bearport Pub. (New York, NY), 2006.

"AMERICA'S LEADERS" SERIES

The Vice President of the United States, Thomson Gale (San Diego, CA), 2002.

The Secretary of Defense, Thomson Gale (San Diego, CA), 2002.

The President of the United States, Thomson Gale (San Diego, CA), 2002.

The FBI Director, Blackbirch Press (San Diego, CA), 2004.

The Secretary of Commerce, Blackbirch Press (San Diego, CA), 2004.

The National Security Adviser, Blackbirch Press (San Diego, CA), 2004.

The Secretary of Treasury, Blackbirch Press (San Diego, CA), 2004.

The Secretary of Labor, Blackbirch Press (San Diego, CA), 2004.

The Postmaster General, Blackbirch Press (San Diego, CA), 2004.

"HISTORY'S VILLAINS" SERIES

Francisco Pizarro, Blackbirch Press (San Diego, CA), 2002.

Adolf Hitler, Blackbirch Press (San Diego, CA), 2002.

Joseph Stalin, Blackbirch Press (San Diego, CA), 2002.

Attila the Hun, Blackbirch Press (San Diego, CA), 2002.
Kim Il Sung, Blackbirch Press (San Diego, CA), 2004.

"LIBRARY OF THE STATES" SERIES: AS W. SCOTT INGRAM

California: The Golden State, World Almanac Library (Milwaukee, WI), 2002.
Missouri: The Show-Me State, World Almanac Library (Milwaukee, WI), 2002.
Kansas: The Sunflower State, World Almanac Library (Milwaukee, WI), 2002.
Pennsylvania: The Keystone State, World Almanac Library (Milwaukee, WI), 2002.
Oregon: The Beaver State, World Almanac Library (Milwaukee, WI), 2002.

"EVENTS THAT SHAPED AMERICA" SERIES

(With Sabrina Crewe) *The Writing of "The Star-Spangled Banner,"* Gareth Stevens (Milwaukee, WI), 2005.
(With Sabrina Crewe) *The Stock Market Crash of 1929,* Gareth Stevens (Milwaukee, WI), 2005.
(With Sabrina Crewe) *The 1963 Civil Rights March,* Gareth Stevens (Milwaukee, WI), 2005.

Sidelights

Working as a managing editor at the company that publishes *Weekly Reader,* an age-graded newspaper for children that is distributed in elementary classrooms throughout the United States since the late 1920s, Scott Ingram has gained a familiarity with the most effective way to explain world events to younger readers. As the prolific author of nonfiction titles ranging from *The Chernobyl Nuclear Disaster, The Song Dynasty,* and *A Basketball All-Star* to the books in the "Events That Shaped America" and "History's Villains" series, he conveys a wealth of information in a clear, well-organized text that reflects his personal fascination with world events. Discussing *Nicolaus Copernicus: Father of Modern Astronomy,* Ingram's biography of the sixteenth-century Polish mathematician who first theorized, correctly, that the Earth moves around the Sun, *School Library Journal* reviewer Ann Joslin praised the book as "clearly written biography," noting that the author includes a discussion of "the forces that impacted the astronomer's life and his work."

Several of Ingram's books focus on the history of the American colonies. Part of the "Triangle Histories of the Revolutionary War" series, *The Battle of Long Is-*

Part of the "Life during Great Civilizations" series, Ingram's **The Song Dynasty** *profiles China's history between 960 and 1279.*

In Nicolaus Copernicus *readers follow the life of the noted astronomer who lived in this monastery in Frombork, Poland, during the early sixteenth century.*

land, *The Battle of Yorktown,* and *The Battle of Bunker Hill* feature "an unbiased reporting of the war" that balances British and colonial strategies and battle goals, according to Kristina Aaronson in *School Library Journal.* Noting Ingram's inclusion of quotes from contemporary commentators, Dona Ratteree wrote in the same periodical that the books are "enlivened with sprightly writing" and enhanced by original documents, paintings, and other graphics to the sustain interest of young scholars. Reviewing Ingram's *Kim Il Sung,* part of the "History's Villains" series, *School Library Journal* reviewer Ann G. Brouse dubbed the book a "fascinating, horrifying" study of the North Korean dictator who drew his country into the Korean War, increasing isolation, and financial difficulties through his rigid communist ideology and the cult of personality that dubbed him the "Great Leader." In *Booklist,* Ed Sullivan praised

the series as "clearly written and well organized," citing their inclusion of a glossary, chronology, and list of additional sources.

Ingram once told *SATA:* "Reading and writing have always been at the center of my life. People who knew me thirty years ago would not be surprised to learn that I make my living with language. As an author, editor, and parent I get a great deal of enjoyment from passing my scary stories under my kids' stern eyes and seeing them make faces as they read something icky that I have invented.

"Oddly enough, I think writing gross stuff has increased my stature with my kids; before this, I was just a regular old dad who wrote news stories for *Weekly Reader.* Now that they know characters in my stories are filled with worms or eaten by sharks, they think I'm really onto something—they actually talk about my work with their friends. Ahhh . . . success."

Biographical and Critical Sources

PERIODICALS

Booklist, July, 2004, Ed Sullivan, review of *Kim Il Sung,* p. 1832.
School Library Journal, January, 1997, Elaine E. Knight, review of *More Scary Stories for Stormy Nights,* p. 112; September, 2002, Donna L. Scanlon, review of *Pennsylvania: The Keystone State,* p. 246; March, 2003, Kristina Aaronson, review of *The Battle of Yorkstown,* p. 252; March, 2003, Marion F. Gallivan, review of *Attila the Hun,* p. 252; May, 2003, Doris Losey, review of *The Secretary of Defense,* p. 135; March, 2004, Dona Ratterree, review of *The Battle of Long Island,* p. 236; May, 2004, Ann G. Brouse, review of *Kim Il Sung,* p. 160, Diane S. Marton, review of *The Indian Americans,* p. 162; June, 2004, Linda Beck, review of *King George III,* p. 167; August, 2004, Peg Glisson, review of *The Song Dynasty,* p. 138; March, 2004, Janice C. Hayes, review of *A Basketball All-Star,* p. 230; June, 2005, Ann Joslin, review of *Nicolaus Copernicus: Father of Modern Astronomy,* p. 178.*

*   *   *

INGRAM, W. Scott
See INGRAM, Scott

J-K

JACKSON, Ellen B.

Personal

Born in Los Angeles, CA; daughter of Merrill O. (an accountant) and Carol (a children's librarian; maiden name, Goldstein) Jackson; married Roger Schlueter; stepchildren: Kyle, Megan. *Education:* University of California, Los Angeles, B.A., 1967; California Family Study Center, M.A., 1977. *Hobbies and other interests:* Hiking, tidepooling and beachcombing after a storm, playing alto, soprano, and bass recorder, fiber arts, volunteering at the library.

Addresses

Home—Santa Barbara, CA. *Agent*—c/o Author Mail, Millbrook Press/Lerner Publishing Group, 1251 Washington Ave. N., Minneapolis, MN 55401. *E-mail*—ellenj@west.net.

Career

Writer. Monte Vista Street School, Los Angeles, CA, kindergarten teacher, 1969-79; Santa Barbara County Schools, Santa Barbara, CA, curriculum writer, 1984-87.

Member

Society of Children's Book Writers and Illustrators, Authors Guild, Author's League, Amnesty International.

Awards, Honors

National Writer's Club certificate, 1991; Children's Choice selection, International Reading Association, 1995, for *The Winter Solstice;* Outstanding Book designation, *Child* magazine, 1995, for *Brown Cow, Green Grass, Yellow Mellow Sun;* Book of the Year award, *Family Fun* magazine, 1996, for *Monsters in My Mailbox;* Pick of the List designation, American Booksellers Association (ABA), 1996, for *The Precious Gift;* ABA Pick of the List designation, and Editor's Choice, *Booklist,* both 1998, both for *Turn of the Century; Storytelling World* Award, 2001, for *Scatterbrain Sam;* 100 Best Books citation, Los Angeles Unified Library Services, Bank Street College Children's Book of the Year designation, and Society of School Librarians International Honor Book designation, all 2001, all for *The Summer Solstice;* Gold Award, Parents' Choice Foundation, 2001, for *Scatterbrain Sam,* and 2005, for *Earth Mother;* Outstanding Science Trade Book for Children citation, National Science Teachers Association/Children's Book Council (CBC), John Burroughs List of Outstanding Nature Books for Young Readers selection, and first runner-up, Society of Midland Authors Children's Nonfiction Award, all 2002, and Children's Literature Choice listee, 2003, all for *Looking for Life in the Universe;* Cooperative Children's Book Center honor, 2003, for *The Spring Equinox;* Notable Children's Trade Book in the Field of Social Studies, National Council for the Social Studies/CBC, 2004, for *It's Back to School We Go.*

Writings

PICTURE BOOKS

The Bear in the Bathtub, illustrated by Margot Apple, Addison-Wesley (Reading, MA), 1981.
The Grumpus under the Rug, illustrated by Scott Gustafson, Follett (Chicago, IL), 1981.
Ants Can't Dance, illustrated by Frank Remkiewicz, Macmillan (New York, NY), 1990.
Boris the Boring Boar, illustrated by Normand Chartier, Macmillan (New York, NY), 1992.
The Tree of Life (nonfiction), illustrated by Judeanne Winter, Prometheus (Buffalo, NY), 1993.
Cinder Edna, illustrated by Kevin O'Malley, Lothrop, Lee & Shepard (New York, NY), 1994.
The Winter Solstice (nonfiction), illustrated by Jan Davey Ellis, Millbrook (Brookfield, CT), 1994.
Brown Cow, Green Grass, Yellow Mellow Sun, illustrated by Victoria Raymond, Hyperion (New York, NY), 1995.

The Impossible Riddle, illustrated by Alison Winfield, Whispering Coyote Press (Boston, MA), 1995.

Monsters in My Mailbox, illustrated by Maxie Chambliss, Troll (Mahwah, NJ), 1995.

(Reteller) *The Precious Gift: A Navajo Creation Myth,* illustrated by Woodleigh Marx Hubbard, Simon & Schuster (New York, NY), 1996.

The Wacky Witch War, illustrated by Denise Brunkus, WhistleStop (Mahwah, NJ), 1996.

Why Coyote Sings to the Moon, illustrated by Eric Joyner, American Education Publishing, 1996.

The Book of Slime (nonfiction), illustrated by Jan Davey Ellis, Millbrook Press (Brookfield, CT), 1997.

Turn of the Century (nonfiction), illustrated by Jan Davey Ellis, Charlesbridge (Watertown, MA), 1998.

Here Come the Brides (nonfiction), illustrated by Carol Heyer, Walker (New York, NY), 1998.

The Autumn Equinox (nonfiction), illustrated by Jan Davey Ellis, Millbrook Press (Brookfield, CT), 2000.

Scatterbrain Sam, illustrated by Matt Faulkner, Whispering Coyote (Watertown, MA), 2001.

The Summer Solstice (nonfiction), illustrated by Jan Davey Ellis, Millbrook Press (Brookfield, CT), 2002.

The Spring Equinox: Celebrating the Greening of the Earth (nonfiction), illustrated by Jan Davey Ellis, Millbrook Press (Brookfield, CT), 2002.

Sometimes Bad Things Happen, photographs by Shelley Rotner, Millbrook Press (Brookfield, CT), 2002.

Looking for Life in the Universe: The Search for Extraterrestrial Intelligence, photographs by Nic Bishop, Houghton Mifflin (Boston, MA), 2002.

It's Back to School We Go: First Day Stories from around the World, illustrated by Jan Davey Ellis, Millbrook Press (Brookfield, CT), 2003.

(Editor) Theodore Roosevelt, *My Tour of Europe: By Teddy Roosevelt, Age Ten,* illustrated by Catherine Brighton, Millbrook Press (Brookfield, CT), 2003.

Earth Mother, illustrated by Leo and Diane Dillon, Walker & Co. (New York, NY), 2005.

Cinnamon Brown and the Seven Dwarfs, illustrated by Elbrite Brown, Viking (New York, NY), 2006.

Worlds around Us: A Space Voyage, illustrated by Ron Miller, Millbrook Press (Minneapolis, MN), in press.

"MONTHS" SERIES; PICTURE BOOKS

January, illustrated by Pat DeWitt and Robin DeWitt, Charlesbridge (Watertown, MA), 2002.

February, illustrated by Pat DeWitt and Robin DeWitt, Charlesbridge (Watertown, MA), 2002.

March, illustrated by Kay Life, Charlesbridge (Watertown, MA), 2002.

April, illustrated by Kay Life, Charlesbridge (Watertown, MA), 2002.

May, illustrated by Kay Life, Charlesbridge (Watertown, MA), 2002.

June, illustrated by Kay Life, Charlesbridge (Watertown, MA), 2002.

July, illustrated by Pat DeWitt and Robin DeWitt, Charlesbridge (Watertown, MA), 2002.

August, illustrated by Pat DeWitt and Robin DeWitt, Charlesbridge (Watertown, MA), 2002.

September, illustrated by Pat DeWitt and Robin DeWitt, Charlesbridge (Watertown, MA), 2002.

October, illustrated by Pat DeWitt and Robin DeWitt, Charlesbridge (Watertown, MA), 2002.

November, illustrated by Pat DeWitt and Robin DeWitt, Charlesbridge (Watertown, MA), 2002.

December, illustrated by Pat DeWitt and Robin DeWitt, Charlesbridge (Watertown, MA), 2002.

OTHER

Stay on the Safe Side (grades 5-6 and 7-8), Office of Criminal Justice Planning (Sacramento, CA), 1985.

Stay on the Safe Side (grades K-4), Office of Criminal Justice Planning (Sacramento, CA), 1987.

Top of the World, Children's Story Scripts, 1991.

Quick Wits and Whiskers, Children's Story Scripts, 1991.

Families Are for Finding, Children's Story Scripts, 1991.

Earthquake Safety, Horizon (Montreal, Quebec, Canada), 1991.

Household Safety, Horizon (Montreal, Quebec, Canada), 1991.

Stranger Danger (safety advice for kids), Horizon (Montreal, Quebec, Canada), 1991.

Contributor to newspapers, including *Critical Times;* contributor of children's stories to periodicals, including *Humpty Dumpty's.* Author of how-to manual *How to Start a Pet Grooming Business;* author of multimedia history book for computer game *Where in Time Is Carmen Sandiego?,* Version 3.0, Broderbund Software, 1997.

Adaptations

Cinder Edna was adapted as a musical stage production produced in Hopkins, MN, 2005-06.

Sidelights

Creating children's books that range from cautionary tales to humorous and informative nonfiction picture books, Ellen B. Jackson is noted for a simple, direct style that appeals to very young children and beginning readers. "Jackson is a gifted writer who can make the simplest language rhyming and interesting," noted Lauralyn Persson in *School Library Journal.* The daughter of a children's librarian, Jackson is well equipped for a career in children's writing. A decade-long career as a kindergarten teacher, as well as a stint as a curriculum writer for the Santa Barbara County Schools, have also helped to prepare her for the job of imparting information to young children concisely and wittily.

Jackson's first book, *The Bear in the Bathtub,* is a funny tale of a young boy, Andrew, who hates to take baths, but learns to appreciate tubby time when a huge bear takes over the bathtub. Unable to bathe for days, Andrew soon becomes so dirty that his friends no longer want to be near him. Unfortunately, no one—not his parents, the police, or even the fire fighters—can re-

Based on a Welsh folktale, Jackson's **Scatterbrain Sam** *finds a young man stumbling upon true love while tracking down the ingredients for a stew that will make him smarter. (Illustration by Matt Faulkner.)*

move the bear from the tub, leaving the boy to finally solve the problem. "Jackson accents the mirth by relating the nonsense with a straight face," wrote a contributor to *Publishers Weekly. The Bear in the Bathtub* was described as an "amusing, well-written story [that] reads aloud well," by Pamela Warren Stebbins in a *School Library Journal* review.

The Grumpus under the Rug is the tale of a mother who refuses to believe that the Grumpus under the rug is causing the mischief in her house. Even though her little boy keeps assuring his mother that the naughty Grumpus is there, she blames her son for the Grumpus's messy habits. Fortunately, the mother finally discovers the Grumpus by looking under the rug before the mischievous creature can disappear, and she throws it into the sky, ridding her home of it. A reviewer for *Booklist* said that Jackson's "spare story, told in mock-tale vein, plunges readers into the crux of its matter."

Another boy has trouble convincing his parents to believe him in *Ants Can't Dance.* Jonathan finds a dancing ant and brings it home to show his parents, but once he is home, the ant refuses to perform. His parents, skeptical to begin with, remain unconvinced, especially when the next day Jonathan brings home a talking peanut that becomes mute in front of them. Jonathan finally discovers a whistling stone that does perform for everybody, even television reporters. A reviewer for *Publishers Weekly* called the book a "whimsical tale" and added that this "lighthearted picture book . . . will be enjoyed by parents and children alike," though the "fresh, witty prose of the opening pages peters out, and the plot and premise become repetitive." Marie Orlando echoed these remarks in a *School Library Journal* review, calling the book "a slight but amusing story," and concluding that "colorful cartoon illustrations blend well with the story, and youngsters will enjoy the clever lad's ultimate triumph." John Murray, reviewing *Ants Can't Dance* in *Magpies,* found the "repetitive language

structures and rhyme accompanying each episode of the story make this a fairly useful book for early reading," while "well marked dialogue and a plot with the three episodes so common in folktales allow for predictability of form and ready dramatization."

There is a lesson in the humor of *Boris the Boring Boar,* in which Boris discovers that it pays to listen. Boris's friends are so tired of his boring monologue about how great he is that no one wants to be around him. Feeling lonely, he meets a smooth-talking wolf who ends up tying him to a tree while preparing to cook the boring bear for dinner. Boris, however, uses his wits to save himself by complimenting the wolf on his fine, sharp teeth and handsome coat. The wolf, as lonely as Boris, eats up these compliments instead of Boris, and sets the fast-talking bear free. After this experience, Boris learns an important lesson, and when he then encounters Pansy Pig, he asks about her day instead of describing his. Martha Topol wrote in *School Library Journal* that the "text makes good use of its verbal pun without going overboard," and that in spite of "some quick transitions, the story is well developed and has a satisfying conclusion. . . . Children will not be bored with Boris." A writer for *Kirkus Reviews* remarked that Boris "is a quintessential bore," and that whether or not "it prompts embarrassed self-appraisal, the comical dialogue here is as much fun as the deft caricatures in the well-crafted art."

Sometimes Bad Things Happen is designed less to show a lesson than it is to help children deal with sad events. Filled with photographs of emergency workers and people helping each other, *Sometimes Bad Things Happen* covers feelings of sadness or fear or anger, offering children comfort at times of struggle. Noting that the title is "undisguised bibliotherapy," John Peters of *Booklist* felt that Jackson's book will "offer comfort in a more visually appealing way" than more old-fashioned titles on emotions. Lucinda Snyder Whitehurst, writing for *School Library Journal,* complimented the book's "brief text and crisp, color photos."

The first day of school is the topic of *It's Back to School We Go.* Instead of discussing the back-to-school anxieties many American children face, Jackson takes a broader world view, showing children from eleven different countries returning to school. With children from such countries as Kazakhstan, China, and Kenya, *It's Back to School We Go* presents U.S. readers with information about the foods that children in other countries eat and the types of games they play at school. "This multinational approach provides material for comparing and contrasting cultures," noted Lynda Ritterman in her *School Library Journal* review.

Jackson retells traditional tales and myths in picture books such as *Cinder Edna,* an alternative Cinderella story; *The Precious Gift,* a Navajo creation myth; and *The Impossible Riddle*, based on a Russian folktale. In *Cinder Edna* Jackson takes a feminist approach to the traditional story, making "the traditional passive Cinderella . . . the neighbor of liberated Cinder Edna," explained *Booklist* contributor Hazel Rochman. While Cinderella needs a fairy godmother to transport her to the ball, the self-reliant Cinder Edna gets herself there. Although she is not beautiful, Cinder Edna is spunky and full of zip. Bored by the prince, she is attracted to his younger brother, Rupert, a young man who is more interested in ecology than in high fashion. Rochman noted that "humor softens the commentary" in Jackson's politically correct tale, and added that there is "fun in the literal reduction of the fantasy as well as in the transformed role models." A reviewer for *Publishers Weekly* commented that the "Cinderella send-up is full of kid-pleasing jokes and, besides, it's never too early to discover the hazards of codependence." Reviewing the book for *School Library Journal,* Susan Hepler called *Cinder Edna* a "clever, double story" and concluded that kids "will love this version for its humor and vibrant artwork."

In *The Precious Gift* Jackson retells part of the Dineh creation myth in which a lowly snail is responsible for bringing water to an arid land. This story has a "relevant ecological theme," according to a critic for *Publishers Weekly,* who also remarked that "the story is clever in its explanation of how other creatures, such as the turtle and frog, acquired their attributes." *The Impossible Riddle* is an adaptation of a Russian folktale about a tsar who loves his daughter and her potato pancakes to distraction. He vows never to let her marry unless a suitor can answer the tsar's prized riddle. A handsome suitor appears, and manages to outsmart the tsar and win the hand of his talented daughter.

Basing a new story on a traditional Welsh folktale, Jackson set her hero in small-town America for *Scatterbrain Sam.* Sam wants brains, but cannot figure out how to organize his thoughts. Widder Woman, the town's wisest woman, agrees to make a potion with which she will glue Sam's brain together. When Sam's sweetheart, Maizie Mae, is at risk due to his potion, he is willing to make the sacrifice to save his lady love. As it happens, Maizie is an on-the-ball figure, so the Widder Woman tells Sam he has some brains after all: Maizie's. The story "is sure to entertain scatterbrained and cool-headed readers alike," stated a reviewer for *Publishers Weekly.* Beth Tegart, writing in *School Library Journal,* considered the book "a funny, folksy tall tale filled with exaggeration and sly humor," while *Booklist* reviewer GraceAnne A. DeCandido felt that Sam "heads straight for the funny bone—and the heart."

Earth Mother, while not a traditional story, is an environmental tale told in a folklore style. The Earth Mother of the title keeps watch over all of creation, walking throughout the land and singing. She encounters a man who is glad for many of the things Earth Mother provides but wishes she could do something about the mosquitoes that bite him. Frog is grateful for the mosquitoes, which he eats, but wishes man would stop eating him. Mosquito is happy that man provides his food, but wishes frog would go away. The story, which is illustrated by award winning artists Diane and Leo Dillon, has little action, but shows a circular pattern of nature. "The Dillons' illustrations capture the spiritual aura of Jackson's graceful words," wrote a *Publishers Weekly* contributor. A critic for *Kirkus Reviews* called the story "beautiful and satisfying; its own teachable moment." Noting that some readers might be frustrated by the story's leisurely pace, Susan Lissim noted in *School Library Journal* that "reading it a few times helps readers realize the book's calming effect."

In addition to fiction, Jackson has produced several highly praised nonfiction books in which she examines topics ranging from the winter solstice to slime. A freelance writer for over two decades, she once told *SATA:* "I live in a house one block from the beach in Santa Barbara, California, with my husband and schnoodle, Abby. I read in many different fields including science, sociology, fiction, eastern philosophy, and history. I do volunteer work for Amnesty International and the Peace Resource Center in Santa Barbara." Her wide-ranging interests have led her to bring science and cultural topics to young readers in picture-book format. She also provides a wealth of information, such as reading guides an experiments, for teachers and parents, using her books in educational settings, on her home page.

In *The Tree of Life* Jackson explains evolution to young readers, introducing the concept by examining the origins of life and how it has diversified. Roger Sutton, writing in the *Bulletin of the Center for Children's Books,* called the book "a mostly successful attempt to explain the complex theory," adding that the vocabulary "is kept simple . . . and the progression is logical." Reviewing the same book for *Science Books and Films,* Erik Scully remarked that Jackson's "language is as nontechnical as possible, and the concept of natural selection is implied throughout the text." "The book is generally successful in presenting the concept of evolution," the critic added, "but the emphasis on a nontechnical presentation sometimes results in a very vague discussion."

Among Jackson's other science books are *The Winter Solstice* and *The Book of Slime.* In the former, she combines science and cultural history, looking at the physical mechanics that bring about the shortest day of the year and then examining a variety of customs surrounding the winter solstice as practiced by ancient Britons, Romans, and Native Americans. "Teachers will value the book's multicultural approach as well as its simple, readable text," noted *Booklist* reviewer Carolyn Phelan.

Kay McPherson commented in *School Library Journal* that Jackson does "a solid job of explaining various peoples' attitudes about the winter solstice and related rituals and traditions." Animal secretions is the subject of *The Book of Slime,* in which Jackson details the beneficial qualities of this seemingly gross substance. From lubricant for snails and slugs to recipes for edible slime bread, the book leavens its yucky topic with jokes, activities, and a short story. "Place this book with its green and black slimy cover face-out and it will simply ooze off the shelves," suggested a critic for *Kirkus Reviews.*

Jackson looks at culture and history in both *Here Come the Brides* and *Turn of the Century.* In the former book

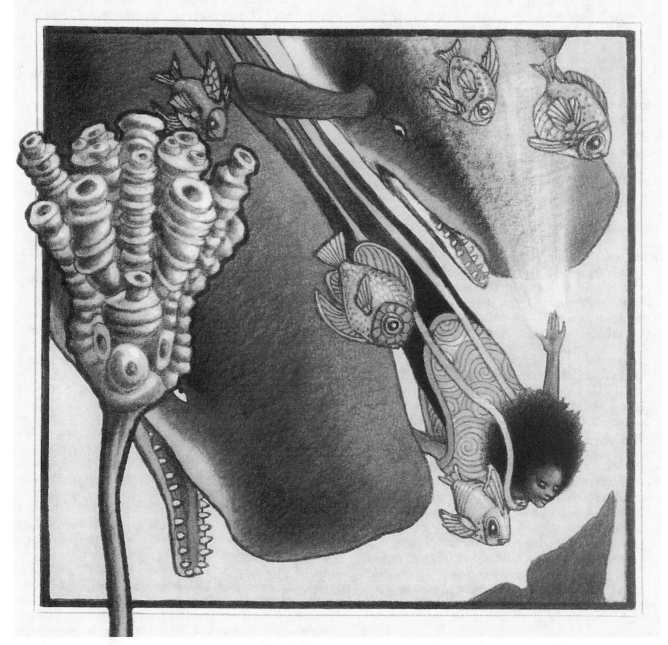

Reflecting the traditions of many ancient cultures, **Earth Mother** *describes the god-like being who gives life and nurture to all Earth's creatures. (Illustration by Leo and Diane Dillon.)*

she discusses wedding costumes and customs from around the world. Kathleen Isaacs, writing in *School Library Journal,* called the book a "lavishly illustrated easy-to-read introduction." *Here Come the Brides* includes information about varying cultural ideas, from the appropriate color for the bride to traditional kinds of flowers and food. In *Turn of the Century* Jackson takes advantage of millennium fever to look at different centuries from the point of view of contemporary, fictional children. "This informative picture book introduces youngsters to history through 11 fictitious children, each living in a different period," explained Susan Knell in *School Library Journal,* dubbing the book "a fine resource to add to any social studies or history curriculum and a delightful and timely choice as the year 2000 approaches." A critic for *Kirkus Reviews* called the work an "ambitious book about children from the past, present, and near future. . . . An astute and provocative book for browsing, or for tying into assignments."

After the success of *The Winter Solstice,* Jackson went on to produce three more titles about the science and cultural histories of the seasonal peaks. With *The Autumn Equinox,* called "informative and succinct" by Jody McCoy in *School Library Journal,* she introduces readers to festivals all over the world that celebrate autumn. *The Summer Solstice* discusses the longest day of the year, and provides a traditional solstice story from Hawaii. *Booklist* reviewer Carolyn Phelan called the title "an attractive resource" while Patricia Manning, writing in *School Library Journal,* considered the book "an interesting conglomeration of folkloric traditions, science, and myth." The end of winter and beginning of spring are celebrated in *The Spring Equinox,* which completes the season quartet. Carolyn Phelan, reviewing this work for *Booklist,* considered it "a spirited overview of spring celebrations around the world." Writing for *School Library Journal,* Lisa Gangemi Kropp called *The Spring Equinox* an "informative look at the vernal equinox."

Jackson crosses biography with science in *Looking for Life in the Universe: The Search for Extraterrestrial Intelligence.* By telling the story of Dr. Jill Tarter, the scientist on whom noted astrophysicist Carl Sagan based the protagonist of his novel *Contact,* Jackson introduces young readers to the concept of the Phoenix-based project of the Search for Extraterrestrial Intelligence (SETI), for which Tarter is the director. While there are other titles for young readers that talk about the possibility of life beyond Earth, "few focus on the scientists as Jackson does," according to Ann G. Brouse in *School Library Journal.* Brouse concluded that the title, filled with photographs by Nic Bishop, is "an exciting, visually awesome look at frontier science." John Peters wrote in *Booklist* that "readers will come away with a clear sense of the lure of this frustrating but exciting endeavor."

There is no science in *My Tour of Europe: By Teddy Roosevelt, Age Ten,* which Jackson edited, but there is plenty of history. When his family traveled through Europe, ten-year-old Theodore Roosevelt kept a diary of his experiences, and in this book Jackson presents excerpts from this document that show the president's childhood view of Europe. Susan Lissim, reviewing the title for *School Library Journal,* wrote that Jackson's "delightful collection of excerpts" come together to make an "interesting and informative book."

Jackson once told *SATA:* "Most of my childhood was spent in Glendale, California. My mother worked for Walt Disney Studios for over thirty years. In the early years, Walt would sometimes give her a ride to work. He was that kind of guy. My mother loved books, music, art, and learning, and she made sure I knew all the classics of children's literature. I grew up with a lot of family trauma, and I coped by retreating into the world of books. My sixth grade teacher complained that I read too much. I still do.

"I went to various schools in southern California and prolonged my education as long as possible because I love learning. After graduating from UCLA, I discovered there were no jobs for English/psychology/history majors. A friend told me about a special program in a nearby school district to train teachers, and I applied and was accepted. Due to overcrowding, some teachers in this program, including me, had no classrooms in which to conduct classes. With no instructional materials, I bought or made everything myself. I taught kindergarten for one year out on the playground in rain, wind, and 100-degree heat.

"In spite of this, I loved teaching. Monday was my favorite day of the week. I decided to go back to school, make teaching my life's work, and earn a degree that would get me a classroom of my own. I got the proper credentials, and taught school for ten years. During that time, I picked up an M.A. in family counseling and traveled in Europe, the Amazon jungle, and the Galapagos Islands. (On the Galapagos, I stayed for a week at a 'hotel' with a unique decor—walls covered with large, hairy-legged spiders.)

"At the end of ten years, I moved to Santa Barbara to take care of my mother, who was ill. It occurred to me that writing might be fun. Having read many books to my students over the years, I thought I could write a children's book if I tried. It seemed so easy. My first book accumulated a stack of form rejection slips in no time. Nevertheless, I kept reworking the same book; I was convinced it was a work of genius (it wasn't; trust me). It was about a snail. While working on this particular book, another idea popped into my head one day. I tried to shoo it away, but it wouldn't be shooed. With no hope of publication, I sent the second book out, and Addison-Wesley promptly took it. Well, not so promptly, actually. It took them a year to make up their minds. This book developed a cult following among my relatives. It was also enjoyed, though rarely bought, by my friends and acquaintances.

"Since then I've written manuals (*How to Start a Pet Grooming Business*), nonfiction books (*The Winter Solstice*), curriculum (*Stay on the Safe Side*), and worked on multimedia projects (*Where in Time Is Carmen Sandiego?*). My role of caretaker has continued. Three years ago, my elderly aunt and uncle moved to Santa Barbara, where they acquired a house and an orchard. Helping them out and supervising the orchard has been both frustrating and rewarding.

"My life is a busy but happy one. I write almost every day. My eccentric miniature schnauzer, Bailey, sleeps under my computer desk and makes cozy dog noises while I work. I love to go beach combing or explore the back hills of Santa Barbara. Currently I volunteer at the local library one day a week. I occasionally cook meals at a local homeless shelter and walk dogs for the Dog Adoption Welfare Group. In my spare time (ha!) I read and play the recorder. Despite periodic bouts of sloth and torpor, I manage to keep it all going."

Biographical and Critical Sources

PERIODICALS

Booklist, December 15, 1981, review of *The Grumpus under the Rug,* p. 553; November 15, 1992, p. 608; February 15, 1994, Carolyn Phelan, review of *The Winter Solstice,* pp. 1085-1086; March 15, 1994, Hazel Rochman, review of *Cinder Edna,* p. 1373; June 1, 1995, p. 1786; January 1, 1996, p. 845; March 15, 1997, p. 1246; July, 1998 p. 1877; January 1, 1999, review of *Turn of the Century,* p. 783; April 1, 2001, Carolyn Phelan, review of *The Summer Solstice,* p. 1459; August, 2001, GraceAnne A. DeCandido, review of *Scatterbrain Sam,* p. 2130; April 15, 2002, Carolyn Phelan, review of *The Spring Equinox,* p. 1397; November 15, 2002, John Peters, review of *Sometimes Bad Things Happen,* p. 605; December 1, 2002, review of *Looking for Life in the Universe,* p. 684.

Bulletin of the Center for Children's Books, December, 1993, Roger Sutton, review of *The Tree of Life,* pp. 123-124; June, 1996, pp. 339-340.

Kirkus Reviews, September 1, 1992, review of *Boris the Boring Boar,* p. 1130; April 1, 1994, p. 480; April 1, 1995, p. 470; January 15, 1997, review of *The Book of Slime,* p. 143; April 1, 1998, p. 496; June 15, 1998, review of *Turn of the Century,* p. 895; August 1, 2005, review of *Earth Mother,* p. 850.

Magpies, November, 1991, John Murray, review of *Ants Can't Dance,* p. 27.

Publishers Weekly, April 17, 1981, review of *The Bear in the Bathtub,* p. 62; April 19, 1991, review of *Ants Can't Dance,* p. 66; February 14, 1994, review of *Cinder Edna,* p. 88; April 24, 1995, p. 70; April 1, 1996, review of *The Precious Gift,* p. 76; July 6, 1998, p. 62; June 25, 2001, review of *Scatterbrain Sam,* p. 71; September 22, 2003, review of *It's Back to School We Go!,* p. 106; October 27, 2003, review of

My Tour of Europe: By Teddy Roosevelt, Age Ten, p. 69; July 18, 2005, review of *Earth Mother,* p. 204; July 18, 2005, review of *Earth Mother,* p. 204.

School Library Journal, September, 1981, Pamela Warren Strebbins, review of *The Bear in the Bathtub,* p. 109; July, 1991, Marie Orlando, review of *Ants Can't Dance,* p. 58; September, 1992, Martha Topol, review of *Boris the Boring Boar,* p. 206; April, 1994, Susan Helper, review of *Cinder Edna,* p. 107; April, 1994, Kay McPherson, review of *The Winter Solstice,* pp. 138-139; May, 1995, Lauralyn Persson, review of *Brown Cow, Green Grass, Yellow Mellow Sun,* pp. 85-86; May, 1996, p. 105; June, 1997, p. 108; April, 1998, Kathleen Isaacs, review of *Here Come the Brides,* p. 118; September, 1998, Susan Knell, review of *Turn of the Century,* p. 174; November, 2000, Jody McCoy, review of *The Autumn Equinox,* p. 144; May, 2001, Patricia Manning, review of *The Summer Solstice,* p. 143; July, 2001, Beth Tegart, review of *Scatterbrain Sam,* p. 83; June, 2002, Lisa Gangemi Kropp, review of *The Spring Equinox,* p. 120; December, 2002, Ann G. Brouse, review of *Looking for Life in the Universe,* p. 162; February, 2003, Lucinda Snyder Whitehurst, review of *Sometimes Bad Things Happen,* p. 132; May, 2003, John Peters, review of *Looking for Life in the Universe,* p. 102; June, 2003, Susan Lissim, review of *My Tour of Europe,* p. 129; October, 2003, review of *Sometimes Bad Things Happen,* p. S28, and review of *Looking for Life in the Universe,* p. S47; November, 2003, Lynda Ritterman, review of *It's Back to School We Go,* p. 126; July, 2004, Lisa G. Kropp, review of *It's Back to School We Go,* p. 45; September, 2005, Susan Lissim, review of *Earth Mother,* p. 174.

Science Books and Films, March, 1994, Erik Scully, review of *The Tree of Life,* p. 47.

Voice of Youth Advocates, April, 2003, review of *Looking for Life in the Universe,* p. 77.

ONLINE

Ellen Jackson Home Page, http://www.ellenjackson.net (January 18, 2006).

*   *   *

KAHN, Katherine Janus 1942-

Personal

Born December 2, 1942, in Washington, DC; daughter of Milton Harold (a labor lawyer) and Edmina (Benish) Janus; married David Fitch Kahn (a history teacher), June 15, 1970; children: Robert Milton. *Education:* University of Chicago, A.B., 1964; attended Bezalel School of Art, 1967-68; attended Corcoran School of Art, 1968; University of Iowa, M.A., 1970; attended Montgomery College, 1985-90. *Religion:* Jewish.

Addresses

Home—4401 Ferrara Dr., Wheaton, MD 20906. *Agent*—c/o Author Mail, Kar-Ben Publishing, 11430 Strand Dr., No. 2, Rockville, MD 20852-4371. *E-mail*—dkahn@ erols.com.

Career

Painter, sculptor, illustrator, and educator. National Institutes of Health, Bethesda, MD, exhibits technician, 1962; U.S. Information Agency, Washington, DC, visual information specialist, 1964-67; Institute of Modern Languages, Washington, DC, art director, 1970-73; Maryland College of Art and Design, Silver Spring, instructor, 1986-87. Part-time and freelance positions include Center for Science in the Public Interest, illustrator, 1970-73; WETA-TV, illustrator of animated television programs, including *The Wizard of Earthsea,* 1973-76, 1985-86; WTTG-TV, courtroom illustrator, 1977-78. *Exhibitions:* Exhibitor in shows, including those sponsored by Pan American Health Organization, Washington, DC; Montgomery College, Montgomery County, MD; and Rockville Civic Mansion, Rockville, MD.

Member

Children's Book Guild, Woman's Honorary Society (University of Chicago), Nu Pi Sigma.

Awards, Honors

Golden Hugo Award, Chicago International Film Festival, 1975, for animated television program *The Wizard of Earthsea.*

Writings

SELF-ILLUSTRATED

Alef Is One: An Alphabet Counting Book, Kar-Ben Copies (Rockville, MD), 1989.

ILLUSTRATOR

Seymour Rossel, *Journey through Jewish History,* edited by Neil Kozodoy, Behrman House (New York, NY), Volume 1, 1981, Volume 2, 1983.

Miriam Schlein, *Hanukah,* Behrman House (New York, NY), 1983.

Miriam Schlein, *Passover,* Behrman House (New York, NY), 1983.

Evelyn Zusman, *The Passover Parrot,* Kar-Ben Copies (Rockville, MD), 1983.

Eileen Bluestone Sherman, *The Odd Potato,* Kar-Ben Copies (Rockville, MD), 1984.

Ruth Esrig Brinn, *More Let's Celebrate,* Kar-Ben Copies (Rockville, MD), 1984.

Howard Cushnir, *The Secret Spinner,* Kar-Ben Copies (Rockville, MD), 1985.

Erwin and Agnes Herman, *The Yanov Torah,* Kar-Ben Copies (Rockville, MD), 1985.

Carol Levin, *A Rosh Hashanah Walk,* Kar-Ben Copies (Rockville, MD), 1987.

Ellie Gellman, *Tamar's Sukkah,* Kar-Ben Copies (Rockville, MD), 1988.

Rosalind Schilder, *Dayenu; or, How Uncle Murray Saved the Seder,* Kar-Ben Copies (Rockville, MD), 1988.

My Play-a-Tune Book of Jewish Songs, JTG of Nashville (Nasville, TN), 1988.

Varda Cohen-Grauman, *Yesh Lanu Lamah,* Behrman House (New York, NY), Volume 1, 1989, Volume 2, 1993.

Shoshana Silberman, *The Whole Megilla (Almost),* Kar-Ben Copies (Rockville, MD), 1990.

Harriet K. Feder, *Judah Who Always Said, No!,* Kar-Ben Copies (Rockville, MD), 1990.

M. Lev, *The Magic Faucet,* Antroll Publishers (Burlington, VT), 1991.

Mindy Avra Portnoy, *Matzah Ball: A Passover Story,* Kar-Ben Copies (Rockville, MD), 1994.

Miriam Ramsfelder Levin, *In the Beginning,* Kar-Ben Copies (Rockville, MD), 1996.

Judyth Groner and Madeline Wikler, *Make Your Own Megallah: The Story of Purim,* Kar-Ben Copies (Rockville, MD), 1998.

Jacqueline Jules, *Once upon a Shabbos,* Kar-Ben Copies (Rockville, MD), 1998.

Judy Silverman, *Rosie and the Mole,* Pitspopany Press (New York, NY), 1999.

Judye Groner, *You Can Do a Mitzvah,* Kar-Ben Copies (Rockville, MD), 1999.

Jacqueline Jules, *The Hardest Word: A Yom Kippur Story,* Kar-Ben Copies (Rockville, MD), 2001.

Tami Lehman-Wilzig, *Tasty Bible Stories: A Menu of Tales and Matching Recipes,* Kar-Ben Publishing (Minneapolis, MN), 2003.

Jacqueline Jules, *Noah and the Ziz,* Kar-Ben Publishing (Minneapolis, MN), 2005.

Jacqueline Jules, *The Ziz and the Hanukkah Miracle,* Kar-Ben Publishing (Minneapolis, MN), 2006.

Contributor of illustrations to various periodicals, including *Defenders of Wildlife, Smithsonian,* and *Washington Post.*

BOARD BOOKS

Ellie Gellman, *It's Chanukah!,* Kar-Ben Copies (Rockville, MD), 1985.

Ellie Gellman, *It's Rosh-Hashanah!,* Kar-Ben Copies (Rockville, MD), 1985.

Myra Shostak, *Rainbow Candles: A Chanukah Counting Book,* Kar-Ben Copies (Rockville, MD), 1986.

Judye Groner and Madeline Wikler, *Let's Build a Succah,* Kar-Ben Copies (Rockville, MD), 1986.

Judye Groner and Madeline Wikler, *The Purim Parade,* Kar-Ben Copies (Rockville, MD), 1986.

Judye Groner and Madeline Wikler, *My First Seder,* Kar-Ben Copies (Rockville, MD), 1986.

Susan Remick Topek, *Israel Is . . . ,* Kar-Ben Copies (Rockville, MD), 1988.

Judye Groner and Madeline Wikler, *The Shofar Calls to Us,* Kar-Ben Copies (Rockville, MD), 1991.

"SAMMY SPIDER" SERIES

Sylvia A. Rouss, *Sammy Spider's First Hanukkah,* Kar-Ben Copies (Rockville, MD), 1993.

Sylvia A. Rouss, *Sammy Spider's First Passover,* Kar-Ben Copies (Rockville, MD), 1995.

Sylvia A. Rouss, *Sammy Spider's First Rosh Hashannah,* Kar-Ben Copies (Rockville, MD), 1996.

Sylvia A. Rouss, *Sammy Spider's First Shabbat,* Kar-Ben Copies (Rockville, MD), 1997.

Sylvia A. Rouss, *Sammy Spider's First Tu B'Shevat,* Kar-Ben Copies (Rockville, MD), 2000.

Sylvia A. Rouss, *Sammy Spider's First Purim,* Kar-Ben Copies (Rockville, MD), 2000.

Sylvia A. Rouss, *Sammy Spider's First Trip to Israel: A Book about the Five Senses,* Kar-Ben Copies (Rockville, MD), 2002.

Sylvia A. Rouss, *Sammy Spider's First Sukkot,* Kar-Ben Publishing (Minneapolis, MN), 2004.

"FAMILY SERVICE" SERIES

Shoshano Silberman, *A Family Haggadah,* Kar-Ben Copies (Rockville, MD), 1987.

Judith Z. Abrams, *Selichot: A Family Service,* Kar-Ben Copies (Rockville, MD), 1990.

Judith Z. Abrams, *Yom Kippur: A Family Service,* Kar-Ben Copies (Rockville, MD), 1990.

Judith Z. Abrams, *Shabbat: A Family Service,* Kar-Ben Copies (Rockville, MD), 1992.

Judith Z. Abrams, *Sukkot: A Family Seder,* Kar-Ben Copies (Rockville, MD), 1993.

Judith Z. Abrams, *Simchat Torah: A Family Service,* Kar-Ben Copies (Rockville, MD), 1995.

Judith Z. Abrams, *Rosh Hashanah: A Family Service,* Kar-Ben Copies (Rockville, MD), 1999.

ACTIVITY BOOKS

Hanukkah Fun for Little Hands, Kar-Ben Copies (Rockville, MD), 1991.

Passover Fun for Little Hands, Kar-Ben Copies (Rockville, MD), 1991.

Shabbat Fun for Little Hands, Kar-Ben Copies (Rockville, MD), 1992.

Ruth Esrig Brinn, with Judye Groner and Madeline Wikler, *Jewish Holiday Crafts for Little Hands,* Kar-Ben Copies (Rockville, MD), 1993.

Purim Fun for Little Hands, Kar-Ben Copies (Rockville, MD), 1994.

Sidelights

Katherine Janus Kahn is a painter, sculptor, and illustrator. Since beginning her work as an illustrator in the early 1980s, she has specialized in works focusing on Jewish culture and traditions. The picture books, board books, and activity books Kahn has created for young children include the "Sammy Spider" stories written by Sylvia A. Rouss. Beginning with *Sammy Spider's First Hanukkah* the series presents preschoolers with an engaging introduction to Jewish traditions by taking the point of view of a spider living in the Shapiro family's home. Kahn's brightly colored collage illustrations for the "Sammy Spider" series have been praised by several reviewers, a *Publishers Weekly* reviewer comparing them to the work of Eric Carle. *School Library Journal* writer Amy Kellman wrote that in *Sammy Spider's First Trip to Israel: A Book about the Five Senses* Kahn's artwork is actually "stronger than the text" of the story. Commenting on Kahn's work for *Once upon a Shabbos,* a story by Jacqueline Jules, a *Publishers Weekly* contributor noted that the illustrator's "deep-hued paintings . . . sustain the playful, warm mood of fantasy," while Kahn's work for Mindy Avra Pornoy's *Matzah Ball: A Passover Story* was described by another *Publishers Weekly* critic as "warmly colored illustrations [that] will gladden" young readers.

Kahn once told *SATA:* "In 1967 I was twenty-four years old and working in Washington, DC, for the U.S. Information Agency in their exhibits division. Although I had always loved to make art, college had awakened other interests and I really wasn't doing much art, nor had I done any to speak of in college. Although I worked with designers in my job, I was actually doing photographic research. There was a vague, unconscious need eating at me.

"There was also a desire to reconnect with my Judaism, and indeed to find out more about it. In June 1967, sudden war broke out between Israel and her neighbors. My roommate was glued to the television set, but I hadn't made the connection for myself yet. In fact, I had begun to think about the Peace Corps, which was very much a part of the thinking of young people at the time. But the connection was there, and obvious; when a friend suggested that I should go to Israel as a volunteer, it immediately struck me as being right. The war was over in an amazing six days, but it wasn't until August that the first airplanes again began flying between the United States and Israel. In those three months, I had done the necessary paper work to leave my job in Washington and become a volunteer in Israel. I was on the plane without a word of Hebrew, and with one small suitcase which held what were to be the three most significant pencils I have ever bought, one eraser, and one table of drawing paper.

"There were many volunteers on that plane, and many more already there from all over the world. I was put with other English speakers and sent down to the Negev Desert to be a part of an archeological dig. We worked out under the hot desert sun all day for a month, and we didn't find any artifacts at all, but I loved it. Months later, I spent a few days digging at the Wailing Wall in Jerusalem, and we found Roman glass and coins.

"From the Negev we were moved to a kibbutz in the Galilee, where I helped harvest olives. That was a wonderful kind of work, out in the olive orchards, with gentle breezes and the shade of the olive trees as protection from the sun. It was quiet work and we talked a great deal. And after work, I drew and drew and didn't stop drawing—not the scenery, which was beautiful, but the other volunteers—portrait after portrait.

"When we had finished the olive harvest and the grape-fruit harvest (harder, because it was already the beginning of the rainy season), they asked me if I would like to go to Bezalel, the art school in Jerusalem. I jumped at the opportunity. Jerusalem was a gorgeous, heady place to be. The city was finally united, and for the first time since 1948, Jews were allowed back into the Old City, where two mosques occupied the Temple Mount and the Wailing Wall itself. The student quarters for the school were overlooking a beautiful, but deserted, Arab village in the valley right below us. My friends and I wandered it endlessly, and I was slowly learning Hebrew. I shopped and cooked. And I was drawing and painting and sculpting. I even started illustrating for the *Volunteer.*

"To make this pivotal year complete, I met an American who was an Orthodox Jew, and he and his family took me in, teaching me the daily rituals of living as a Jew. This has informed my life from then until now. I draw most of my inspiration from the wealth of my religion, getting both subject matter and understanding from the Torah and the cycles of the Jewish year.

"I have built my life around what I learned in the year of August 1967 to August 1968."

Biographical and Critical Sources

PERIODICALS

Publishers Weekly, November 8, 1991, review of *The Shofar Calls to Us,* p. 63; September 20, 1993, review of *Sammy Spider's First Hanukkah,* p. 32; March 28, 1994, review of *Matzah Ball: A Passover Story,* p. 97; March 20, 1995, review of *Sammy Spider's First Passover,* p. 59; January 25, 1999, review of *Once upon a Shabbos,* p. 89.

School Library Journal, October, 1993, p. 47; July, 1995, Marcia W. Posner, review of *Sammy Spider's First Passover,* p. 68; May, 1997, Libby K. White, review of *Sammy Spider's First Rosh Hashanah,* p. 113; August, 2001, Martha Link, review of *Sammy Spider's First Tu B'Shevat,* p. 160; December, 2002, Amy Kellman, review of *Sammy Spider's First Trip to Israel,* p. 107.

ONLINE

JBooks.com, http://www.jbooks.com/ (January 3, 2006), Gershom Gorenberg, "Waiter, There's a Spider in My Sukkah."

Katherine Janus Kahn Home Page, http://www.katherine-januskahn.com (January 3, 2006).*

* * *

KAY, Guy Gavriel 1954-

Personal

Born November 7, 1954, in Weyburn, Saskatchewan, Canada; son of Samuel Kopple (a surgeon) and Sybil (an artist; maiden name, Birstein) Kay; married Laura Beth Cohen (a marketing consultant), July 15, 1984; children: two sons. *Education:* University of Manitoba, B.A., 1975; University of Toronto, LL.B., 1978.

Addresses

Home—Toronto, Ontario, Canada. *Agent*—c/o Author Mail, Roc Books, 375 Hudson St., New York, NY 10014.

Career

Practicing attorney, 1981-82; Canadian Broadcasting Corporation Radio, Toronto, Ontario, writer and producer in drama department, 1982-89; writer.

Member

Association of Canadian Television and Radio Artists, Law Society of Upper Canada.

Awards, Honors

Scales of Justice Award for best media treatment of a legal issue, Canadian Law Reform Commission, 1985, for *Second Time Around;* Casper Award for best speculative fiction novel in Canada, 1986, for *The Wandering Fire;* Casper Award, 1987; World Fantasy Award nominee, and Aurora Award, both 1991, both for *Tigana;* Geffen Award for translation nomination, Israeli Society for Science Fiction and Fantasy, 2005, for *The Lions of Al-Rassan;* Canadian Sunburst Award nomination, 2005, for *The Last Light of the Sun.*

Writings

FANTASY FICTION

(Editor with Christopher Tolkien) J.R.R. Tolkien, *The Silmarillion,* Houghton (Boston, MA), 1977.
Tigana, Viking (New York, NY), 1990.
A Song for Arbonne, Crown (New York, NY), 1992.
The Lions of Al-Rassan, Viking (New York, NY), 1995.
The Last Light of the Sun, Roc (New York, NY), 2004.

"FIONAVAR TAPESTRY" SERIES; FANTASY FICTION

The Summer Tree, McClelland & Stewart (Toronto, Ontario, Canada), 1984, Arbor House, 1985, reprinted, Roc (New York, NY), 2001, 20th anniversary edition, HarperPerennial Canada (Toronto, Ontario, Canada), 2004.
The Wandering Fire, McClelland & Stewart (Toronto, Ontario, Canada), 1984, Arbor House, 1986, reprinted, Roc (New York, NY), 2001, 20th anniversary edition, HarperPerennial Canada (Toronto, Ontario, Canada), 2004.
The Darkest Road, Arbor House, 1986, reprinted, Roc (New York, NY), 2001.

"SARANTINE MOSAIC" SERIES; FANTASY FICTION

Sailing to Sarantium, HarperPrism (New York, NY), 1999.
Lord of Emperors, HarperPrism (New York, NY), 2000.

OTHER

Beyond This Dark House: Poems, Penguin Canada (Toronto, Ontario, Canada), 2003.

Also author of radio drama *Second Time Around.*

Kay's novels have been translated into Swedish, Spanish, Serbian, Bulgarian, German, French, Greek, Croatian, Polish, Minumsa, and Russian.

Adaptations

The Lions of Al-Rassan was optioned for film, 2005.

Sidelights

The fantasy novels of Canadian writer Guy Gavriel Kay have become bestsellers and have won critical acclaim for their appealing protagonists, lively pacing, and deft interweaving of complex plot lines. Best known for his "Fionavar Tapestry" trilogy from the mid-1980s, Kay has progressed from the pure fantasy genre into novels such as *The Last Light of the Sun* and *Lord of Emperors,* works of fiction that mine the treasures of medieval British and European history for inspiration. "Kay creates complex psychological characters and a rich sense of ambience, place and time," declared *Washington Post Book World* writer John H. Riskind, adding that Kay's novels are "resonant and powerful, almost impossible to put down, satisfying the reader on multiple levels."

Kay was born in a small town in the prairie province of Saskatchewan in 1954, and he grew up in nearby Winnipeg, Manitoba. His father was a surgeon, and his mother an artist. Kay went on to pursue a degree in philosophy from the University of Manitoba, but his education was interrupted by a fortuitous opportunity. Through a connection to the family of the woman who had become the second wife of famed British novelist J.R.R. Tolkien, Kay was introduced to Tolkien's son, Christopher. A medievalist by profession, the elder Tolkien gained a cult following with his 1937 fantasy novel *The Hobbit,* and continued the story about the mythological Middle Earth kingdom with a trilogy of books in the 1960s known as "The Lord of the Rings." Tolkien left behind a cache of other fantasy writings when he died in 1973, and Kay, a devoted enthusiast of the Tolkien books, was invited by Christopher Tolkien to England to help assemble the materials for publication. The result was *The Silmarillion,* published in 1977 to great success; Kay and Christopher Tolkien were listed as joint editors. "The public didn't have any idea who I was, except for the dyed-in-the-wool Tolkien junkies," Kay recalled to *Maclean's* writer Ann Jansen. "But the industry did, because *The Silmarillion* was a monstrous success."

Kay went on to earn a law degree from the University of Toronto in 1978, but practiced only briefly. Instead, he found an opportune way to merge his literary ambitions with his training, taking a job with the Canadian Broadcasting Corporation (CBC) in 1982 as a writer and producer of radio and television dramas. Kay was particularly associated with the television series *The Scales of Justice,* which dramatized landmark cases in Canadian history for seven years.

When publication of *The Silmarillion* not surprisingly incited a spate of derivative fantasy novels, Kay was dismayed by the second-rate imitators of Tolkien and the other masters of the genre that he found on bookstore and library shelves. As a result, he set to work writing his own series, "The Fionavar Tapestry." Its first installment, *The Summer Tree,* was published in 1984, and like all of Kay's books it became a tremendous commercial success. The novel introduces five University of Toronto students who find themselves suddenly immersed in an entirely different realm—that of Fionavar—and realize that they must fight to save both it and themselves.

As *The Summer Tree* opens, the Canadian students have been invited to a Celtic studies conference by a reclusive academic named Lorenzo Marcus. Marcus is actually an ambassador from Fionavar who has been charged with the task of bringing representatives from other universes back to Fionavar for a royal jubilee. Thus the students find themselves in a meta-world that possesses characteristics of many other worlds and mythologies; Fionavar is the "Weaver's World" where all of these other belief systems—Celtic tenets, Norse legends, matriarchal practices—find common ground. A magical Tapestry of Life is the repository for the answers as to how and why all these philosophies are interrelated.

Each of the five Toronto students featured in Kay's series has distinctive strengths and weaknesses, and these personality traits interweave during their interactions on Fionavar as well: Dave's self-esteem has been damaged by a father who favors his brother over him; Paul is grieving the breakup with his girlfriend, who recently died in an accident; Kevin is handsome and well-liked, but realizes his world is shallow; Jennifer's heart has been saddened by the end of a relationship; and Kim is a loner. As *The Summer Tree* gets underway, the students learn that Fionavar is in grave danger: the malevolent Rakoth Maugrim, imprisoned for a thousand years, has escaped and plans to abscond with the Tapestry of Life. The group of five ally with an exiled prince to save Fionavar, and in the course of their quest discover that they each possess a special power. In the end, one has sacrificed his life, and Jennifer has been sexually assaulted by Rakoth.

Booklist reviewer Sally Estes called *The Summer Tree* "an ambitious undertaking that succeeds in itself and as a precursor of what is to come." Though the work does invoke comparisons to Tolkien's writings, in the *St. James Guide to Fantasy Writers* essayist Maureen Speller called Kay "among the foremost modern fantasy writers on the strength of the Fionavar Tapestry." Speller noted that while Kay's books and Tolkien's classic cycle share some similarities, the former "nevertheless set a new standard in what could be achieved in original fantasy writing."

The second installment of the "Fionavar Tapestry" trilogy, *The Wandering Fire,* was published in 1986. Set a year after the first novel, the book finds the students returning to Fionavar, and Jennifer is carrying Rakoth's child, which is not expected to survive. A perpetual winter has descended upon Fionovar, the curse of a wicked magician who has allied with Rakoth. However, the students have brought with them representatives from the Arthurian legends to assist them in saving the Tapestry of Life. Jennifer emerges as the Arthurian female Guinevere, and a cabal of virtuous deities help the students shatter the magic cauldron and end the world's

MASTER STORYTELLER

GUY GAVRIEL KAY

Bestselling author of *Tigana* and *A Song for Arbonne*

THE LIONS OF AL·RASSAN

In Kay's compelling fantasy, two kingdoms, one cultivating pleasure and the other hungry for power, are destined to clash as their leaders are linked through their relationships with a beautiful physician. (Cover illustration by Mel Odem.)

long winter. While one student ultimately loses his life in a sacrifice to the Mother Goddess on Midsummer's Eve, he remains a guiding spirit in the plot. *Booklist* reviewer Estes termed *The Wandering Fire* "a most satisfying sequel" and a book "rich in mythological lore."

Critics also commended Kay for creating a believable cast of innocents who, like readers, are utterly unfamiliar with the strange universe of Fionavar. His deft and full delineation of each character is considered one of the trilogy's primary strengths, and his convincing description of a complex world has won additional praise.

Kay concluded the "Fionavar Tapestry" trilogy with *The Darkest Road,* published in 1986. As it opens, spring finally arrives, but the seasonal rains bring disease. Kim persuades a nation of giants known as the Paraiko to take their side, and the armies of good arrive at Rakoth's fortress to do battle. "Even the prose weighs a ton," noted a *Kirkus Reviews* assessment of *The Darkest Road,* commenting that Kay's intricate layering of plot, action, and cast creates "a density that's often impenetrable." In the novel, Jennifer's son Darien, feeling that the pro-Fionavar forces have rejected him because of his mixed heritage, steals a dagger with magical properties and leaves home, ostensibly to fight on Rakoth's side. Darien becomes "the random thread in the Weaver's story, the one who can control many destinies by his choice," explained Penny Blubaugh in the *Voice of Youth Advocates*. "Like Tolkien, Kay recognizes that there must be sacrifice as well as a happy ending and the Fionavar trilogy is more successful than most modern fantasies for acknowledging this," observed Speller in the *St. James Guide to Fantasy Writers.*

The "Fionavar Tapestry" books were a success for Kay and were published in both English and foreign-language editions. By 1989 he had quit his job with the CBC, although he later acknowledged that his years writing radio and television dramas helped give his works the gripping pace so often cited by critics. "I proudly acknowledge my sense of the operatic and theatrical," he told Ann Jansen for *Maclean's*. "I want to give the readers that page-turning energy." Having traveled to Crete and New Zealand to write two of the "Fionavar" books, Kay now arrived in Tuscany, beginning the research for his next project, *Tigana,* which was published in 1990. Here he created another fantasy world, one that bears some resemblance to Renaissance Italy.

In the novel, Tigana is threatened by sorcerer-king Brandin, who battles to erase from history the very word "Tigana." The Mediterranean realm was once a powerful and noble kingdom, but Brandin's beloved son died in a battle against it, and he has made its destruction his revenge. After erasing its borders, he has been able to cast a spell that renders the very word Tigana unhearable. A few surviving Tiganans band together to fight him, and their lost prince, Alessan, and a troubadour named Devin also join the cause. The courtesan Dianora becomes a spy in Brandin's camp, and achieves in the end what bloodshed could not. Reviewing the novel for *Voice of Youth Advocates,* Edith S. Tyson termed *Tigana* an even more intricate creation than the "Fionavar Tapestry" trilogy. "This well crafted, fully realized mega-fantasy is designed to appeal to the fans of Tolkien and Donaldson," Tyson wrote. "It is not for casual readers or for the faint of heart."

Other reviewers found problems with Kay's post-"Fionavar" effort, and commented that the characters in *Tigana* do not emerge as clearly as the well-rounded personalities who saved Fionavar. The troubadours, outlaws, exiles, and magicians who make up the novel's large cast were faulted for being too attractive and heroic. Some critics also found that the intersection of an array of mythologies and worlds was confusing. "There is a sense that this novel was intended to be much more closely related to the Fionavar trilogy than it is now," assessed Speller in the *St. James Guide to Fantasy Writers.*

Kay returns to the Mediterranean world for his 1992 fantasy *A Song for Arbonne,* which takes place in a medieval Europe where Christianity never took hold. Arbonne is located in Provence, a region that is now part of the south of France; here, a more progressive outlook on gender issues fostered the rise of the troubadour in the twelfth century. These wandering poets/musicians sang verse in a dialect called langue d'oc, addressing romantic love, nature, and war in their songs. In Kay's novel, the most famous among them is Bertran of Arbonne. In contrast to the peace in Arbonne, the disintegrating patriarchal kingdom of Gorhaut is ruled by the brutal, corrupt King Ademar. Blaise, an honorable young man from Ademar's court, flees south to Arbonne, where he becomes a mercenary soldier in the war now raging between the two countries due to Arbonne's defense of its heretical worship of a female deity. Blaise eventually challenges Ademar for the throne.

The liberal climate and revolutionary rethinking of masculine and feminine behaviors in Provence and the Languedoc region—before they became an actual part of France—came to a repressive close with the real-life events surrounding the Albigensian Crusade. Kay's novel, however, has a more positive ending. As the author explained to Ann Jansen in *Maclean's,* "I'm basing my works on a period, but I'm not writing about that period. I reinterpret it in order to allow for some reflection on how we didn't have to end up where we are today."

A Song for Arbonne was published to positive reviews. "This panoramic, absorbing novel beautifully creates an alternate version of the medieval world," wrote a *Publishers Weekly* reviewer. Candace Smith, writing in *Booklist,* described it as a "lush, lengthy medieval saga" with a "compelling narrative," although *St. James Guide to Fantasy Writers* essayist Speller faulted *A Song for*

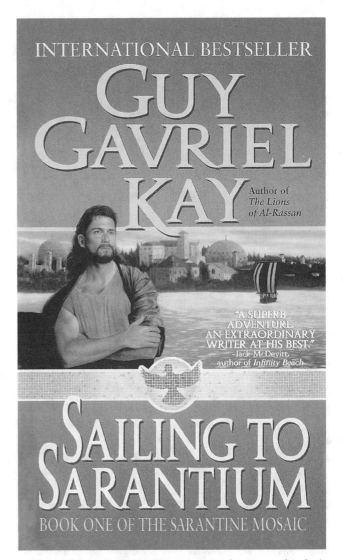

A talented artisan discovers intrigue, magic, and romance when he is summoned to the fabled city of Sarantium and confront his destiny as artisan to the Emperor Valerius. (Cover illustration by Keith Birdsong.)

Arbonne for its scope. "The novel is strong on background flavor, and many of its characters are as attractive as those in *Tigana,* but the plot might easily have been accomplished in half the pages," Speller remarked.

Kay's next novel, *The Lions of Al-Rassan,* also tackles an historically significant epoch by creating a complex series of nations and alliances under entirely fictitious names. Many critics remarked that *The Lions of Al-Rassan* recalls a period of Spanish medieval history when Christians, Moors, and Jews enjoyed a tenuous but culturally rich coexistence. The novel is set on a peninsular land called Esperana that is ruled by Asharites who had come from desert lands. As the story opens, this once-powerful group's hold on the conquered land is waning. Esperana has disintegrated into rival city-kingdoms, and a holy war against the imperialist Jaddites seems imminent. The Jaddites are led by Rodrigo Belmonte, and two other characters who play crucial roles: a female physician and a poet-courtier. The novel comes to an emotionally wrenching conclu-

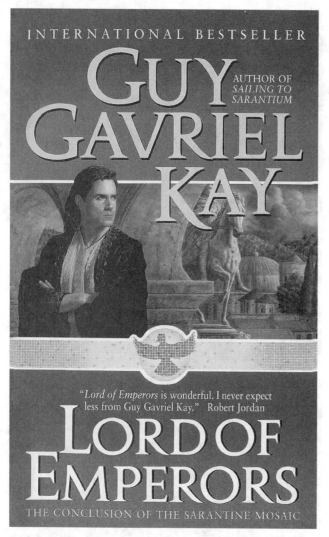

In this sequel to **The Sarantine Mosaic,** *mosaicist Crispin completes his commission for the emperor; meanwhile, conspiracies, rumors, and jealousies threaten not only the city but his homeland as well.*

sion. Margaret Miles, writing in *Voice of Youth Advocates,* called *The Lions of Al-Rassan* "yet another monumentally impressive historical novel." Kay's heroes and the wide cast of other figures "come vividly to life," Miles added, noting that the book is "set in the matrix of an equally vivid and complex society and involved in a plot as intricate and subtle as the characters themselves."

Sailing to Sarantium begins Kay's "Sarantine Mosaic" series, and also features a Mediterranean backdrop. The book's protagonist is a mosaic artisan living in Rome at the time of the Visigoths in the sixth century. The Roman Empire has fallen, and the center of power has shifted eastward to Sarantium, an ersatz Byzantine empire. The artisan, Caius Crispin, plans to travel to Sarantium's capital to work on a massive mosaic project for the city's famous church. The invitation had been extended to Crispin's mentor, Martinian, but because of his age, Martinian asked Crispin to go in his place. Since Crispin has recently lost his entire family in a plague, he accepts the mission. Before he departs, the

queen learns of his plans and she sends with Crispin a secret message to deliver to Sarantium's brutal emperor. Along the way, Crispin rescues a prostitute, and after arriving in Sarantium he becomes embroiled in local political and religious discord between the competing Blues and Greens, gangs of charioteers that rule the city. "*Sarantium* also harbors intriguing elements of magic, adding the chiaroscuro of pagan blood-worship and alchemic transmutation to this tale about a people terrified of darkness and night," observed John Burns, writing in *Quill & Quire*. A *Publishers Weekly* reviewer remarked that "Kay is at his best when describing the intertwining of art and religion or explicating the ancient craft of mosaic work."

In the concluding book in the series, *Lord of Emperors,* Crispin finds his work on the mosaic disrupted by Sarantium's political infighting. His involvement with a physician and spy from Bassania, as well as an exiled queen and others connected with the palace soon draws him into the escalating battle between the city's competing political factions. Writing in *Booklist,* Roland Green praised the novel for "fulfilling the promise of *Sailing to Sarantium* magnificently," while in *The Magazine of Fantasy and Science Fiction* Charles De Lint praised Crispin as a man with "a clever wit and a strong sense of honor." De Lint also noted that the two-book series represents a transition for Kay, because *Lord of Emperors* isn't a fantasy novel. . . . And since the entire story is set in a world that never was, it's not exactly an historical novel either." Instead, Kay creates a quasi-history that "allows him to rewrite history as we know it so that he can play out the struggle of his characters as best suits the requirements of his story," De Lint explained, adding that the novel exhibits "Kay's sheer gift with language."

Kay sets *The Last Light of the Sun* in a harsh world that melds the histories of Celts, Anglo-Saxons, and Vikings. In Kay's story, the Anglycyns and Erlings are competing island tribes. Into this world comes Bern Thorkellson, driven from his home country due to the transgressions of his father and determined to vengeance for his mis-treatment. Thorkellson leads raiding parties into to the southern lands of his new island home and becomes allied with the Erlings, whereupon Aeldred, king of the Anglycyns, musters forces to stop him. Praising the novel as a "wonderfully imaginative historical fantasy," a *Publishers Weekly* reviewer added that Kay's novel contains several plot threads that "come together to weave a dazzling tapestry of conjoined fates." In *Booklist,* Freida Murray noted that the novel "poses intriguing historical riddles" regarding the ancient British and Welsh history it draws on, while a *Library Bookwatch* contributor deemed it a "compelling fantasy saga."

Regarding his chosen genre, Kay told a *Locus* interviewer: "I'm beginning to see fantasy as a way of looking at history, as an antidote to what they call 'faction'—fiction using real people, real lives, and

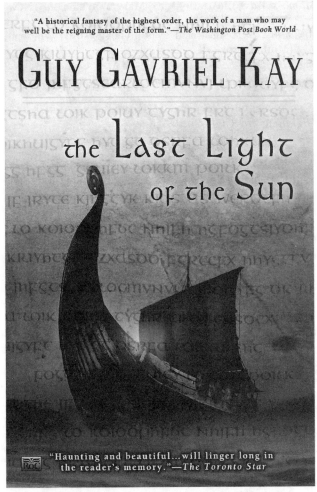

"A historical fantasy of the highest order, the work of a man who may well be the reigning master of the form."—*The Washington Post Book World*

GUY GAVRIEL KAY

the Last Light of the Sun

"Haunting and beautiful...will linger long in the reader's memory."—*The Toronto Star*

Kay continues to spin historical fantasy with this 2004 novel, which draws readers back in time to the brutal world inhabited by Beowulf and Grendel. (Cover illustration by Mel Odem.)

embedding them in narrative." "In *Sailing to Sarantium* and *Lord of Emperors*," he explained, "the reign of Justinian and Theodora, with Count Belisarius and the eunuch Narses, is clearly my source, but I'm saying right from the beginning that this is not even pretending to know what the real people were like. It's a fantasy on themes."

Kay's novels usually take up to a year to research, and another year to write. Creating entirely fictional characters who participate in actual historic events and sometimes even alter their outcome has allowed his creativity to flourish and gained him a committed readership among both fantasy and history buffs. "I lack the utter autonomy some writers have," Kay told a writer for *Maclean's.* "I don't want to write on the back of a real person. That smacks of hubris."

Biographical and Critical Sources

BOOKS

St. James Guide to Fantasy Writers, St. James Press (Detroit, MI), 1996, pp. 318-319.

PERIODICALS

Booklist, September 1, 1985, Sally Estes, review of *The Summer Tree,* p. 4; May 15, 1986, Sally Estes, review of *The Wandering Fire,* p. 1361; January 15, 1993, Candace Smith, review of *A Song for Arbonne,* p. 878; January 1, 1999, p. 842; March 15, 2000, review of *Lord of Emperors,* p. 1335; March 1, 2004, Freida Murray, review of *The Last Light of the Sun,* p. 1146.

Fantasy Review, January, 1985; December, 1986.

Financial Post, July 8, 1995, Shlomo Schwartzberg, review of *The Lions of Al-Rassan,* p. 23.

Globe and Mail (Toronto, Ontario, Canada), February 9, 1985; June 28, 1986; September 8, 1990.

Kirkus Reviews, May 15, 1986, p. 752; October 1, 1986, review of *The Darkest Road,* p. 1475.

Kliatt, July, 2005, Lesley Farmer, review of *The Last Light of the Sun,* p. 30.

Library Bookwatch, May, 2005, review of *The Last Light of the Sun.*

Library Journal, October 15, 1985, p. 104; November 15, 1986, p. 112; August, 1990, p. 147; December, 1998, p. 161; March 15, 2004, Jackie Cassada, review of *The Last Light of the Sun,* p. 110.

Locus, June, 1990; September, 1992; November, 1992; May, 2000, "Guy Gavriel Kay: Lord of Fantasy," pp. 6-7, 63-64; April, 2005, interview with Kay.

Maclean's, March 23, 1987; December 14, 1992, Ann Jansen, "Castles in the Air: Guy Gavriel Kay Mixes History and Fantasy"; July 1, 1995; October 26, 1998, "Playing Fast and Fun with Past Events," p. 82; April 3, 2000, Brian Bethune, "The Man Who Sailed to an Alternate Byzantium," p. 58.

Magazine of Fantasy and Science Fiction, December, 1995; October, 2000, Charles De Lint, review of *The Lord of Emperors,* p. 39; January, 2004, Charles De Lint, review of *Beyond This House,* p. 25.

New Statesman, November 28, 1986.

Publishers Weekly, May 16, 1986, pp. 72-73; October 10, 1986, p. 81; November 23, 1992, review of *A Song for Arbonne,* pp. 56-57; February 8, 1999, review of *Sailing to Sarantium,* p. 199; February 9, 2004, review of *The Last Light of the Sun,* p. 62.

Quill & Quire, May, 1995, p. 33; October, 1998, John Burns, review of *Sailing to Sarantium,* p. 35.

Time International, March 13, 2000, Katherine Govier, "Fantastic Voyager," p. 54.

Voice of Youth Advocates, December, 1986, p. 237; April, 1987, Penny Blubaugh, review of *The Darkest Road,* p. 38; April, 1991, Edith S. Tyson, review of *Tigana,* p. 44; October, 1995, Margaret Miles, review of *The Lions of Al-Rassan,* p. 234.

Washington Post Book World, July 28, 1996, John H. Riskind, review of *The Lions of Al-Rassan,* p. 8.

ONLINE

Guy Gavriel Kay Home Page, http://www.brightweavings. com (January 3, 2006).

January Online, http://www.januarymagazine.com/ (January 3, 2006), Lincoln Cho, "Fantastic Journey," review of *The Last Light of the Sun.**

KETTEMAN, Helen 1945-

Personal

Born July 1, 1945, in Augusta, GA; daughter of Jack (a physician) and Mary Helen (a teacher; maiden name, Walker) Moon; married Charles Harry Ketteman, Jr. (an accountant), 1969; children: William Gregory, Mark David. *Education:* Young Harris College, A.A., 1965; attended Georgia Southern College, 1965-66; Georgia State University, B.A., 1968.

Addresses

Home—Dallas, TX. *Agent*—Ginger Knowlton, Curtis Brown Ltd., 10 Astor Pl., New York, NY 10003.

Career

Writer.

Awards, Honors

Best Books of the Year listee, *Boston Globe,* 1995, for *Luck with Potatoes;* Pick of the Lists designation, American Booksellers Association, 1998, for *I Remember Papa;* Georgia Children's Book Award for Picture Storybook nomination, 2002-03, for *Armadillo Tattletale. Bubba, the Cowboy Prince* has been named to the reading award lists in seven states.

Writings

Not Yet, Yvette, illustrated by Irene Trivas, Albert Whitman (Morton Grove, IL), 1992.
Aunt Hilarity's Bustle, illustrated by James Warhola, Simon & Schuster (New York, NY), 1992.
The Year of No More Corn, illustrated by Robert Andrew Parker, Orchard Books (New York, NY), 1993.
One Baby Boy: A Counting Book, illustrated by Maggie Flynn-Staton, Simon & Schuster (New York, NY), 1994.
The Christmas Blizzard, illustrated by James Warhola, Scholastic (New York, NY), 1995.
Luck with Potatoes, illustrated by Brian Floca, Orchard Books (New York, NY), 1995.
Grandma's Cat, illustrated by Marsha Lynn Winborn, Houghton Mifflin (Boston, MA), 1996.
Bubba, the Cowboy Prince: A Fractured Texas Tale, illustrated by James Warhola, Scholastic (New York, NY), 1997.
Heat Wave, illustrated by Scott Goto, Walker (New York, NY), 1998.
I Remember Papa, illustrated by Greg Shed, Dial (New York, NY), 1998.
Shoeshine Whittaker, illustrated by Scott Goto, Walker (New York, NY), 1999.
Armadillo Tattletale, illustrated by Keith Graves, Scholastic (New York, NY), 2000.

Mama's Way, illustrations by Mary Whyte, Dial (New York, NY), 2001.
Armadilly Chili, illustrated by Will Terry, Albert Whitman (Morton Grove, IL), 2004.
The Great Cake Bake, illustrated by Matt Collins, Walker (New York, NY), 2005.

Also contributor to periodicals, including *Spider* and *Highlights for Children.*

Sidelights

Picture-book author Helen Ketteman is known for spinning tall tales and introducing rambunctious protagonists. She weaves stories out of droughts and blizzards, out of bustles and a cowboy prince closely resembling Cinderella. Many of her stories, which include *The Christmas Blizzard, Mama's Way,* and *The Year of No More Corn,* reflect a nostalgia for bygone days and are rich with the sights and sounds of rural America. Reviewing *Mama's Way,* a story about a single, hardworking mother who, despite the lack of money, manages to make her sixth-grade daughter's dream come true, was praised by *Booklist* reviewer Shelley Townsend Hudson as a "celebration of old-fashioned values," while in *Publishers Weekly* a reviewer noted that Ketteman "ably outlines both the friction and the underlying love between mother and daughter."

Ketteman's first book, *Not Yet, Yvette,* tells of a girl who waits impatiently while she and her dad busily prepare a surprise birthday party for her mother. Together this African-American father and daughter vacuum, dust, and bake. Excited by the preparations, young Yvette must repeatedly be cautioned by her father that it is not yet time for the celebration. "In this homey picture book, excitement and anticipation run high for a girl and her father," according to a reviewer in *Publishers Weekly,* the critic adding: "It would be hard to find more likable party givers . . . who aptly illustrate just how much fun giving can be." *Booklist* contributor Carolyn Phelan predicted that the book "will appeal to any child old enough to enjoy secrets and surprises," while a *Kirkus Reviews* contributor noted that the "simple story is deftly conveyed in natural-sounding dialogue," and with its accompanying illustrations by Irene Trivas, "nicely reflect[s] this black family's warm pleasure in each other's company."

Fashion foibles are put on display in *Aunt Hilarity's Bustle,* a "funny story about a heroine with plenty of spark," according to Michelle M. Strazer writing in *School Library Journal.* Unable to find a high-fashion bustle in the backwater town of Willow Flats, Aunt Hilarity determines to make one herself. Her initial creation, made out of a hay-filled grain sack, has fleas; when she uses paint rags as stuffing for a bustle, these scraps of cloth quickly catch fire when Aunt Hilarity backs too close to a candle flame. A bystander spills a glass of punch onto her bustled backside to extinguish the flames, but unfortunately much of the punch drenches Mrs. Anna Belle Prather, precipitating a food fight of gargantuan proportions. Finally a chicken-wire frame provides support for the dress Hilarity wears to a Christmas party, but when the wire begins to unravel, the woman is forced to don the Christmas tree. *Aunt Hilarity's Bustle* "is bound to be a winner with the pre-school set and with early readers," commented *Booklist* reviewer Sheilamae O'Hara.

Beanie and his grandfather are at opposite ends of the age cycle in *The Year of No More Corn*. Neither can help out with the corn planting on the family farm this year: one is too young and the other too old. Instead, Old Grampa tells Beanie of the dreadful year 1928 when local farmers had to plant and replant their corn crop because of weather conditions, and Old Grampa himself finally resorted to planting corn kernels carved out of wood. He grew a forest of corncob-bearing trees from such ingenuity and saved the day. *Booklist* reviewer Phelan applauded Ketteman's wild tall tale, noting that, "with its well-written text and accessible story and art-work, [*The Year of No More Corn*] . . . be a good choice to read aloud, even to somewhat older children studying tall tales." A *Publishers Weekly* reviewer commented that "Ketteman spins her tall tale in a pleasingly folksy deadpan style, her vivid descriptions bringing the old man's outrageous account to life until the reader, like Beanie, would like nothing better than to believe every word." A *Kirkus Reviews* critic concluded that *The Year of No More Corn* is a "lively, likable tall tale."

The Yuletide season is at the center of Ketteman's *The Christmas Blizzard*, a "tale taller than the Empire State Building," according to a reviewer for *School Library Journal*. The winter of 1922 saw weather so crazy, according to Maynard Jenkins, that the North Pole became a slush pond and Santa had to pull up stakes and set up shop at narrator Maynard's hometown of Lizzard, Indiana. Although cold, there was no snow in Lizzard, until a visit to a local weather spell-caster made the suitable climactic corrections. "This is a fun-filled story with more hyperbole than a Christmas turkey has stuffing," a critic wrote in the *School Library Journal*. "Ketteman's rollicking original tall tale has a true Christmasy flavor," noted a reviewer for *Publishers Weekly*, while Kay Weisman commented in *Booklist* that the book is an "appealing choice for holiday read-alouds or for older children learning to write their own tall tales."

The weather once more goes haywire when a passing heat wave gets snagged on a weather vane at a Kansas farm in Ketteman's *Heat Wave*. In fact, it gets so hot on the farm that the corn in the fields starts popping and the cattle are almost cooked. Finally it is left to the young girl of the farm—who has repeatedly been told that girls cannot farm—to save the family by planting iceberg lettuce to cool things off. A critic writing in *Publishers Weekly* called *Heat Wave* a "rollicking original tall tale that would do Paul Bunyan proud." Lee Bock, in a *School Library Journal* review, also praised

A big-eared armadillo who enjoys passing along everything he hears learns a lesson in discretion in Ketteman's humorous picture book **Armadillo Tattletale.** *(Illustration by Keith Graves.)*

Ketteman's "rollicking American tall tale," noting that while "things go from bad to worse," "younger children will enjoy the prescribed exaggeration and silliness, and older children might well be encouraged to create their own."

Farming again provides a venue for a tall tale in *Luck with Potatoes*, in which giant potatoes pop out of the earth at a farm where there was never any luck before. One huge potato fills the bed of the farmer's pick-up truck, and several cause earthquakes as they grow. In fact, the tubers are so big that the farmer, Clemmon Hardigree, starts cutting them into planks to sell to the local lumber company. "Ketteman has a firm grasp on the humor and stylistic elements of the tall tale," noted Janice Del Negro in a *Booklist* review. "Her narrative voice is bemused yet down-to-earth, retaining its laconic style even as the situation becomes more and more outlandish." *Horn Book* contributor Ann A. Flowers called Ketteman's creation a "cheerful story," while Virginia Opocensky, writing in *School Library Journal*, cautioned young readers: "Don't miss the fun!"

In one of her most popular books, Ketteman revises the famous Cinderella fairy tale; in *Bubba, the Cowboy Prince* a Texas cowboy serves as something of a Cinderella stand-in. The Prince Charming of the story—or rather *Princess* Charming—is Miz Lurleen, a rich and feisty young cowgirl who decides it is time to find a husband and throws a ball in order to do so. The fairy godmother's role is taken over by a cow. Poor Bubba is overworked and under-appreciated by his step-dad and no-account stepbrothers, Milton and Dwayne, but manages, Cinderella-like, to attend Lurleen's ball courtesy of his fairy godcow. "Ketteman wisely leaves the [Cinderella] plot unchanged," noted Lauren Peterson in *Booklist,* "but the story has a distinct western flair and a humorous tall-tale feel." A *Kirkus Reviews* contributor remarked that this "Cinderella parody features the off-the-wall, whang-dang Texas hyperbole of Ketteman," while a *Publishers Weekly* critic joined in the linguistic fun: "Rustler lingo and illustrations chock-ablock with Texas kitsch make this ranch-spun Cinder-fella a knee-slappin' tale. . . . Just the ticket for buckaroos lookin' fer a good read."

An armadillo is at the heart of both *Armadillo Tattletale* and *Armadilly Chili* In *Armadillo Tattletale,* the creature's habit of eavesdropping and then spreading gossip makes Armadillo persona non grata with the other animals, until they finally find a way to cure him of the bad habit of listening in on private conversations. In *Armadilly Chili* Miss Billy Armadilly decides to mix up some of her special-recipe chili for a passel of friends, but when she passes out a list of ingredients—beetles, a peck of hot peppers, and even a piece of prickly pear cactus—excuses abound. In *Booklist* Julie Cummins described *Armadilly Chili* as "a surefire hit for the lap-sit crowd," while a *Kirkus Reviews* writer noted that Ketteman's "is a tale guaranteed to warm the bones on a cold night."

More mischief is served up in *The Great Cake Bake,* as well as in Ketteman's counting book *One Baby Boy,* in which the baby in question performs a series of rather naughty deeds that introduce, in rhyme, the numbers from one to ten. In *The Great Cake Bake* a young woman with more imagination than cooking skill is nonetheless determined to win the local July 4th cake-baking contest. With the town mayor as her judge, she tries several ill-conceived cakes, and when contest-day

Determined to win Mayor Fargenberg's July 4th bake-off, Donna Rae becomes frustrated after her patriotic-themed confection falls flat in **The Great Cake Bake.** *(Illustration by Matt Collins.)*

arrives, the disaster her cake causes is balanced by the announcement that she will become a judge from now on. Dubbing the story a "lightly amusing tale," *Booklist* reviewer GraceAnne A. DeCandido called special attention to illustrator Matt Collins's use of "vivid colors" in his "hyperrealistic" art.

In *Grandma's Cat,* a book written from a child's point of view, a little girl visiting her grandmother tries to make a friend of an aloof cat. The girl has no idea how to go about her task; she makes the cat hiss and spit at her by treating it roughly and pulling its tail. Finally the kindly grandmother intervenes, showing her granddaughter how to befriend the animal. "The story will appeal to the many children whose ideas of befriending animals work better in their dreams than in reality," commented *Booklist* reviewer Phelan, the critic adding that "the story reads aloud well, making this a good choice for storytime." Christina Linz, writing in *School Library Journal,* noted that *Grandma's Cat* "is delightfully told in brief, rhymed sentences that make a charming group or individual read-aloud, yet are simple enough for beginning readers to try on their own." A reviewer for *Publishers Weekly* felt that "Ketteman delivers a full roller coaster of emotion with an economy of words." The same reviewer went on: "Her rhythmic, rhyming (mostly) couplets speak to every child who has tried desperately to express fondness for a pet."

Another family story forms the core of *I Remember Papa,* featuring young Audie who has saved his allowance for months in hopes of buying a baseball mitt. He gets his chance one Saturday when he and his dad take the morning train to Cincinnati to see a Reds game. While shopping before gametime, Audie finds the perfect baseball glove, while his dad finds a pair of new work boots, and plans to return to the store and purchase them after the game. When Audie loses his money in the stands, his dad sacrifices his new boots to buy his son the prized mitt. Christine A. Moesch called *I Remember Papa* a "warm story set in the past" in a *School Library Journal* review, and also noted that the story "is warm without being treacly." *Booklist* contributor Weisman felt that "baseball fans will appreciate this rich family story," while a *Kirkus Reviews* critic concluded that "the theme at the center of the story is the hallowed relationship between father and son in a bygone era, fondly remembered."

The rag-snapping hero of *Shoeshine Whittaker* discovers the town of Mudville and thinks he has found the perfect place to ply his trade. But freshly shined boots are quick to lose their luster on the soggy streets of this aptly named town, and Shoeshine's satisfaction guarantee soon gets him into trouble. Quick thinking and a creative solution save the day, however. "Ketteman's colorful yarn is all twang and swagger, sheer catnip to read-aloud enthusiasts," declared a *Publishers Weekly* reviewer.

Ketteman once told *SATA:* "I believe children should be exposed to books early and often. If children learn at an

A boy who dreams of playing baseball finds that the values of hard work and sacrifice instilled by a loving parent help him attain his goal in I Remember Papa. *(Illustration by Greg Shed.)*

early age that books can be fun and entertaining, I think the battle with television and video games can be won. Readers that are created early will be lifelong readers."

Biographical and Critical Sources

PERIODICALS

Booklist, February 15, 1993, Sheilamae O'Hara, review of *Aunt Hilarity's Bustle,* p. 1067; September 15, 1993, Carolyn Phelan, review of *The Year of No More Corn,* p. 158; September 15, 1995, Kay Weisman, review of *The Christmas Blizzard,* p. 170; October 1, 1995, Janice Del Negro, review of *Luck with Potatoes,* p. 326; April 1, 1996, Carolyn Phelan, review of *Grandma's Cat,* p. 1372; December 1, 1997, Lauren Peterson, review of *Bubba, the Cowboy Prince,* p. 641; February 1, 1998, p. 922; March 15, 1998, Kay Weisman, review of *I Remember Papa,* p. 1249; December 15, 2000, Kelly Milner Halls, review of *Armadillo Tattletale,* p. 827; February 15, 2001, Shelley Townsend Hudson, review of *Mama's Way,* p. 1140; June 1, 2004, Julie Cummins, review of *Armadilly Chili,* p. 1742; June 1, 2005, GraceAnne A. DeCandido, review of *The Great Cake Bake,* p. 1821.
Bulletin of the Center for Children's Books, June, 1992, p. 265; September, 1993, p. 14; December, 1997, p. 131; November, 2000, review of *Armadillo Tattletale,* p. 108.

Horn Book, January-February, 1996, Ann A. Flowers, review of *Luck with Potatoes,* pp. 64-65.

Kirkus Reviews, February 1, 1992, review of *Not Yet, Yvette,* p. 186; August 1, 1993, review of *The Year of No More Corn,* p. 1003; November 1, 1997, review of *Bubba, the Cowboy Prince,* p. 1646; December 1, 1997, p. 1776; January 15, 1998, review of *I Remember Papa,* p. 114; February 15, 2004, review of *Armadilly Chili,* p. 180.

Magpies, September, 1993, p. 29.

New York Times Book Review, November 29, 1992, p. 34; August 25, 1996, p. 23.

Publishers Weekly, February 24, 1992, review of *Not Yet, Yvette,* p. 53; March 15, 1992, Carolyn Phelan, review of *Not Yet, Yvette,* p. 1388; July 26, 1993, review of *The Year of No More Corn,* p. 70; May 30, 1994, p. 54; September 18, 1995, review of *The Christmas Blizzard,* p. 100; April 15, 1996, review of *Grandma's Cat,* p. 67; November 17, 1997, review of *Bubba, the Cowboy Prince,* p. 61; December 15, 1997, review of *Heat Wave,* p. 58; November 15, 1999, review of *Shoeshine Whittaker,* p. 66; January 29, 2001, review of *Mama's Way,* p. 89.

Reading Today, August, 2001, Lynne T. Burke, review of *Mama's Way,* p. 30.

School Library Journal, May, 1992, p. 90; February, 1993, Michelle M. Strazer, review of *Aunt Hilarity's Bustle,* pp. 72-73; October, 1995, review of *The Christmas Blizzard,* p. 38, and Virginia Opocensky, review of *Luck with Potatoes,* p. 105; May, 1996, Christina Linz, review of *Grandma's Cat,* p. 93; March, 1998, Lee Bock, review of *Heat Wave,* p. 182; June, 1998, Christine A. Moesch, review of *I Remember Papa,* p. 112; March, 2001, Rosalyn Pierini, review of *Mama's Way,* p. 214; May, 2004, Mary Elam, review of *Armadilly Chili,* p. 133; May, 2005, Linda M. Kenton, review of *The Great Cake Bake,* p. 86.*

*   *   *

KINSEY-WARNOCK, Natalie 1956-

Personal

Born November 2, 1956, in Newport, VT; daughter of Frederick (a farmer) and Louise (Rowell) Kinsey; married Tom Warnock (a teacher), May 8, 1976. *Education:* Johnson State College, B.A. (art and athletic training), 1978. *Religion:* Presbyterian. *Hobbies and other interests:* Running, cross-country skiing, windsurfing, rollerblading, kayaking, rock climbing, hiking, bird watching, painting, playing bagpipes and fiddle, rescuing abused animals, traveling with family in Scotland.

Addresses

Home—3590 Country Rd., Barton, VT 05822. *Agent*—Gina Maccoby Agency, P.O. Box 60, Chappaqua, NY 10514.

Career

Writer. University of Vermont Extension Service, Newport, energy auditor, 1980-85; Craftsbury Sports Center,

Natalie Kinsey-Warnock

Craftsbury, VT, elderhostel director and cross-country ski instructor, 1987-91. Albany Library trustee, 1988-90; leader of East Craftsbury Recreation Program, 1983-2000; elder of East Craftsbury Presbyterian Church, 1989—. Member, Catamount Pipe Band, 1999—

Awards, Honors

American Library Association Notable Book citation, 1989, New York Library's 100 Best Books citation, 1989, and Joan Fassler Memorial Book Award, Association for Children's Health, 1991, all for *The Canada Geese Quilt;* American Booksellers Pick-of-the-List citation, 1991, for *The Night the Bells Rang; The Wild Horses of Sweetbriar* and *The Night the Bells Rang* selected as Children's Books of the Year by Bank Street College; Children's Choice Award, International Reading Association/Children's Book Council, 1993, for *The Bear That Heard Crying; Smithsonian* Notable Books for Children Award, 1996, for *The Fiddler of the Northern Lights,* and 1997, for *The Summer of Stanley*; Award for Children's Books, New England Booksellers Association; Vermont Humanities Council Vermont Reads selection, 2006, for *As Long as There Are Mountains.*.

Writings

CHAPTER BOOKS

The Canada Geese Quilt, illustrated by Leslie W. Bowman, Cobblehill Books (New York, NY), 1989.

The Night the Bells Rang, illustrated by Leslie W. Bowman, Cobblehill Books (New York, NY), 1991.

Sweet Memories Still, illustrated by Laurie Harden, Cobblehill Books (New York, NY), 1997.

As Long as There Are Mountains, Cobblehill Books (New York, NY), 1997.

In the Language of Loons, Cobblehill Books (New York, NY), 1998.

If Wishes Were Horses, Dutton (New York, NY), 2000.

What Emma Remembers, illustrated by Kathleen Kolb, Cobblehill Books (New York, NY), 2001.

A Farm of Her Own, illustrated by Kathleen Kolb, Dutton (New York, NY), 2001.

Lumber Camp Library, illustrated by James Bernardin, HarperCollins (New York, NY), 2002.

A Doctor like Papa, illustrated by James Bernardin, HarperCollins (New York, NY), 2002.

Gifts from the Sea, illustrated by Judy Pedersen, Knopf (New York, NY), 2003.

PICTURE BOOKS

The Wild Horses of Sweetbriar, illustrated by Ted Rand, Cobblehill Books (New York, NY), 1990.

Wilderness Cat, illustrated by Mark Graham, Cobblehill Books (New York, NY), 1992.

When Spring Comes, illustrated by Stacey Schuett, Dutton (New York, NY), 1993.

The Bear That Heard Crying, illustrated by Ted Rand, Cobblehill Books (New York, NY), 1993.

On a Starry Night, illustrated by David McPhail, Orchard Books (New York, NY), 1994.

The Fiddler of the Northern Lights, illustrated by Leslie W. Bowman, Cobblehill Books (New York, NY), 1996.

The Summer of Stanley, illustrated by Donald Gates, Cobblehill Books (New York, NY), 1997.

From Dawn till Dusk, illustrated by Mary Azarian, Houghton Mifflin (Boston, MA), 2002.

A Christmas like Helen's, illustrated by Mary Azarian, Houghton Mifflin (Boston, MA), 2004.

Nora's Ark, illustrated by Emily Arnold McCully, HarperCollins (New York, NY), 2005.

Adaptations

The Canada Geese Quilt was adapted for audio cassette, Recorded Books, 1998.

Sidelights

Natalie Kinsey-Warnock was born, raised, and still lives in Vermont, a fact that is reflected in almost all of her picture books and juvenile novels. Kinsey-Warnock tells warm stories of rural families and country home truths, coming-of-age tales, and epiphanies that involve the natural world and the close and loving sphere of families and best friends. In novels such as *The Canada Geese Quilt, The Night the Bells Rang, Sweet Memories Still,* and the heavily autobiographical *As Long as There Are Mountains,* the Vermont writer places stories in history and near-history, recreating the flavor of bygone times and scenes. Her picture books, such as *The Wild Horses of Sweetbriar, Wilderness Cat, When Spring Comes, The Bear That Heard Crying,* and *The Summer of Stanley,* often feature animals in realistic ways, another favorite Kinsey-Warnock motif.

"My Scottish ancestors settled here in the Northeast Kingdom of Vermont almost two hundred years ago," Kinsey-Warnock once told *SATA.* "It is this land that they settled—where I grew up and still live—that means so much to me and provides the setting for almost all of my stories. I feel a part of this hill country and I'm grateful to the legacy these ancestors passed down. I grew up on a dairy farm, along with a sister and three

Feeling overlooked in favor of her older sister, Lily holds out hope of having a horse to love, but when tragedy strikes her family she is forced to let even that dream go in Kinsey-Warnock's highly praised novel. (Cover illustration by James Yamasaki.)

brothers. This fostered a strong connection to the land, a sense of nurturing and caring for the earth. My father was a baseball and track star before he became a farmer and passed on both his love of sports and of history to us, while my mother, a former teacher, instilled in us her insatiable appetite for books and words. It is because of her that my brother Leland and I are writers."

Kinsey-Warnock married while still in college and then went on to graduate from Johnson State College with a B.A. in both art and athletic training, twin passions. She held various jobs, including a position as a cross-country ski instructor, until the time she penned her first children's book and decided that she had finally found her career. "My first children's book, *The Canada Geese Quilt*, grew out of my love and admiration for my grandmother and a special quilt we made together. My grandmother began quilting when she was in her sixties, and over the next fifteen years she made 250 quilts. I designed about twenty of the quilts, most of them of birds, wild flowers, and starry skies, including one of Canada geese which inspired the book. My grandmother died in February, 1991, at age eighty-nine."

The Canada Geese Quilt tells the story of ten-year-old Ariel, who loves the Vermont farm where she lives with her parents and grandmother. Ariel is fearful that her life will change for the worse when a new baby is born and her grandmother then suffers a stroke and seems unable to recover. Finally, Ariel combines her grandmother's skill at quilt-making and her artistic abilities to make a very special quilt, crafting a gift for the new baby that also makes her grandmother want to join the living once again. As a *Publishers Weekly* reviewer wrote, "In one gorgeous, slim volume, Kinsey-Warnock tells a story of a particular time, from spring to fall, in a 10-year-old's life. . . . Kinsey-Warnock's language is simple and direct as it conveys both the loving relationship between the old woman and the girl, and the girl's love of the land." An American Library Association Notable Book, *The Canada Geese Quilt* set Kinsey-Warnock's career off on the right foot.

"Many of my books come from family stories," Kinsey-Warnock once told *SATA*. "My sister Helen is the family genealogist, and I have often joined her in reading town histories and walking old cemeteries. Most of my stories take place before I was born; I enjoy putting my characters into time periods I'm interested in. I guess I feel that in some small way I get to live in that time period, at least while I'm writing the story."

With *The Night the Bells Rang*, Kinsey-Warnock pushes the clocks back to 1918, and a nation that still views World War I as a European war. For young Mason, who lives on a farm in rural Vermont, the war is closer to home in the shape of an older bully, Aden Cutler. Mason wishes for Aden's death, and gets his wish when Aden enlists and goes to war, never to return. Thereafter, Mason must deal with his guilt feelings over this incident, as well as come to terms with his younger

In **Lumber Camp Library** *an orphaned girl resigned to giving up her dreams of an education to care for her younger siblings finds new hope in an unlikely friendship. (Illustration by James Bernardin.)*

brother. *Horn Book* critic Ellen Fader, in her review of *The Night the Bells Rang*, called attention to details of farm life, such as maple sugaring and birthing a foal, which "realistically evoke life in another time and place." Fader concluded, "This quiet, affecting coming-of-age story, marked by its fluid, graceful prose, is a natural for reading aloud in classrooms."

Kinsey-Warnock returns to an intergenerational theme with a grandmother who figures prominently in *Sweet Memories Still*. In this chapter book, Shelby is initially put off by having to spend time with her ailing grandmother, but gradually understands that the older woman has much to teach her. Her grandmother's gift to her on her birthday, an old box camera, does little to cement Shelby's love for the woman, but ultimately the camera becomes a metaphor for the stories of her childhood that Grandmother shares with Shelby. *Booklist* reviewer Carolyn Phelan felt that while its author tries to take on too much for a chapter book, the story is "written with skill and sensitivity" and "the narrative is more vivid than many longer novels written for children." A *Publishers Weekly* critic noted that Kinsey-Warnock "continues to show a gentle touch in peeling back the small layers of life to reveal simple epiphanies."

"*As Long as There Are Mountains* is my longest and most autobiographical book," Kinsey-Warnock explained. "It centers on twelve-year-old Iris Anderson and her family on their northern Vermont farm in 1956. Her father wants to pass on the farm to Iris's brother, who wants to be a writer instead. Then her father loses his leg, and the farm must be sold unless her brother can be persuaded to give up his dream and come home." Reviewing the novel in *Booklist,* Hazel Rochman concluded: "Most moving is Iris' quiet, lyrical, first-person narrative, which expresses her closeness to the land and her sense of freedom in taking care of a farm." Writing in *School Library Journal,* Carol Schene remarked that the novel "is a powerful and beautifully written story of love and determination set during the 1950s." As Schene went on to note, Kinsey-Warnock "masterfully captures the gamut of Iris's feelings from passion for the land and compassion for a classmate whose family is homeless." A *Kirkus Reviews* contributor commented that "the profound pleasure of living on a farm . . . pervades this story of a Vermont farm family."

The summer of 1969 is the setting for 1998's *In the Language of Loons,* the story of young Arlis, who spends the months with his grandparents in Vermont and learns some home truths about responsibility that he takes back home with him in the fall. Arlis's grandfather teaches the boy about nature and also encourages his participation in cross-country running. "This is a touching and poignant story of a boy starting on his journey to manhood," reflected Arwen Marshall in a *School Library Journal* review. "The emotions and relationships are the true driving force of this story, and they are timeless."

Kinsey-Warnock's chapter book *If Wishes Were Horses* is set in an earlier period of American history: the Great Depression of the 1930s. Lily's greatest desire is to have a horse, but due to her sister Emily's illness, all of the family's money goes into keeping Emily well. As Emily's condition worsens, however, Lily has to decide whether to put her own desires or her family first. Gillian Engberg, writing in *Booklist,* considered the writing in the novel to be uneven, noting that readers find "beautifully articulated scenes alternating with melodrama." While *School Library Journal* reviewer Corrine Camarata noted that the plot lacks "subtlety," "the first-person narrative flows gracefully between the present and the recent past." Camarata also complimented the growth Lily experiences in the book, ultimately becoming more caring toward others. Family is also the focus of *A Farm of Her Own.* Emma, a ten-year-old girl, spends a summer with her aunt and uncle on their farm, which she grows to love. Although her aunt and uncle cannot keep the farm and eventually have to sell it, when Emma grows up she is able to buy the property back for her family. Lee Bock, writing for *School Library Journal,* found the novel's text "is poetic, rhythmically listing joyous details" of life on the farm and the people in Emma's life. *Booklist* reviewer Denise Wilms considered the tale a "sweet, sturdy story."

Lumber Camp Library, A Doctor like Papa, and *Gifts from the Sea* all feature girls growing up to make choices that turn them from children into responsible young women. In *Lumber Camp Library,* set in the early 1900s, Ruby longs to be a teacher, but when her father, a lumberjack, is killed in an accident, Ruby has to stay home and help take care of the family. At the lumber camp, however, she discovers she can be true to her calling by teaching the lumberjacks to learn how to read. "This spare and moving chapter book will hold readers from the first page," assured Kristen Oravec in her *School Library Journal* review.

Despite the winter months of snow and slush and the summers full of hard work, life on a northern New England farm yields magical moments, as Kinsey-Warnock shows in **From Dawn till Dusk.** *(Illustration by Mary Azarian.)*

A Vermont native, Kinsey-Warnock mines her state's history during the tragic flood of 1927 in spinning the hopeful story **Nora's Ark.** *(Illustration by Emily Arnold McCully.)*

In *A Doctor like Papa,* set in 1918, Margaret wants to become a doctor, even though she is told that being a doctor is not a woman's job. In spite of this, she accompanies her father, a doctor, and acts as his assistant. When she finds a child alone after his family has all died from the flu, it takes all of her skills to keep the child from dying, too. "Young readers will be engrossed," promised a *Kirkus Reviews* contributor. JoAnn Jonas, in *School Library Journal,* commented: "Good suspense and believable characters are the hallmarks of this short but well-written story." Based on a true story, *Gifts from the Sea* is also set in the early 1900s. It tells the story of Quila, whose family keeps a lighthouse on an island. When Quila's mother dies, she and her father have difficulty coming to terms with their loss, until a new baby washes up on their island, bound between two mattresses, and helps the grieving process. But when a woman claiming to be the child's aunt shows up, Quila tries something desperate to keep her family together. A *Publishers Weekly* contributor felt that readers will identify with "Quila's sturdy independence and resilience," and commented on the author's "emphasis on warmth and family."

"My interests are varied—athletics, nature, art and writing—but all of them are rooted to this area where I live," Kinsey-Warnock once told *SATA.* "Sports are an integral part of my life: I run five to ten miles each morning, cross-country ski, mountain bike, roller blade, swim, play tennis, and I played field hockey all across the country for thirteen years. I love the outdoors, and study and sketch birds and wild flowers, which are most often the subjects of my watercolor paintings. . . . My husband, Tom, . . . shares my love of the land, sports and animals; we have three horses, seven dogs and seven cats. I always wished I could open a shelter for animals—and I guess I have!"

Many of Kinsey-Warnock's picture books for children display this love for animals. *The Wild Horses of Sweetbriar* recounts the severe winter of 1903 during which a young girl lives on a small island with her father, who works for the Coast Guard. They share the island with ten wild horses, and the young girl feeds these horses when the cold becomes such that the animals cannot find feed. "Kinsey-Warnock's appealing, poetic text is a stirring account of the struggle between people and the forces of nature," declared a reviewer for *Publishers Weekly.*

A heroic cat follows the family that left it from Vermont to Canada in *Wilderness Cat,* a true family story set in the late 1700s. "A fine book for cat lovers," wrote *Horn Book* contributor Ann A. Flowers. In *When Spring Comes* a little girl and her dog gaze out the window at early spring in Vermont, imagining the many activities of the season: maple sugaring, planting, witnessing the return of the Canada geese. This picture book is a "convincing portrait of a close-knit farm family living decades ago," *Booklist* contributor Deborah Abbott wrote.

"*The Bear That Heard Crying,* is a collaboration between my sister and me and is the true story of our great-great-great-great-aunt Sarah Whitcher," Kinsey-Warnock once explained to *SATA.* "In 1783, when she was three years old, she was lost in the woods for four days and was found and protected by a bear." The 1993 tale was dubbed "an unusually appealing slice of Americana" by a *Kirkus Reviews* critic. "Plainly told, this sturdy tale exudes comfort," concluded a reviewer for *Publishers Weekly.* Another animal figures in *The Summer of Stanley:* a troublesome goat that comes to the rescue.

Overcoming a child's fear of the dark and a love of fanciful stories form the storylines of *On a Starry Night* and *The Fiddler of the Northern Lights* respectively. Of the former title, Shirley Wilton wrote in *School Library Journal* that the book is "a gentle story that celebrates a family's enveloping warmth." Quebec is the setting for *The Fiddler of the Northern Lights,* in which a grandfather's stories of the mythical fiddler entertain eight-year-old Henry. Kinsey-Warnock's tale of the Aurora Borealis "delivers the anticipated magic," according to a *Publishers Weekly* reviewer.

Kinsey-Warnock and Mary Azarian team up for a pair of picture books about Vermont country life: *From Dawn till Dusk* and *A Christmas like Helen's.* In *From Dawn till Dusk* a group of siblings talk about the tasks they undertake from season to season, such as sugaring, finding new kittens, or helping neighbors get their tractors unstuck from the mud. Kinsey-Warnock and Azarian "remain on this side of nostalgia by grounding the story in . . . specific details," commented a *Publishers Weekly* contributor. "It should be eye-opening to readers for whom life on the farm is quite different" from their own lives, commented Margaret Bush in *School Library Journal.* Commenting on the narrative pattern showing both the chores the children complete and the rewards for getting them done, *Booklist* contributor Ilene Cooper noted that "the author's memories are not idealized," but are grounded in real life. *A Christmas like Helen's* focuses on Christmas traditions of a young girl growing up in Vermont in the days before cars and electricity reached the area. "The language is lovely," praised Ilene Cooper for *Booklist,* the critic concluding that the book is "warm and welcoming." A *Kirkus Reviews* contributor cited the author for her "poetic, understated text."

Nora's Ark relates another Vermont tale; set in 1927, the picture book tells how Wren and her family take in many of their neighbors and local livestock during the flood of 1927. Before the flood, Wren's grandmother felt that the new house on the hill was a luxury she did not need—but it proved to be the only house to stay clear of the water, Wren's grandmother came to appreciate her home. A *Kirkus Reviews* contributor called the tale "a well-told adventure," while a *Publishers Weekly* reviewer noted that Kinsey-Warnock "blends history, drama, and good old-fashioned storytelling in a picture book that makes these true events relevant to young readers." In *School Library Journal,* Kathy Piehl wrote that *Nora's Ark* "offers reassurance that lives can be rebuilt with the support of family and friends."

While Kinsey-Warnock takes inspiration from her native Vermont and from the world of nature surrounding her, she blends these elements with small and touching stories that reflect individual human truths. She once concluded for *SATA:* "I've had such strong role models in my life—especially strong, enduring women have influenced me: women like my grandmother, Helen Urie Rowell, my great-aunt Ada Urie (who was featured in a book titled *Enduring Women* by Diane Koos Gentry), and down to my mother. I want my books to portray strong female characters, and I hope they honor these women."

Biographical and Critical Sources

PERIODICALS

Booklist, August, 1992, p. 2018; March 1, 1993, Deborah Abbott, review of *When Spring Comes,* p. 1236; August, 1993, p. 2070; November 15, 1996, p. 594; February 15, 1997, Carolyn Phelan, review of *Sweet Memories Still,* p. 1023; August, 1997, Hazel Rochman, review of *As Long as There Are Mountains,* p. 1901; November 15, 2000, Gillian Engberg, review of *If Wishes Were Horses,* p. 642; July, 2001, Denise Wilms, review of *A Farm of Her Own,* p. 2019; April 1, 2002, Julie Cummins, review of *A Doctor like Papa,* p. 1328; April 15, 2002, Kay Weisman, review of *Lumber Camp Library,* p. 1401; November 15, 2002, Ilene Cooper, review of *From Dawn till Dusk,* p. 602; June 1, 2003, Kathleen Odean, review of *Gifts from the Sea,* p. 1777; October 15, 2004, Ilene Cooper, review of *A Christmas like Helen's,* p. 405.

Horn Book, January-February, 1992, Ellen Fader, review of *The Night the Bells Rang,* pp. 71-72; March-April, 1993, Ann A. Flowers, review of *Wilderness Cat,*

p. 197; July-August, 1994, p. 441; November-December, 1998, p. 766; July-August, 2005, Robin Smith, review of *Nora's Ark,* p. 452.

Kirkus Reviews, August 1, 1993, review of *The Bear That Heard Crying,* p. 1003; November 15, 1996, pp. 1670-1671; May 1, 1997, p. 723; June 1, 1997, review of *As Long as There Are Mountains,* p. 875; December 1, 1997, pp. 1776-1777; April 15, 2002, reviews of *Lumber Camp Library* and *A Doctor like Papa,* p. 572; September 1, 2002, review of *From Dawn till Dusk,* p. 1312; June 1, 2003, review of *Gifts from the Sea,* p. 806; November 1, 2004, review of *A Christmas like Helen's,* p. 1051; June 15, 2005, review of *Nora's Ark,* p. 684.

Publishers Weekly, July 28, 1989, review of *The Canada Geese Quilt,* p. 222; October 26, 1990, review of *The Wild Horses of Sweetbriar,* p. 67; October 12, 1992, p. 78; February 1, 1993, p. 95; September 6, 1993, review of *The Bear That Heard Crying,* p. 95; February 21, 1994, p. 252; November 11, 1996, review of *The Fiddler of the Northern Lights,* p. 74; December 30, 1996, review of *Sweet Memories Still,* p. 67; April 21, 1997, p. 71; September 2, 2002, review of *From Dawn till Dusk,* p. 76; May 12, 2003, review of *Gifts from the Sea,* p. 68; September 27, 2004, review of *A Christmas like Helen's,* p. 61; August 29, 2005, review of *Nora's Ark,* p. 55.

School Library Journal, February, 1992, p. 86; October, 1992, p. 90; April, 1993, p. 98; May, 1994, Shirley Wilton, review of *On a Starry Night,* p. 96; November, 1996, p. 87; June, 1997, p. 94; August, 1997, Carol Schene, review of *As Long as There Are Mountains,* p. 157; November, 1998, Stephanie Bange, review of *The Canada Geese Quilt,* p. 69; March, 1998, Arwen Marshall, review of *In the Language of Loons,* p. 214; December, 2000, Corrine Camarata, review of *If Wishes Were Horses,* p. 146; June, 2001, Lee Bock, review of *A Farm of Her Own,* p. 122; May, 2002, Kristen Oravec, review of *Lumber Camp Library,* p. 118; July, 2002, JoAnn Jonas, review of *A Doctor like Papa,* p. 94; October, 2002, Margaret Bush, review of *From Dawn till Dusk,* p. 115; June, 2003, review of *Gifts from the Sea,* p. 144; September, 2005, Kathy Piehl, review of *Nora's Ark,* p. 175.

ONLINE

Natalie Kinsey-Warnock Home Page, http://www.kinsey-warnock.com (January 22, 2006).

*   *   *

KIRK, Connie Ann 1957-

Personal

Born February 14, 1957, in Wellsville, NY; daughter of Leonard A. and Mary Arlene Lewis; married Kenneth A. Kirk, 1983; children: Benjamin, Johnathan. *Ethnicity:* "Irish American and Native American (Seneca)."

Education: Binghamton University, B.A., 1985, M.A. (English and creative writing), 1988, Ph.D. (English), 2004.

Addresses

Office—P.O. Box 337, Painted Post, NY 14870. *E-mail*—connieannkirk@hotmail.com.

Career

Mansfield University, Mansfield, PA, adjunct professor of English, 1988—.

Member

Modern Language Association, American Literature Association, Emily Dickinson International Society, Society of Children's Book Writers and Illustrators.

Awards, Honors

Everett Helm fellowship, University of Indiana—Bloomington, 2003; Mark Twain research fellowship, Center for Mark Twain Studies at Elmira College, 2003;

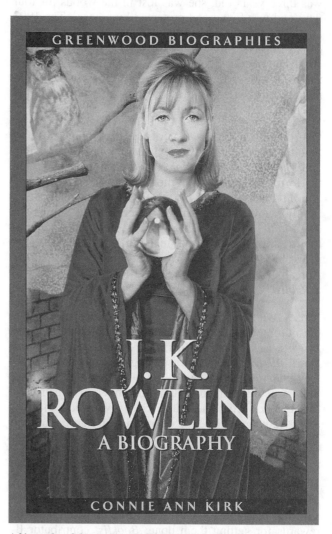

A biography of the popular British author who penned the "Harry Potter" novels is one of Kirk's nonfiction books for younger readers. (Cover image by Rafael Fuchs.)

Ezra Jack Keats/deGrummond children's literature research fellowship, University of Mississippi, 2004; Kerlan grant, University of Minnesota—Minneapolis, 2004.

Writings

FOR CHILDREN

Sky Dancers (picture book), illustrated by Christy Hale, Lee & Low (New York, NY), 2004.

NONFICTION

The Mohawks of North America ("First Peoples" series), Lerner (Minneapolis, MN), 2002.

J.K. Rowling: A Biography, Greenwood Press (Westport, CT), 2003.

Emily Dickinson: A Biography, Greenwood Press (Westport, CT), 2004.

Mark Twain: A Biography, Greenwood Press (Westport, CT), 2004.

Sylvia Plath: A Biography, Greenwood Press (Westport, CT), 2004.

A Student's Guide to Robert Frost, Enslow Publishers (Berkeley Heights, NJ), 2005.

Companion to American Children's Picture Books, Greenwood Press (Westport, CT), 2005.

Work in Progress

Emily Dickinson and Children, for University Press of New England; research on American literature and culture, children's literature, and Emily Dickinson.

Sidelights

In addition to teaching English on the college level, Connie Ann Kirk is the author of several literary biographies as well as the picture book *Sky Dancer.* Her book *J.K. Rowling: A Biography* was praised by *School Library Journal* contributor Kathleen Simonetta, who wrote that the volume's "scholarly writing style" and discussion of the literary analysis of Rowling's "Harry Potter" novels would be useful to high-school students.

In *Sky Dancers* Kirk tells a story about a young Mohawk boy whose father and uncle are steel-workers helping to build New York City's Empire State Building during the 1930s. One of many Native Americans hired to work on the structural steel beams high in the sky, John Cloud's brave father inspires his young son to conquer his own fear of heights. A *Kirkus Reviews* writer praised Kirk's detailed research into relevant Native-American culture and called the book a "true-to-life portrait of [Mohawk] family life and traditions," while in *Booklist* Jennifer Mattson noted that *Sky Dancers* "will work nicely to extend children's understanding of Native American traditions."

Awed by his father and grandfather's ability to walk along steel beams while working atop one of New York City's giant skyscrapers, a young Mohawk boy also tales pride in his family's special gift to the growing city in Sky Dancers. *(Illustration by Christy Hale.)*

Kirk told *SATA:* "I started out writing fiction in college and am somewhat surprised to find that most of my currently published books are nonfiction. However, I do love research, so I am pleased to be doing scholarly work—at least for now.

"I expect that eventually the lure of characters, narrative, and language will draw me back to fiction. I have always seen myself as a novelist. I think it is the novelist in me that provides the curiosity about people as well as the narrative technique necessary to write biography. If each piece of writing is a journey, then a writing career is also a journey, where the scenery changes from time to time."

Biographical and Critical Sources

PERIODICALS

Booklist, November 15, 2004, Jennifer Mattson, review of *Sky Dancers,* p. 590.

Kirkus Reviews, October 15, 2004, review of *Sky Dancers,* p. 1009.

School Library Journal, August, 2003, Kathleen Simonetta, review of *J.K. Rowling: A Biography,* p. 179;

January, 2005, Kathy Krasniewicz, review of *Sky Dancers*, p. 94.

Voice of Youth Advocates, February, 2004, Roxy Ekstrom, review of *J.K. Rowling,* p. 516.

ONLINE

Connie Ann Kirk Home Page, http://www.connieannkirk. com (January 5, 2006).

* * *

KORMAN, Gordon 1963-
(Gordon Richard Korman)

Personal

Born October 23, 1963, in Montreal, Quebec, Canada; son of C.I. (an accountant) and Bernice (a journalist; maiden name, Silverman) Korman; married; children: two sons, one daughter. Avocation: Music, travel, sports. *Education:* New York University, B.F.A., 1985.

Addresses

Agent—c/o Author Mail, Scholastic, Inc., 555 Broadway, New York, NY 10012.

Career

Writer, 1975—.

Member

Writers Union of Canada, Canadian Society of Children's Authors, Illustrators, and Performers, Society of Children's Book Writers.

Writings

"BRUNO & BOOTS" SERIES

This Can't Be Happening at Macdonald Hall!, illustrated by Affie Mohammed, Scholastic (New York, NY), 1977.

Go Jump in the Pool!, illustrated by Lea Daniel, Scholastic (New York, NY), 1979.

Beware the Fish!, illustrated by Lea Daniel, Scholastic (New York, NY), 1980, reprinted, Scholastic Canada (Markham, Ontario, Canada), 2003.

The War with Mr. Wizzle, Scholastic (New York, NY), 1982, published as *The Wizzle War,* Scholastic Canada (Markham, Ontario, Canada), 2003.

The Zucchini Warriors, Scholastic (New York, NY), 1988, reprinted, Scholastic Canada (Markham, Ontario, Canada), 2004.

Macdonald Hall Goes Hollywood, Scholastic (New York, NY), 1991, published as *Lights, Camera, Disaster!,* Scholastic Canada (Markham, Ontario, Canada), 2004.

Something Fishy at Macdonald Hall, Scholastic (New York, NY), 1995, published as *The Joke's on Us,* Scholastic Canada (Toronto, Ontario, Canada), 2004.

"MONDAY NIGHT FOOTBALL CLUB" SERIES

Quarterback Exchange: I Was John Elway, Hyperion (New York, NY), 1997.

Running Back Conversion: I Was Barry Sanders, Hyperion (New York, NY),1997.

The Super Bowl Switch: I Was Dan Marino, Hyperion (New York, NY), 1997.

Heavy Artillery: I Was Junior Seau, Hyperion (New York, NY), 1997.

Ultimate Scoring Machine: I Was Jerry Rice, Hyperion (New York, NY), 1998.

(With James Buckley, Jr. and Brian C. Peterson) *NFL Rules: Bloopers, Pranks, Upsets, and Touchdowns,* Hyperion (New York, NY), 1998.

"NOSE PICKERS" SERIES

Nose Pickers from Outer Space!, illustrated by Victor Vaccaro, Hyperion (New York, NY), 1999.

Planet of the Nose Pickers, illustrated by Victor Vaccaro, Hyperion (New York, NY), 2000.

Your Mummy Is a Nose Picker, illustrated by Victor Vaccaro, Hyperion (New York, NY), 2000.

Invasion of the Nose Pickers, illustrated by Victor Vaccaro, Hyperion (New York, NY), 2001.

The Ultimate Nose-Picker Collection, Hyperion (New York, NY), 2006.

"SLAPSHOTS" SERIES

Stars from Mars, Scholastic (New York, NY),1999.

All-Mars All-Stars, Scholastic (New York, NY), 1999.

The Face-Off Phony, Scholastic (New York, NY), 2000.

Cup Crazy, Scholastic (New York, NY), 2000.

"ISLAND" TRILOGY

Shipwreck, Scholastic (New York, NY), 2001.

Survival, Scholastic (New York, NY), 2001.

Escape, Scholastic (New York, NY), 2001.

Island Trilogy (contains *Shipwreck, Survival,* and *Escape*), Scholastic (New York, NY), 2005.

"DIVE" TRILOGY

The Discovery, Scholastic (New York, NY), 2003.

The Deep, Scholastic (New York, NY), 2003.

The Danger, Scholastic (New York, NY), 2003.

"ON THE RUN" SERIES

Chasing the Falconers, Scholastic (New York, NY), 2005.

The Fugitive Factor, Scholastic (New York, NY), 2006.

Now You See Them, Now You Don't, Scholastic (New York, NY), 2006.

The Stowaway Solution, Scholastic (New York, NY), 2006.

Public Enemies, Scholastic (New York, NY), 2006.

Hunting the Hunter, Scholastic (New York, NY), 2006.

OTHER

Who Is Bugs Potter?, Scholastic (New York, NY), 1980.

I Want to Go Home!, Scholastic (New York, NY), 1981, reprinted, Scholastic Canada (Markham, Ontario, Canada), 2004.

Our Man Weston, Scholastic (New York, NY), 1982.

Bugs Potter: Live at Nickaninny, Scholastic (New York, NY), 1983.

No Coins, Please, Scholastic (New York, NY), 1984, reprinted, Scholastic Canada (Markham, Ontario, Canada), 2005.

Don't Care High, Scholastic (New York, NY), 1985.

Son of Interflux, Scholastic (New York, NY), 1986.

A Semester in the Life of a Garbage Bag, Scholastic (New York, NY), 1987.

Radio Fifth Grade, Scholastic (New York, NY), 1989.

Losing Joe's Place, Scholastic (New York, NY), 1990.

(With Bernice Korman) *The D-minus Poems of Jeremy Bloom,* Scholastic (New York, NY), 1992.

The Twinkie Squad, Scholastic (New York, NY), 1992.

Why Did the Underwear Cross the Road?, Scholastic (New York, NY), 1994.

The Chicken Doesn't Skate, Scholastic (New York, NY), 1996.

The Last-Place Sports Poems of Jeremy Bloom, Scholastic (New York, NY), 1996.

Liar, Liar, Pants on Fire!, illustrated by JoAnn Adinolflt, Scholastic (New York, NY), 1997.

The Sixth-Grade Nickname Game, Scholastic Canada (Toronto, Ontario, Canada), 1998.

No More Dead Dogs, Hyperion (New York, NY), 2000.

Son of the Mob, Scholastic Canada (Markham, Ontario, Canada), 2002.

Maxx Comedy: The Funniest Kid in America, Hyperion (New York, NY), 2003.

Jake Reinvented, Hyperion (New York, NY), 2003.

Son of the Mob: Hollywood Hustle, Hyperion (New York, NY), 2003.

Born to Rock, Hyperion (New York, NY), 2006.

Short stories have appeared in anthologies and magazines, including *From One Experience to Another,* edited by Dr. M. Jerry Wiess and Helen S. Weiss, 1997; *Connections,* edited by Donald R. Gallo, 1989, and *SCOPE* magazine. Creative developer, "Mad Science" series.

Korman's books have been translated into French, Japanese, Dutch, Italian, Spanish, Portuguese, Swedish, Danish, Norwegian, and Chinese.

Adaptations

The "Monday Night Football Club" series has been adapted for the Disney Channel TV series, *The Jersey.*

Work in Progress

"Kidnapped," a trilogy featuring the "On the Run" characters Aiden and Meg; *Schooled,* a YA novel.

Sidelights

Since publishing his first book when he was only fourteen years old, Canadian author Gordon Korman has written dozens of novels for children and young adults. Korman's trademark storylines—featuring slapstick humor, madcap adventures, and high-spirited, rebellious characters—have helped make him a favorite author of school-age readers—particularly boys—across Canada and the United States. The novels in Korman's "Bruno & Boots" series "revolve around the frustrations of rambunctious boys forced to submit to stuffy academic authorities," noted Leslie Bennetts in the *New York Times,* and feature two recurring characters "who are roommates, best friends and incorrigible troublemakers." Korman, whose books have sold millions of copies, strives to write stories that provide a healthy dose of humor for his young readers. "My books are the kind of stories I wanted to read and couldn't find when I was ten, eleven, and twelve," he once remarked. "I think that, no matter what the subject matter, kids' concerns are important, and being a kid isn't just waiting out the time between birth and the age of majority. I hope other kids see that in my work." Other book series by Korman include "Slap Shots," "Nose Pickers," and "On the Run."

Korman was born in 1963 in Montreal, Quebec, where his father worked as an accountant and his mother wrote an "Erma Bombeck-type column" for a local newspaper, as he told Bennetts. In elementary and middle school Korman was always fond of writing—especially his own brand of zany stories and scenarios. "I wasn't a big reader for some reason," he remarked to Chris Ferns in *Canadian Children's Literature.* "But I always tried to put in creativity where I could: if we had (to write) a sentence with all the spelling words for that week, I would try to come up with the stupidest sentences, or the funniest sentences, or the craziest sentences I could think of."

Korman's writing career began at the age of twelve with a story assignment for his seventh-grade English class. "The big movies at the time were 'Jaws' and 'Airplane,' and everyone decided they were going to write action stories," he told Bennetts. "It was my mother who brought me down to earth. She told me to write about something a little closer to home." Korman created the characters Boots and Bruno, whose escapades create havoc in their small private school, Macdonald Hall. "I got kind of carried away . . . and I accidentally wrote the first book," he told Ferns. "The characters sort of became real people to me, and they more or less wrote the book for me. The class had to read all the assignments at the end of the whole business, and a lot of people were coming to me and saying how they really liked it. I suppose anyone who writes

120 pages for class is going to attract a certain amount of attention anyway—and I just got the idea of seeing if I could get the book published." Korman sent his manuscript to the publisher Scholastic Canada, and two years later, at the age of fourteen, witnessed the publication of both his first book and first best seller, *This Can't Be Happening at Macdonald Hall!*.

After his initial success, Korman published books at the rate of one per year, writing them during summers when he was on vacation from school. At age eighteen he was voted the Most Promising Writer under Thirty-five by the Canadian Author's Association, and he became a popular author on school and reading tours across Canada and the United States. Adding six more titles to his "Bruno and Boots" series, he has also created several other popular series, including "Monday Night Football Club," "Slapshots," and the "Island" trilogy.

Korman has also created memorable characters in humorous standalone novels: Bugs Potter, a rock-and-roll drummer who lives for his music, is the star of *Bugs Potter: Live at Nickaninny;* Simon Irving, the hero of *Son of Interflux,* organizes a middle-school campaign to save school land from being purchased by his father's

Aiden and Meg Falconer must find a way to escape from a juvenile detention facility in order to help their parents avoid an injust prison sentence in Korman's fast-paced YA adventure. (Cover design by Tim Hall.)

corporation; Artie, in *No Coins, Please,* pulls off scams for money whenever his summer-camp group visits the city; and an eleven year old on the fast-track to a career as a stand-up comic is the focus of *Maxx Comedy: The Funniest Kid in America.* While Korman's characters display a healthy disrespect for authority, part of their wider appeal is that they respect the line between disrespect and anarchy. "I was writing at the time of 'Animal House,' and things like that," he explained to Ferns. "I think one of the things which makes the books fairly strong, so that they defy being compared to things like that, is that they don't cross that line. Considering how crazy the books are, I keep a firm foot in reality."

Zany humor is a staple in most of Korman's work, as seen in his "Nose Pickers" series. These books feature residents of the planet Pan. The Pants, as they are called, have developed sophisticated digitally activated computer systems implanted in their noses—which serve as the basis for much gross-out humor. *Booklist* reviewer Karen Hutt found *Nose Pickers from Outer Space!* filled with "slapstick humor" and "frenzied action." A *Publishers Weekly* contributor enjoyed the book's "fast-fire . . . wordplay and amusingly preposterous plot," and commended it as a "light and silly caper that will . . . bring on ample laughs."

Serious challenges and a more serious tone imbue the books in Korman's "Island" trilogy, an adventure series. In these novels, six troubled teenagers are enrolled in an Outward Bound-type program that requires them to spend a few weeks at sea together in a small sailboat. The titles of the novels—*Shipwreck, Survival,* and *Escape*—suggest the adventures that await this unusual crew as they deal with treacherous weather, the death of their captain, and other serious challenges.

Chasing the Falconers is the first volume in Korman's "On the Run" series, which focuses on a brother and sister who find themselves pursued by FBI agents after their psychologist parents are apprehended and accused of being spies. Escaping from a juvenile detention facility during a fire, Aiden and Meg Falconer make the journey from Nebraska to Vermont, hoping to track down a man they know only as "Uncle Frank," who they believe will help them prove their parents' innocence. The series continues in *The Fugitive Factor.* Calling the novel "fast-paced" and "action-packed," *School Library Journal* reviewer Connie Tyrrell Burns wrote that *Chasing the Falconers* is "appropriate for reluctant readers and those addicted to television action shows." As Korman noted on his home page, the tension in the projected six-part series comes from the fact that "when you're a fugitive, the entire world becomes dangerous for you. In a way, it's scarier than an eighteen-foot shark."

In addition to humor and fast pace, Korman attributes one reason for his books' popularity to the fact that he portrays characters achieving power and success in an adult world. "Whatever an adult can do, somewhere in the world there's one sixteen year old who can do it as well," he commented to Ferns. "The problem is with the age level where kids are starting to be able to do things, but it still seems unnatural. And I think that's one of the reasons why books do well in that age bracket, which they're not really supposed to because of their presentation—because they address that situation of kids being able to triumph over the adults, and in many cases with the adults coming to terms with it."

Biographical and Critical Sources

BOOKS

Authors and Artists for Young Adults, Volume 10, Thomson Gale (Detroit, MI), 1993.

Children's Literature Review, Volume 25, Thomson Gale (Detroit, MI), 1991.

St. James Guide to Children's Writers, 5th edition, edited by Sara Pendergast and Tom Pendergast, St. James Press (Detroit, MI), 1999.

PERIODICALS

Booklist, November 15, 1996, Bill Ott, review of *The Chicken Doesn't Skate,* p. 588; October 15, 1998, Carolyn Phelan, review of *The Sixth-Grade Nickname Game,* p. 422; August 19, 1999, Karen Hutt, review of *Nose Pickers from Outer Space!,* p. 2058.

Bulletin of the Center for Children's Books, November, 1985; December, 1985; November, 1986; November, 1992, p. 77; November, 1998, Janice M. Del Negro, review of *The Sixth-Grade Nickname Game,* p. 103.

Canadian Children's Literature, number 38, 1985, Chris Ferns, interview with Korman, pp. 54-65; number 52, 1988, Chris Ferns, "Escape from New Jersey," pp. 63-64.

Canadian Statesman, January 23, 1980.

Globe and Mail (Toronto, Ontario, Canada), June 28, 1980; November 18, 1980; October 19, 1985; December 2, 1989.

Horn Book, March-April, 1986; November-December, 1987; November-December 1997, Nancy C. Hammond, review of *Liar, Liar, Pants on Fire!,* p. 724.

Jam, spring, 1981.

Journal of Commonwealth Literature, February, 1982.

Kirkus Reviews, June 1, 1997, p. 876.

New York Times, July 24, 1985, Leslie Bennetts, "Gordon Korman: Old-Pro Author of 10 Books at 21," section 3, p. 17.

Publishers Weekly, June 30, 1989, review of *Radio Fifth Grade,* p. 106; March 15, 1991, review of *Macdonald Hall Goes Hollywood,* p. 59; July 26, 1993, review of *The Toilet Paper Tigers,* p. 73; August 2, 1999, review of *Nose Pickers from Outer Space!,* p. 85; June 16, 2003, review of *Maxx Comedy: The Funniest Kid in America,* p. 71.

Quill & Quire, November, 1983, Peter Carver, "From the Gripping Yarn to the Gaping Yawn," p. 24; October, 1994, Phyllis Simon, review of *Why Did the Underwear Cross the Road?,* p. 44; August, 1995, Dave Jenkinson, review of *Something Fishy at Macdonald Hall,* p. 34; January, 1999, Sheree Haughian, review of *The Sixth-Grade Nickname Game,* p. 46.

School Library Journal, September, 1989, Todd Morning, review of *Radio Fifth Grade,* p. 252; May, 1990, Jack Forman, review of *Losing Joe's Place,* p. 124; January, 1995, Suzanne Hawley, review of *Why Did the Underwear Cross the Road?,* p. 108; September, 1995, Connie Tyrrell Burns, review of *Something Fishy at Macdonald Hall,* p. 202; November, 1996, Burns, review of *The Chicken Doesn't Skate,* pp. 107-108; September 1997, Robin L. Gibson, review of *Liar, Liar, Pants on Fire!,* p. 724; January, 2000, Elaine E. Knight, review of *Nose Pickers from Outer Space!,* p. 106; April, 2001, Anne Connor, review of *Your Mummy Is a Nose Picker,* p. 114; June, 2005, Steven Engelfried, review of *No More Dead Dogs,* p. 57; August, 2005, Connie Tyrell Burns, review of *Chasing the Falconers,* p. 129.

Toronto Star, July 29, 1978; December 14, 1982.

Voice of Youth Advocates, June, 1990, Shirley Carmony, review of *Losing Joe's Place,* p. 106; December, 1992, Patsy H. Adams, review of *The Twinkie Squad,* p. 281.

ONLINE

Gordon Korman Home Page, http://www.gordonkorman.com (January 3, 2006).

*   *   *

KORMAN, Gordon Richard
See KORMAN, Gordon

L-M

LLOYD, David
    See LLOYD, David T.

*   *   *

LLOYD, David T. 1954-
  (David Lloyd)

Personal

Born February 25, 1954, in Utica, NY; son of Richard Glynne (a minister) and Mair Elvira (Thomas) Lloyd; married Kim G. Waale (a sculptor and professor), June 15, 1990; children: Nia Mair Waale. *Education:* St. Lawrence University, B.A., 1975; University of Vermont, M.A., 1978; Brown University, M.A. (creative writing) and Ph.D., 1985.

Addresses

Office—English Department, Le Moyne College, Syracuse, NY 13214. *E-mail*—Lloyd@lemoyne.edu.

Career

Le Moyne College, Syracuse, NY, 1985—, assistant professor, associate professor, then professor of English and director of creative-writing program, Rev. Francis J. Fallon, SJ, professor, 1999-2001, Rev. Kevin G. O'Connell, SJ, professor in the humanities, 2005-08; freelance writer. Poet-in-residence, Constance Saltonstall Foundation for the Arts, Ithaca, NY, 2001, and Anderson Center for Interdisciplinary Studies, 2002.

Awards, Honors

Scholar of the Year, Le Moyne University, 1995; New York State Foundation for the Arts/Upper Catskill Community Council of the Arts stipend, 2000, 2002, 2004; first prize, TallGrass Anthology Contest, 2000, for poems "Expedition" and "Creatures within Give Advice";

David T. Lloyd

Robert H. Winner Memorial Award, Poetry Society of America, 2000, and first place in tradition verse category, Oregon State Poetry Association, 2001, both for "Sestinas for the Everyday Apocalypse"; Fulbright Distinguished Scholar Award, 2000-01; Pushcart Award nomination, 2001, for story "As Always, Jason"; Maryland State Poetry & Literary Society chapbook contest winter, 2002, for *The Everyday Apocalypse;* New American Press poetry book contest winner, 2003, for *The Gospel according to Frank.*

Writings

(Editor) *The Urgency of Identity: Contemporary English-Language Poetry from Wales,* TriQuarterly Books (Evanston, IL), 1994.

Writing on the Edge: Interviews with Writers and Editors of Wales, Rodopi (Atlanta, GA), 1997.

The Everyday Apocalypse (poetry), Three Conditions Press (Baltimore, MD), 2002.

The Gospel according to Frank (poetry), New American Press (Greensboro, NC), 2003.

(Under name David Lloyd) *Boys: Stories and a Novella,* Syracuse University Press (Syracuse, NY), 2004.

Contributor of poetry to books, including *Knowing Stones: Poems of Exotic Places,* John Gordon Burke Publishing, 2000; *Earth Beneath, Sky Beyond,* Outrider Press, 2000; *A Storied Singer: Frank Sinatra as Literary Conceit,* Greenwood Press, 2001; and *A Due Voci: The Photographs of Rita Hammond,* Syracuse University, 2003; and periodicals, including *Crab Orchard Review, Denver Quarterly, Verseweavers,* and *Doubletake.* Contributor of essays and interviews to books, including *The Writer in Our World,* edited by Reginald Gibbons, Atlantic Monthly Press, 1986; *Poetry Wales: 25 Years,* Seren Books, 1990; *Self, World, Poem: Essays on Contemporary Poetry,* Kent State University Press, 1990; *Contiguous Traditions in Post-War British Poetry,* 1994; *Seamus Heaney: The Shaping Spirit,* University of Delaware Press, 1996; and *Twayne Companion to Contemporary World Literature,* 2003; and to periodicals, including *Twentieth Century Literature.* Contributor of fiction to periodicals, including *Del Sol Review* and *Salt Hill.*

Sidelights

Poet and fiction writer David T. Lloyd is also a professor of English and director of the creative writing program at Le Moyne College in upstate New York. In his published poems and articles, Lloyd shares his interest in post-World War II literature as well as other aspects of Irish/Welsh studies. The anthology *The Urgency of Identity: Contemporary English-Language Poetry from Wales,* which Lloyd edited, appeared in 1994; his first poetry collection, 2002's *The Everyday Apocalypse,* was a winner of the Maryland State Poetry and Literary Society chapbook contest; his second collection, 2003's *The Gospel according to Frank,* won the New American Press poetry book contest. Lloyd has also received the Poetry Society of America's Robert H. Winner Memorial Award.

Lloyd's first published collection of prose, *Boys: Stories and a Novella,* focuses on the lives of adolescent boys growing up in New York during the mid-1960s. The protagonists of Lloyd's tales face obstacles, sometimes

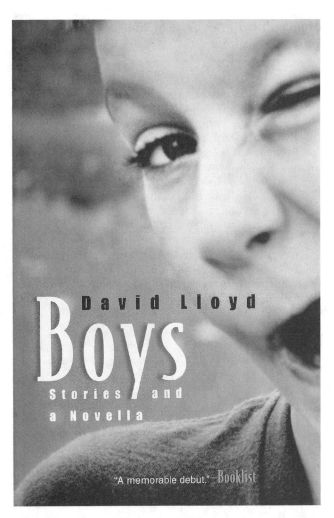

Lloyd's collection of short fiction has been praised for its sensitively observed portraits of boys' experiences while growing up in rural America during the 1960s. (Cover photograph by Catrin Lloyd-Bolland.)

throwing caution to the wind as they test their physical and emotional limitations. In the novella *Boys Only* thirteen-year-old Chris takes a risk by joining best friends Joey and Frank in forming an exclusive gang, gains his first insight into adult sexuality, and suffers his first romantic crush. Other stories include "No Boundaries," about a combative dodge ball game; "As Always, Jason," about a boy's efforts to gain attention by dispensing information in fact-filled notes; and "Spider," in which a teen wrestler takes the upper hand against a weaker sparring partner. Revealing and yet sometimes brutal, the collection was praised for its accurate portrayal of modern teen boys' sometimes troubled coming of age. "Sharply observed," Lloyd's fiction is "filled with scenes both mundane and shocking that capture those strange, private moments of shame, fear, pride, and creativity," stated Gillian Engberg in *Booklist,* while a *Publishers Weekly* reviewer commented that the "quiet, sometimes chilling stories remind us of childhood's unique travails." Lloyd proves himself to be "a writer with unique insight into that world," added the *Publishers Weekly* contributor.

Biographical and Critical Sources

PERIODICALS

Booklist, March 1, 2004, Gillian Engberg, review of *Boys: Stories and a Novella,* p. 1138

Choice, January, 1995, E.M. Slotkin, review of *The Urgency of Identity: Contemporary English-Language Poetry from Wales,* p. 787.

Georgia Review, summer, 2005, Paul Zimmer, review of *The Everyday Apocalypse,* pp. 410-421.

Main Street Rag, spring, 2003, Todd Hester, review of *The Gospel according to Frank,* pp. 83-85.

New Welsh Review, autumn, 2003, Kate North, review of *Boys,* pp. 112-113; winter, 2004, Matthew Jarvis, review of *The Everyday Apocalypse,* pp. 115-117.

Publishers Weekly, March 8, 2004, review of *Boys,* p. 51.

World Literature Today, winter, 1998, review of *Writing on the Edge,* p. 223.

ONLINE

Le Moyne College Web site, http://www.lemoyne.edu/ (December 19, 2005), "David T. Lloyd."

*　　*　　*

LUCKETT, Dave 1951-

Personal

Born February 9, 1951, in Stanmore, New South Wales, Australia; son of Terence (a minister) and Gwyneth Elizabeth (a secretary; maiden name, Williams) Luckett; married Sally Barbara Beasley (a psychologist), January 7, 1984; children: Evan John. *Education:* Teachers College of Western Australia (now Edith Cowan University), diploma in education, 1974; University of Western Australia, B.A., 1983.

Addresses

Home—69 Federal St., Tuart Hill 6060, Western Australia, Australia. *E-mail*—home@daveluckett.com.

Career

Writer. Teacher at secondary schools in Western Australia, 1974-75; Perth, Australia, federal public servant, 1977-97.

Awards, Honors

Aurealis Award for Best Australian Fantasy Novel, 1998, and Western Australia Premier's Book Award shortlist, and Tin Duck Award, Western Australia Sci-Fi Awards, both 1999, all for *A Dark Winter;* Aurealis Award shortlist for Best Novel, 1999, for both *A Dark Journey* and *A Dark Victory;* Western Australia Premier's Book Award, 2001, for *Rhianna and the Wild Magic;* Aurealis Award shortlist for Best Children's Novel, 2002, for *Rhianna and the Dogs of Iron.*

Writings

FOR CHILDREN

The Adventures of Addam, illustrated by Timothy Ide, Omnibus Books (Norwood, South Australia, Australia), 1995.

Night Hunters, Omnibus Books (Norwood, South Australia, Australia), 1995.

The Best Batsman in the World, illustrated by David Kennett, Omnibus Books (Norwood, South Australia, Australia), 1996.

The Wizard and Me, Omnibus Books (Norwood, South Australia, Australia), 1996.

The Last Eleven, illustrated by David Kennett, Omnibus Books (Norwood, South Australia, Australia), 1997.

Cricket Australia: Kids' Ultimate Fan Handbook (nonfiction), illustrated by Don Hatcher, Omnibus Books (Norwood, South Australia, Australia), 2004.

Iron Soldiers: A Story of Arms and Armour (nonfiction), illustrated by Joseph Bond, Omnibus Books (Norwood, South Australia, Australia), 2005.

(With Max Fatchen) *Howzat!: A Celebration of Cricket* (nonfiction), illustrated by David Cox, Don Hatcher, and David Kennett, Omnibus Books (Norwood, South Australia, Australia), 2005.

In the first volume of Luckett's "Rhianna Chronicles," a young magician in training hopes her uncontrollable power is enough to tame a troublemaking dragon. (Cover illustration by Dan Andreasen.)

The Truth about Magic ("School of Magic" series), Omnibus Books (Malvern, South Australia, Australia), 2005.

The Return of Rathalorn ("School of Magic" series), Omnibus Books (Malvern, South Australia, Australia), 2005.

Luckett's novels have been translated into Polish.

"TENABRAN TRILOGY"

A Dark Winter, Omnibus Books (Norwood, South Australia, Australia), 1998.

A Dark Journey, Omnibus Books (Norwood, South Australia, Australia), 1999.

A Dark Victory, Omnibus Books (Norwood, South Australia, Australia), 1999.

"RHIANNA CHRONICLES" SERIES

Rhianna and the Wild Magic, Omnibus Books (Norwood, South Australia, Australia), 2000, published as *The Girl, the Dragon, and the Wild Magic,* Scholastic (New York, NY), 2003.

Rhianna and the Dogs of Iron, Omnibus Books (Norwood, South Australia, Australia), 2002, published as *The Girl, the Apprentice, and the Dogs of Iron,* Scholastic (New York, NY), 2004.

Rhianna and the Castle of Avalon, Omnibus Books (Norwood, South Australia, Australia), 2002, published as *The Girl, the Queen, and the Castle,* Scholastic (New York, NY), 2004.

Sidelights

Australian children's writer Dave Luckett is the author of several titles for young and juvenile readers. He began his career in children's literature with junior novels and chapter books, and has gained critical attention and praise for his "Tenabran Trilogy," the first installment of which received the Aurealis Award for Best Australian Fantasy Novel. Luckett has continued his success with other fantasy series, including the "Rhianna Chronicles" and his "School of Magic" novels.

One of Luckett's first chapter books, *Night Hunters,* began to build his reputation for writing enjoyable science-fiction and fantasy novels for young readers. *Night Hunters* was one of several books published by Omnibus Books for reluctant teen readers, and was praised as "accessible, pacy literature" by Nicola Robinson in the *Australian Book Review.* The novel tells the story of two twenty-first-century teens who get drawn into an all-too-real virtual reality program

With *A Long Winter* Luckett established himself as an up-and-coming Australian writer of science fiction and fantasy. The first book of the "Tenabran Trilogy," *A Long Winter* introduces readers to Willan Parkin, a squire and experienced warrior who is bored with his current duties. Willan's adventures begin when he and

When Rhianna's temper gets the better of her, so does her magic when she brings two fierce iron dogs to life and evil forces take control. (Cover illustration by Dan Andreasen.)

his knight companion embark on a quest to defeat an evil magician. Jonathan Strahan, writing for *Eidolon. net,* called *A Dark Winter* "dryly humorous," while *Viewpoints* reviewer Luigi Guadagnuolo noted that Luckett's experience writing fantasy and science fiction "shines through as he produces vivid descriptions detailing the surroundings, emotions, smells, and images."

In *A Dark Journey* Willan is introduced to the Great Wandini, a magician who hopes to found a magic school, and to Wandini's lovely assistant, Arienne, who would like nothing more than to be free of her master. When Arienne escapes, Willan pledges to help her, and the two begin a romance that is threatened by Wandini, by political struggles between the ruler of Tenabran and the local goblins, and by the prince of Tenabran's own henchmen. Strahan noted that Luckett returns to themes of *A Dark Winter,* such as honor, decency, independence, and responsibility, "expanding upon them, and telling a story that is sufficiently satisfying that it manages to end *A Dark Journey,* but not the series." In the concluding book of the trilogy, *A Dark Victory,* Luckett tells the story of Asta, a young girl able to use magic but unaware of her own potential. Ongoing issues from earlier books, including Willan and Arienne's struggle and the plight of the goblins, are brought to a conclusion. Strahan called the novel "a stand out from the run-of-the-mill fantasy."

The "Rhianna Chronicles" books, written for slightly younger readers than the "Tenabran Trilogy" had been, recount the adventures of a young, would-be wizard named Rhianna. In spite of her schooling, Rhianna is unable to master the simplest spells; far from being a failure, however, she is revealed to have the Wild Talent—a gift that could endanger all the realm unless she learns to control it. In the first novel, *Rhianna and the Wild Magic,* Rhianna must learn to harness her talent to keep a dragon from harming her home and family. A reviewer for *Viewpoint* called the book "a delightful novel which combines adventure, warmth and humour." In the second novel, *Rhianna and the Dogs of Iron,* the girl's jealousy toward her father's apprentice causes her to unleash two magical iron dogs which she alone can stop. "Luckett's writing addresses issues such as jealousy and envy and the importance of overcoming these," noted a *Viewpoints* contributor. In *Rhianna and the Castle of Avalon* Rhianna must face off against another user of Wild Magic for the sake of her kingdom. "Rhianna is a strong character full of flaws but [ultimately with] an innate desire to do the right thing," wrote a critic for *Viewpoints.*

As well as writing books of science fiction and fantasy, Luckett has also penned several nonfiction titles: *Iron Soldiers* deals with early development of arms and armor for knights, while both *Cricket Australia* and *Howzat* focus on the sport of cricket. Discussing his primary writing focus, however, Luckett once told *SATA:* "I write science fiction and fantasy because I love it. It has its dark moments, but generally it assumes a future (or at least a heroic past) that means more to me than all the kitchen-sink realism of the mainstream—a realism that is no more real than any fiction, when you come right down to it. My great regret is that I won't be around to see the ships leave for the stars. My great hope is that they will go anyway."

Biographical and Critical Sources

PERIODICALS

Australian Book Review, July 1-2, 1995, Nicola Robinson, review of *Night Hunters*; August, 1995, p. 62; December, 1996, p. 86.
Magpies, May, 1996, p. 43; September, 1999, review of *A Dark Victory,* p. 40; November, 2000, review of *Rhianna and the Wild Magic,* p. 35; May, 2005, review of *The Truth about Magic,* p. 35, and review of *Iron Soldiers: A Story of Arms and Armour,* p. 44.
Viewpoint, winter, 1998, Luigi Guadagnuolo, review of *A Dark Winter;* autumn, 2001, review of *Rhianna and the Wild Magic;* summer, 2002, review of *Rhianna and the Dogs of Iron;* autumn, 2003, review of *Rhianna and the Castle of Avalon.*

ONLINE

Dave Luckett Home Page, http://www.daveluckett.com (December 27, 2004).
Eidolon.net, http://eidolon.net/ (April 29, 2003), Jonathan Strahan, reviews of *A Dark Journey* and *A Dark Victory;* review of *Rhianna and the Dogs of Iron.*

*   *   *

MANZANO, Sonia 1950-

Personal

Born June 12, 1950, in New York, NY; daughter of Bonifacio (a construction worker) and Isidra (a seamstress; maiden name Rivera) Manzano; married Richard Scott Reagan (a foundation director); children: Gabriela Rose Reagan. *Ethnicity:* "Puerto Rican." *Education:* Attended Carnegie-Mellon University, 1968-71. *Politics:* Democrat. *Hobbies and other interests:* Kayaking.

Addresses

Office—Sesame Workshop, 1 Lincoln Plaza, New York, NY 10023. *Agent*—Sara Jane Freymann, Stepping Stone Literary Agency, 59 W. 71st St., New York, NY 10023. *E-mail*—Soniamanzano2@aol.com.

Career

Actress and writer. Sesame Workshop, New York, NY, actress and writer, performing role of María on *Sesame Street,* 1971—. Actor in stage productions, including in *Godspell,* 1971; and *The Exonerated,* produced off-Broadway. Actor in television films, including (as María) *Christmas Eve on Sesame Street,* 1978; *A Special Sesame Street Christmas,* 1978; *Sesame Street in Puerto Rico,* 1979; *Sesame Street: Put down the Duckie,* 1988; *Sesame Street: 20 and Still Counting,* 1989; *Sesame Street Jam: A Musical Celebration,* 1994; *Elmo Saves Christmas,* 1996; *The Adventures of Elmo in Grouchland,* 1999; and *Sesame Street Presents: The Street We Live On,* 2004. Actress in television series, including *B.J. and the Bear,* 1981, and *Law & Order,* 2004. Actress in films, including (as grocery clerk) *Death Wish,* 1974; and (as María) *Sesame Street Presents: Follow That Bird,* 1985. March of Dimes, former member of board; George Foster Peabody Awards, member of board, 1997-2001; Symphony Space, New York, NY, member of board; member, Bronx River Alliance, 2004—. Lecturer. Affiliated with Three Amigas (design licensing company).

Awards, Honors

Education 2003 Hispanic Heritage honor, Hispanic Heritage Foundation; Parents' Choice honor designation, *Child* magazine Best Children's Book selection, and Miami-Dade County One Picture Book, One Community selection, all 2004, all for *No Dogs Allowed!;* hon-

In No Dogs Allowed! *Manzano introduces a spunky young narrator whose family is determined to include the family pet in a much-anticipated weekend outing. (Illustration by John J. Muth.)*

orary doctorate, Notre Dame University, 2005; two Emmy Award nominations for Outstanding Performer in a Children's Series; awards from Association of Hispanic Arts, Congressional Hispanic Caucus, National Hispanic Media Coalition, and Committee for Hispanic Children and Families.

Writings

No Dogs Allowed!, illustrated by Jon J. Muth, Atheneum Books for Young Readers (New York, NY), 2004.

Contributor to *Thanks and Giving: All Year,* Simon & Schuster (New York, NY), 2004. Author of numerous scripts for television series *Sesame Street,* beginning 1985; author of video scripts, including *The Best of Elmo, Big Bird Visits the Hospital, Sing along with Sonia Mazano,* and *Sing, Hoot, and Howl.* Author of column "Talking Outloud Parenting," for Sesame Street Web site.

Adaptations

No Dogs Allowed! was adapted as a video recording, Spoken Arts, 2005.

Work in Progress

A memoir, titled *This Is My Story and I'm Sticking to It;* a children's picture book titled *A Box Full of Kittens,* for Simon & Schuster, 2007.

Sidelights

Sonia Manzano is known to several generations of Americans as María, the role she has performed on the long-running Public Television series *Sesame Street* for over two decades. Although she continues to devote much of her time to both acting and writing for the popular program, Manzano has also become active as a role model for Hispanic children. One of the first Hispanics to appear regularly on a U.S. television series, Manzano has also been active as a speaker and as a member of several community organizations. As a writer, she has also engaged her core audience—young children—with the 2005 picture book *No Dogs Allowed!*

With engaging illustrations by John J. Muth, *No Dogs Allowed!* carries young readers along as six-year-old Iris describes a family outing to a nearby park. Packing up everything they can think of to ensure a day of fun, Iris's large extended family—along with the family dog—overcome a series of setbacks and mishaps en route, only to learn that no dogs are allowed inside the park gates once they arrive. Manzano's story "reflects loving family ties and the value of shared responsibilities," noted Teresa Bateman in a review for *School Library Journal,* while a *Kirkus Reviews* critic wrote that "children will happily hitch a ride" and "laugh at the exaggerated but believable details and misadventures" included in "Iris's sunny account."

Manzano told *SATA:* "After playing 'Maria' on *Sesame Street* for several years, I decided to add to the experience by writing for the show as well. I watched a lot of television as a child and felt that kids deserved better.

"The first children's book author I admired was Cynthia Rylant. Fiction is what I read the most—fiction about the fascinating things that people do. A good story, read or written, can take you places. I love reading about the human condition and attempting to describe it from my point of view. The things people do fascinate me and I try to share that interest with both children and adults.

"I write everyday—first thing in the morning if possible. My parenting column, called "Talking Outloud," can be found at www.sesameworkshop.org."

Biographical and Critical Sources

PERIODICALS

Booklist, June 1, 2004, Jennifer Mattson, review of *No Dogs Allowed!,* p. 1744.

Books in Canada, June-July, 2004, Olga Stein, review of *No Dogs Allowed!,* p. 44.

Kirkus Reviews, March 1, 2004, review of *No Dogs Allowed!,* p. 227.

Library Media Connection, January, 2005, Pam Watts Flavin, review of *No Dogs Allowed!,* p. 72.

School Library Journal, July, 2004, Jane Marino, review of *No Dogs Allowed,* p. 82.

ONLINE

Sonia Manzano Home Page, http://www.soniamanzano. com (December 19, 2005).

Soy Unica! Soy Latina! Web site, http://www.soyunica. gov/ (December 19, 2005), "Spotlight on Sonia Manzano."*

*   *   *

MARCIANO, John Bemelmans 1970-

Personal

Born 1970; son of Barbara Bemelmans; grandson of Ludwig Bemelmans (a writer and illustrator). *Education:* Majored in art history.

Addresses

Home—Brooklyn, NY. *Agent*—c/o Author Mail, Viking, Penguin Putnam, 375 Hudson St., New York, NY 10014.

Career

Writer and illustrator

Writings

SELF-ILLUSTRATED CHILDREN'S BOOKS

Madeline Says Merci: The Always-Be-Polite Book, Viking (New York, NY), 2001.

Delilah, Viking (New York, NY), 2002.

Harold's Tail, Viking (New York, NY), 2003.

There's a Dolphin in the Grand Canal!, Viking (New York, NY), 2005.

OTHER

(With Ludwig Bemelmans) *Madeline in America, and Other Holiday Tales* (contains "The Count and the Cobbler," "Bemelmans' Christmas Memory," and "Sunshine"), Scholastic (New York, NY), 1999.

Bemelmans: The Life and Art of Madeline's Creator, edited by C. Hennessy, illustrated by Ludwig Bemelmans, Viking (New York, NY), 1999.

Sidelights

Author and illustrator John Bemelmans Marciano began his career in children's literature in an almost magical fashion: The grandson of award-winning writer Ludwig Bemelmans, John discovered an unfinished manuscript for a children's story featuring Bemelmans' beloved picture-book heroine Madeline while rummaging through his late relative's memorabilia. Although Marciano had never met his grandfather, who passed away in 1962, his mother introduced him to the six "Madeline" books and Bemelmans' engaging artwork. *Madeline in America, and Other Holiday Tales* is based on Bemelman's unfinished manuscript, "Madeline's Christmas in Texas," completed and illustrated by Marciano. Basing his illustrations on the pencil sketches left by his grandfather, Marciano completes the story of Madeline who, with teacher Miss Clavel and the other eleven girls from her school in Paris, travels to Texas after she inherits a cattle ranch, gold mines, and oil wells. Including two other stories by Bemelmans, *Madeline in America, and Other Holiday Tales* also features an essay by Marciano's mother, Barbara Bemelmans, describing Christmas festivities in her artistic father's home.

Since reintroducing Madeline to generations of new audiences, Marciano has featured the perky French schoolgirl in his original work, *Madeline Says Merci: The*

Red the farmer unknowingly threatens a special relationship when he tries to multiply his happiness by ordering a dozen more lambs just like his special favorite in Marciano's self-illustrated Delilah.

A little boy living in Venice for the summer finds the city more exciting than usual after he spots something unbelievable swimming up a nearby waterway in There's a Dolphin in the Grand Canal!

Always-Be-Polite Book, in which Madeline is transformed into what *School Library Journal* contributor Carol Schene dubbed "a mini 'Miss Manners.'" Taking place in the streets of Paris, the book finds Madeline exhibiting proper behavior in a variety of situations, each captured in illustrations that, according to Schene, show that Bemelmans' "impish Parisian is still alive and well." In addition to reprising his grandfather's picture-book character, Marciano has produced *Bemelmans: The Life and Art of Madeline's Creator,* a study of the Caldecott Medal-winning author/illustrator and journalist that was praised by a *Horn Book* critic as "an entirely affectionate biography."

Marciano has gone on to expand his repertoire beyond the antics of Madeline. In *Delilah* he tells a tale of friendship between a farmer and a frisky lamb that soon becomes the farmer's constant companion. Enjoying the lamb, named Delilah, so much, the farmer acquires a whole flock of sheep, only to realize that the value of one thing is not always increased when it is acquired in large numbers. Calling *Delilah* "a charmer," Jeanne Clancy Watkins predicted that young readers "will not be able to resist these engaging friends," while a *Kirkus Reviews* critic concluded that the book "is sure to become a bedtime favorite." Most critics praised Marciano's illustrations, a *Publishers Weekly* reviewer noting that the author/illustrator "draws faces with the evocative simplicity of his grandfather's draftsmanship." The *Kirkus Reviews* writer deemed the pencil and gouache artwork "delightfully simple."

Other books by Marciano include *Harold's Tail,* about a Manhattan-dwelling squirrel who learns what life is like for the less fortunate when he takes a dare, shaves the fluff from his tail, and finds himself reviled due to his resemblance to a city rat. In *Booklist,* Julie Cummins described *Harold's Tail* as a "clever, urban animal survival tale," while a *Kirkus Reviews* contributor viewed Marciano's illustrated story as a "study of prejudice and elitism" disguised as a lively children's book. Animals also star in *There's a Dolphin in the Grand Canal!,* as a boy living in Venice, Italy, discovers a dolphin frolicking in the waters of the city's canal but has a difficult time convincing his parents. Noting that the Venice scenery, with its "meticulous painted brickwork and golden touches," is the author/illustrator's "strong suit," a *Publishers Weekly* critic wrote that *There's a Dolphin in the Grand Canal!* "makes for an entertaining introduction to Venice." *School Library Journal* critic Wendy

Just as the clothes make the man, so, too, the fluffy tail makes the squirrel; at least that is the lesson Harold the squirrel learns in Marciano's bittersweet picture book Harold's Tail.

Lukehart maintained that Marciano's picture-book "romp" effectively "capture[s] the grandeur and diversity of Venetian architecture and the magical quality of the liquid streets."

Biographical and Critical Sources

PERIODICALS

Booklist, August, 2002, Helen Rosenberg, review of *Delilah,* p. 1973; September 1, 2003, Julie Cummins, review of *Harold's Tale,* p. 119; June 1, 2005, Karin Snelson, review of *There's a Dolphin in the Grand Canal!,* p. 1822.

Bulletin of the Center for Children's Books, April, 2000, review of *Bemelmans: The Life and Art of Madeline's Creator,* p. 297.

Horn Book, January, 2000, review of *Bemelmans,* p. 106.

Kirkus Reviews, May 1, 2002, review of *Delilah,* p. 660; August 2, 2003, review of *Harold's Tale,* p. 1020; May 15, 2005, review of *There's a Dolphin in the Grand Canal!,* p. 592.

Oakland Press, January 12, 2000, p. D3.

Publishers Weekly, November 19, 2001, review of *Madeline Says Merci: The Always-Be-Polite Book,* p. 70; April 15, 2002, review of *Delilah,* p. 63; August 11, 2003, review of *Harold's Tale,* p. 280; June 27, 2005, review of *There's a Dolphin in the Grand Canal!,* p. 62.

School Library Journal, December, 2001, Carol Schene, review of *Madeline Says Merci,* p. 124; February, 2000, Lisa Falk, review of *Madeline in America, and Other Holiday Tales,* p. 91; August, 2002, Jeanne Clancy Watkins, review of *Delilah,* p. 161; November, 2003, Susan Helper, review of *Harold's Tale,* p. 108; August, 2005, Wendy Lukehart, review of *There's a Dolphin in the Grand Canal!,* p. 102.

Voice of Youth Advocates, August, 2000, review of *Bemelmans,* p. 206.

ONLINE

BookPage, http://www.bookpage.com/ (June, 2002), Heidi Henneman, interview with Marciano.

Canadian Review of Materials Online, http://www.umanitoba.ca/cm/ (February 18, 2000), Dave Jenkinson, review of *Madeline in America, and Other Holiday Tales.*

*   *   *

MARSTEN, Richard
See HUNTER, Evan

*   *   *

MARSZALEK, John F. 1939-

Personal

Born July 5, 1939, in Buffalo, NY; son of John and Regina (Sierakowski) Marszalek; married Jeanne Kozmer, October 16, 1965; children: John, Chris, Jamie. *Ethnicity:* "Polish-American." *Education:* Canisius College, B.A., 1961; University of Notre Dame, M.A., 1963, Ph. D., 1968. *Politics:* Democrat. *Religion:* Roman Catholic.

Addresses

Home and office—108 Grand Ridge Rd., Starkville, MS 39759. *E-mail*—JohnMarsz@yahoo.com.

Career

Writer and educator. Canisius College, Buffalo, NY, instructor in history, 1967-68; Gannon University, Erie, PA, assistant professor, then associate professor of his-

John F. Marszalek

tory, 1968-73; Mississippi State University, Mississippi State, associate professor, 1973-80, professor, 1980-94, Giles distinguished professor of history, 1994-2002, then emeritus, 2002—, director and mentor of distinguished scholars, 2004—. *Military service:* U.S. Army, 1965-67; attained rank of captain; served in Vietnam.

Member

Organization of American Historians, Southern Historical Association, Mississippi Historical Society, Society of Civil War Historians, Historians of the Civil War Western Theatre.

Awards, Honors

Richard Wright Literary Award for Lifetime Achievement; Distinguished Alumnus, Canisius College, 1999; Natchez Literary and Cinema Celebration, 2002; B.L.C. Wailes AWard for National Distinction in the Field of History; Mississippi Historical Society, 2004.

Writings

Court-Martial; A Black Man in America, Scribner (New York, NY), 1972, published with new afterword as

Assault at West Point: The Court-Martial of Johnson Whittaker, Collier Books (New York, NY), 1994.

(With Sadye H. Wier) *A Black Businessman in White Mississippi, 1886-1974,* University Press of Mississippi (Jackson, MS), 1977.

The Diary of Miss Emma Holmes, 1861-1866, Louisiana State University Press (Baton Rouge, LA), 1979, published with new preface, 1994.

Sherman's Other War: The General and the Civil War Press, Memphis State University Press (Memphis, TN), 1981, revised edition, Kent State University Press (Kent, OH), 1999.

(With Douglas L. Conner) *A Black Physician's Story: Bringing Hope in Mississippi,* University Press of Mississippi (Jackson, MS), 1985.

Grover Cleveland: A Bibliography, foreword by Arthur M. Schlesinger, Jr., Meckler (Westport, CT), 1988.

(Editor with Charles D. Lowery) *Encyclopedia of African-American Civil Rights: From Emancipation to the Present,* Greenwood Press (New York, NY), 1992, expanded as *The Greenwood Encyclopedia of African-American Civil Rights: From Emancipation to the Twenty-first Century,* 2 volumes, 2004.

Sherman: A Soldier's Passion for Order, Free Press (New York, NY), 1993.

(Editor with Wilson D. Miscamble) *American Political History: Essays on the State of the Discipline,* University of Notre Dame Press (Notre Dame, IN), 1997.

The Petticoat Affair: Manners, Mutiny, and Sex in Andrew Jackson's White House, Free Press (New York, NY), 1997.

The Civil War in the Western Theater, Mississippi State University Department of History (Mississippi State, MS), 2001.

Commander of All Lincoln's Armies: A Life of General Henry W. Halleck, Belknap Press of Harvard University (Cambridge, MA), 2004.

(Author of introduction) Samuel W. Hankins, *Simple Story of a Solider,* new edition, University of Alabama Press (Tuscaloosa, AL), 2004.

Sherman's March to the Sea, Grace McWhiney Foundation Press (Abilene, TX), 2005.

Adaptations

Court-Martial was adapted as the television film *Assault at West Point,* 1994.

Work in Progress

Battling Discrimination in the Age of Jim Crow: A Life of South Carolina Black Congressman George W. Murray; Civil War in the Western Theatre, expected, 2009.

Sidelights

John F. Marszalek told *SATA:* "I do not remember how old I was, but my first exposure to the world of books came when my mother took me by the hand and we walked into a branch library in Buffalo, New York. There were people of all ages sitting and reading, and I was immediately struck by the huge number of books which seemed to be everywhere. It was in fact a small room, but to me at that early age it was enormous. I frequently went back to that library on my own for story hours and once I remember getting in trouble with my parents for not telling them that I was going there.

"In fifth grade, my family moved to the suburbs of Buffalo, to an area where there was no library. My school, in fact, consisted of only four rooms, two grades per room. It had no school library, but every week or two the mobile library truck came and we excitedly climbed aboard to find books to read. I was stuck on sports books, eventually reading every book on the topic on the truck. I remember thinking that books had to be important—how else could one explain this marvelous visiting truck full of them.

"My high school, the Jesuit Canisius High School in Buffalo, had as its library a grand ball room with chandeliers and high ceilings. I joined the library club so I could be there, once again impressed both by the setting and the books themselves.

"When I attended Canisius College and later went to graduate school at the University of Notre Dame, I was exposed to professors who not only read vociferously but actually wrote books themselves. I had to write papers for every course, and the magnificent circular building that served as the research library for the Buffalo and Erie County Public Library and the multistoried Notre Dame Library became second homes. I was hooked. My life was gong to center on research, writing, and publishing books. And I have been lucky. That is what happened. As I write this essay, right at my elbow is the library my wife and I put into our Mississippi home. It is full of history books in my areas of interest, but on the bottom shelf are children's books—for visiting grandchildren but also as a memorial to that first day my mother took me to that small library in Buffalo."

Biographical and Critical Sources

PERIODICALS

American Historical Review, December, 1998, John M. Belohlavek, review of *The Petticoat Affair: Manners, Mutiny, and Sex in Andrew Jackson's White House,* p. 1694.

Booklist, June 1, 2004, review of *The Greenwood Encyclopedia of African-American Civil Rights: From Emancipation to the Twenty-first Century,* p. 1789.

Choice, July-August, 2004, L.K. Speer, review of *The Greenwood Encyclopedia of African-American Civil Rights,* p. 2026.

Chronicle of Higher Education, February 6, 1998, review of *The Petticoat Affair,* p. 17.

Civil War History, December, 1998, Kenneth R. Stevens, review of *The Petticoat Affair,* p. 292.

History: Review of New Books, fall, 1998, Gary J. Tocchet, review of *American Political History: Essays on the State of the Discipline,* p. 5.

Journal of American History, December, 1982; June, 1994, pp. 282; December, 1998, Elizabeth R. Varon, review of *The Petticoat Affair,* p. 1061; December, 2006, Paul D. Casdorph, review of *Commander of All Lincoln's Armies: A Life of General Henry W. Halleck,* p. 994.

Journal of Southern History, August, 1999, Joel H. Silbey, review of *American Political History,* p. 679.

Library Journal, January, 1998, Stephen G. Weismar, review of *The Petticoat Affair,* p. 116; October 1, 2004, David Lee Poremba, review of *Commander of All Lincoln's Armies,* p. 91.

Reviews in American History, December, 1997, Donald A. Ritchie, review of *American Political History,* p. 698; December, 1998, Norma Basch, review of *The Petticoat Affair,* p. 687.

School Library Journal, October, 2004, Julie Webb, review of *The Greenwood Encyclopedia of African-American Civil Rights,* p. 95.

*   *   *

MARTINEZ, Agnes

Personal

Born in New York, NY; daughter of Victor (a mechanic) and Doris N. (a homemaker and poet) Martinez. *Ethnicity:* "Puerto Rican." *Education:* Syracuse University, B.A., 1983; New York University, M.A. (educational theatre), 1989; Fordham University, M.A. (educational administration), 2000; attended Barbara Seuling Manuscript workshop, 1992-2000. *Religion:* Roman Catholic. *Hobbies and other interests:* Marathon runner.

Addresses

Home—73-12 35th Ave., No. F3, Jackson Heights, NY 11372.

Career

Educator, writer, and artist. New York City Board of Education, New York, NY, elementary teacher, staff developer, and mentor, 1983-85, 1989—; visual artist. Member, Queens Council of the Arts, Flushing Town Hall Arts Council, and Women's Studio. *Exhibitions:* Artwork included in collection at Woodhull Hospital Maternity Ward and exhibited in galleries.

Member

Queens Council of the Arts, Flushing Town Hall Arts Council, Women's Studio.

Awards, Honors

Books for Young People award (Peterson, NJ), 2005.

Writings

Poe Park, Holiday House (New York, NY), 2004.

Work in Progress

Number One Chica, a young-adult novel; *When Tito Plays Timbales,* a picture book.

Sidelights

A teacher and visual artist who has exhibited her artwork in and around her New York City home, Agnes Martinez made her writing debut with the 2004 novel *Poe Park,* the story of a young boy who overcomes life-altering devastation with courage. Starting out the summer after fifth grade, eleven-year-old Enoch Morales is looking forward to several months of freedom, where he can relax and have fun with his friends. All thoughts of fun come to an abrupt halt, however, when his best friend Spencer is shot and killed, a tragic casualty of the area's gang violence. To further complicate matters, Enoch's older half-brother Miguel arrives from Puerto Rico. Miguel, who has come to live with Enoch and his family, is soon drawn to the allure of gang life, and although he sometimes behaves like a concerned older brother, Miguel's behavior leaves Enoch unsure how to deal with him.

Martinez brings to life both her characters and the story's setting "in a vivid and accessible manner that will make readers care about the boy's problems and their

After gang violence takes the life of his best friend, fifth-grader Enoch fears things will go from bad to worse with the arrival of his half-brother from Puerto Rico. (Cover photograph by Marc Tauss.)

resolution," commented Carolyn Phelan in *Booklist,* while *School Library Journal* writer Faith Brautigam praised *Poe Park* for reflecting "the sights and sounds of a large city." Reviewing *Poe Park* for *Black Issues Book Review,* Suzanne Rust wrote that, "in a poignant and well-written story, Martinez captures the voice of the spirited" young protagonist, and in *Kirkus Reviews* a contributor praised the book's narrative as "beautiful without losing street credibility."

Biographical and Critical Sources

PERIODICALS

Black Issues Book Review, January-February, 2005, Suzanne Rust, review of *Poe Park,* p. 70.
Booklist, November 15, 2004, Carolyn Phelan, review of *Poe Park,* p. 602.
Bulletin of the Center for Children's Books, December, 2004, Timnah Card, review of *Poe Park,* p. 174.
Kirkus Reviews, October 1, 2004, review of *Poe Park,* p. 964.
Language Arts, May, 2005, review of *Poe Park,* p. 402.
School Library Journal, October, 2004, Faith Brautigam, review of *Poe Park,* p. 172; July, 2005, Coop Renner, review of *Poe Park,* p. 45.

ONLINE

Queens Council on the Arts Web site, http://www.queenscouncil arts.org/ (December 19, 2005), "Agnes Martinez."

*   *   *

MATTHEWS, Nicola
See BROWNE, N.M.

*   *   *

MAZER, Harry 1925-

Personal

Born May 31, 1925, in New York, NY; son of Sam (a dressmaker) and Rose (a dressmaker; maiden name, Lazevnick) Mazer; married Norma Fox (a novelist), February 12, 1950; children: Anne, Joseph, Susan, Gina. *Education:* Union College, B.A., 1948; Syracuse University, M.A., 1960.

Addresses

Agent—George Nicholson, Sterling Lord Literistic, 65 Bleeker St., New York, NY 10012.

Career

New York Central Railroad, brake man and switchtender, 1950-55; New York Construction, Syracuse, sheet metal worker, 1957-59; Central Square School, Central

Square, NY, English teacher, 1959-60; Aerofin Corp., Syracuse, welder, 1960-63; full-time writer, 1963—. *Military service:* U.S. Army Air Force, 1943-45; became sergeant; received Purple Heart and Air Medal with four bronze oak leaf clusters.

Member

Authors Guild, Authors League of America, Society of Children's Book Writers and Illustrators, American Civil Liberties Union.

Awards, Honors

Best of the Best Books designation, American Library Association (ALA), 1970-73, for *Snow Bound; Kirkus* Choice designation, 1974, for *The Dollar Man;* Best Books for Young Adults designation, ALA, 1977, and Children's Choice designation, International Reading Association (IRA)/Children's Book Council (CBC), 1978, both for *The Solid Gold Kid;* Best Books for Young Adults designation, ALA, and Dorothy Canfield Fisher Children's Book Award nominee, Vermont Congress of Parents and Teachers/Vermont Department of Libraries, both 1979, both for *The War on Villa Street;* Best Books designation, *New York Times,* 1979, Books for the Teen Age inclusion, New York Public Library, 1980, Best Books for Young Adults designation, ALA, 1981, and Best of the Best Books 1970-83 listee, ALA, all for *The Last Mission; Booklist* Contemporary Classics listee, 1984, and Preis der Lesseratten (West Germany), both for *Snow Bound;* Arizona Young Readers Award nominee, Arizona State Library Association, 1985, for *The Island Keeper;* Best Books for Young Adults designation, ALA, 1986, for *I Love You, Stupid!;* Books for the Teen Age inclusion, New York Public Library, 1986, and IRA/CBC Young Adult Choice listee, 1987, both for *Hey, Kid! Does She Love Me?;* Best Books for Young Adults designation, ALA, 1987, inclusion in Iowa Teen Award Master list, 1988, and West Australian Young Reader's Book Award, Australian Library and Information Association, 1989, all for *When the Phone Rang;* Best Books for Young Adults designation, ALA, named among Books for Reluctant Young Adult Readers, ALA, 1988, and Books for the Teen Age inclusion, New York Public Library, 1988, all for *The Girl of His Dreams;* Books for the Teen Age inclusion, New York Public Library, 1989, for *Heartbeat;* named among Books for Reluctant Young Adult Readers, ALA, 1989, for *City Light;* Quick Picks for Reluctant Young Adult Readers designation, ALA, 1998, for *Twelve Shots: Outstanding Short Stories about Guns;* Best Books selection, *School Library Journal,* 1998, and Fanfare listee, *Horn Book,* 1999, both for *The Wild Kid.*

Writings

NOVELS; FOR YOUNG ADULTS

Guy Lenny, Delacorte (New York, NY), 1971.
Snow Bound, Delacorte (New York, NY), 1973.
The Dollar Man, Delacorte (New York, NY), 1974.

The War on Villa Street, Delacorte (New York, NY), 1978.
The Last Mission, Delacorte (New York, NY), 1979.
The Island Keeper: A Tale of Courage and Survival, Delacorte (New York, NY), 1981.
I Love You, Stupid!, Crowell (New York, NY), 1981.
Hey, Kid! Does She Love Me?, Crowell (New York, NY), 1984.
When the Phone Rang, Scholastic (New York, NY), 1985.
Cave under the City, Crowell (New York, NY), 1986.
The Girl of His Dreams, Crowell (New York, NY), 1987.
City Light, Scholastic (New York, NY), 1988.
Someone's Mother Is Missing, Delacorte (New York, NY), 1990.
Who Is Eddie Leonard?, Delacorte (New York, NY), 1993.
(Editor) *Twelve Shots: Outstanding Short Stories about Guns,* Delacorte (New York, NY), 1997.
The Dog in the Freezer: Three Novellas, Simon & Schuster (New York, NY), 1997.
The Wild Kid, Simon & Schuster (New York, NY), 1998.
A Boy at War: A Story of Pearl Harbor, Simon & Schuster (New York, NY), 2001.
A Boy No More (sequel to *A Boy at War*), Simon & Schuster (New York, NY), 2004.
Heroes Don't Run: A Novel of the Pacific War (sequel to *Heroes Don't Run*), Simon & Schuster (New York, NY), 2005.

Author's works have been translated into German, French, Finnish, and Danish.

WITH WIFE, NORMA FOX MAZER

The Solid Gold Kid, Delacorte (New York, NY), 1977.
Heartbeat, Bantam (New York, NY), 1989.
Bright Days, Stupid Nights, Bantam (New York, NY), 1992.

OTHER

Contributor of short story to *Places I Never Meant to Be: Original Short Stories by Censored Writers,* edited by Judy Blume, Simon & Schuster (New York, NY), 1999.

Adaptations

Snow Bound was produced as a National Broadcasting Company (NBC) "After School Special" in 1978. *Snow Bound* and *The Last Mission* were recorded on audiocassette by Listening Library, 1985.

Sidelights

In addition to being part of a writing family that includes wife Norma Fox Mazer and daughter Anne Mazer, novelist Harry Mazer has received critical acclaim for his many young-adult novels. His books, which include *The Island Keeper: A Tale of Courage and Survival, Who Is Eddie Leonard?,* and *A Boy at War: A Story of Pearl Harbor,* illustrate the values of perseverance, self-esteem, and inner fortitude. Noting that, "despite their predicaments, Mazer's protagonists usually emerge morally victorious," *Twentieth-Century Young-Adult Writers* contributor Mary Lystad cited as Mazer's strength his depiction of the "emotional turmoil, the humor and pain" of adolescence. "His characters are resilient and strong," Lystad continued. "His endings emphasize compassion, understanding, resourcefulness, and honesty." As Kenneth L. Donelson asserted in *Voice of Youth Advocates,* "Mazer writes about young people caught in the midst of moral crises, often of their own making. Searching for a way out, they discover themselves, or rather they learn that the first step in extricating themselves from their physical and moral dilemmas is self-discovery. Intensely moral as Mazer's books are," continued Donelson, "they present young people thinking and talking and acting believably," a characteristic that accounts for Mazer's continued popularity among readers and critics alike.

The son of hard-working Polish-Jewish immigrants, Mazer grew up in the Bronx, New York, where his family lived in an apartment in a two-block complex called the Coops. As the author recalled in *Something about the Author Autobiography Series* (*SAAS*), "you could feel the optimistic spirit that built these houses—in the central courtyards with their gardens and fountains, in the library, the gymnasium, and the kindergarten. The Coops were special, an island, a community, a village in a great city built on a shared dream of cooperation and social justice." Mazer shared the only bedroom with his brother, while his parents slept in the living room, which also served as a dining room and kitchen. The halls and stairs were Mazer's playground, and he grew up between two worlds—the park and the street—both of which he would later use in his novels. "The park was mine, so big it was limitless," recalled Mazer. The many games that the street offered, such as marbles and chalk-drawing, also appealed to Mazer, as did the huge fires built in empty lots after dark.

While retaining few memories of his school days, Mazer remembered lying on the couch with his nose in a book and "a pile of apple cores on the floor." He read everything from series books and adventure stories to the collected works of Charles Dickens. "Two of my all-time favorite books were *Robinson Crusoe,* the story of a man alone on a desert island, and *Tarzan of the Apes,*" he recalled in *SAAS.*

Mazer took the competitive exam for the Bronx High School of Science and got in, but the courses that most interested him were English and history. In high school, questions about his future occupied his mind. Jobs were scarce at the time, and many employers would not hire Jews. If he had been a dutiful son, Mazer later reflected, he would have become a teacher; "but I was in rebellion. I was impatient. I wanted to be great, famous. . . . My secret desire was to be a writer, but I knew nothing about how to make it happen. I had the idea that if I could only write it down, if I could only put all my feelings into words, I would finally figure everything out (whatever everything was)."

World War II was on Mazer's mind also. At age seventeen he qualified to join the U.S. Army Air Force Cadets, but had to wait until he was eighteen to serve. "I prayed that the war didn't end before I got in," he remembered in his *SAAS* essay. Mazer served for two and a half years, starting out as an airplane mechanic, then training as a ball-turret and waist gunner. He was assigned to a crew on a B-17 bomber and in December of 1944 headed for Europe, where the crew flew their first mission two months later. In April their plane was shot down over Czechoslovakia, and only Mazer and one other crew member survived. "I remember thinking afterward that there had to be a reason why I had survived," recalled the author. "I didn't think it was God. It was chance. Luck. But why me? Chance can't be denied as a factor in life, but I clung to the thought that there was a reason for my survival."

Mazer was discharged from the army in October of 1945, and days later began attending classes at a liberal arts college. He began writing, but his work "was too serious and self-conscious. I turned each word over in my head before I allowed it out into the open. . . . I wrote, but I was full of doubt, my standards were miles higher than my abilities. I suffered over what I wrote and didn't write any more than I had to." After graduation, he trained as a welder and got a job in an autobody shop. "I was dramatizing myself," Mazer later admitted, "imagining myself a leader of the downtrodden, pointing the way to the future. . . . I was idealistic. I was unrealistic. Most of all I was avoiding the real issues of my life. I didn't have the belief or the nerve to say I was a writer, to begin writing and let everything else take care of itself."

While working on a political campaign, Mazer met Norma Fox. It was their second meeting; they had been introduced two years earlier when she was fifteen and he was twenty-one. Now they began an on-again, off-again romance. A year later Norma began college, and Mazer pressed her to get married. "Norma said yes, we'd get married, then she said no," Mazer remembered. "When she was with me it was yes, but when she went back to school it was no again." The couple finally married and settled in a tiny apartment in New York City, but soon moved back upstate to Schenectady, and then to Utica, finally settling in Syracuse. Mazer worked at various jobs, doing welding, sheet metal work, and track work for the railroad, but still avoided writing.

After ten years of factory work, Mazer became a teacher. It was at this point that he and Norma discovered that they both longed to be writers. In the meantime, Mazer lost his teaching job and returned to factory work, taking paperbacks with him, trying to understand how a story worked. The insurance money from an accident finally enabled him to quit his job and begin writing full-time.

Now in his mid-thirties, Mazer and his wife began to write every day, supporting their family by penning articles for the true-confessions market. These stories demanded that I develop a character, a plot, action that rose to a climax, and a satisfying ending. And I had to do it every week, week after week. It was a demanding school. I was being forced to write to stay out of the factory," Mazer wrote in *SAAS.* He also tried other forms of writing, including television scripts and pieces for literary magazines. The Mazers' agent finally suggested they try the children's field.

Mazer's first serious effort produced the 1971 novel *Guy Lenny,* which marked the beginning of his successful career in children's literature. The story was inspired by a piece in a "Dear Abby" column about a boy who was concerned about an older girl he liked. She was going with someone else who was no good for her, and the boy wanted to know how he could break them up. *Guy Lenny* is the story of a boy whose parents are

After bluffing his way into the Air Force and onto a bomber flying missions over Europe during World War II, a fifteen year old faces a new challenge when he is taken captive by German soldiers. (Cover illustration by Tom Freeman.)

divorced, a situation children's books of the time did not deal with. Guy's mother has left, and he is living with his father when she returns to claim him. "It's a children's story because it's about a boy and is told from his point of view," explained Mazer in *SAAS;* "it's also an adult story because it's about growing up and having to live with some of the hard, intractable things of life. And that's what made it a young-adult book, a new category of fiction that was still to be named."

Many of Mazer's novels use characters from earlier books, and father-and-son relationships like the one in *Guy Lenny* often appear. Romance also plays a part, as in *The Girl of His Dreams,* in which Mazer relates the romance of Willis and Sophie, two ordinary young adults, with "a credibility apart from [the book's] fairy-tale ending," in the opinion of Marianne Gingher writing in the *Los Angeles Times.* Willis is a factory worker and dedicated runner who has a clear vision of exactly what the girl of his dreams should be like. Sophie does not fit this image, and their relationship develops slowly and awkwardly. "No run-of-the-mill, boy meets girl story here," stated Libby K. White in *School Library Journal,* adding that the novel "is romantic without being either mushy or explicitly sexual. Willis and Sophie are attractive characters who will interest and involve readers."

Snow Bound is another tale of two mismatched teens who are caught unprepared in a winter blizzard and must cooperate in order to survive. Tony is a spoiled rich kid who sets out to get revenge on his parents for not letting him keep a stray dog. He steals his mother's car and takes off in the middle of a snowstorm, picking up hitchhiker Cindy along the way. After getting lost, Tony wrecks the car in a desolate area, and he and Cindy must survive both the frigid cold and a pack of wild dogs. "The relationship that develops between the two of them is sensitively handled, never foolishly romanticized, and will probably be an easy thing for young readers to identify with," maintained Tom Heffernan in *Children's Literature. New York Times Book Review* contributor Cathleen Burns Elmer concluded that "the final measure of the book's capacity to enthrall lies in the *mature* reader's willingness to suspend disbelief. *Snow Bound* is a crackling tale; Mazer tells it with vigor and authority."

The main character in Mazer's *I Love You, Stupid!* is faced with more typical adolescent problems: High school senior Marcus wants to be a writer and is also obsessed with sex. *School Library Journal* contributor Kay Webb O'Connell pointed out that Marcus's erotic dreams include almost every young female he meets—everyone but Wendy, a girl he knew in grade school. Marcus even goes so far as to babysit for a young divorced woman, hoping she will become his lover. Wendy and Marcus finally make love, but the boy's aggressive pursuit of sex eventually drives Wendy away. "It takes most of the book to get them together, but it's better that way; Marcus and Wendy are friends who become lovers," observed O'Connell, concluding that Mazer's teen protagonists are "honest and humorous; their conversations and adventures are fresh and funny."

Who Is Eddie Leonard? introduces readers to a fifteen year old who lives with an eccentric elderly woman he calls Grandmother. When the woman dies, Eddie is left alone, but feels he must belong somewhere. A poster of a missing child named Jason Diaz changes everything for Eddie. Seeing the resemblance between himself and the missing boy, and calculating that Jason would now also be fifteen years old, Eddie hunts down the boy's family and introduces himself as their missing son. Now divorced and having given up their son as lost forever, Jason's parents are skeptical, and the missing boy's sister has been happy living as an only child. When the truth about his birth is finally discovered, Eddie must suffer further loss due to his emotional attachment to this new family. "Mazer has written a book teens will respond to," maintained *Voice of Youth Advocates* contributor Ruth E. Dishnow, calling *Who Is Eddie Leonard?* "a story about the often painful search for self-identity." While *School Library Journal* reviewer Lucinda Snyder Whitehurst felt that Mazer's terse, detached style makes the novel more a "series of strong character studies" than a cohesive story, Chris Sherman praised the book, writing in *Booklist* that Mazer's is "an emotionally charged story that readers will not be able to put down."

The Wild Kid finds Sammy, a twelve year old with Down's syndrome, building a reputation as a no-goodnik. Leaving the house without permission, Sammy gets his bike stolen and becomes lost in the woods outside of town while following the thief. In the forest he meets Kevin, a teen on the run. As Kevin's prisoner, Sammy gradually becomes the wild teen's friend, and Kevin ultimately helps the younger boy find his way home. Mazer's story was praised by several reviewers for its positive portrayal of an impaired child. *School Library Journal* contributor Carol A. Edwards asserted: "Vividly and with a fast pace, Mazer describes Sammy's world, his awful predicament, his magnificent spirit, and his incredible determination." Edwards concluded that *The Wild Kid* is "for anyone looking for an adventure, a survival story on many levels, or a compelling read."

Highly praised by critics, *The Last Mission* is based in part on Mazer's own experiences in World War II and "represents an amazing leap in writing," according to Donelson in *Voice of Youth Advocates.* Jewish fifteen-year-old Jack Raab is so desperate to fight against Hitler's Germany that he borrows his older brother's identification to enlist in the U.S. Army Air Forces. Jack is trained as a gunner, and he and his fellow crew members fly more than twenty missions out of England before being hit by enemy fire. The only one to survive, he ends up a German prisoner of war. *The Last Mission*

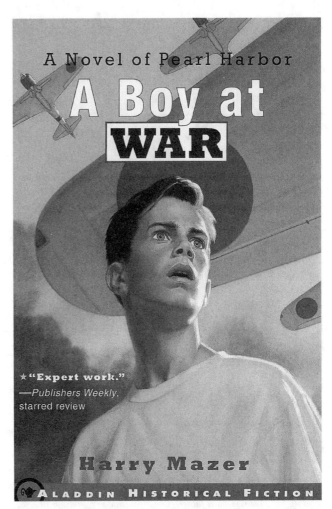

Adam is fishing with a friend near Honolulu when Japanese bombers attack nearby Pearl Harbor. Now his father's ship, the USS Arizona, *is in flames and Adam is determined to locate his missing dad. (Cover illustration by Tristan Elwell.)*

"conveys better than any other young adult novel, and better than most adult novels, the feeling of war and the desolation it leaves behind," Donelson noted, adding that the novel "is a remarkable achievement, both for its theme and its portrait of a young man who searches and acts and finds the search futile and the actions incoherent."

Mazer returns to the World War II era in a novel trilogy that includes *A Boy at War, A Boy No More,* and *Heroes Don't Run: A Novel of the Pacific War.* In *A Boy at War* readers meet fourteen-year-old Adam Pelko, whose naval officer father's reassignment to Hawaii has prompted the family's move to Pearl Harbor. Despite his father's disapproval, Adam makes friends with a Japanese-American boy named Davi Mori; the fateful morning that Japanese bombers begin making their deadly runs over the U.S. naval base on the harbor, the two boys are out fishing together. Focusing on racism and the violence of war, the novel presents what a *Horn Book* contributor called "a thought-provoking, sobering account of the human cost of war," while in *Publishers Weekly* a reviewer praised Mazer for presenting a

With his widowed mother and sister, Adam moves to California, but is drawn back into his old life when his best friend Davi asks for help in locating his Japanese-born father. (Cover illustration by Tristan Elwell.)

"vivid" depiction of the Japanese bombing while inserting in his story "subtle suggestions of the complexities of Japanese-American relations as played out in particular lives."

Adam's story continues in *A Boy No More,* as he comes to terms with his father's death in the bombing of the USS *Arizona* and moves with his mother and younger sister to California as the United States enters World War II. While he endeavors to live according to his late father's wishes, when Davi asks for Adam's help in locating his Japanese-born father, who has been transported to a California internment camp, the teen must decide what friendship is worth. In *Booklist,* Carolyn Phelan noted Mazer's inclusion of factual information about the war period and called *A Boy No More* "a satisfying coming-of-age story in a well-documented historical setting." Adam's story comes to a close in *Heroes Don't Run,* as Adam enlists in the U.S. Marines, makes it through boot camp, and is then sent to the Pacific theatre in time to participate in the battle for Okinawa in 1945. Commending the novel's first-person narration of a young soldier's experiences, Carol A. Edwards wrote in *School Library Journal* that Mazer's story is "more realistic than many novels about combat" written for a young-adult audience. In "telegraphic,

first-person prose," Mazer tells a story that a *Kirkus Reviews* critic praised for its "interesting detail," while noting that *Heroes Don't Run* is "strong on plot but short on character development." In *Kliatt,* Paula Rohrlick deemed Mazer's "spare, action-filled tale" "a good choice for reluctant readers and fans of historical fiction."

Other novels by Mazer include *The War on Villa Street,* about a boy's attempts to find stability in a family where his father's alcoholism and his mother's passivity mean constant upheaval and relocation. Ultimately his own passivity and sense of shame at his father's abuse cause the boy to fight back, building his self-confidence in the process. Also set in an urban area, *Cave under the City* takes place during the Great Depression, as two brothers find themselves parentless after their father's departure in search of work and their mother's subsequent collapse and hospitalization. When social workers attempt to separate the boys, they flee and live among New York City's homeless population until their father returns. *The War on Villa Street* was called "a moving, fast-paced story that once more proves Mazer's understanding of adolescence" by *School Library Journal* contributor Robert Unsworth, while Christine Behrmann noted in the same periodical that *Cave under the City* resonates with "the plight of today's homeless."

In addition to novel-length books and several collaborative efforts with his wife, Mazer has also written *The Dog in the Freezer: Three Novellas,* and edited the fiction collection *Twelve Shots: Outstanding Short Stories about Guns.* Focusing on dogs, the boys who own them, and the fathers who rule the family home, each of the stories in *The Dog in the Freezer* has a slightly quirky perspective. "My Life as a Boy" finds the family dog trading places with his human master for a day, while "Puppy Love" weaves a teen boy's summer crush on a pretty dog trainer with his growing affection for the puppy he adopted in order to gain the young woman's attention. In the title story, a boy struggles to figure out how to bury a neighbor's dead dog rather than leave it lying on the street. While of the opinion that Mazer is more adept at longer fiction, a *Kirkus Reviews* contributor praised *The Dog in the Freezer* as "an interesting departure."

Drawing on Mazer's personal concerns about modern society, *Twelve Shots* contains stories from a dozen authors who were asked to write about "not the politics of the gun, not the heated arguments or the polemics, but the way guns are present in people's lives." Mazer assembles works by well-known children's authors Walter Dean Myers, Chris Lynch, Frederick Busch, and Rita Williams-Garcia, among others, and also contributes his own short story, based on his novel *The Last Mission.* While the stories range from serious commentary on the devastation wrought by gun-related violence in modern society to humorous folk-like tales, Mazer's personal anti-gun slant is made clear. "Destruction clearly outweighs redemption in the bulk of these stories,"

Determined to take some action to avenge his father's death, Adam bluffs his way into the Marines and ultimately sees a different side of war after being deployed to Okinawa. (Cover illustration by Tristan Elwell.)

Elizabeth Bush commented in the *Bulletin of the Center for Children's Books,* "with manipulative power, paranoia, or profound despair generally behind the trigger." Including statistics about guns and other helpful information, *Twelve Shots* is "timely and thought provoking" as well as "an excellent springboard for discussion," in the opinion of *Booklist* contributor Helen Rosenberg.

In his novels as well as his shorter works of fiction, Mazer's writing reflects his overarching belief in the essential goodness of people, particularly young people, according to critics. As *Horn Book* reviewer Margaret A. Bush observed, the author's "characters are down to earth, very ordinary people who are flawed, inept, good. Their eccentricities, loneliness, and dreams are lightly touched with humor." In his *SAAS* essay, Mazer concluded: "I think underlying all my writing has always been the belief that beneath the surface of our differences there is a current, a dark stream that connects all of us, readers and writers, parents and children, the young and the old. Despite the erosion of time the child in us never dies. The search for love never ends, the need for connection, the desire to know who we are, and the need to find someone of our own to love. How else do I keep writing for young readers?"

Biographical and Critical Sources

BOOKS

Authors and Artists for Young Adults, Volume 5, Thomson Gale (Detroit, MI), 1990.
Beacham's Guide to Literature for Young Adults, Volume 6, Beacham Publishing (Osprey, FL), 1994.
Butler, Francelia, editor, *Children's Literature Review,* Volume 16, Thomson Gale (Detroit, MI), 1989, pp. 125-133.
Dreyer, Sharon Spredemann, *The Bookfinder: A Guide to Children's Literature about the Needs and Problems of Youth Aged 2-15,* Volume 1, American Guidance Service, 1977.
Nilsen, Alleen Pace, and Kenneth L. Donelson, *Literature for Today's Young Adults,* Scott, Foresman, 1985.
Reed, Arthea J.S., *Presenting Harry Mazer,* Twayne (New York, NY), 1996.
St. James Guide to Young Adult Writers, 2nd edition, St. James Press (Detroit, MI), 1999.
Sherrard-Smith, Barbara, *Children's Books of the Year: 1982,* Julia MacRae, 1983.
Something about the Author Autobiography Series, Volume 11, Thomson Gale (Detroit, MI), 1991, pp. 223-240.
Wilkin, Binnie Tate, *Survival Themes in Fiction for Children and Young People,* Scarecrow Press (Metuchen, NJ), 1978.

PERIODICALS

Booklist, November 15, 1993, Chris Sherman, review of *Who Is Eddie Leonard?,* p. 615; March 15, 1997, p. 1236; August, 1997, Helen Rosenberg, review of *Twelve Shots: Outstanding Short Stories about Guns,* p. 1899; August, 1998, John Peters, review of *The Wild Kid,* p. 2007; September 2, 2004, Carolyn Phelan, review of *A Boy No More,* p. 108.
Bulletin of the Center for Children's Books, October, 1997, Elizabeth Bush, review of *Twelve Shots,* p. 61; November, 1997, p. 109; December, 2004, Elizabeth Bush, review of *A Boy No More,* p. 175.
Children's Literature (annual), 1975, p. 206.
Horn Book, August, 1977; February, 1980; March-April, 1988, Margaret A. Bush, review of *The Girl of His Dreams,* pp. 209-210; September-October, 1998, Kitty Flynn, review of *The Wild Kid,* p. 611; May, 2001, Kitty Flynn, review of *A Boy at War: A Novel of Pearl Harbor,* p. 331.
Kirkus Reviews, August 15, 1974; January 1, 1980; May 15, 1985; September 15, 1985; October 1, 1986; March 15, 1997, review of *The Dog in the Freezer: Three Novellas,* p. 466; July 1, 1997, p. 1033; September 1, 2004, review of *A Boy No More,* p. 879; June 15, 2005, review of *Heroes Don't Run: A Novel of the Pacific War,* p. 687.
Kliatt, July, 2005, Paula Rohrlick, review of *Heroes Don't Run,* p. 13.
Los Angeles Times, March 12, 1988, Marianne Gingher, "A Boy Who Runs Meets a Girl Anxious to Catch Up."

New York Times Book Review, August 12, 1973, Cathleen Burns Elmer, review of *Snow Bound,* p. 8; November 17, 1974; December 2, 1979, Paxton Davis, review of *The Last Mission,* p. 41; September 13, 1981; November 15, 1981.

Publishers Weekly, November 1, 1985, p. 65; August 10, 1990, p. 446; February 10, 1997, review of *The Dog in the Freezer,* p. 84; May 7, 2001, review of *A Boy at War,* p. 247.

School Library Journal, October, 1971; December, 1978, Robert Unsworth, review of *The War on Villa Street,* p. 62; November, 1979; September, 1980; April, 1981; October, 1981, Kay Webb O'Connell, review of *I Love You, Stupid!,* p. 152; November, 1985; December, 1986, Christine Behrmann, review of *Cave under the City,* pp. 105-106; January, 1988, Libby K. White, review of *The Girl of His Dreams,* pp. 86-87; November, 1993, Lucinda Snyder Whitehurst, review of *Who Is Eddie Leonard?,* p. 125; October, 1998, Carol A. Edwards, review of *The Wild Kid,* p. 140; May, 2001, William McLoughlin, review of *A Boy at War,* p. 156; May, 2004, Vicki Reutter, review of *Snowbound,* p. 65; September, 2004, Denise Moore, review of *A Boy No More,* p. 212; August, 2005, Carol A. Edwards, review of *Heroes Don't Run,* p. 131.

Voice of Youth Advocates, February, 1983, Ken Donelson, "Searchers and Doers: Heroes in Five Harry Mazer Novels," pp. 19-21; October, 1984; August, 1985; April, 1994, Ruth E. Dishnow, review of *Who Is Eddie Leonard?,* p. 29; August, 1997, p. 190; June, 2001, review of *A Boy at War,* p. 124; August, 2005, Jay Wise, review of *Heroes Don't Run,* p. 221.

Washington Post Book World, July 10, 1977.

ONLINE

Writers Block Web site, http://www.writersblock.ca/ (summer, 1998), Diana Bocco, interview with Mazer.

*   *   *

McBAIN, Ed
See HUNTER, Evan

*   *   *

MEDINA, Jane 1953-

Personal

Born June 13, 1953, in Alhambra, CA; daughter of Harry R. (a civil engineer) and Anna M. (a secretary) Peirce; married Pablo Medina (a carpenter), June 14, 1980; children: Anna Maria, Joel. *Ethnicity:* "White by birth, Latina in my heart." *Education:* Azusa Pacific University, B.A., 1975; California State University, Fullerton, M.S., 1999. *Religion:* Christian. *Hobbies and other interests:* "Walking by the ocean, in the mountains, or just down the street—especially with my family."

Jane Medina

Addresses

Home—773 South Breezy Way, Orange, CA 92869. *Office*—California Elementary School, 1080 North California St., Orange, CA 92869. *E-mail*—Demedina@cs.com.

Career

Orange Unified School District, Orange, CA, elementary music teacher, 1977-82, bilingual education teacher, 1982-96, parent educator, 1995-97, English-as-a-second-language skills center teacher, 1996-97, elementary education teacher, 1997-99, reading specialist, starting 1999. California State University, Fullerton, guest instructor, 1997, model lesson teacher, 1998, adjunct professor of education, 1999-2003. *Reading Teacher,* member of review team, 1999, member of executive review board, beginning 1999. Presenter at elementary schools.

Member

International Reading Association, National Council of Teachers of English, National Educators Association, National Education Association, National Association of Bilingual Educators, Teachers of English to Speakers of Other Languages, Society of Children's Book Writers and Illustrators, Southern California Council on Literature for Children and Young People, California Teachers of English to Speakers of Other Languages, California Reading Association, Orange County Reading Association, Orange Unified Education Association.

Awards, Honors

Edwin Carr fellowship, California State University, Fullerton, 1999; finalist, Tomas Rivera Mexican-American Children's Book of the Year award, and Notable Book Award, National Council of Teachers of English, both 2000, both for *My Name Is Jorge on Both Sides of the River;* Américas Commended List, Consortium of Latin American Studies Programs, 2005, for *The Dream on Blanca's Wall.*

Writings

My Name Is Jorge on Both Sides of the River, illustrated by Fabricio Vanden Broeck, Boyds Mills Press (Honesdale, PA), 1999.

The Dream on Blanca's Wall: Poems in English and Spanish, illustrated by Robert Casilla, Boyds Mills Press (Honesdale, PA), 2004.

Tomás Rivera (easy-reader biography), illustrated by Edward Martinez, Harcourt (Orlando, FL), 2004.

Contributor of articles to educational journals, including *Language Arts* and *NEA Today,* and to books, including *Portfolios in the Classrooms.* Contributor of poetry to children's anthologies, teachers' magazines, and journals.

Work in Progress

Mr. Feather Saves the Weather, The Magic Chili Pot, Pablo, Lily and Suzette, and "various poems, short stories, and picture books."

Sidelights

Growing up in Garden Grove, California, writer and teacher Jane Medina recalled in a Boyds Mills Press release that she began writing letters and poems while still a teenager. Sensitive to criticism from others, the budding poet refused to share her work with anyone but her closest friends. Then, while writing a letter to thank the editor of an inspiring instructional volume, Medina decided to enclose a short poem as well. "To my surprise," Medina explained, "the editor wrote back—not to thank me for the letter, but to ask if I had any more poetry." Soon after, Medina realized that she had a talent for capturing the emotions of children in verse, and she began work on the collection of children's poems that was eventually published as *My Name Is Jorge on Both Sides of the River.*

In *My Name Is Jorge on Both Sides of the River,* a book of poems written in both Spanish and English, Medina describes the thoughts and feelings of a young boy trying to adjust to life in the United States. After his family crosses the river from Mexico, Jorge finds himself in a different world. While his parents retain their Mexican traditions and way in their new country, Jorge is torn between fitting in with U.S. society and preserving his Mexican heritage. Throughout the collection of poems, Medina illustrates the challenges Jorge faces as he learns the language and customs of his adopted country. Describing the verses as "insightful," *School Library Journal* reviewer Ann Welton wrote that *My Name Is Jorge on Both Sides of the River* "depicts the sometimes painful experience of adjusting to a new language and a new culture." A reviewer for *Horn Book* praised the seriousness of Medina's collection, concluding: "Finally—bilingual poems that aren't overflowing with happy colors and tortilla chips."

Medina presents a second collection of bilingual poetry in *The Dream on Blanca's Wall.* Blanca is in sixth grade and hopes to become a teacher. Unfortunately, she is afraid to pursue her goal, and worries that she will never be able to accomplish it. With encouragement from her loving family, a neighbor, and an insightful teacher, Blanca strengthens her confidence in achieving her dream. Medina's poems serve as an "excellent . . . teaching tool, both as a pattern for writing verse and as a discussion starter," wrote Ann Welton in *School Library Journal.* A *Kirkus Reviews* contributor commented that the "easy-to-read free verse encourages even the reluctant reader" for both languages.

In Tomás Rivera *Medina describes the childhood of the noted Hispanic author who, despite his family's poverty, gained a love of stories through his grandfather's tales and an early visit to the library. (Illustration by Edward Martinez.)*

Medina's bilingual poetry collection **The Dream on Blanca's Wall** *relates the thoughts and feelings of a young immigrant with dreams of one day becoming a teacher. (Illustration by Robert Casilla.)*

In an article for *Yellow Brick Road,* Medina explained how affected she has been as a teacher recognizing the difficulties confronting the Spanish-speaking students in her classrooms. "I think things are getting better for immigrant children in today's schools," she commented. "I don't think they'll ever be perfect, but I think people are trying harder to accept one another and we're more aware of the sense of our forefathers and our past." Medina dedicated *The Dream on Blanca's Wall* to the faculty members in the College of Education at California State University—Fullerton who worked with her on her master's degree. "I think every student deserves to be encouraged by at least one teacher," she told *Dateline* contributor Valerie Orleans. "I was in my 40s before I found the teachers to encourage me. I am so thankful to them."

A noted Mexican-American writer and teacher is the subject of Medina's easy-reader biography, *Tomás Rivera.* As a child, Rivera toiled as a migrant worker alongside the other members of his family, harvesting crops on farms. Rivera's grandfather always told stories after the day's work. Learning of Rivera's love for stories, his grandfather took the boy to the public library; this experience led Rivera to begin writing his own tales and to his later career as an educator. Carolyn Phelan, writing in *Booklist,* found the biography to be "a good introduction to Rivera for young children."

Discussing the influences in her own life, Medina explained to *SATA* that many are reflected in her book *The Dream on Blanca's Wall.* "Blanca is just like me: she wants something so bad, so bad and she thinks she'll never get it. And, like me, she's blessed with something much greater than her ambition . . . she just doesn't realize it. Blanca [also] symbolizes many of my students who have dreams about their futures, dreams they think will never come true. Blanca dreams of becoming a teacher, but is afraid even to think too much about it. It's just impossible.

"Blanca has gifts that help her believe in her dream. But the gifts are, themselves, even better than what she desires. Blanca has a family who loves her, a neighbor who creates a friendship from their differences, and Blanca has one teacher—just one—who sees her abilities and believes in her. I am blessed in these same ways: a loving family, supportive friends, and teachers who believed in me.

"Yes, I believe Blanca will become a teacher someday . . . just as I became a children's author. But richer and sweeter than any dream come true is the love of the people who surround me."

Biographical and Critical Sources

PERIODICALS

Booklist, July, 2004, Carolyn Phelan, review of *Tomás Rivera,* p. 1851.

Dateline (University of California—Fullerton), May 19, 2005, "CSUF Alumna Dedicates Book to Education Faculty," p. 2.
Horn Book, July-December, 1999, review of *My Name Is Jorge on Both Sides of the River,* p. 153.
Instructor, October, 2001, Alice Quiocho, review of *My Name Is Jorge on Both Sides of the River,* p. 18.
Kirkus Reviews, April 1, 2004, review of *The Dream on Blanca's Wall,* p. 334.
School Library Journal, February, 2000, Ann Welton, review of *My Name Is Jorge on Both Sides of the River,* p. 136; April, 2004, Ann Welton, review of *The Dream on Blanca's Wall,* p. 146.
Skipping Stones, September-October, 2005, review of *The Dream on Blanca's Wall,* p. 30.
Yellow Brick Road, November-December, 2004, "Jane Medina," pp. 1-3.

OTHER

Press release from Boyds Mills Press, 1999.*

*   *   *

METZENTHEN, David 1958-

Personal

Born December 27, 1958, in Melbourne, Victoria, Australia; son of Ron Arthur (a sharebroker) and Joan (Grey) Metzenthen; married; wife's name Fiona Miriam (a business manager); children: Ella, Liam. *Politics:* "Green." *Religion:* "Agnostic."

Addresses

Home—Melbourne, Victoria, Australia. *Agent*—c/o Author Mail, Penguin Group/Pearson Australia 250 Camberwell Rd., Camberwell, Victoria 3124, Australia.

Career

Writer. Formerly worked in advertising; Radio 3DB, former copywriter. Once worked variously as a gardener and grave digger. Victorian Premier's Reading Challenge, ambassador, 2005.

Awards, Honors

Children's Book Council of Australia (CBCA) Book of the Year for Younger Readers shortlist, and Multicultural Book of the Year Award shortlist, both 1995, both for *Brocky's Bananagram;* Ethel Turner Prize, New South Wales Premier's Literary Awards, 1996, for *Johnny Hart's Heroes,* and 2004, for *Tiff and the Trout;* CBCA Book of the Year for Older Readers Honor Book, 1997, for *Johnny Hart's Heroes,* 1998, for *Gilbert's Ghost Train,* and 2004, for *Boys of Blood and Bone;* Western Australia Young Readers Book Award for Older Reader, 1999, for *Finn and the Big Guy;* New South Wales Premier's Literary Award, and CBCA Book of the Year Award for Older Readers shortlist, both 2000, both for *Stony Heart Country;* State of Victoria Prize for Young-Adult Fiction shortlist, 2003, for *Wildlight.*

Writings

Danger Wave, Scholastic (Gosford, New South Wales, Australia), 1990.

Lee Spain, Scholastic (Gosford, New South Wales, Australia), 1991.

Brocky's Bananagram, Scholastic (Gosford, New South Wales, Australia), 1994.

Roadie, Omnibus Books (Norwood, South Australia, Australia), 1995.

Johnny Hart's Heroes, Puffin (Ringwood, Victoria, Australia), 1996.

Animal Instinct, Omnibus Books (Norwood, South Australia, Australia), 1996.

Gilbert's Ghost Train, Ashton Scholastic (Gosford, New South Wales, Australia), 1997.

Cody and Zero, Addison Wesley Longman (Melbourne, Victoria, Australia), 1997.

Lefty Lemon Kicks Goals, Addison Wesley Longman (Melbourne, Victoria, Australia), 1997.

Finn and the Big Guy, Penguin (Ringwood, Victoria, Australia), 1997.

The Diary of Fat Robby Pile, Addison Wesley Longman (Melbourne, Victoria, Australia), 1997.

Rodney the Surfing Duck, illustrated by Steve Axelson, Addison Wesley Longman (Melbourne, Victoria, Australia), 1997, Sundance (Littleton, MA), 1999.

Falling Forward, Omnibus Books (Norwood, South Australia, Australia), 1998.

Fort Island, illustrated by Peter Gouldthorpe, Penguin (Ringwood, Victoria, Australia), 1998.

Mick the Mimic, illustrated by Matt Golding, Addison Wesley Longman (Melbourne, Victoria, Australia), 1998.

The Red Hot Footy Fiasco, illustrated by Matt Golding, Addison Wesley Longman (Melbourne, Victoria, Australia), 1998.

Stony Heart Country, Penguin (Ringwood, Victoria, Australia), 1999.

The Hand-Knitted Hero, illustrated by David Cox, Penguin (Ringwood, Victoria, Australia), 1999.

Adrian Goes out There, Addison Wesley Longman (Melbourne, Victoria, Australia), 1999.

Last Chance Hut, Addison Wesley Longman (Melbourne, Victoria, Australia), 1999.

The Colour of Sunshine, Penguin (Ringwood, Victoria, Australia), 2000.

The Red Boxing Gloves, Word Weavers Press (Bulimba, Queensland, Australia), 2002.

Wildlight: A Journey, Penguin (Camberwell, Victoria, Australia), 2002.

The Really Really High Diving Tower, Puffin Books (Camberwell, Victoria, Australia), 2003.

Boys of Blood and Bones, Penguin (Camberwell, Victoria, Australia), 2003.

Spider!, illustrated by Peter Sheehan, Puffin Books (Camberwell, Victoria, Australia), 2004.

Tiff and the Trout, Puffin Books (New York, NY), 2004.

Anton Rocks On, Puffin Books (Camberwell, Victoria, Australia), 2004.

Time Turns on Spooky Hill, illustrated by Philip Webb, Word Weavers Press (Bulimba, Queensland, Australia), 2004.

Falling Forward, Penguin (Camberwell, Victoria, Australia), 2005.

The Rollercoaster, illustrated by Peter Sheehan, Puffin Books (Camberwell, Victoria, Australia), 2005.

The Really Really Epic Mini-Bike Ride, Puffin Books (Camberwell, Victoria, Australia), 2006.

Adaptations

Wildlight was adapted as an audiobook read by Michael Veitch, Bolinda Audio, 2003.

Sidelights

David Metzenthen is an award-winning author of books for children of many ages that are set in his native Australia. *Magpies* contributor Anne Briggs commended the delightful language employed in Metzenthen's young-adult novel *Falling Forward,* which tells the poignant story of the relationship between two "damaged" young men. Briggs maintained that the novel "is studded with memorable scenes expressed with delicacy and tenderness." Describing the author's text in *Johnny Hart's Heroes,* where two drifters leave a sideshow to become drovers for a sheep farmer, critic Kerry Neary observed in the same publication that "Metzenthen uses a laconic prose . . . that mirrors the heat-burdened laziness of an outback summer" and "is sparked with an imagery that is sometimes breathtaking in its originality."

Another novel for young adults, *Wildlight: A Journey* is a high-action story that recounts the life and adventures of Dirk Wildlight, an orphaned young man who is determined to find a new life in Greater Australia during the 1840, a time when the country was largely uninhabited. Reviewing the audiobook version of the novel, Julie Scordato wrote in *Kliatt* that Metzenthen's story "is packed with action as Dirk moves from place to place in search of a better life" and "he learns about his past, about love and how he is the opposite in every way to what the people who 'adopted' him believed him to be."

Written for younger children, *The Red Boxing Gloves* relates the story of two young boys, Bicky and Miles, who decide to solve their differences, and some mutual aggressions, in an official boxing match at their local youth club. "This is a fast moving story, with more than a touch of humour," noted Claire Saxby in *Aussie Reviews* online, adding that the easy-reading novel, which alternates points of view between the two boys, "is sure to capture the target reader," particularly elementary-grade boys who are note keen on reading but who will be attracted by the boxing motif.

Metzenthen once told *SATA:* "I write to give to my reader what I feel to be the most important things that I know or think about. I am interested in what we all seek in life, how we pursue happiness and fulfillment. I am a realist Australian writer who believes that place and landscape influence character and, because I care deeply about my country, I spend a lot of my writing time trying to show the 'soul' of the land of this place. I try to write simply, but I also try to present complex issues that face us all as we go about our lives. I love words and the way that good prose can be almost magical in its ability to convey deeply felt and complex meaning.

"I also believe I owe my readers the best, most entertaining work I can possible create."

Biographical and Critical Sources

PERIODICALS

Australian Book Review, July, 1996, p. 60; December, 1996, p. 86; May, 1997, p. 60.
Kliatt, March, 2004, Julie Scordato, review of *Wildlight: A Journey,* p. 58.
Magpies, March, 1992, p. 33; July, 1995, p. 26; May, 1996, Kerry Neary, review of *Johnny Hart's Heroes,* p. 50; May, 1997, p. 36; September, 1998, Anne Briggs, review of *Falling Forward,* p. 39; July, 2000, review of *Danger Wave,* p. 18; July, 2000, review of *Brockey's Bananagram,* p. 18; November, 2000, review of *The Colour of Sunshine,* p. 35; July, 2002, review of *Wildlight,* p. 39; July, 2002, review of *The Red Boxing Gloves,* p. 35; July, 2003, review of *Boys of Blood and Bone,* p. 41; November, 2003, review of *The Really Really High Diving Tower,* p. 35; November, 2004, Neville Barnard, review of *Time Turns on Spooky Hill,* p. 36; March, 2005, Kevin Steinberger, review of *Anton Rocks On,* p. 36.
Reading Time, August, 1998, p. 10; February, 1999, p. 31.

ONLINE

Aussie Reviews Online, http://www.aussiereviews.com/ (September 26, 2005), Claire Saxby, review of *The Red Boxing Gloves.*
Curriculum Materials Information Services Web site, http://www.amlib.eddept.wa.edu.au/ (September 27, 2005), Martin Turner, review of *Boys of Blood and Bone;* Jennifer Riggs, review of *Wildlight.*
Puffin at Penguin Books Australia Web site, http://www.penguin.com.au/ (September 26, 2005).
State Library of Victoria Web site, http://www.slv.vic.gov.au/ (September 26, 2005).
Victorian Premier's Reading Challenge Web site, http://www.sofweb.vic.edu.au/ (September 26, 2005), "David Metzenthen."
Word Weavers Press Web site, http://www.wordweaverspress.com.au/ (September 26, 2005).*

MORROW, Barbara Olenyik 1952-

Personal

Born March 3, 1952, in St. Louis, MO; daughter of Robert (a businessman) and Janet (a homemaker) Olenyik; married Douglas C. Morrow (an optometrist), July 31, 1976; children: Matthew, James, Andrew, Nathan. *Education:* Indiana University, B.A., 1974, M.A. (journalism), 1975. *Religion:* Presbyterian.

Addresses

Agent—c/o Author Mail, Holiday House, 425 Madison Ave., New York, NY 10017. *E-mail*—writolen@ctlnet.com.

Career

Journalist and author. Reporter for *Herald-Telephone,* Bloomington, IN, and *Louisville Times,* KY; *Journal-Gazette,* Fort Wayne, IN, editorial writer; freelance writer.

Awards, Honors

Pulitzer Prize finalist for editorial writing, 1986; honorable mention for children's literature, Best Books of Indiana award, 2005.

Writings

Those Cars of Auburn, privately published, 1987.
From Ben-Hur to Sister Carrie: Remembering the Lives and Works of Five Indiana Authors, Guild Press of Indiana (Indianapolis, IN), 1995.
A Good Night for Freedom, illustrated by Leonard Jenkins, Holiday House (New York, NY), 2004.

Sidelights

Barbara Olyenik Morrow told *SATA:* "When I moved to a small town in northern Indiana in 1979, a librarian mentioned to me that the Hoosier state had a rich liter-

Barbara Olenyik Morrow

The discovery that her neighbors are harboring runaway slaves forces a young girl to act on her own beliefs when confronted by slave hunters in **A Good Night for Freedom.** *(Illustration by Leonard Jenkins.)*

ary heritage. Not being a native of Indiana, I knew very little about any aspect of the state's history. So I began reading books by and about Indiana authors, and discovered that the librarian was correct—Indiana's literary heritage was exceptionally rich. In the early decades of the twentieth century Hoosier authors regularly penned best-sellers and some, such as naturalist and nature writer Gene Stratton-Porter, had fans in nearly every corner of the world.

"Eventually I wrote *From Ben-Hur to Sister Carrie: Remembering the Lives and Works of Five Indiana Authors,* in which I profiled the lives of five prominent Hoosier writers. Along with Stratton-Porter, I told the story of U.S. Civil War general Lew Wallace, whose novel *Ben-Hur: A Tale of the Christ* was among America's first literary blockbusters. In addition, I wrote about the beloved poet James Whitcomb, the Pulitzer Prize-winning novelist Booth Tarkington, and Theodore Dreiser, whose novel *Sister Carrie* was extremely contro-

versial in its day but is now recognized as a classic in modern American literature.

"Researching these writers taught me much about the history of America, including its literary coming-of-age in the late 1800s and early 1900s. Through these writers' lives, I came to better understand the impact the U.S. Civil War had on our nation's political and cultural life. As my interest in the Civil War era grew, I began reflecting anew on a subject that had long fascinated me: the Underground Railroad. Before long I discovered that Indiana had another claim to fame. It was home to Levi and Catharine Coffin, an abolitionist couple who worked tirelessly to help more than 2,000 runaway slaves escape north to freedom.

"In *A Good Night for Freedom,* an historical fiction picture book for children, I acquaint readers with the Coffins, whose Hoosier home was known as the "Grand Central Station" of the Underground Railroad. I also introduce two real-life runaways, whose names I learned researching nineteenth-century court records. The story, as a *Kirkus Reviews* contributor noted, 'presents young readers with a powerful dilemma.'

"For me, life is all about dilemmas and the choices we make in response. History teaches us that, though the particulars may differ, each generation struggles with essentially the same vexing problems: how to be happy, how to treat others fairly, how to live peacefully. As a writer, I have been inspired by the lives of historical figures—from Lew Wallace to the Coffins. As I've shared their stories, I hope that readers will find some truth to guide them as they weigh their choices and make decisions."

Biographical and Critical Sources

PERIODICALS

Booklist, March 1, 2004, Hazel Rochman, review of *A Good Night for Freedom,* p. 1206.

Bulletin of the Center for Children's Books, March, 2004, Timnah Card, review of *A Good Night for Freedom,* p. 289.

Kirkus Reviews, January 15, 2004, review of *A Good Night for Freedom,* p. 86.

Publishers Weekly, January 12, 2004, review of *A Good Night for Freedom,* p. 52.

School Library Journal, February, 2004, Beth Tegart, review of *A Good Night for Freedom,* p. 118.

N

NICKELL, Joe 1944-

Personal

Born December 1, 1944, in Lexington, KY; son of J. Wendell Nickell (a postmaster) and Ella Kathleen (a bookkeeper; maiden name, Turner) Nickell; children: Cherette Roycroft. *Education:* University of Kentucky, B.A., 1967, M.A., 1982, Ph.D., 1987. *Hobbies and other interests:* Collecting antique writing materials.

Addresses

Office—Center for Inquiry, P.O. Box 703, Amherst, NY 14226.

Career

Paranormal investigator, author, and educator. Volunteers in Service to America (VISTA), Washington, DC, volunteer worker in Carroll County, GA, 1967-68; professional stage magician in Toronto, Ontario, Canada, 1968-73; private investigator with Toronto agency, 1973-75; Dawson City Museum, Dawson City, Yukon Territory, Canada, museologist, 1975-76; freelance investigative writer, beginning 1976; University of Kentucky, Lexington, instructor in technical writing, 1980-95; Committee for the Scientific Investigation of Claims of the Paranormal, Amherst, NY, senior research fellow, 1995—. Presenter at conferences; lecturer at colleges and universities, including University of Kentucky, Heidelberg University, Old Dominion University, Yale University, Colgate University, University of Ghent, University of Toronto, University of Brussels, University of California at Berkeley, and California Institute of Technology. Has appeared on numerous radio and television programs.

Member

Historical Confederation of Kentucky (member of executive committee, 1988-95), Committee for the Scientific Investigation of Claims of the Paranormal (technical consultant, 1984-88; member of executive council, 1988).

Joe Nickell

Awards, Honors

Committee for the Scientific Investigation of Claims of the Paranormal fellow, 1988-2005.

Writings

FOR CHILDREN

(And illustrator) *The Magic Detectives,* Prometheus Books (Buffalo, NY), 1989.
(And illustrator) *Wonderworkers! How They Perform the Impossible,* Prometheus Books (Buffalo, NY), 1991.

FOR ADULTS

Inquest on the Shroud of Turin, Prometheus Books (Amherst, NY), 1983, reprinted, 1998.

(With John F. Fischer) *Secrets of the Supernatural,* Prometheus Books (Buffalo, NY), 1988.

Pen, Ink, and Evidence: A Study of Writing and Writing Materials for the Penman, Collector, and Document Detective, University Press of Kentucky (Lexington, KY), 1990.

Ambrose Bierce Is Missing, and Other Historical Mysteries, University Press of Kentucky (Lexington, KY), 1992, published as *Unsolved History: Investigating Mysteries of the Past,* 2005.

(With Robert A. Baker) *Missing Pieces: How to Investigate Ghosts, UFOs, Psychics, and Other Mysteries,* Prometheus Books (Buffalo, NY), 1992.

Looking for a Miracle: Weeping Icons, Relics, Stigmata, Visions, and Healing Cures, Prometheus Books (Buffalo, NY), 1993.

(Editor) *Psychic Sleuths: ESP and Sensational Cases,* Prometheus Books (Buffalo, NY), 1994.

Camera Clues: A Handbook for Photographic Investigation, University Press of Kentucky (Lexington, KY), 1994.

Entities: Angels, Spirits, Demons, and Other Alien Beings, Prometheus Books (Amherst, NY), 1995.

Detecting Forgery: Forensic Investigation of Documents, University Press of Kentucky (Lexington, KY), 1996.

(Editor with Kendrick Frazier and Barry Karr) *The UFO Invasion: The Roswell Incident, Alien Abductions, and Government Coverups,* Prometheus Books (Amherst, NY), 1997.

(With John F. Fischer) *Crime Science: Methods of Forensic Detection,* University Press of Kentucky (Lexington, KY), 1999.

Real-Life X-Files: Investigating the Paranormal, University Press of Kentucky (Lexington, KY), 2001, published as *Investigating the Paranormal,* Fine Communications (New York, NY), 2004.

The Kentucky Mint Julep, University Press of Kentucky (Lexington, KY), 2003.

The Mystery Chronicles: More Real-Life X-Files, University Press of Kentucky (Lexington, KY), 2004.

Secrets of the Sideshows, University Press of Kentucky (Lexington, KY), 2005.

Contributor to periodicals, including *Popular Photography, Journal of Police Science and Administration, Law Enforcement Technology, Indiana Folklore, Journal of Forensic Identification, Virginia Magazine of History and Biography, Canada West, Filson Club History Quarterly, International Journal of Forensic Document Examiners, Humanist, Fate, Science et Vie, Skeptical Inquirer, American Rationalist, Performing Arts in Canada, Christian Life, Current Anthropology, Fire and Arson Investigator, Lincoln Herald, Appalachian Heritage, Free Inquiry, Journal of Kentucky Studies, Identification News, Manuscripts,* and *Behavioral and Social Sciences Librarian.*

Sidelights

In addition to a career in document analysis that has prompted him to write the books *Pen, Ink, and Evidence: A Study of Writing and Writing Materials for the Penman, Collector, and Document Detective* and *Detecting Forgery: Forensic Investigation of Documents,* Joe Nickell has been described by *New Yorker* writer Burkhard Bilger as "the country's most accomplished investigator of the paranormal." In his job as senior researcher for the Committee for the Scientific Investigation of Claims of the Paranormal (CSCIOP), Nickell attends séances, healing services, and other events wherein connections with otherworldly entities are claimed to occur. He also publishes a column in *Skeptical Inquirer,* which is published by CSICOP, an organization founded in 1976 to evaluate paranormal and pseudoscientific claims within a rational framework. Nickell stands as a skeptic in a world in which, according to Bilger, "half of all Americans believe in E.S.P., more than forty per cent believe in demonic possession and haunted houses, and about a third believe in astrology, clairvoyance, and ghosts." Not surprisingly, Nickell's books *Real-Life X-Files: Investigating the Paranormal* and *The UFO Invasion: The Roswell Incident, Alien Abductions, and Government Coverups* have gained a teen readership due to their fascinating premise, while *Crime Science: Methods of Forensic Detection* has an attraction to fans of the mega-popular *CSI* television series.

In *Real-Life X-Files,* as well as its sequel, *The Mystery Chronicles: More Real-Life X-Files,* Nickell collects dozens of articles he has written for *Skeptical Inquirer* magazine that debunk claims of paranormal activity. In addition to research, Nickell describes on-site experiences that range from visits to crop circles to meetings with spiritualists and witnessing stigmata and other seemingly unearthly manifestations. In *Booklist* George Eberhart noted that "skeptical teens will enjoy the debunking of these 'paranormal'" phenomena, an activity that is approached in a serious manner in *Real-Life X-Files.* Also praising Nickell's reasoned approach in studying everything from mind-reading dogs to haunted houses, *Skeptical Inquirer* reviewer Kendrick Frazier wrote that the investigator "demonstrates the power of his neither too-credulous nor too-dismissive attitude" in the process of revealing far more plausible explanations for these unusual events.

Nickell told *SATA:* "In my childhood I wanted to be many things—magician, detective, museum curator, artist, and writer, among others—and I played at being each. For example, with a glued-on mustache and a kit of tricks, I gave magical performances in my grandmother's parlor. An extra upstairs room in our home became alternately a 'crime lab,' 'museum,' 'artist's studio,' and so on.

"I grew up to do all these things and more, becoming (as one source dubbed me) 'a man with a hundred

Nickell studies everything from New England graveyard ghouls to Louisiana swamp monsters in his book The Mystery Chronicles: More Real-Life X Files.

faces.' I call them *personas*. Growing up, I worked as a popcorn vendor, surveyor's chainman, sign painter, and (in high school) athletic trainer and scoreboard operator.

"At one time or another, I have been a carnival pitchman, stage magician (I was resident magician at the Houdini Magical Hall of Fame in Niagara Falls, Canada, from 1970 to 1972), clown, political cartoonist, blackjack dealer, freelance broadcaster, prospector, riverboat manager, museum-exhibit designer, armed guard, movie extra, and many more, including private investigator (with undercover 'roles' such as mail clerk, steelworker, lens polisher, forklift driver, tavern waiter, and shipper-receiver). I also have an avocation as a questioned-document examiner, having been involved in many famous cases of suspected historical texts.

"I am currently a paranormal investigator—perhaps the only full-time, salaried one in the world—meaning I am alternately (as a skeptic) a ghost hunter, UFOlogist, cryptozoologist (one who studies unknown animals like Bigfoot), etc. As part of this work, I am an investigative writer for *Skeptical Inquirer* science magazine, which occasionally finds me also wearing the hats of illustrator, photographer, and proofreader.

"Even as a writer, I've been something of a chameleon: children's author, poet, forensic-science writer, carnival historian, editor, advertising copywriter, columnist, newspaper stringer, historical reporter, and so on.

"Why have I done so many things? Like every child, I think, I had changing ideas of what I wanted to be when I 'grew up.' Maybe I never really grew up. But since I began to think of myself primarily as an author (which kept me from having an identity crisis!), it made sense to try on different 'costumes,' so to speak (sometimes quite literally), in order to learn about people and the world. I have been able to view life from different windows, different perspectives, and thus to learn more about myself as well. In fact, I believe the most creative thing one can do is to shape one's own life, not merely to drift along at the mercy of circumstances. I realize I've been very fortunate to be able to follow Thoreau's advice: 'Go confidently in the direction of your dreams. Live the life you've imagined.' Others who influenced me were George Plimpton, the participatory journalist, and Ferdinand Waldo Demara, the 'Great Impostor.'

"Some of my roles—notably Vietnam War protester, civil-rights organizer, and teacher—have involved expressions of my most deeply held values. As to new personas, while continuing to be an investigative writer, I have also become a part-time antiques dealer and virtual-museum curator (see www.skeptiseum.org). I am currently a Toastmaster in training. Born in 1944 (you can do the math!), I am of sufficient age that it's unlikely I'll become an astronaut, and I never realized my childhood role of pirate. But I can still dream, can't I?"

Biographical and Critical Sources

PERIODICALS

Booklist, October 15, 2001, George Eberhart, review of *Real-Life X-Files: Investigating the Paranormal,* p. 357; March 15, 2004, George Eberhart, review of *The Mystery Chronicles: More Real-Life X-Files,* p. 1245.

Criminal Justice Review, spring, 2000, Jeffrey D. Lane, review of *Crime Science: Methods of Forensic Detection,* p. 143.

Library Journal, February 15, 1999, Michael Sawyer, review of *Crime Science,* p. 168;.

Library Quarterly, July, 2001, Clay Stalls, review of *Pen, Ink, and Evidence: A Study of Writing and Writing Materials for the Penman, Collector, and Document Detective,* p. 421.

New Yorker, December 23-30, 2002, Burkhard Bilger, "Waiting for Ghosts: The Many Careers of Joe Nickell, Paranormal Investigator," pp. 86-88, 93-100.

Publishers Weekly, November, 9, 1998, review of *Crime Science,* p. 65.

Skeptical Inquirer, May-June, 1995, Robert A. Baker, review of *Psychic Sleuths: ESP and Sensational Cases,* p. 44; July-August, 2002, Robert A. Baker, "Truth Really Is Stranger than Fiction—and More Entertaining," review of *Real-Life X Files,* p. 55; July-August, 2004, Kendrick Frazier, review of *The Mystery Chronicles,* p. 58.

USA Today, May, 1999, Gerald F. Kreyche, review of *Crime Science,* p. 80.

ONLINE

Joe Nickell Home Page, http://www.joenickell.com (January 10, 2006).

R

RANDALL, David 1972-

Personal

Born March 25, 1972, in New York, NY; son of Francis (a history professor) and Laura Rosenbaum (an economics professor) Ballard; married Laura Congleton, June 2, 2001. *Education:* Swarthmore College, B.A., 1993; Columbia University, M.F.A., 1996; Fordham University, M.A., 2000; Rutgers University, Ph.D., 2005.

Addresses

Home—New York, NY. *Agent*—Simon Lipskar, Writer's House, 21 W. 26th St., New York, NY 10010.

Career

Writer.

Writings

Clovermead: In the Shadow of the Bear (young-adult fantasy novel), Margaret K. McElderry Books (New York, NY), 2004.

Work in Progress

A sequel to *Clovermead.*

Sidelights

While still a graduate student, David Randall wrote *Clovermead: In the Shadow of the Bear,* a fantasy adventure novel. The story tells of Clovermead Wickward, a twelve-year-old tomboy, as she attempts to assist the innkeeper Waxmelt, a man who has raised her as if she were his own daughter. Clovermead's journey leads her into a battle between good and evil that allows her to see past society's many deceptions and find her own place in the adult world.

Jennifer Mattson, in a review of *Clovermead* for *Booklist,* commented on Randall's decision to add a dark side to his young heroine's personality, noting that it "puts an intriguing spin on the otherwise archetypal fantasy plot." A *Kirkus Reviews* contributor called Clovermead "vivacious, loquacious, precocious," and "a delightful heroine," while in *School Library Journal,* Jane G. Conner deemed the novel "a challenging high fantasy for those who can keep straight many details and forces, and who don't mind a good bit of violence." Dubbing Randall "a writer to watch," a *Publishers Weekly* contributor concluded that *Clovermead* will attract "fantasy buffs" due to its "fast-paced plotting and the turn of events at the end."

In discussing his novel and its influences, Randall explained: "*Clovermead* looks with admiration to L.N. Montgomery, Lloyd Alexander, Ursula K. LeGuin, C.S. Lewis, and of course, J.R.R. Tolkien. Unlike my heroine, I am not twelve years old, blonde, or female, but I have been known to fence, and I am told we talk alike."

Biographical and Critical Sources

PERIODICALS

Booklist, July, 2004, Jennifer Mattson, review of *Clovermead: In the Shadow of the Bear,* p. 1834.
Kirkus Reviews, June 15, 2004, review of *Clovermead,* p. 580.
Publishers Weekly, August 2, 2004, review of *Clovermead,* p. 71.
School Library Journal, July, 2004, Jane G. Connor, review of *Clovermead,* p. 112.

ONLINE

Fables.org, http://www.fables.org/ (April 16, 2005), "David Randall."

NimbleSpirit.com, http://www.nimblespirit.com/ (June 28, 2005), Christy Risser-Milne, review of *Clovermead.*

WritersWrite.com, http://www.writerswrite.com/ (June 28, 2005), Claire E. White, review of *Clovermead.*

*   *   *

RAPPOPORT, Ken 1935-

Personal

Born February 14, 1935, in Brooklyn, NY; son of Jacob (in sales) and Margie (in business; maiden name, Geller) Rappoport; married Bernice Goodman (a teacher and artist), March 26, 1961; children: Felicia Lowenstein, Sharon Bell, Larry. *Education:* Rider College, B.S., 1956. *Politics:* Democrat. *Religion:* Jewish. *Hobbies and other interests:* Photography, cooking, travel.

Addresses

Home—29 Owens Rd., Old Bridge, NJ 08857.

Career

Journalist and author. Dorf Feature Service, Newark, NJ, feature writer and reporter, 1960-61; *Doylestown Intelligencer,* Doylestown, PA, reporter, 1961-63; Associated Press, reporter in Philadelphia, PA, 1963-69, sports writer in New York, NY, 1969-99; freelance writer. *Military service:* U.S. Army, 1958-60, served in Germany; became private first class.

Member

Professional Hockey Writers Association, Baseball Writers Association of America.

Awards, Honors

Sports Digest Best Story of the Month designation, November, 1973; second-place award, *Writer's Digest* National Writing Competition, 1991; Books for the Teen Age citation, New York Public Library, 1993, for *Bobby Bonilla,* and 1994, for *Shaquille O'Neal; Voice of Youth Advocates* honor list, 1996, for *Grant Hill;* New York Public Library Books for the Teen Age designation, 1997, for *Guts and Glory;* Sugarman Children's Biography Award nominee, 2005, for *Ladies First.*

Writings

NONFICTION

The Nittany Lions: A Story of Penn State Football, Strode, 1973, revised edition, 1979.

The Trojans: A Story of Southern California Football, Strode, 1974.

The Syracuse Football Story, Strode, 1975.

Wake up the Echoes: Notre Dame Football, Strode, 1975, revised edition, 1979.

Tar Heel: North Carolina Football, Strode, 1976.

Tar Heel: North Carolina Basketball, Strode, 1976, revised edition, 1979.

Great College Football Rivalries, Grosset (New York, NY), 1978.

The Classic: The History of the NCAA Basketball Playoffs, National Collegiate Athletic Association-Lowell Press, 1979.

Diamonds in the Rough, Grosset (New York, NY), 1979.

Super Sundays, Grosset (New York, NY), 1980.

Pigskin Power, Grosset (New York, NY), 1981.

Doubleheader: Yankees and Dodgers, Grosset (New York, NY), 1982.

Football's Special Teams: Cowboys and Raiders, Grosset (New York, NY), 1982.

Nolan Ryan: The Ryan Express, Dillon Press (Minneapolis, MN), 1992.

Bobby Bonilla, Walker & Co. (New York, NY), 1993.

Shaquille O'Neal, Walker & Co. (New York, NY), 1994.

Top Ten Basketball Legends, Enslow (Berkeley Heights, NJ), 1995.

Sports Great Wayne Gretzky, Enslow (Berkeley Heights, NJ), 1996.

Grant Hill, Walker & Co. (New York, NY), 1996.

Sports Great Eric Lindros, Enslow (Springfield, NJ), 1997.

Guts and Glory: Making It in the NBA, Walker & Co. (New York, NY), 1997.

Mario Lemieux: Star Center, Enslow (Springfield, NJ), 1998.

(With Barry Wilner) *They Changed the Game: Sports Pioneers of the Twentieth Century,* Andrews-McMeel (Kansas City, MO), 1999.

Scottie Pippen: Star Forward, Enslow (Springfield, NJ), 1999.

(With Barry Wilner) *Girls Rule!: The Glory and Spirit of Women in Sports,* foreword by Billie Jean King, Andrews McMeel (Kansas City, MO), 2000.

Tim Duncan: Star Forward, Enslow (Berkeley Heights, NJ), 2000.

(With Barry Wilner) *Villains: The Bad Boys and Girls of Sports,* Stark Books (Kansas City, MO), 2000.

Super Sports Star Penny Hardaway, Enslow (Berkeley Heights, NJ), 2001.

Tales from the Tar Heel Locker Room, Sports Publishing, 2002.

Super Sports Star Glen Rice, Enslow (Berkeley Heights, NJ), 2002.

Sheryl Swoopes, Star Forward, Enslow (Berkeley Heights, NJ), 2002.

Super Sports Star Peyton Manning, Enslow (Berkeley Heights, NJ), 2003.

Tales from Penn State Football, Sports Publishing, 2003.

Super Sports Star Jerome Bettis, Enslow (Berkeley Heights, NJ), 2003.

Super Sports Star Derek Jeter, Enslow (Berkeley Heights, NJ), 2004.

Jason Kidd: Leader on the Court, Enslow (Berkeley Heights, NJ), 2004.

Super Sports Star Alex Rodriguez, Enslow (Berkeley Heights, NJ), 2004.

Super Sports Star Ichiro Suzuki, Enslow (Berkeley Heights, NJ), 2004.

Ladies First: Women Athletes Who Made a Difference, Peachtree (Atlanta, GA), 2005.

(With Barry Wilner) *Gridiron Glory: The Story of the Army-Navy Football Rivalry,* Taylor Trade Publishing (Lanham, MD), 2005.

Penn State: Where Have You Gone?, Sports Publishing (Champaign, IL), 2005.

Profiles in Sports Courage, Peachtree (Atlanta, GA), 2006.

Contributor to books, including *A Century of Sports,* edited by Will Grimsley, Associated Press, 1971; *The Sports Immortals,* edited by Grimsley, Prentice-Hall, 1972; *The World in 1974,* edited by Tom Hoge, Associated Press; *A Century of Champions,* edited by Ben Olan, Associated Press, 1976; *Football's Fifty Greatest Games,* Bobbs-Merrill, 1983; and *101 Greatest Athletes of the Century,* Bonanza Books, 1987. Contributor to national sports journals, *Saturday Evening Post,* and *USA Today.*

Sidelights

Long-time journalist Ken Rappoport spent many years on the sidelines as a sports reporter for the Associated Press. He covered professional sports for over three decades, following the teams, coaches, players, and plays in football, basketball, hockey, and baseball, from season opener to nail-biting playoff. In more recent years he has channeled his vast knowledge of professional sports into a number of books for children and adults, from player profiles that include *Sheryl Swoopes, Star Forward, Super Sports Star Glen Rice,* and *Top Ten Basketball Legends* to broader sports-related books such as *Profiles in Sports Courage, Ladies First: Women Athletes Who Made a Difference,* and *Gridiron Glory: The Story of the Army-Navy Football Rivalry.*

In *Ladies First* Rappoport profiles twelve of the top twentieth-century women athletes, including four-time Iditarod winner Susan Butcher, African-American tennis pro Althea Gibson, and champion American swimmer Gertrude Ederle, in what *School Library Journal* contributor Janice C. Hayes described as a "lively" prose that results in an "entertaining and easy read." A collaboration with fellow writer Barry Wilner, *Gridiron Glory* presents a history as well as a profile of the best players to appear on the field during one of the country's most widely followed football face-offs: the Army-Navy rivalry. In the 240-page sports history, the co-authors "compellingly portray the pathos and irony" that players have invested in the team competition since it started back in 1890, according to Wes Lukowsky in *Booklist.* Commenting on Rappoport's skill as a biographer, *Booklist* contributor Julie Corsaro noted that in *Grant Hill* the author writes in "smart, energetic prose" and "never talks down to his audience," while Shelley Townsend-Hudson wrote in the same periodical that Rappoport's "readable style" in *Guts and Glory: Making It in the NBA* brings to life each athlete's "dedica-

Joining the newly formed Women's National Basketball Association along with Rebecca Lobo (left) is one of the many achievements made by Sheryl Swoopes (right) and outlined in Rappaport's 2002 biography. (Photograph from Sheryl Swoopes, Star Forward.*)*

tion and perseverance" in the face of sometimes intimidating obstacles.

Rappoport once told *SATA:* "This may sound corny, but I believe I was born to be a writer. Nothing I have ever done in my life has ever given me this kind of satisfaction—particularly in the area of books. I love the idea of putting a book together, watching it grow day by day from a seed. The work itself is the most important thing—from original idea, library research, interviews, writing, rewriting, to finished product. I could no less stop writing than stop breathing. I have combined my love of writing with my love of sports, and most of my work feeds off my career as a sportswriter with the Associated Press in New York. My only object is to become a better writer with each project. It goes without saying that there is great satisfaction in knowing I have made a contribution to our society and will leave something lasting for future generations.

"My advice to aspiring writers is: Always follow your dream."

Biographical and Critical Sources

PERIODICALS

Booklist, January 1, 1997, Julie Corsaro, review of *Grant Hill,* p. 840; August, 1997, Shelley Townsend-Hudson, review of *Guts and Glory: Making It in the NBA,* p. 1895; October 15, 2001, Carolyn Phelan, review of *Super Sports Star Penny Hardaway,* p. 420; Septem-

The accomplishments of a host of women within sports ranging from competitive distance swimming and organized basketball to the grueling Iditarod dogsled race are the subject of Rappaport's inspiring 2005 book. (Cover design by Melanie McMahon Ives.)

ber 1, 2002, Gillian Engberg, review of *Sheryl Swoopes,* p. 130; November 1, 2005, Wes Lukowsky, review of *Gridiron Glory: The Story of the Army-Navy Football Rivalry,* p. 12.

School Library Journal, January, 1997, Tom S. Hurlburt, review of *Grant Hill,* p. 133; July, 1997, Tom S. Hurlburt, review of *Guts and Glory,* p. 111; June, 2005, Janice C. Hayes, review of *Ladies First: Women Athletes Who Made a Difference,* p. 185.

Sentinel (East Brunswick, NJ), November 14, 2002, Dick Metzgar, "Pair Merges Artwork for Local Library," p. 1.

*   *   *

RAU, Dana Meachen 1971-

Personal

Born October 15, 1971, in CT; married Christopher Rau (a teacher), July 2, 1994. *Education:* Trinity College (Hartford, CT), B.A., 1993. *Hobbies and other interests:* Reading, watching movies, knitting, playing with her children.

Addresses

Home—22 Candlewood Rd., Burlington, CT 06013.

Career

Children's book writer and editor.

Member

Society of Children's Book Writers and Illustrators, Phi Beta Kappa.

Awards, Honors

Trumbull (CT) Arts Festival Literary Competition first-place award, 1993, for story "The Date," and honorable mentions, 1996, for stories "The Traveler" and "Delusions of Grandeur"; International Reading Association/Children's Book Council Children's Choice designation, 1998, for *A Box Can Be Many Things; Booklist* Top-Ten Sci-Tech Books, 2002, for *A Star in My Orange; Learning* magazine Teachers' Choice designation, 2004, for "Our Solar System" series; Association of Educational Publishers Distinguished Achievement award finalist, 2005, for *The Amazing Body: The Five Senses.*

Writings

FOR CHILDREN

Robin at Hickory Street, illustrated by Joel Snyder, Soundprints (Norwalk, CT), 1995.

One Giant Leap: The First Moon Landing, illustrated by Thomas Buchs, Soundprints, 1996.

A Box Can Be Many Things, illustrated by Paige Billin-Frye, Children's Press (New York, NY), 1997.

Undersea City: A Story of a Caribbean Coral Reef, illustrated by Katie Lee, Soundprints (Norwalk, CT),1997.

Arctic Adventure: Inuit Life in the 1800s, illustrated by Peg Magovern, Soundprints (Norwalk, CT), 1997.

The Secret Code, illustrated by Bari Weissman, Children's Press (New York, NY), 1998.

(Self-illustrated) *Bob's Vacation,* Children's Press (New York, NY), 1999.

Circle City, illustrated by Susan Miller, Children's Press (New York, NY), 1999.

Panama, Children's Press (New York, NY), 1999.

Purple Is Best, illustrated by Mike Cressy, Children's Press (New York, NY), 1999.

(With Christopher Rau) *George Lucas: Creator of Star Wars,* Franklin Watts (New York, NY), 1999.

Explore in a Cave, photographs by Romie Flanagan, Rourke Press (Vero Beach, FL), 2000.

Christmas, Children's Press (New York, NY), 2000.

Chanukah, Children's Press (New York, NY), 2000.

Feet, illustrated by Rick Stromoski, Children's Press (New York, NY), 2000.

Hands, illustrated by Rick Stromoski, Children's Press (New York, NY), 2000.

Kwanzaa, Children's Press (New York, NY), 2000.

New Year's Day, Children's Press (New York, NY), 2000.

(Self-illustrated) *My Book by Me,* Children's Press (New York, NY), 2000.

Stroll by the Sea, Rourke Press (Vero Beach, FL), 2000.

Thanksgiving, Children's Press (New York, NY), 2000.

Chilly Charlie, illustrated by Martin Lemelman, Children's Press (New York, NY), 2001.

Climb up a Mountain, photographs by Romie Flanagan, Rourke Press (Vero Beach, FL), 2001.

Clown Around, illustrated by Nate Evans, Compass Point Books (Minneapolis, MN), 2001.

Favorite Foods, illustrated by Grace Lin, Compass Point Books (Minneapolis, MN), 2001.

Halloween, Children's Press (New York, NY), 2001.

Harriet Tubman, Compass Point Books (Minneapolis, MN), 2001.

Harry Houdini: Master Magician, Franklin Watts (New York, NY), 2001.

Hats!, illustrated by Paul Harvey, Compass Point Books (Minneapolis, MN), 2001.

In the Yard, illustrated by Elizabeth Wolf, Compass Point Books (Minneapolis, MN), 2001.

Lots of Balloons, illustrated by Jayoung Choi, Compass Point Books (Minneapolis, MN), 2001.

Marie Curie, Compass Point Books (Minneapolis, MN), 2001.

Martin Luther King, Jr., Day, Children's Press (New York, NY), 2001.

Rosh Hashanah and Yom Kippur, Children's Press (New York, NY), 2001.

Shoo Crow! Shoo!, illustrated by Mary Rojas, Compass Point Books (Minneapolis, MN), 2001.

So Many Sounds, illustrated by Kristin Sorra, Children's Press (New York, NY), 2001.

Splash in a Pond, Rourke Press (Vero Beach, FL), 2001.

Uncle's Bakery, illustrated by Janie Baskin, Compass Point Books (Minneapolis, MN), 2001.

Valentine's Day, Children's Press (New York, NY), 2001.

Visit the Desert, photographs by Romie Flanagan, Rourke Press (Vero Beach, FL), 2001.

Walk in the Woods, photographs by Romie Flanagan, Rourke Press (Vero Beach, FL), 2001.

Ways to Go, illustrated by Jane Conteh-Morgan, Compass Point Books (Minneapolis, MN), 2001.

Wonderful Things, illustrated by Viki Woodworth, Compass Point Books (Minneapolis, MN), 2001.

Australia, Smart Apple Media (Mankato, MN), 2002.

I'll Make You a Card, illustrated by Jan Bryan-Hunt, Compass Point Books (Minneapolis, MN), 2002.

"Ladies and Gentlemen!", illustrated by Jim Caputo, Compass Point Books (Minneapolis, MN), 2002.

Life on the Oregon Trail, Kidhaven Press (San Diego, CA), 2002.

Look down Low, illustrated by Bernard Adnet, Compass Point Books (Minneapolis, MN), 2002.

Making Music, illustrated by Maureen Ivy Fisher, Compass Point Books (Minneapolis, MN), 2002.

Mount Rushmore, Compass Point Books (Minneapolis, MN), 2002.

My Red Rowboat, illustrated by Miriam Sagasti, Compass Point Books (Minneapolis, MN), 2002.

Pet Your Pet, illustrated by Jeffrey Scherer, Compass Point Books (Minneapolis, MN), 2002.

Rubber Duck, illustrated by Patrick Girouard, Compass Point Books (Minneapolis, MN), 2002.

Say "Hi!" up High, illustrated by Mike Dammer, Compass Point Books (Minneapolis, MN), 2002.

A Star in My Orange: Looking for Nature's Shapes, Millbrook Press (Brookfield, CT), 2002.

The Statue of Liberty, Compass Point Books (Minneapolis, MN), 2002.

Uncle's Bakery, illustrated by Janie Baskin, Compass Point Books (Minneapolis, MN), 2002.

Yahoo for You, illustrated by Cary Pillo, Compass Point Books (Minneapolis, MN), 2002.

Albert Einstein, Compass Point Books (Minneapolis, MN), 2003.

Dr. Seuss, Children's Press (New York, NY), 2003.

Frederick Douglass, Compass Point Books (Minneapolis, MN), 2003.

George Armstrong Custer, Compass Point Books (Minneapolis, MN), 2003.

The Moon, Compass Point Books (Minneapolis, MN), 2003.

Moon Walk, illustrated by Thomas Buchs, Soundprints (Norwalk, CT), 2003.

Neil Armstrong, Children's Press (New York, NY), 2003.

Neptune, Compass Point Books (Minneapolis, MN), 2003.

My Special Space, Children's Press (New York, NY), 2003.

Tired of Waiting, illustrated by Brad Fitzpatrick, Picture Window Books (Minneapolis, MN), 2004.

North America, Child's World (Chanhassen, MN), 2004.

Iraq, Benchmark Books (New York, NY), 2004.

Antarctica, Child's World (Chanhassen, MN), 2004.

I Am in Charge of Me, illustrated by Shirley Beckes, Picture Window Books (Minneapolis, MN), 2005.

The Harlem Renaissance, Compass Point Books ("We the People" series), Compass Point Books (Minneapolis, MN), 2005.

Great Women of the Suffrage Movement, Compass Point Books (Minneapolis, MN), 2005.

Sounds like Fun, illustrated by Marcelo Elizalde, Picture Window Books (Minneapolis, MN), 2005.

(With Jonatha A. Brown) *Pennsylvania,* Gareth Stevens (Milwaukee, WI), 2005.

Let's Share, illustrated by Béatrice Favereau, Picture Window Books (Minneapolis, MN), 2005.

The Whale in the Water, Marshall Cavendish Benchmark (New York, NY), 2005.

Stickers, Shells, and Snow Globes, illustrated by Claude Thivierge, Picture Window Books (Minneapolis, MN), 2005.

The Robin in the Tree, Marshall Cavendish Benchmark (New York, NY), 2006.

The Lion in the Grass, Marshall Cavendish Benchmark (New York, NY), 2006.

The Butterfly in the Sky, Marshall Cavendish Benchmark (New York, NY), 2006.

Andrew Carnegie: Captain of Industry, Compass Point Books (Minneapolis, MN), 2006.

The Frog in the Pond, Marshall Cavendish Benchmark (New York, NY), 2006.

Flying, Marshall Cavendish Benchmark (Tarrytown, NY), 2006.

Floating, Marshall Cavendish Benchmark (New York, NY), 2006.

Elizabeth Dole: Public Servant and Senator, Compass Point Books (Minneapolis, MN), 2006.

Driving, Marshall Cavendish Benchmark (New York, NY), 2006.

Climbing, Marshall Cavendish Benchmark (New York, NY), 2006.

Rolling, Marshall Cavendish Benchmark (New York, NY), 2006.

Riding, Marshall Cavendish Benchmark (New York, NY), 2006.

"OUR SOLAR SYSTEM" SERIES

The Solar System, Compass Point Books (Minneapolis, MN), 2001.

Mars, Compass Point Books (Minneapolis, MN), 2002.

Mercury, Compass Point Books (Minneapolis, MN), 2002.

Saturn, Compass Point Books (Minneapolis, MN), 2002.

Venus, Compass Point Books (Minneapolis, MN), 2002.

Jupiter, Compass Point Books (Minneapolis, MN), 2002.

Comets, Asteroids, and Meteoroids, Compass Point Books (Minneapolis, MN), 2003.

Earth, Compass Point Books (Minneapolis, MN), 2003.

Pluto, Compass Point Books (Minneapolis, MN), 2003.

Space Exploration, Compass Point Books (Minneapolis, MN), 2003.

The Sun, Compass Point Books (Minneapolis, MN), 2003.

Uranus, Compass Point Books (Minneapolis, MN), 2003.

The International Space Station, Compass Point Books (Minneapolis, MN), 2005.

Constellations, Compass Point Books (Minneapolis, MN), 2005.

Black Holes, Compass Point Books (Minneapolis, MN), 2005.

The Milky Way and Other Galaxies, Compass Point Books (Minneapolis, MN), 2005.

Space Walks, Compass Point Books (Minneapolis, MN), 2005.

"WHAT'S INSIDE ME" SERIES

My Skin, Benchmark Books (New York, NY), 2004.

My Bones and Muscles, Benchmark Books (New York, NY), 2004.

My Stomach, Benchmark Books (New York, NY), 2005.

My Lungs, Benchmark Books (New York, NY), 2005.

My Heart and Blood, Benchmark Books (New York, NY), 2005.

My Brain, Benchmark Books (New York, NY), 2005.

"VERBS IN ACTION" SERIES

Grow Up, Benchmark Books (New York, NY), 2005.

Fall Down, Benchmark Books (New York, NY), 2005.

Dig In, Benchmark Books (New York, NY), 2005.

On the Run, Benchmark Books (New York, NY), 2005.

Spring Out, Benchmark Books (New York, NY), 2005.

Spin Around, Benchmark Books (New York, NY), 2005.

Play Ball, Benchmark Books (New York, NY), 2006.

Move Along, Benchmark Books (New York, NY), 2006.

Make a Face, Benchmark Books (New York, NY), 2006.

Carry On, Benchmark Books (New York, NY), 2006.

Blow Out, Benchmark Books (New York, NY), 2006.

Turn Into, Benchmark Books (New York, NY), 2006.

"GAMES AROUND THE WORLD" SERIES

Jump Rope, Compass Point Books (Minneapolis, MN), 2005.

Chess, Compass Point Books (Minneapolis, MN), 2005.

Card Games, Compass Point Books (Minneapolis, MN), 2005.

Spinning Toys, Compass Point Books (Minneapolis, MN), 2005.

"MONEY AND BANKS" SERIES

The History of Money, Weekly Reader Early Learning Library (Milwaukee, WI), 2005.

Coins, Weekly Reader Early Learning Library (Milwaukee, WI), 2005.

Saving Money, Weekly Reader Early Learning Library (Milwaukee, WI), 2005.

Paper Money, Weekly Reader Early Learning Library (Milwaukee, WI), 2005.

What Is a Bank?, Weekly Reader Early Learning Library (Milwaukee, WI), 2005.

Spending Money, Weekly Reader Early Learning Library (Milwaukee, WI), 2005.

"AMAZING BODY" SERIES

Soft and Smooth, Rough and Bumpy: A Book about Touch, Picture Window Books (Minneapolis, MN), 2005.

Sniff, Sniff: A Book about Smell, Picture Window Books (Minneapolis, MN), 2005.

Shhh . . . : A Book about Hearing, Picture Window Books (Minneapolis, MN), 2005.

Look!: A Book about Sight, illustrated by Rick Peterson, Picture Window Books (Minneapolis, MN), 2005.

Yum!: A Book about Taste, illustrated by Rick Peterson, Picture Window Books (Minneapolis, MN), 2005.

"AMAZING SCIENCE" SERIES

Spots of Light: A Book about Stars, illustrated by Denise Shea, Picture Window Books (Minneapolis, MN), 2006.

Spinning in Space: A Book about the Planets, illustrated by Denise Shea, Picture Window Books (Minneapolis, MN), 2006.

Space Leftovers: A Book about Comets, Asteroids, and Meteoroids, illustrated by Denise Shea, Picture Window Books (Minneapolis, MN), 2006.

Night Light: A Book about the Moon, illustrated by Denise Shea, Picture Window Books (Minneapolis, MN), 2006.

Hot and Bright: A Book about the Sun, illustrated by Denise Shea, Picture Window Books (Minneapolis, MN), 2006.

Fluffy, Flat, and Wet: A Book about Clouds, illustrated by Denise Shea, Picture Window Books (Minneapolis, MN), 2006.

"INSIDE STORY" SERIES

Igloo, Marshall Cavendish Benchmark (New York, NY), 2006.

Castle, Marshall Cavendish Benchmark (New York, NY), 2006.

Skyscraper, Marshall Cavendish Benchmark (New York, NY), 2006.

Pyramid, Marshall Cavendish Benchmark (New York, NY), 2006.

Teepee, Marshall Cavendish Benchmark (New York, NY), 2006.

Log Cabin, Marshall Cavendish Benchmark (New York, NY), 2006.

"SHAPE OF THE WORLD" SERIES

Circles, Marshall Cavendish Benchmark (Tarrytown, NY), 2006.

Rectangles, Marshall Cavendish Benchmark (New York, NY), 2006.

Ovals, Marshall Cavendish Benchmark (New York, NY), 2006.

Many-sided Shapes, Marshall Cavendish Benchmark (New York, NY), 2006.

Triangles, Marshall Cavendish Benchmark (New York, NY), 2006.

Squares, Marshall Cavendish Benchmark (New York, NY), 2006.

OTHER

Wall (play), produced in Hartford, CT, 1993.

Also author of short stories for adults.

Sidelights

Dana Meachen Rau is an editor as well as a prolific author of fiction and nonfiction for younger readers. In her work as a book editor, Rau once explained to *SATA,* "I coordinate the entire book process and collaborate with a diverse group of authors and illustrators." She also writes stories for children of all ages during her free time, specializing in fictional tales for beginning readers and elementary-grade nonfiction covering a range of topics, including biographies and the books in her "Amazing Body," "Shape of the World," and "Games around the World" series.

The world of make believe plays a large role in much of Rau's fiction, such as *A Box Can Be Many Things,* in which a discarded cardboard box sets the stage for a series of new adventures for two young children. Praising *A Box Can Be Many Things,* Carolyn Phelan wrote in *Booklist* that Rau's beginning reader "will appeal to imaginative preschoolers" as well as to children in the early elementary grades. Other easy readers include *Shoo, Crow! Shoo!,* a story about two children's efforts to make a scarecrow that was praised by Phelan for its "cheerful tone." The game-filled day spent by a boy and his tubby toy is the subject of *Rubber Duck,* wherein the illustrations by Patrick Girouard "add to the playfulness of the text," according to *School Library Journal* reviewer Janie Schomberg.

The world of imagination is also central to Rau's nonfiction biography *Harry Houdini: Master Magician,* which profiles the life of the most famous escape artist of the early twentieth century. Born in Budapest in 1914, Houdini became a trapeze artist before enthralling audiences with his escapes from handcuffs, ropes, and straitjackets while locked in boxes, suspended in mid-air, or immersed underwater. Noting that Rau draws on Houdini's actual records, *School Library Journal* contributor Edith Ching cited *Harry Houdini* as "well researched" and noted that the book serves as "a useful resource for reports."

In *The Solar System,* part of the "Our Solar System" series designed for grades two and three, Rau brings readers on a tour of the planets surrounding Earth, as well as discussing meteors, comets, moons, and the possibilities that exist beyond the solar system. The "intellectually stimulating" series was praised by *School Library Journal* reviewer John Peters for providing enough information to engage budding scholars "without overwhelming them." Discussing Rau's other contributions to the series, which includes *Black Holes, The International Space Station,* and *The Milky Way and Other Galaxies* in addition to profiles of each planet in Earth's solar system, Peters awarded the books "high marks for visual appeal" and praised Rau for her "clear, specific presentation" of scientific topics. Reviewing Rau's volumes on Jupiter, Mars, and Mercury, the reviewer also wrote that "the level of detail is nicely calibrated to inform and fascinate readers."

With its more down-to-earth focus, *The Statue of Liberty* pairs color photographs with Rau's "clear and concise" explanation of New York's Lady Liberty and how she came to be, according to Dorcas Hand in *School Library Journal.* Moving from man-made art to the wonders of nature, *A Star in My Orange* serves as an "interesting introduction" to the art of observation, according to David J. Whitin in *Teaching Children Mathematics.* In the well-illustrated book, which features brilliantly colored photographs, Rau reveals the wealth of stars, spirals, hexagons, and other shapes and common formations that occur in nature. In her *Booklist* review, Phelan deemed the book "well-designed and effective," while in *School Library Journal* Jessica Snow wrote that *A Star in My Orange* presents parents with the opportunity to take children "on a journey of discovery in the natural world."

"I have always thought that one of the most important things an author can have is an active imagination,"

Rau once told *SATA*. "When I was little, my brother and I always used our imaginations. We pretended our beds were pirate ships, and the hallway was a bowling alley. The best creation of all was setting up the boxes in the basement to look like a palace!

"Now that I am an adult, I find that I am still always using my imagination. I pretend that driving my car is a roller coaster ride. I pretend that a walk in the woods is a safari adventure. When I look around my [home], I still pretend that I live in a palace!"

Biographical and Critical Sources

PERIODICALS

Booklist, October 15, 1996, Hazel Rochman, review of *One Giant Leap,* p. 419; May 1, 1997, Carolyn Phelan, review of *A Box Can Be Many Things,* p. 1504; December 1, 1999, Ilene Cooper, review of *Purple Is Best,* p. 716; April 15, 2001, Hazel Rochman, review of *Chilly Charlie,* p. 1569; July, 2001, Carolyn Phelan, review of *Shoo, Grow! Shoo!,* p. 2023; February 1, 2002, Carolyn Phelan, review of *A Star in My Orange: Looking for Nature's Shapes,* p. 944; May 1, 2002, Ilene Cooper, review of *Yahoo for You,* p. 1535; May 15, 2002, Carolyn Phelan, review of *Venus* and *Jupiter,* p. 1596; July, 2002, John Peters, review of *Mars* and *Mercury,* p. 110; June 1, 2003, Lauren Peterson, review of *Neil Armstrong,* p. 1800; October 15, 2005, Stephanie Zvirin, review of *What Is a Bank?,* p. 78.

School Library Journal, January, 2001, Ellen Heath, review of *Explore in a Cave* and *Climb up a Mountain,* p. 122; February, 2001, John Peters, review of *The Solar System,* p. 111; August, 2001, Melinda Piehler, review of *Hats!,* and Laura Scott, review of *Shoo, Crow! Shoo!,* p. 158; September, 2001, Laura Scott, review of *My Favorite Foods,* p. 204, Edith Ching, review of *Harry Houdini,* p. 252; January, 2002, Dorcas Hand, review of *The Statue of Liberty,* p. 118; February, 2002, Janie Schomberg, review of *Lots of Balloons,* p. 111; March, 2002, Janie Schomberg, review of *Rubber Duck,* p. 200; May, 2002, Jessica Snow, review of *A Star in My Orange,* p. 143; August, 2002, Mary Ann Carcich, review of *I'll Make You a Card,* p. 165; September, 2002, Andrew Medlar, review of *Life on the Oregon Trail,* p. 217; August, 2003, Maryann H. Owen, review of *Dr. Seuss,* p. 151; October, 2003, review of *Jupiter, Mars,* and *Mercury,* p. S27; February, 2004, Jennifer England, review of *Frederick Douglass,* p. 136; February, 2005, Melinda Piehler, review of *Tired of Waiting,* p. 94, and Christine E. Carr, review of *My Bones and Muscles,* p. 126; August, 2005, John Peters, review of *Black Holes,* p. 116.

Teaching Children Mathematics, March, 2004, David J. Whitin, review of *A Star in My Orange,* p. 382.

RAYBAN, Chloë 1944-
[A pseudonym]
(Carolyn Bear)

Personal

Born April 10, 1944, in Exeter, England; daughter of Richard Eric Leo (a banker) and Marjorie (a homemaker; maiden name, Rix) Salter; married Peter Julian Bear (an advertising director), 1967; children: Claudia Bear, Leonora Clare Bear. *Education:* University of Newcastle upon Tyne, B.A. (philosophy; with honors); attended University of Western Australia. *Politics:* "Socialist." *Religion:* Church of England (Anglican). *Hobbies and other interests:* Painting.

Addresses

Agent—Laura Cecil, 17 Alwyne Villas, London N1 2HG, England.

Career

Novelist and scriptwriter. McCann Erickson, London, England, advertising copywriter, beginning 1965; Craton, Lodge & Knight (product development agency), creative director, until 1980; freelance copywriter and scriptwriter for videos and multimedia installations.

Member

Societé d'Emulation du Bourbonnais (France), VMF Paris, Hurlingham Club (London, England).

Awards, Honors

Guardian Fiction Prize shortlist, 1995, and Carnegie Medal shortlist, 1996, both for *Love in Cyberia.*

Writings

YOUNG-ADULT NOVELS

(Under name Carolyn Bear) *Under Different Stars,* Methuen (London, England), 1988, published under name Chloë Rayban, Mammoth (London, England), 1998.

Footprints in the Sand ("Back2back" series), Collins (London, England), 1999.

Watching You, Watching Me ("Back2back" series), Collins (London, England), 1999.

Drama Queen, Bloomsbury (London, England), 2004.

Wrong Number, Barrington Stoke (London, England), 2004.

Author's books have been translated into German, Danish, Swedish, Italian, Russian, Polish, French, Icelandic, and Greek.

"JUSTINE" SERIES; YOUNG-ADULT NOVELS

Wild Child, Bodley Head (London, England), 1991, revised, Red Fox (London, England), 1998.

Chloë Rayban

Virtual Sexual Reality, Bodley Head (London, England), 1994.

Love in Cyberia, Bodley Head (London, England), 1996.

Terminal Chic, Bodley Head (London, England), 2000.

"MODELS" SERIES; YOUNG-ADULT NOVELS

Screen Kiss, Hodder Children's (London, England), 1997.

Clash on the Catwalk, Hodder Children's (London, England), 1997.

Havana to Hollywood, Hodder Children's (London, England), 1997.

Street to Stardom, Hodder Children's (London, England), 1997.

"MODELS MOVE ON" SERIES; YOUNG-ADULT NOVELS

The Starring Role, Hodder Children's (London, England), 1998.

Skin Deep, Hodder Children's (London, England), 1998.

Typecast, Hodder Children's (London, England), 1999.

Boy Babe, Hodder Children's (London, England), 1999.

PICTURE BOOKS

(Under name Carolyn Bear) *The Last Loneliest Dodo,* Roger Schlesinger, 1974.

(Under name Carolyn Bear) *No Time for Dinosaurs,* Roger Schlesinger, 1975.

(Under name Carolyn Bear) *Digby the Biggest Dog in the World,* Lexington Press, 1976.

(Under name Carolyn Bear) *Johnny Tomorrow,* Heinrich Hanau, 1977.

(Under name Carolyn Bear) *The Tangled Spell,* Methuen (London, England), 1986.

(Under name Carolyn Bear) *Scrapman,* Oxford University Press (Oxford, England), 1996.

(Under name Carolyn Bear) *Scrapman and Scrapcat,* Oxford University Press (Oxford, England), 1999.

(Under name Carolyn Bear) *Scrapman and the Incredible Flying Machine,* Oxford University Press (Oxford, England), 2000.

Tiger Boy (picture book), illustrated by John Prater, Red Fox (London, England), 2000.

(Under name Carolyn Bear) *Psid and Bolter,* Oxford University Press (Oxford, England), 2002.

(Under name Carolyn Bear) *Town Dog,* Oxford University Press (Oxford, England), 2003.

Adaptations

Johnny Tomorrow was adapted as an audio book; *Virtual Sexual Reality* was adapted by Nick Fisher as the film *Virtual Sexuality,* directed by Nick Hurran and starring Kieran O'Brien and Laura Fraser, Columbia TriStar, 1998.

Work in Progress

Two volumes in "My Life Starring Mum" series, for Bloomsbury.

Sidelights

Chloë Rayban is the pseudonym of British writer Carolyn Bear. Beginning her writing career as an advertising copywriter and creative director for several top London agencies, she began writing books for younger children in the 1980s, after becoming a freelance writer. Under her Rayban pseudonym, Bear has gained popularity among teen girls for her popular series featuring sixteen-year-old Justine Duval. Justine is part of the materialistic social scene of 1990s London, but through the experiences she encounters in novels such as *Wild Child, Love in Cyberia, Terminal Chic,* and *Virtual Sexual Reality*—the last which was also adapted as a motion picture—she is prompted to question the values her peers live by. Cited for its sharp wit and likeable teen heroine, Rayban's *Wild Child* was praised by a *School Librarian* reviewer as a novel that "is funny, doesn't lecture, and [is sure to] . . . provoke some interesting reaction." In a review of *Love in Cyberia* for *Books for Keeps,* a reviewer also commended Rayban's time-travel novel, writing that its "journalistic style" "makes an art out of the hectic and fashionably eccentric" 1960s society in which the "stylish" and lovelorn Justine finds herself during a surf on the Web.

Rayban told *SATA:* "I started writing books for children because I had a daughter who didn't like reading. A life without books seemed to me the ultimate deprivation, so I set about writing something I thought would appeal to her. My second daughter then got in on the act. As teenagers, they told me precisely what they wanted—books that were funny, fast-paced, and contemporary.

So I came up with the "Justine" books, for which they, inadvertently, provided most of the source material. Rather ruefully, they admitted they enjoyed the books.

"As my children have grown up my prime source material is no longer on my doorstep. I am now forced to sink to such devious things as eavesdropping—the tops of buses are ideal territory—and the advent of mobile phones has been a literary blessing (people don't seem to realize how loud they're talking).

"Currently, I'm writing a series for Bloomsbury about the daughter of a pop-idol. It's a satire on celebrity whose heroine is a girl who doesn't want to be famous—to her mother's horror she wants to be a vet. I'm working on book two of the series right now and it's set in the States. Once again the daughters have proved handy. I have one who is currently a freelance journalist in L.A. As my on-location researcher she's updating me on all the latest gossip on the stars, the star-struck, and the star-crossed (she's having boyfriend trouble right now).

Featuring one of Rayban's characteristically sharp-witted, independent-minded, know-everything, and surprisingly endearing teen sophisticates, this 2004 novel finds Jessica in matchmaking mode. (Cover illustration by Joy Gosney.)

"I am also working on a novel for adults (or a *real* book as my husband calls it). However, I believe firmly that novels for teenagers are *real* books. Teenagers are a tough audience to please but refreshingly open to original ideas. Sadly, it's during the teenage years that we lose most readers. I just hope that I've helped a few burgeoning adults not to miss out on one of life's greatest pleasures: curling up with a good book." Rayban makes her home in both England and France.

Biographical and Critical Sources

PERIODICALS

Books for Keeps, January 1, 1997, review of *Love in Cyberia.*
Just Seventeen, November 6, 1996, review of *Love in Cyberia.*
Nature, November 30, 2000, review of *Terminal Chic,* p. 49.
School Librarian, May, 1992, review of *Wild Child,* p. 72; November, 1994, review of *Virtual Sexual Reality,* p. 166; November, 1997, review of *Screen Kiss,* p. 214; autumn, 2004, Chris Brown, review of *Drama Queen,* p. 156.
Times Educational Supplement, May 2, 1997, review of *Love in Cyberia,* p. 8; July 3, 1998, review of *Wild Child,* p. 11; July 23, 1999, review of *Watching You, Watching Me,* p. 31; August 11, 2000, review of *Terminal Chic,* p. 22.

ONLINE

Chloë Rayban Home Page, http://www.chloerayban.com (September 27, 2005).

* * *

ROOP, Connie 1951-
(Constance Betzer Roop)

Personal

Born June 18, 1951, in Elkhorn, WI; daughter of Robert Sterling (a funeral director) and Marjorie (a homemaker; maiden name, Gary) Betzer; married Peter G. Roop (an educator and author), August 4, 1973; children: Sterling Gray, Heidi Anne. *Education:* Lawrence University, B.A., 1973; attended University of Wisconsin—Madison and Colorado School of Mines, 1974; Boston College, M.S.T., 1980. *Politics:* "Independent." *Religion:* Unitarian-Universalist. *Hobbies and other interests:* Reading, traveling, camping, sewing, skiing, and activities with her husband and children.

Addresses

Home and office—2601 North Union St., Appleton, WI 54911. *E-mail*—peterroop@aol.com.

Career

Appleton Area School District, Appleton, WI, science teacher, beginning 1973. Fulbright exchange teacher at Lady Hawkins School, Kingston, England, 1976-77. D.C. Heath Company, consultant, 1986-87; Duquesne University, workshop coordinator, beginning 1986; "Belize Bound" participant, 1997, 1998.

Member

American Association of University Women (chairperson of international relations, 1984-87; issue chairman, 1987-88), National Education Association, Society of Children's Book Writers and Illustrators, Wisconsin Society of Science Teachers, Wisconsin Society of Earth Science Teachers (treasurer, 1987—), Wisconsin Regional Writers, American Field Service, Friends of the Appleton Library (member of board of directors for community nursery school, 1986-87), Wild Ones.

Awards, Honors

Children's Choice Award, International Reading Association/Children's Book Council (CBC), 1984, for *Out to Lunch!* and *Space Out!*; Children's Book of the Year designation, Child Study Association, 1985, for *Keep the Lights Burning, Abbie,* and 1986, for *Button for General Washington;* Irma Simonton Black Award Honor Book, and Children's Book of the Year Award, both from Bank Street College of Education, and Outstanding Trade Book in the Language Arts, National Council of Teachers of English, all 1986, all for *Keep the Lights Burning, Abbie;* Outstanding Trade Book in the Field of Social Studies designation, National Council for the Social Studies (NCSS)/CBC, 1986, for *Buttons for General Washington;* Florida Sunshine Award, 1992, for *Ahyoka and the Talking Leaves;* Wisconsin Library Association Award, and Outstanding Trade Book in the Field of Social Studies designation, NCSS/CBC, both 1993, both for *Off the Map: The Journals of Lewis and Clark;* Kansas Reading Circle Book award, 1999, for *Girl of the Shining Mountains: Sacagawea's Story.*

Writings

WITH HUSBAND, PETER ROOP

Keep the Lights Burning, Abbie, illustrated by Peter E. Hanson, Carolrhoda (Minneapolis, MN), 1985.
Buttons for General Washington, illustrated by Peter E. Hanson, Carolrhoda (Minneapolis, MN), 1986.
Snips the Tinker, Milliken, 1988.
Seasons of the Cranes, Walker (New York, NY), 1989.
(Editor) *I, Columbus: My Journal, 1492-93,* illustrated by Peter E. Hanson, Walker (New York, NY), 1990.
Ahyoka and the Talking Leaves, illustrated by Yoshi Miyake, Lothrop (New York, NY), 1992.

One Earth, a Multitude of Creatures, illustrated by Valerie A. Kells, Walker (New York, NY), 1992.
(Editor) *Off the Map: The Journals of Lewis and Clark,* illustrated by Tim Tanner, Walker (New York, NY), 1993.
(Editor) *Capturing Nature: The Writings and Art of John James Audubon,* illustrated by Rick Farley, Walker (New York, NY), 1993.
Pilgrim Voices: Our First Year in the New World, illustrated by Shelley Pritchett, Walker (New York, NY), 1995.
Take Command, Mr. Farragut!, illustrated by Henri Sorensen, Lothrop (New York, NY), 1996.
Westward, Ho, Ho, Ho!, illustrated by Anne Canevari Green, Millbrook Press (Brookfield, CT), 1996.
Walk on the Wild Side!, illustrated by Anne Canevari Green, Millbrook Press (Brookfield, CT), 1997.
Let's Celebrate Christmas, illustrated by Katy Keck Arnsteen, Millbrook Press (Brookfield, CT), 1997.
Let's Celebrate Halloween, illustrated by Katy Keck Arnsteen, Millbrook Press (Brookfield, CT), 1997.
Grace's Letter to Lincoln, illustrated by Stacey Schuett, Hyperion (New York, NY), 1998.
If You Lived with the Cherokee, illustrated by Kevin Smith, Scholastic (New York, NY), 1998.
Martin Luther King, Jr., Heinemann (Chicago, IL), 1998.
Susan B. Anthony, Heinemann (Chicago, IL), 1998.
Brazil, Heinemann (Chicago, IL), 1998.
China, Heinemann (Chicago, IL), 1998.
Egypt, Heinemann (Chicago, IL), 1998.
India, Heinemann (Chicago, IL), 1998.
Israel, Heinemann (Chicago, IL), 1998.
Japan, Heinemann (Chicago, IL), 1998.
Vietnam, Heinemann (Chicago, IL), 1998.
A Home Album, Heinemann (Chicago, IL), 1998.
A City Album, Heinemann (Chicago, IL), 1998.
A Farm Album, Heinemann (Chicago, IL), 1999.
A School Album, Heinemann (Chicago, IL), 1999.
A City, Heinemann (Chicago, IL), 1999.
A Suburb, Heinemann (Chicago, IL), 1999.
A Town, Heinemann (Chicago, IL), 1999.
A Farming Town, Heinemann (Chicago, IL), 1999.
Let's Celebrate Thanksgiving, illustrated by Gwen Connelly, Millbrook Press (Brookfield, CT), 1999.
Let's Celebrate Valentine's Day, illustrated by Katy Keck Arnsteen, Millbrook Press (Brookfield, CT), 1999.
Girl of the Shining Mountains: Sacagawea's Story, Hyperion (New York, NY), 1999.
Good-Bye for Today: The Diary of a Young Girl at Sea, illustrated by Thomas B. Allen, Atheneum (New York, NY), 2000.
Whales and Dolphins, illustrated by Carol Schwartz, Scholastic (New York, NY), 2000.
Let's Celebrate Presidents' Day, illustrated by Gwen Connelly, Millbrook Press (Brookfield, CT), 2001.
Octopus under the Sea, illustrated by Carol Schwartz, Scholastic (New York, NY), 2001.
Let's Celebrate Earth Day, illustrated by Gwen Connelly, Millbrook Press (Brookfield, CT), 2001.
Escape from the Ice: Shackleton and the Endurance, illustrated by Bob Doucet, Scholastic (New York, NY), 2001.

California Gold Rush, Scholastic Reference (New York, NY), 2002.

Starfish: Stars of the Sea, illustrated by Carol Schwartz, Scholastic (New York, NY), 2002.

Take Command, Captain Farragut!, illustrated by Michael McCurdy, Simon & Schuster (New York, NY), 2002.

Let's Celebrate St. Patrick's Day, Scholastic (New York, NY), 2003.

Over in the Rain Forest, illustrated by Carol Schwartz, Scholastic (New York, NY), 2003.

Millions of Monarchs, illustrated by Mike Maydak, Scholastic (New York, NY), 2003.

Louisiana Purchase, illustrated by Sally Wern Comport, Aladdin (New York, NY), 2004.

Holiday Howlers: Jokes for Punny Parties, illustrated by Brian Gable, Carolrhoda (Minneapolis, MN), 2004.

(With Diane L. Burns) *Backyard Beasties: Jokes to Snake You Smile,* illustrated by Brian Gable, Carolrhoda (Minneapolis, MN), 2004.

The Declaration of Independence, illustrated by Jim Madsen, Aladdin (New York, NY), 2005.

Authors' works have been translated into French and Spanish.

"MAKE ME LAUGH" SERIES; WITH PETER ROOP

Space Out! Jokes about Outer Space, illustrated by Joan Hanson, Lerner (Minneapolis, MN), 1984.

Go Hog Wild! Jokes from down on the Farm, illustrated by Joan Hanson, Lerner (Minneapolis, MN), 1984.

Out to Lunch! Jokes about Food, illustrated by Joan Hanson, Lerner (Minneapolis, MN), 1984.

Stick out Your Tongue! Jokes about Doctors and Patients, illustrated by Joan Hanson, Lerner (Minneapolis, MN), 1986.

Going Buggy! Jokes about Insects, illustrated by Joan Hanson, Lerner (Minneapolis, MN), 1986.

Let's Celebrate! Jokes about Holidays, illustrated by Joan Hanson, Lerner (Minneapolis, MN), 1986.

"GREAT MYSTERIES" SERIES; WITH PETER ROOP

Dinosaurs: Opposing Viewpoints, Greenhaven (San Diego, CA), 1988.

Poltergeists: Opposing Viewpoints, Greenhaven (San Diego, CA), 1988.

The Solar System: Opposing Viewpoints, Greenhaven (San Diego, CA), 1988.

Stonehenge: Opposing Viewpoints, Greenhaven (San Diego, CA), 1989.

"IN THEIR OWN WORDS" SERIES; WITH PETER ROOP

Betsy Ross, Scholastic (New York, NY), 2001.

Sojourner Truth, Scholastic (New York, NY), 2002.

Sitting Bull, Scholastic (New York, NY), 2002.

"IN MY OWN WORDS" SERIES; EDITOR WITH PETER ROOP

The Diary of John Wesley Powell: Conquering the Grand Canyon, illustrated by Laszlo Kubinyi, Benchmark Books (New York, NY), 2001.

The Diary of Joseph Plumb Martin, a Revolutionary War Soldier, illustrated by Laszlo Kubinyi, Benchmark Books (New York, NY), 2001.

The Diary of David R. Leeper: Rushing for Gold, Benchmark Books (New York, NY), 2001.

The Diary of Mary Jemison, Captured by the Indians, Benchmark Books (New York, NY), 2001.

"BEFORE I MADE HISTORY" SERIES; WITH PETER ROOP

Sew What, Betsy Ross?, Scholastic (New York, NY), 2002.

Let's Split Logs, Abe Lincoln!, Scholastic (New York, NY), 2002.

Let's Play Soldier, George Washington!, Scholastic (New York, NY), 2002.

Turn on the Light, Thomas Edison!, Scholastic (New York, NY), 2003.

Let's Fly Wilbur and Orville!, Scholastic (New York, NY), 2003.

Go Fly a Kite, Ben Franklin!, Scholastic (New York, NY), 2003.

Let's Ride, Paul Revere!, Scholastic (New York, NY), 2004.

Let's Drive, Henry Ford!, Scholastic (New York, NY), 2004.

Let's Dream, Martin Luther King, Jr.!, Scholastic (New York, NY), 2004.

Give Me a Sign, Helen Keller!, Scholastic (New York, NY), 2004.

Take a Stand, Rosa Parks!, Scholastic (New York, NY), 2004.

Take a Giant Leap, Neil Armstrong!, Scholastic (New York, NY), 2005.

Thank You, Squanto!, Scholastic (New York, NY), 2005.

Lead Us to Freedom, Harriet Tubman!, Scholastic (New York, NY), 2006.

Sidelights

Together with her husband and collaborator, Peter Roop, Connie Roop enjoys focusing on the lives of actual men and women in the many books she writes for children. Drawing from actual journals as well as sometimes traveling to the locations they write about in their books, the Roops—both former educators—have contributed substantially to the growing number of nonfiction titles designed to capture the imagination of young readers. Among their books are biographies of David Farragut, Sacagawea, Martin Luther King, Jr., and Susan B. Anthony, while other nonfiction titles range from the lighthearted "Let's Celebrate" series describing holiday traditions to the science-based volume *One Earth, a Multitude of Creatures.*

Born in 1951 in Elkhorn, Wisconsin, Roop was raised in a family where reading was encouraged. "I loved school and was an avid reader," she once explained to *SATA,* noting that she also "actively participated in everything from bassoon and forensics to scouting where I gained a love for the outdoors." Although her writing skills brought Roop recognition during her middle-school years, she did not consider them significant enough to consider a career as an author. Instead, she fed her natural curiosity; during the summer of her junior year in high school, she traveled to Italy and lived with a family there as an American Field Service student. "This experience confirmed my desire to learn," Roop recalled, "and to discover the uniqueness of different cultures."

Roop enrolled at Lawrence University in 1969, with the intention of becoming a physician. However, a field camp experience changed all that; instead, she decided to study geology. "The vastness of geologic time still humbles me," she noted. Combining her fascination with nature with her empathy for people, Roop decided to go into education, and became a junior-high science teacher. She also married "an equally adventurous and curious person," fellow educator Peter Roop. Together, the Roops took advantage of travel and study opportunities, among them a year's stint teaching in England as part of the Fulbright Exchange Program.

Content with her choice of career, Roop did not branch out into her second career as a children's book author until the late 1970s, while pursuing a master's degree in science teaching at Boston College. "I began to read many of the books assigned to my husband in his master's of children's literature program as a welcome change from [the] science journals [I was required to read for my own degree]. Based on this reading, I developed a fiction booklist to supplement the science curriculum in my junior high school science classes. These scientifically accurate and exciting books provided my entry into the world of writing for children and young adults."

With this grounding in the juvenile nonfiction market, Roop wrote several articles for educational journals and worked as a reviewer and science specialist for *Appraisal* magazine. From there, she and her husband began their first book-length project, a series of illustrated joke and riddle books that includes *Space Out! Jokes about Outer Space* and *Holiday Howlers: Jokes for Punny Parties.*

While researching a travel article off the coast of Maine, the Roops learned the story of a young heroine named Abbie Burgess who, according to local legend, in 1856 singlehandedly kept two lighthouses lit during weeks of stormy weather. The resulting book, *Keep the Lights Burning, Abbie,* was published in 1985, beginning the Roops' long and prolific writing collaboration. Whereas *Buttons for General Washington* is a work of fiction, the many other books stemming from the Roops' fascination with exceptional men and women from the past have been nonfiction efforts. They often draw on original writings, as in *Pilgrim Voices: Our First Year in the New World* and *Sojourner Truth,* the latter part of Scholastic's "In Their Own Words" series. In *Pilgrim Voices* the Roops' use of actual writings from the period they profile "contributes authenticity and vitality to the text,"

in the opinion of *Booklist* contributor Karen Hutt. In profiling former slave and social reformer Truth, the Roops gather letters, contemporary newspaper accounts, and the text from Truth's famous work *Ain't I a Woman?* to weave together what Ajoke' T.I. Kokodoko described in *School Library Journal* as a biography that provides "facts and insights into the woman's character and convictions." Focusing, in another collaboration, on the works of William Bradford and other pilgrims, the Roops modernize the seventeenth-century language but retain the journal format of the original writings in *Pilgrim Voices,* resulting in a work that "is successful at creating a human sense of history beyond facts and timelines," according to Heide Piehler in a review for *School Library Journal.*

Other fact-based projects authored by the Roops include series of books profiling nations around the world, as well as the "In My Own Words" series, comprised of edited journals by explorers Lewis and Clark, ornithologist John James Audubon, Indian captive Mary Jemison, and others that are geared for upper-elementary-aged readers. *The Diary of Mary Jemison: Captured by the Indians,* for example, is based on Jemison's account, as published by James Seaver in 1824, and describes the girl's capture at age twelve and her life with a Seneca tribe. In another series installment, *The Diary of David R. Leeper: Rushing for Gold,* the Roops bring to life the excitement and hardships of the California gold rush of the late nineteenth century. Noting that the books are "especially appealing in their immediacy," *School Library Journal* contributor Dona J. Helmer praised the Roops' editing, noting that the "resulting texts are polished readable, and reliable." In *Booklist,* Carolyn Phelan noted that, due to modernized spellings, a glossary, and informative sidebars, the "In My Own Words" books "look appealing, read well, and carry the conviction of original accounts."

Drawing on her background in science, Roop has also worked with her husband on several titles for Greenhaven Press's "Great Mysteries" series, which explores quandaries still unsolved by scientific methods. "Scientific debate, key to the scientific process, is a critical element of these books," Roop once explained to *SATA.* "I believe young people need to realize that there are many unanswered questions in science and that they can be part of solving these questions." Among the "Great Mysteries" included in the series are unanswered questions surrounding dinosaurs, poltergeists, and Stonehenge.

Another science-related text, the Roops' *One Earth, a Multitude of Creatures* profiles a dozen creatures that live in the Pacific Northwest, among them black bears, rainbow trout, foxes, humpback whales, and owls. Illustrated with detailed drawings by Valerie A. Kells, the book outlines the survival chain existing within the region's contained ecosystem, and provides "a gentle, nonpreachy introduction to the interdependence and diversity of animals in an environment," according to

Booklist contributor Leone McDermott. *Let's Celebrate Earth Day* also touches on science as it profiles the history of the holiday started in 1970 and the introduction of concepts such as "endangered species" and started Americans' move toward recycling, composting, and restoring native environments.

The Roops' other nonfiction titles range from studies of the way different people live in *A City, A Suburb,* and *A Town* to a series describing holiday traditions in the United States. In *Let's Celebrate Valentine's Day,* for example, the origins of the February holiday are discussed, and riddles, little-known facts, and Valentine's Day trivia are presented. In addition, heart-shaped cookie recipes, poetry, and holiday activities allow readers to create a special day for those they love. Other holidays included in the series are Halloween, Christmas, and Thanksgiving; praising one series installment, *School Library Journal* reviewer Patricia Mahoney Brown commented that the "book offers facts and fun from beginning to end. . . . This is no trick; it's a treat!"

"I look forward to writing projects on a variety of topics as my involvement with science, literature, history, and reading continues," Roop once wrote. "Peter and I are committed to children. I hope to always be able to look at the world with the eyes of a young person—full of fresh wonder, awe, and surprise. I am hopeful that through our books we can help young people discover the joy of learning. This is a precious gift that Peter and I possess and treasure and hope to share with others."

Biographical and Critical Sources

PERIODICALS

Booklist, November 15, 1992, Leone McDermott, review of *One Earth, a Multitude of Creatures,* p. 603; September 1, 1993, Carolyn Phelan, review of *Off the Map: The Journals of Lewis and Clark,* pp. 54-55; February 1, 1996, Karen Hutt, review of *Pilgrim Voices: Our First Year in the New World,* p. 929; December 15, 1996, p. 723; September 1, 1997, p. 137; February 14, 1999, p. 1073; June 1, 2000, Gillian Engberg, review of *Good-Bye for Today: The Diary of a Young Girl at Sea,* p. 1897; February 15, 2001, Carolyn Phelan, review of *The Diary of David R. Leeper: Rush for Gold* and *The Diary of Mary Jemison: Captured by Indians,* p. 1133; May 1, 2001, Kay Weisman, review of *Let's Celebrate Earth Day,* p. 1687; April 15, 2002, Carolyn Phelan, review of *Take Command, Captain Farragut!,* p. 1400; February 15, 2003, Hazel Rochman, review of *Sojourner Truth,* p. 1082.

Kirkus Reviews, January 15, 2002, review of *Take Command, Captain Farragut!,* p. 107.

Publishers Weekly, May 17, 1993, review of *Off the Map: The Journals of Lewis and Clark,* p. 82; September 18, 1995, p. 92; October 6, 1997, p. 52; June 19, 2000, review of *Good-Bye for Today,* p. 80; May 20, 2002, review of *Take Command, Captain Farragut!,* p. 70.

School Library Journal, December, 1992, p. 107; June, 1993, p. 122; January, 1996, Heide Piehler, review of *Pilgrim Voices,* p. 125; August, 1997, Patricia Mahoney Brown, review of *Let's Celebrate Valentine's Day,* p. 150; April, 1999, p. 122; December, 2000, Sue Sherif, review of *Good-Bye for Today,* p. 124; March, 2001, Dona J. Helmer, review of *The Diary of David R. Leeper,* p. 276; April, 2002, Carolyn Janssen, review of *Take Command, Captain Farragut!,* p. 140; July, 2003, Ajoke' T.I. Kokodoko, review of *Sojourner Truth,* p. 148; April, 2004, Cynde Suite, review of *Holiday Howlers: Jokes for Punny Parties,* p. 142; June, 2005, Ann Joslin, review of *Louisiana Purchase,* p. 142.

ONLINE

Peter and Connie Roop Home Page, http://www.author-illustr-source.com/ (January 3, 2006).

*   *   *

ROOP, Constance Betzer
See ROOP, Connie

*   *   *

ROOP, Peter 1951-
(Peter G. Roop)

Personal

Born March 8, 1951, in Winchester, MA; son of Daniel Morehead (an engineer) and Dorothy (a homemaker; maiden name, Danenhower) Roop; married Constance Betzer (an educator and author), August 4, 1973; children: Sterling Gray, Heidi Anne. *Education:* Lawrence University, B.A., 1973; Simmons College, M.A., 1980; also attended University of Wisconsin—Madison. *Politics:* Democrat. *Religion:* Unitarian-Universalist. *Hobbies and other interests:* Reading, traveling, speaking to educators, librarians, and writers, playing with his children.

Addresses

Home and office—2601 N. Union St., Appleton, WI 54911-2141. *E-mail*—peterroop@aol.com.

Career

Appleton Area School District, Appleton, WI, teacher, 1973-99; writer, beginning 1977. Fulbright exchange teacher at Kingston County Primary School, Kingston, England, 1976-77; University of Wisconsin-Fox Valley, Menasha, instructor, 1983-84; University of Wisconsin, School of the Arts, Rhinelander, instructor, 1986-87. Workshop coordinator, Duquesne University, 1986-99; D.C. Heath Company, consultant, 1986-87; *Learning* magazine, teacher consultant, 1988-99. Member of board directors, Friends of the Appleton Public Library, 1974-84, and board of trustees, Appleton Public Library, 1983-89.

Member

Society of Children's Book Writers and Illustrators, National Education Association, Wisconsin Regional Writers (president, 1983-86), Authors and Illustrators Who Visit Schools, Council for Wisconsin Writers.

Awards, Honors

Jade Ring Award, Wisconsin Regional Writers Association, 1979, for play *Who Buries the Funeral Director?,* and 1982, for *The Cry of the Conch;* Reading Teacher of the Year award, Mideast Wisconsin Reading Council, 1983; Children's Choice Award, International Reading Association/Children's Book Council (CBC), 1985, for *Out to Lunch!* and *Space Out!;* Child Study Association Children's Books of the Year, 1985, for *Keep the Lights Burning, Abbie,* and 1986, for *Buttons for General Washington;* Teacher of the Year, and Outstanding Elementary Educator for Wisconsin, both from Wisconsin Department of Public Instruction, both 1986; named Outstanding Elementary Educator in Appleton, Mielke Foundation, 1986; Children's Book of the Year Award, and Irma Simonton Black Award Honor Book, both from Bank Street College, and Outstanding Trade Book in the Language Arts, National Council of Teachers of English, all 1986, all for *Keep the Lights Burning, Abbie;* Outstanding Trade Book in the Field of Social Studies, National Council for the Social Studies (NCSS)/CBC, 1986, for *Buttons for General Washington;* In Honor of Excellence Award, Burger King Corp., 1987, for excellence in education; Florida Sunshine Award, 1992, for *Ahyoka and the Talking Leaves;* Wisconsin Library Association Award, and Outstanding Trade Book in the Field of Social Studies, NCSS/CBC, both 1993, both for *Off the Map: The Journals of Lewis and Clark;* finalist for Storyteller Award, Western Writers of America, 1996, for *The Buffalo Jump;* Kansas Reading Circle Book award, 1999, for *Girl of the Shining Mountains: Sacagawea's Story.*

Writings

FOR CHILDREN

The Cry of the Conch, illustrated by Patric, Press Pacifica, 1984.

Little Blaze and the Buffalo Jump, illustrated by Jesse Wells, Montana Council for Indian Education, 1984, published as *The Buffalo Jump,* Northland Press, 1996.

Sik-Ki-Mi, illustrated by Shawn Running Crane, Montana Council for Indian Education, 1984.

Natosi: Strong Medicine, illustrated by Shawn Running Crane, Montana Council for Indian Education, 1984.

WITH WIFE, CONNIE ROOP

Keep the Lights Burning, Abbie, illustrated by Peter E. Hanson, Carolrhoda (Minneapolis, MN), 1985.

Buttons for General Washington, illustrated by Peter E. Hanson, Carolrhoda (Minneapolis, MN), 1986.

Snips the Tinker, Milliken, 1988.

Seasons of the Cranes, Walker (New York, NY), 1989.

(Editor) *I, Columbus: My Journal, 1492-93,* illustrated by Peter E. Hanson, Walker (New York, NY), 1990.

Ahyoka and the Talking Leaves, illustrated by Yoshi Miyake, Lothrop (New York, NY), 1992.

One Earth, a Multitude of Creatures, illustrated by Valerie A. Kells, Walker (New York, NY), 1992.

(Editor) *Off the Map: The Journals of Lewis and Clark,* illustrated by Tim Tanner, Walker (New York, NY), 1993.

(Editor) *Capturing Nature: The Writings and Art of John James Audubon,* illustrated by Rick Farley, Walker (New York, NY), 1993.

Pilgrim Voices: Our First Year in the New World, illustrated by Shelley Pritchett, Walker (New York, NY), 1995.

Take Command, Mr. Farragut!, illustrated by Henri Sorensen, Lothrop (New York, NY), 1996.

Westward, Ho, Ho, Ho!, illustrated by Anne Canevari Green, Millbrook Press (Brookfield, CT), 1996.

Walk on the Wild Side!, illustrated by Anne Canevari Green, Millbrook Press (Brookfield, CT), 1997.

Let's Celebrate Christmas, illustrated by Katy Keck Arnsteen, Millbrook Press (Brookfield, CT), 1997.

Let's Celebrate Halloween, illustrated by Katy Keck Arnsteen, Millbrook Press (Brookfield, CT), 1997.

Grace's Letter to Lincoln, illustrated by Stacey Schuett, Hyperion (New York, NY), 1998.

If You Lived with the Cherokee, illustrated by Kevin Smith, Scholastic (New York, NY), 1998.

Martin Luther King, Jr., Heinemann (Chicago, IL), 1998.

Susan B. Anthony, Heinemann (Chicago, IL), 1998.

Brazil, Heinemann (Chicago, IL), 1998.

China, Heinemann (Chicago, IL), 1998.

Egypt, Heinemann (Chicago, IL), 1998.

India, Heinemann (Chicago, IL), 1998.

Israel, Heinemann (Chicago, IL), 1998.

Japan, Heinemann (Chicago, IL), 1998.

Vietnam, Heinemann (Chicago, IL), 1998.

A Home Album, Heinemann (Chicago, IL), 1998.

A City Album, Heinemann (Chicago, IL), 1998.

A Farm Album, Heinemann (Chicago, IL), 1999.

A School Album, Heinemann (Chicago, IL), 1999.

A City, Heinemann (Chicago, IL), 1999.

A Suburb, Heinemann (Chicago, IL), 1999.

A Town, Heinemann (Chicago, IL), 1999.

A Farming Town, Heinemann (Chicago, IL), 1999.

Let's Celebrate Thanksgiving, illustrated by Gwen Connelly, Millbrook Press (Brookfield, CT), 1999.

Let's Celebrate Valentine's Day, illustrated by Katy Keck Arnsteen, Millbrook Press (Brookfield, CT), 1999.

Girl of the Shining Mountains: Sacagawea's Story, Hyperion (New York, NY), 1999.

Good-Bye for Today: The Diary of a Young Girl at Sea, illustrated by Thomas B. Allen, Atheneum (New York, NY), 2000.

Whales and Dolphins, illustrated by Carol Schwartz, Scholastic (New York, NY), 2000.

Let's Celebrate Presidents' Day, illustrated by Gwen Connelly, Millbrook Press (Brookfield, CT), 2001.

Octopus under the Sea, illustrated by Carol Schwartz, Scholastic (New York, NY), 2001.

Let's Celebrate Earth Day, illustrated by Gwen Connelly, Millbrook Press (Brookfield, CT), 2001.

Escape from the Ice: Shackleton and the Endurance, illustrated by Bob Doucet, Scholastic (New York, NY), 2001.

California Gold Rush, Scholastic Reference (New York, NY), 2002.

Starfish: Stars of the Sea, illustrated by Carol Schwartz, Scholastic (New York, NY), 2002.

Take Command, Captain Farragut!, illustrated by Michael McCurdy, Simon & Schuster (New York, NY), 2002.

Let's Celebrate St. Patrick's Day, Scholastic (New York, NY), 2003.

Over in the Rain Forest, illustrated by Carol Schwartz, Scholastic (New York, NY), 2003.

Millions of Monarchs, illustrated by Mike Maydak, Scholastic (New York, NY), 2003.

Louisiana Purchase, illustrated by Sally Wern Comport, Aladdin (New York, NY), 2004.

Holiday Howlers: Jokes for Punny Parties, illustrated by Brian Gable, Carolrhoda (Minneapolis, MN), 2004.

(With Diane L. Burns) *Backyard Beasties: Jokes to Snake You Smile,* illustrated by Brian Gable, Carolrhoda (Minneapolis, MN), 2004.

The Declaration of Independence, illustrated by Jim Madsen, Aladdin (New York, NY), 2005.

Authors' works have been translated into French and Spanish.

"MAKE ME LAUGH" SERIES; WITH CONNIE ROOP

Space Out! Jokes about Outer Space, illustrated by Joan Hanson, Lerner (Minneapolis, MN), 1984.

Go Hog Wild! Jokes from down on the Farm, illustrated by Joan Hanson, Lerner (Minneapolis, MN), 1984.

Out to Lunch! Jokes about Food, illustrated by Joan Hanson, Lerner (Minneapolis, MN), 1984.

Stick out Your Tongue! Jokes about Doctors and Patients, illustrated by Joan Hanson, Lerner (Minneapolis, MN), 1986.

Going Buggy! Jokes about Insects, illustrated by Joan Hanson, Lerner (Minneapolis, MN), 1986.

Let's Celebrate! Jokes about Holidays, illustrated by Joan Hanson, Lerner (Minneapolis, MN), 1986.

"GREAT MYSTERIES" SERIES; WITH CONNIE ROOP

Dinosaurs: Opposing Viewpoints, Greenhaven (San Diego, CA), 1988.

Poltergeists: Opposing Viewpoints, Greenhaven (San Diego, CA), 1988.

The Solar System: Opposing Viewpoints, Greenhaven (San Diego, CA), 1988.

Stonehenge: Opposing Viewpoints, Greenhaven (San Diego, CA), 1989.

"IN THEIR OWN WORDS" SERIES; WITH CONNIE ROOP

Betsy Ross, Scholastic (New York, NY), 2001.

Sojourner Truth, Scholastic (New York, NY), 2002.

Sitting Bull, Scholastic (New York, NY), 2002.

"IN MY OWN WORDS" SERIES; EDITOR WITH CONNIE ROOP

The Diary of John Wesley Powell: Conquering the Grand Canyon, illustrated by Laszlo Kubinyi, Benchmank Books (New York, NY), 2001.

The Diary of Joseph Plumb Martin, a Revolutionary War Soldier, illustrated by Laszlo Kubinyi, Benchmark Books (New York, NY), 2001.

The Diary of David R. Leeper: Rushing for Gold, Benchmark Books (New York, NY), 2001.

The Diary of Mary Jemison: Captured by the Indians, Benchmark Books (New York, NY), 2001.

"BEFORE I MADE HISTORY" SERIES; WITH CONNIE ROOP

Sew What, Betsy Ross?, Scholastic (New York, NY), 2002.

Let's Split Logs, Abe Lincoln!, Scholastic (New York, NY), 2002.

Let's Play Soldier, George Washington!, Scholastic (New York, NY), 2002.

Turn on the Light, Thomas Edison!, Scholastic (New York, NY), 2003.

Let's Fly Wilbur and Orville!, Scholastic (New York, NY), 2003.

Go Fly a Kite, Ben Franklin!, Scholastic (New York, NY), 2003.

Let's Ride, Paul Revere!, Scholastic (New York, NY), 2004.

Let's Drive, Henry Ford!, Scholastic (New York, NY), 2004.

Let's Dream, Martin Luther King, Jr.!, Scholastic (New York, NY), 2004.

Give Me a Sign, Helen Keller!, Scholastic (New York, NY), 2004.

Take a Stand, Rosa Parks!, Scholastic (New York, NY), 2004.

Take a Giant Leap, Neil Armstrong!, Scholastic (New York, NY), 2005.

Thank You, Squanto!, Scholastic (New York, NY), 2005.

Lead Us to Freedom, Harriet Tubman!, Scholastic (New York, NY), 2006.

Sidelights

Peter Roop credits his years spent working in elementary school classrooms as "one of the prime motivations for my writing for children. When I began my career in education, teaching grades one through four, I was reading numerous children's books," he once explained to

Readers follow a young man on his trip west during the California gold rush in The Diary of David R. Leeper: Rushing for Gold, *an actual mid-nineteenth-century journal edited by the Roops. (Illustration by Laszlo Kubinyi.)*

SATA. "I said to myself, 'I can write these stories.' Little then did I realize the scope of children's literature and the skills it would take to write quality stories for children. The 'easy' appearance of many children's books hides the hours of hard work involved in creating a worthwhile book for young readers." Together with his wife, Connie Roop, Roop has invested those hours, producing such highly praised books as *Grace's Letter to Lincoln, Buttons for General Washington,* and numerous other works of nonfiction. In addition, the Roops have edited actual journals of such individuals as Christopher Columbus, Indian captive Mary Jemison, and several of the Pilgrim immigrants who founded New England's Plymouth Colony, sometimes traveling to the locations featured in their books to bring past lives to life. Other works by the Roops include biographies of Sacagawea, Martin Luther King, Jr., and Susan B. Anthony, as well as a collection of lighthearted joke and riddle books.

Born in Winchester, Massachusetts, in 1951, Roop attended Lawrence University. After graduating in 1973, he married fellow Lawrence University student Connie Betzer and began a teaching career. Although he had talked about doing some writing for children his students' age, he did not set pen to paper until he was inspired to do so while teaching in England as a Fulbright exchange teacher in 1976. "I decided to stop talking and start writing," Roop once noted. "That year I wrote four children's stories and articles, two of which were eventually published in magazines. My route to writing children's books was focused first on writing for the many children's magazines. By taking this approach I hoped to gain the necessary background in the profession, to hone my writing skills, and to establish a name in preparation for writing my books."

In 1980 Roop earned a master's degree at Simmons College's Center for the Study of Children's Literature. "The work at Simmons was pivotal in my understanding of children's literature and in writing for children," he explained, counting among his favorite teachers fellow children's authors Nancy Bond and Scott O'Dell. In fact, O'Dell's work—especially *Island of the Blue Dolphins*—Roop counts as "the mainstay of my perspective on writing for children. O'Dell's style, sensitivity, and adept mixing of history and fiction are models for my own writing efforts."

After Roop had been writing for magazines for several years, he published his first book, *The Cry of the Conch,* in 1984. This story about ancient Hawai'i was followed by three books for the Blackfeet Indian Nation: *Little Blaze and the Buffalo Jump, Sik-Ki-Mi,* and *Natosi: Strong Medicine. Little Blaze and the Buffalo Jump,* originally published by the Montana Council for Indian Education in 1984, was republished as *The Buffalo Jump* in 1996. Focusing on a young runner of the Blackfeet Indian tribe, Roop's story describes the manner in which Montana's Native American tribes hunted buffalo by using a decoy to lead them over a steep cliff to their death. In *School Library Journal,* contributor Celia A. Huffman called Roop's story "well-researched" and "compelling," praised its "engaging main character," and noted that *The Buffalo Jump* "recreates and important part of Native American history and livelihood." While less enthusiastic about Roop's "romanticizing" of his Native American characters, a reviewer for *Publishers Weekly* also had praise for the work, noting that it "keeps alive the memory of a traditional Native American practice."

In 1985 Roop began his long-running collaboration with his wife, Connie, who also worked as a teacher of elementary-age children. "Inspired by a walk along the coast of Maine, we wrote a joke and riddle book about the seashore," Roop recalled. This first effort, while not published, developed into other similar books that include such wacky titles as *Space Out! Jokes about Outer Space, Going Buggy! Jokes about Insects,* and *Backyard Beasties: Jokes to Snake You Smile.*

One of the reasons the Roops' books are so popular with readers is that they feature young people of history, "children who, like Abbie, are 'footnotes in history,'" according to Roop. "By researching and writing these heroic stories, we hope to provide children with an exciting glimpse into the past." In fact, it has been Roop's personal interest in history—an interest he shares with his wife—that has inspired most of his writing, even from the start of his career. "As a writer on assignment for *Cobblestone,* a history magazine, I researched and wrote about topics ranging from the origins of Native Americans to the creation of video games," Roop noted. These *Cobblestone* assignments inspired several books, including *Girl of the Shining Mountains: Sacagawea's Story* and *Good-Bye for Today: The Diary of a Young Girl at Sea,* the story of nine-year-old Laura Jernegan who leaves her home to sail with her father aboard his whaling ship in the Arctic Ocean. In a *Publishers Weekly* review of *Good-Bye for Today* a contributor wrote that "careful research underpins this intriguing tale," while *Booklist* reviewer Gillian Engberg noted that by creating a "believable first-person voice" and telling their story in a diary format, the Roops "convey the often dangerous life" endured by those at sea during the nineteenth century.

In the fictional letters that comprise *Take Command, Captain Farragut!* the Roops bring to life a boy that is more than a footnote in history; distinguished Admiral David Glasgow Farragut, who captured New Orleans during the U.S. Civil War, began his sailing career at age ten. Sometimes overlooked in Farragut's later military accomplishments is the fact that, as a boy he swiftly rose through the ranks to become captain of the U.S. Navy vessel *Essex* during the war of 1812. Farragut, who was only twelve when the captaincy was thrust upon him, was ultimately captured by the British, and the Roops frame their biography as a series of letters written by thirteen-year-old David to his father while the teen was a British captive held in Valparaiso, Chile. While noting that the book "seems to straddle fiction and nonfiction," *Booklist* reviewer Carolyn Phelan dubbed *Take Command, Captain Farragut!* an "intriguing read-aloud," while in *School Library Journal* Carolyn Janssen noted that the "well-researched" book "can help students relate to history."

Other books inspired by the Roops' fascination with history have included several edited journals, among them *Pilgrim Voices: Our First Year in the New World,* and the diaries of explorers Lewis and Clark, ornithologist John James Audubon, and Christopher Columbus. In *Pilgrim Voices* the Roops' use of actual writings from the period they profile "contributes authenticity and vitality to the text," according to *Booklist* reviewer Karen Hutt. Based on the seventeenth-century writings of William Bradford and his fellow New England colonists, the text in *Pilgrim Voices* has been modernized for twenty-first-century readers while retaining the flavor of the original writing. This technique by the Roops has resulted in a book that *School Library Journal* contributor Heide Piehler deemed "successful at creating a human sense of history beyond facts and timelines."

Off the Map: The Journals of Lewis and Clark is based on the explorers' eight-volume work recounting their explorations in the western territories during the years 1804-1806. Beginning with Thomas Jefferson's letter to Meriweather Lewis wherein the president sets forth guidelines and objectives for the trip, *Off the Map* follows Lewis and Clark's impressions of the natural world they encountered, their interactions with the region's native people, and other aspects of their historic trek to the Pacific Ocean. Deeming the book's editing "judicious," a *Publishers Weekly* contributor added that the Roops' creative approach and organization of the material, "impart[s] . . . a feel for the challenges and dangers of the 8,000-mile trip through the Louisiana Purchase." In *Booklist,* Carolyn Phelan called *Off the Map* a "vivid source . . . [that] would be a welcome part of any classroom study of the subject."

In an interesting take on biographies of notable Americans, the Roops' "Before I Made History" series presents the early years of notable individuals ranging from Benjamin Franklin and Abraham Lincoln to civil rights leader Rosa Parks and astronaut Neil Armstrong. Books in this series, which include *Take a Giant Leap, Neil Armstrong!, Give Me a Sign, Helen Keller!,* and *Let's Drive, Henry Ford!,* describe the formative years of many notable Americans, showing the influences and experiences that shaped their achievements as grown ups.

Another interest the Roops share is science; in fact, Connie Roop began her teaching career as a junior-high-school science teacher. This interest has resulted in several books, including a three-volume series published by Greenhaven Press that explores such great mysteries as the extinction of the dinosaurs, the existence of poltergeists, and the marvels of the solar system. Another science-related book, *One Earth, a Multitude of Creatures,* includes descriptions of twelve creatures that call the Pacific Northwest region home. Illustrated with detailed drawings of black bears, rainbow trout, foxes, humpback whales, and owls by artist Valerie A. Kells, *One Earth, a Multitude of Creatures* depicts the links between creatures in an ecosystem, and serves as what *Booklist* contributor Leone McDermott called "a gentle, nonpreachy introduction to the interdependence and diversity of animals in an environment."

Roop's interest in travel has allowed him to effectively bring to life many of the topics he presents to young readers. "As a writer I believe that getting the right sense of setting is critical to the impact of a story," he once explained to *SATA.* "Experiencing the sacredness of a *pu'unhonua* in Hawaii was essential to *The Cry of the Conch.* Feeling the chilling blasts of a nor'easter was vital in creating the atmosphere of *Keep the Lights Burning, Abbie.* Walking the cobbled streets of Philadelphia established the feeling of place in *Buttons for George Washington.*" Taking his responsibility as an author of books for children seriously has also contributed to Roop's success. "Writing the best books possible for young readers is my goal," he maintained. "By providing the best for children, I can open more vistas and distant horizons to their wondering eyes and minds. What better role for a writer?"

Biographical and Critical Sources

PERIODICALS

Booklist, November 15, 1992, Leone McDermott, review of *One Earth, a Multitude of Creatures,* p. 603; September 1, 1993, Carolyn Phelan, review of *Off the Map: The Journals of Lewis and Clark,* pp. 54-55; February 1, 1996, Karen Hutt, review of *Pilgrim Voices: Our First Year in the New World,* p. 929; December 15, 1996, p. 723; September 1, 1997, p. 137; February 14, 1999, p. 1073; June 1, 2000, Gillian Engberg, review of *Good-Bye for Today: The Diary of a Young Girl at Sea,* p. 1897; February 15, 2001, Carolyn Phelan, review of *The Diary of David R. Leeper: Rush for Gold* and *The Diary of Mary Jemison: Captured by Indians,* p. 1133; May 1, 2001, Kay Weisman, review of *Let's Celebrate Earth Day,* p. 1687; April 15, 2002, Carolyn Phelan, review of *Take Command, Captain Farragut!,* p. 1400; February 15, 2003, Hazel Rochman, review of *Sojourner Truth,* p. 1082.

Kirkus Reviews, January 15, 2002, review of *Take Command, Captain Farragut!,* p. 107.

Publishers Weekly, May 17, 1993, review of *Off the Map: The Journals of Lewis and Clark,* p. 82; September 18, 1995, p. 92; October 6, 1997, p. 52; June 19, 2000, review of *Good-Bye for Today,* p. 80; May 20, 2002, review of *Take Command, Captain Farragut!,* p. 70.

School Library Journal, December, 1992, p. 107; June, 1993, p. 122; January, 1996, Heide Piehler, review of *Pilgrim Voices,* p. 125; August, 1997, Patricia Mahoney Brown, review of *Let's Celebrate Valentine's Day,* p. 150; April, 1999, p. 122; December, 2000, Sue Sherif, review of *Good-Bye for Today,* p. 124; March, 2001, Dona J. Helmer, review of *The Diary of David R. Leeper,* p. 276; April, 2002, Carolyn Janssen, review of *Take Command, Captain Farragut!,* p. 140; July, 2003, Ajoke' T.I. Kokodoko, review of *Sojourner Truth,* p. 148; April, 2004, Cynde Suite, review of *Holiday Howlers: Jokes for Punny Parties,* p. 142; June, 2005, Ann Joslin, review of *Louisiana Purchase,* p. 142.

ONLINE

Peter and Connie Roop Home Page, http://www.author-illustr-source.com/ (January 3, 2006).

*   *   *

ROOP, Peter G.
See ROOP, Peter

S

SAN JOSÉ, Christine 1929-

Personal

Born July 26, 1929, in Leicester, Leicestershire, England; daughter of Albert George (an engineer) and Annie May (Wright) Griffin; children: James Martinez, Christian Martinez, Chad Martinez. *Education:* London University, B.A. Dip.Ed.; Syracuse University, Ph.D. *Politics:* "Part of one's effort to be thoughtful, compassionate, and constructive."

Addresses

Home—1501 N. Main St., Honesdale, PA 18431. *Agent*—c/o Author Mail, Publicity Director, Boyds Mills Press, 815 Church St., Honesdale, PA 18431.

Career

Educator, editor, and writer. Worked as a teacher at elementary, secondary, and college level. *Highlights for Children,* Columbus, OH, senior editor for twelve years.

Awards, Honors

National Council of Teachers of English award for research into children's writing; educational award for teacher center program.

Writings

Ketchup Goes to Town, illustrated by Ethel Gold, Highlights for Children (Columbus, OH), 1990.

Sir Good Is on His Way, illustrated by Marilyn Thomason, Highlights for Children (Columbus, OH), 1992.

(Reteller) *Cinderella,* illustrated by Deborah Santini, Boyds Mills Press (Honesdale, PA), 1994.

The Adventures of the Amazing Mazers: Hidden Pictures and Maze Games, illustrated by Charles Jordan, Boyds Mills Press (Honesdale, PA), 1994.

(Reteller) *The Little Match Girl,* illustrated by Anastassiaja Archipowa, Carline House (Honesdale, PA), 1994, illustrated by Kestutis Kasparavicius, 2002.

(Reteller) *The Hidden Picture Book of Aesop's Fables,* illustrated by Charles Jordan, Boyds Mills Press (Honesdale, PA), 1995.

(Reteller) *Sleeping Beauty,* illustrated by Dominic Catalano, Boyds Mills Press (Honesdale, PA), 1997.

(Reteller) *The Emperor's New Clothes,* illustrated by Anastassiaja Archipowa, Boyds Mills Press (Honesdale, PA), 1998.

Work in Progress

Poetry anthologies for Boyds Mills Press; a picture-book retelling of *The Six Wild Swans;* and an historical trilogy for young adults.

Sidelights

English-born author, editor, and teacher Christine San José worked as a teacher before devoting twelve years to work as senior editor of *Highlights for Children* magazine. Writing throughout her adult life, she has penned teaching materials for instructors as well as students, and stories for adults, but her best-known works are the picture books she has published, many based on classic tales. San José's titles include *Cinderella* and *The Little Match Girl,* the latter based on the story by Hans Christian Andersen.

San José presents readers with a fresh take on Charles Perrault's 1697 version of the classic story of Cinderella by setting the backdrop for the story in turn-of-the-twentieth-century Manhattan. Cinderella is no longer a passive lead character; in San José's version the young woman takes on a more assertive, modern outlook. In *The Bridge,* a Boyds Mills Press press release, the author explained: "I knew my starting point had to be a Cinderella far stronger than the vapid if good-natured girl Charles Perrault bequeathed to us. . . . I reasoned that if she's strong, she must have gained her strength from someone who believed in her at some stage of her young life. So, in the very first sentence I gave her a mama."

Faced with rewriting *The Little Match Girl* for younger readers, San José found herself with a bit of a dilemma from the start: How to portray a world in which death is viewed as a means to deal with hardship, as in Andersen's original tale? She decided the best option would be to stick to the true essence of the story and maintain what Andersen so poignantly crafted. "I also pointed out as much as I could the contrast between a spiritual world and the match girl's world and showed the little girl consciously choosing the spiritual," San José explained in *The Bridge*. Reacting to the 2002 book, which features illustrations by Kestutis Kasparavicius, Virginia Walter wrote in a *School Library Journal* review that it represents "a faithful" version of the original tale. Carolyn Phelan commented in a *Booklist* review of San José's *The Little Match Girl* that the book focuses on "surely the most pathetic figure in children's literature," yet also stands as a "a respectful rendering of the classic tale."

Biographical and Critical Sources

PERIODICALS

Booklist, September 15, 1995, April Judge, review of *The Little Match Girl,* p. 172; October 15, 1997, Julie Corsaro, review of *Sleeping Beauty,* p. 410; April 1, 1998, Carolyn Phelan, review of *The Emperor's New Clothes,* p. 1334; October 1, 2002, Carolyn Phelan, review of *The Little Match Girl,* p. 329.

Publishers Weekly, November 4, 2002, review of *The Little Match Girl,* p. 86.

Reading Teacher, December, 1995, review of *Cinderella,* p. 329; September, 1998, review of *Sleeping Beauty,* p. 58.

School Library Journal, September, 1994, Donna L. Scanlon, review of *Cinderella,* p. 235; November, 1995, Donna L. Scanlon, review of *The Little Match Girl,* p. 64; September, 1997, Donna L. Scanlon, review of *Sleeping Beauty,* p. 208; April, 1998, Marilyn Iarusso, review of *The Emperor's New Clothes,* p. 112; October, 2002, Virginia Walter, review of *The Little Match Girl,* p. 56.

ONLINE

Boyds Mills Press Web site, http://www.boydsmillspress.com/ (December 19, 2005), "Christine San José."

OTHER

The Bridge (Boyds Mills Press press release), Christine San José, "Retelling the Grand Old Tales."

*   *   *

SCHNEIDER, Antonie 1954-

Personal

Born 1954, in Mindelheim im Allgau, Germany. *Education:* College graduate.

Addresses

Home—Allgau, Germany. *Agent*—c/o Author Mail, Aufbau Verlag, Postfach 193, 10105 Berlin, Germany.

Career

Writer and former teacher in Germany.

Awards, Honors

Prix Chronos (France), 1999; National Parenting Publications Award, 1999, 2000.

Writings

Schatzsuche und Finderglück, illustrated by Nathalie Duroussy, Findling, 1995, translated as *Treasure Hunt,* 1995.

Ich bin der kleine König, illustrated by Christa Unzer, 1995, translated by J. Alison James as *You Shall Be King!,* North-South Books (New York, NY), 1995.

Der Geburtstags-Bär, illustrated by Uli Waas, 1996, translated by J. Alison James as *The Birthday Bear,* North-South Books (New York, NY), 1996.

Das Buch vom Schaf (title means "The Book of the Sheep"), illustrated by Marion Goedelt, 1997.

Leb wohl, Chaja!, illustrated by Maja Dusíková, 1998, translated by J. Alison James as *Good-bye, Vivi!,* North-South Books (New York, NY), 1998.

Gustl Löenmut, illustrated by Cristina Kadmon, 1998, translated by J. Alison James as *Luke the Lionhearted,* North-South Books (New York, NY), 1998.

Das Buch vom Nashorn (title means "The Book of the Rhinoceros"), 1998.

Rosie und der Riese, 1998.

Das Buch vom Walfisch, 1998.

Ich bin ich und wer bist Du?, 1999.

Die wunderbare Reise des Jungen, 1999.

Eine Taube für Bollibar, illustrated by Uli Waas, 1999, translated by J. Alison James as *Come Back Pigeon,* North-South Books (New York, NY), 1999.

Sankte Martin und der kleine Bär, illustrated by Maja Dusikova, Nord-Sud Verlag, 2000.

Oskars Weihnachtstraum, illustrated by Uli Waas, Findling, 2001.

Max hebt ab!, 2001.

Das Zirkuspony ist mein Freund, 2001.

Mol, 2001.

Du Bist die liebste kleine Maus, illustrated by Quentin Gréban, 2002, translated by J. Alison James as *The Dearest Little Mouse in the World,* North-South Books (New York, NY), 2004.

Lea und König Wuff, DTV, 2002.

Ritter Brumm, 2002.

Ich kann night schlafen, sagte die kleine Maus, illustrated by Eugen Sopko, Findling, 2002.

Kleiner Hase, Osterhase, illustrated by Roser Rius, Ravensburg (Zurich, Switzerland), 2003.

Die Geschichte vom Heiligen Nikolaus, 2003.

Kleiner König, wer bist du? (title means "Small King, Who Are You?"), illustrated by Isabel Pin, Aufbau Verlag (Berlin, Germany), 2003.

Wann ist endlich Weihnachten?, illustrated by Maja Dusíková, Nord-Sud Verlag, 2004, translated as *Advent Storybook: 24 Stories to Share before Christmas,* North-South Books (New York, NY), 2004.

Die Amstel und der Papagei, illustrated by Josef Wilkon, Bohem, 2004.

Still und leise kommt der Sandmann, illustrated by Ulrike Mülhoff, Coppenrath (Münster, Germany), 2005.

Jako, Bajazzo Verlag (Zurich, Switzerland), 2005.

Petö der Zauberer, illustrated by Renate Grünewald, Freies Geistesleben, 2005.

Die Verwandlung, illustrated by Helga Bansch, Bloomsbury, 2005, translated as *Leo's Dream,* Bloomsbury (London, England), 2006.

Fuchs und Gans, illustrated by Helga Bansch, Bajazzo Verlag (Zurich, Switzerland), 2006.

Biographical and Critical Sources

PERIODICALS

Booklist, January 1, 1999, April Judge, review of *Goodbye, Vivi!,* p. 890.

School Librarian, August, 1995, review of *Treasure Hunt,* p. 106; summer, 1999, reviews of *Luke the Lionhearted* and *Good-bye, Vivi!,* p. 76; summer, 2000, review of *Come Back Pigeon,* p. 90; summer, 2005, Jennifer Taylor, review of *Dearest Little Mouse in the World,* p. 78.

School Library Journal, July, 1995, Jeanne Clancy Watkins, review of *You Shall Be King!,* p. 68; December, 1996, Martha Topol, review of *The Birthday Bear,* p. 105; January, 1999, Maura Bresnahan, review of *Luke the Lionhearted,* p. 102; January, 1999, Ann Cook, review of *Good-bye, Vivi!,* p. 102; November, 1999, review of *Come Back, Pigeon,* p. 129; January, 2005, Suzanne Meyers Harold, review of *The Dearest Little Mouse in the World,* p. 98.

ONLINE

Perlentaucher Web site, http://www.perlentaucher.de/ (December 19, 2005), "Antonie Schneider."*

*   *   *

SHADOW, Jak
See SUTHERLAND, Jon

*   *   *

SMEE, Nicola 1948-

Personal

Born February 9, 1948, in Shrewesbury, Salop, England; daughter of Richard (a carpenter, antique restorer, and author) and Fara (a homemaker; maiden name, Bartlett) Gethin; married Michael Smee (a painter and art lecturer), November 15, 1969; children: Oliver, Milo, Leo. *Education:* Attended Birmingham College of Arts. *Religion:* Roman Catholic.

Addresses

Agent—c/o Author Mail, Bloomsbury Publishing, 36 Soho Square, London W1D 3QY, England.

Career

Author and illustrator. Graphic artist; designer of greeting cards and book jackets. Former illustrator for children's television program *Rainbow.*

Member

British Association of Illustrators.

Awards, Honors

Children's Book of the Year citations, Anderson Press/ Children's Book Foundation, 1991, for *The Invitation,* and 1992, for *Finish the Story, Dad;* Sainsbury Baby Books Award shortlist, 2001, for *Sleepyhead.*

Writings

SELF-ILLUSTRATED PICTURE BOOKS

Down in the Woods, Collins (London, England), 1985.

Beach Boy, Collins (London, England), 1987.

The Invitation, Collins (London, England), 1989, Little, Brown (Boston, MA), 1991.

ABC, Collins (London, England), 1990.

Finish the Story, Dad, Simon & Schuster (New York, NY), 1991.

Teacher's Pet, HarperCollins (New York, NY), 1992.

Noah's Ark (six board books in "ark" box), Little, Brown (Boston, MA), 1993.

The Tusk Fairy, Orchard Books (London, England), 1993, BridgeWater Books (Mahwah, NJ), 1994.

The Christmas Story, Orchard (London, England), 1994, published as *My First Christmas Story,* 2000.

Charlie's Choice, Orchard (London, England), 1995.

Little Rabbit (board book), Orchard (London, England), 1996.

Little Piglet (board book), Orchard (London, England), 1996.

Little Duckling (board book), Orchard (London, England), 1996.

Little Chick (board book), Orchard (London, England), 1996.

Where's My Special Bed? (puppet book), Orchard (London, England), 1996.

Sleepyhead!, Campbell Books (London, England), 2001, Barron's Educational (Hauppauge, NY), 2002.

Peek-a-boo Baby, Campbell Books (London, England), 2001, Barron's Educational (Hauppauge, NY), 2002.

Splish! Splash!, Campbell Books (London, England), 2001, Barron's Educational (Hauppauge, NY), 2002.

Tickle Me Too!, Campbell Books (London, England), 2001, Barron's Educational (Hauppauge, NY), 2002.

No Bed without Ted (lift-the-flap book), Bloomsbury (New York, NY), 2005.

Funny Face, Bloomsbury (London, England), 2006.

Clip-Clop!, Sterling Publishing (New York, NY), 2006.

Author's books have been translated into Welsh.

"THREE LITTLE ..." SERIES; SELF-ILLUSTRATED PUPPET BOOKS

Three Little Bunnies, Scholastic (New York, NY), 1994.

Three Little Chicks, Scholastic (New York, NY), 1994.

Three Little Mice, David Bennett (St. Albans, England), 1995.

Three Little Teddies, David Bennett (St. Albans, England), 1995.

"FREDDIE" SERIES; SELF-ILLUSTRATED

Freddie Visits the Doctor, Orchard (London, England), 1996, Little Barron's (Hauppauge, NY), 1999.

Freddie Gets Dressed, Orchard (London, England), 1997, Little Barron's (Hauppauge, NY), 1999.

Freddie Goes Swimming, Orchard (London, England), 1998, published as *Freddie Learns to Swim,* Barron's Educational (Hauppauge, NY), 1999.

Freddie Goes to Playgroup, Orchard (London, England), 1998, Little Barron's (Hauppauge, NY), 1999.

Freddie Has a Haircut, Orchard (London, England), 1998, published as *Freddie Gets a Haircut,* Little Barron's (Hauppauge, NY), 1999.

Freddie Goes to the Seaside, Orchard (London, England), 1999, published as *Freddie Goes to the Beach,* Little Barron's (Hauppauge, NY), 1999.

Freddie Visits the Dentist, Little Barron's (Hauppauge, NY), 2000.

Freddie Goes on an Airplane, Little Barron's (Hauppauge, NY), 2000.

ILLUSTRATOR

Colin Stone, *The Legend of the Gnomes,* Chappell, 1976.

Dorothea King, *Rex Q.C.,* Pavilion Books (London, England), 1983.

Diane Wilmer, *Benny: The Story of a Dog,* Collins (London, England), 1985.

Diane Wilmer, *Benny and the Football Match,* Collins (London, England), 1986.

Diane Wilmer, *Benny and the Fair,* Collins (London, England), 1986.

Diane Wilmer, *Benny and the Builders,* Collins (London, England), 1986.

Diane Wilmer, *Benny and the Jumble Sale,* Collins (London, England), 1986.

Ruth Craft, *Wise Dog,* Collins (London, England), 1986.

Baby's First Year, Heinemann (London, England), 1987.

Ruth Craft, *Fancy Nancy,* Collins (London, England), 1988.

Diane Wilmer, *Step by Step* (twelve-book series), Albion Press/Macmillan, 1988.

Robert Robinson, *Going to the Dentist,* Conran Octopus/Mothercare (London, England), 1989, published as *Danny Goes to the Dentist,* McGraw-Hill Children's (Columbus, OH), 2002.

Barbara Taylor Cork, *Going to School,* Conran Octopus/Mothercare (London, England), 1989, published as *Sam Starts School,* McGraw-Hill Children's (Columbus, OH), 2002.

My Birthday [and] *Animals* (includes activity book, wall chart, and story book), Carnival/Collins (London, England), 1989.

Judy Bastyra, *Busy Little Cook,* Conran Octopus (London, England), 1990.

Ruth Craft, *Something Old: Jets,* A. & C. Black (London, England), 1992.

Fiona Waters, *The Star-Spangled Pandemonium: A Collection of Exceptionally Silly Stories and Verse,* World International (Manchester, England), 1994.

Margaret Mayo, reteller, *First Bible Stories,* Barron's Educational (Hauppauge, NY), 1998.

Jeannie Billington, *Six Feet Long and Three Feet Wide,* Candlewick Press (Cambridge, MA), 2000.

Sidelights

Nicola Smee is an illustrator and writer with many published picture and story books in her list of credits. After studying at the Birmingham College of Art, Smee started her career as an illustrator, designing greeting cards and book covers, as well as doing illustrations for the British television show *Rainbow.* She illustrated a number of picture-book texts by other authors before trying her hand at writing and illustrating her own books in the mid-1980s. *Down in the Woods,* Smee's first solo picture book, was commended by a London *Observer* reviewer for its "admirable plot, pictures and text. Among the many picture books, board books, and lift-the-flap books she has produced since, two of Smee's creations have been honored as Children's Books of the Year by the Children's Book Foundation: *The Invitation* in 1991, and *Finish the Story, Dad* in 1992. Among her most popular works are her "Three Little . . ." series, which feature small puppets that help tell the story, and her "Freddie" series, which have been published in both the United States and Smee's native England.

The Invitation, illustrated in cartoon style complete with dialogue "balloons," describes how a boy named Leo finds an unexpected prize in his cereal box. The prize is an invitation to dine at the fanciest restaurant in town, and Leo and his parents quickly set out to enjoy the experience. Smee's book serves as lively look, from the child's perspective, of "what grown-ups do on Saturday night," with "brightly colored, motion-filled illustrations" of people eating and dancing, according to Ilene Cooper in her *Booklist* review.

Through Smee's engaging art and rhyming text, readers can help a determined young girl find her beloved lost teddy in No Bed without Ted.

In *Finish the Story, Dad* Ruby wants her father to finish the bedtime story he has begun reading. When her father does not give in to Ruby's pleading, the girl returns to her bed and dreams of animals in the jungle, asking each of them in turn to tell her the ending to the interrupted story. Like *The Invitation, Finish the Story, Dad* is illustrated in watercolor cartoons featuring stylized people and animals. Calling *Finish the Story, Dad* "a charming little tale," a *Junior Bookshelf* reviewer noted that "body language and facial expressions are . . . well observed, and the colours delightful." Virginia E. Jeschelnig, writing in *School Library Journal,* observed that Smee's illustrations, in which "colors are subdued with a sprinkling of pattern to add interest," are "best for sharing one-on-one."

Other books authored and illustrated by Smee include *The Tusk Fairy,* in which a young girl's favorite toy, a hand-knitted elephant, meets a sorry end but is given new meaning by the girl's loving grandmother. Another child-and-favorite-toy relationship is the subject of *No Bed without Ted,* a lift-the-flap book that finds a girl postponing bedtime when her must-have teddy is nowhere to be found. In contrast, *Clip-Clop!* features rambunctious imaginative play between a small child and loving parents in a simple, rhyming story. Smee's "economical text" in *The Tusk Fairy* is enhanced by "soft, winsome watercolors that demonstrate the girl's attachment" to her well-worn knitted elephant, wrote a *Publishers Weekly* contributor. Praising *No Bed without Ted* for its reassuring ending, Beverly Combs added in

School Library Journal that the author/illustrator's "illustrations are big and colorful, [and] the story is fun."

Biographical and Critical Sources

PERIODICALS

Booklist, March 15, 1990, Ilene Cooper, review of *The Invitation,* p. 1459.
Independent on Sunday, June 27, 1993.
Junior Bookshelf, October, 1990, p. 221; December, 1991, review of *Finish the Story, Dad,* p. 245.
Kirkus Reviews, September 1, 1991, p. 1169.
Magpies, September, 1991, review of *Beach Boy,* p. 37.
Observer (London, England), April 7, 1985, review of *Down in the Woods,* p. 21.
Practical Parenting, July, 1993.
Publishers Weekly, December 14, 1984, review of *Rex Q.X.,* p. 54; October 18, 1993, review of *Noah's Ark,* p. 74; April 11, 1994, review of *The Tusk Fairy,* p. 63; September 19, 1994, review of *The Christmas Story,* p. 28; April 25, 2005, review of *No Bed without Ted,* p. 58.
School Librarian, September, 1985, review of *Down in the Woods,* p. 231; May, 1990, review of *The Invitation,* p. 60; August, 1993, review of *Teacher's Pet,* p. 106; November, 1993, review of *The Tusk Fairy,* p. 152; February, 1996, review of *Charlie's Choice,* p. 17; spring, 2001, review of *Freddie Visits the Dentist* and *Freddie Goes on an Airplane,* p. 20.
School Library Journal, July, 1990, Linda Boyles, review of *The Invitation,* p. 64; December, 1991, Virginia E. Jeschelnig, review of *Finish the Story, Dad,* p. 107; August, 1994, Susan Hepler, review of *The Tusk Fairy,* p. 146; July, 2005, Beverly Combs, review of *No Bed without Ted,* p. 82.*

*   *   *

STAUNTON, Ted 1956-

Personal

Born March 29, 1956, in Toronto, Ontario, Canada; son of Frederick William (a real estate executive and dance band leader) and Ethel Marjorie Staunton (a homemaker; maiden name, Stewart); married Melanie Catherine Browne (a visual artist); children: William. *Education:* University of Toronto, B.A., B.Ed. *Hobbies and other interests:* Playing guitar, basketball, running.

Addresses

Home—202 Yeovil St., Port Hope, Ontario L1A 1W9, Canada. *Agent*—Transatlantic Literary Agency, 72 Glengowan Rd., Toronto, Ontario M4N 1G4, Canada.

Career

Children's book writer and musician. Performer with group Born Yesterday. Parks and Recreation Department, City of Etobicoke, Ontario, Canada, community programmer, 1974-80; St. Michael's College Library, University of Toronto, Ontario, library technician, 1983-84; Ministry of Consumer and Commercial Relations, Toronto, education officer, 1984-85; full-time writer and speaker, 1985—.

Member

Writers' Union of Canada, Society of Composers, Authors and Music Publishers of Canada, Canadian Society of Children's Authors, Illustrators, and Performers, Canadian Children's Book Centre.

Awards, Honors

Puddleman and *Taking Care of Crumley,* named "Our Choice" selections, Canadian Children's Book Centre; Silver Birch Award shortlist, 1999, and Hackmatack Award shortlist, 2000, both for *Hope Springs a Leak;* Canadian Literature Association Outstanding Children's Book of the Year nomination, c. 2000, for *Two False Moves.*

Writings

PICTURE BOOKS

Puddleman, illustrated by Maryann Kovalski, Kids Can Press (Tonawanda, NY), 1983, revised edition illustrated by Brenda Clark, 1988.

Taking Care of Crumley, illustrated by Tina Holdcroft, Kids Can Press (Tonawanda, NY), 1984.

Simon's Surprise, illustrated by Sylvie Daigneault, Kids Can Press (Tonawanda, NY), 1986.

Miss Fishley Afloat, illustrated by Eric Parker, Kids Can Press (Tonawanda, NY), 1990.

Anna Takes Charge, illustrated by Michael Martchenko, Yorkdale Shopping Centre, 1993.

"MORGAN" SERIES

Morgan Makes Magic, illustrated by Bill Slavin, Formac (Halifax, Nova Scotia, Canada), 1997.

Morgan and the Money, illustrated by Bill Slavin, Formac (Halifax, Nova Scotia, Canada), 1998.

Morgan's Secret, illustrated by Bill Slavin, Formac (Halifax, Nova Scotia, Canada), 2000.

Great Play, Morgan!, illustrated by Bill Slavin, Formac (Halifax, Nova Scotia, Canada), 2001.

Morgan's Birthday, illustrated by Bill Slavin, Formac (Halifax, Nova Scotia, Canada), 2002.

Morgan's Pet Plot, illustrated by Bill Slavin, Formac (Halifax, Nova Scotia, Canada), 2003.

Morgan Makes a Splash, illustrated by Bill Slavin, Formac (Halifax, Nova Scotia, Canada), 2004.

Morgan Makes a Deal, illustrated by Bill Slavin, Formac (Halifax, Nova Scotia, Canada), 2005.

"KIDS FROM MONKEY MOUNTAIN" SERIES

Two False Moves, Red Deer Press (Calgary, Alberta, Canada), 2000.

Forgive Us Our Travises, Red Deer Press (Calgary, Alberta, Canada), 2000.

The Monkey Mountain Monster, Red Deer Press (Calgary, Alberta, Canada), 2000.

Princess, Red Deer Press (Calgary, Alberta, Canada), 2001.

Second Banana, Red Deer Press (Calgary, Alberta, Canada), 2001.

Trouble with Girls, Red Deer Press (Calgary, Alberta, Canada), 2002.

Stinky, Red Deer Press (Calgary, Alberta, Canada), 2002.

"MAGGIE AND CYRIL" SERIES

Maggie and Me, Kids Can Press (Tonawanda, NY), 1986, revised edition illustrated by Jacqui Thomas, Penguin, 1989.

Greenapple Street Blues, Kids Can Press (Tonawanda, NY), 1987.

Mushmouth and the Marvel, Kids Can Press (Tonawanda, NY), 1988.

Great Minds Think Alike, Kids Can Press (Tonawanda, NY), 1989.

Taking the Long Way Home, Kids Can Press (Tonawanda, NY), 1992.

NOVELS

Hope Springs a Leak, Red Deer Press (Calgary, Alberta, Canada), 1998.

Sounding Off, Red Deer Press (Calgary, Alberta, Canada), 2004.

OTHER

(Reviser and editor) Maggie Della Leigh-Burton, *Grandma Burton's Book: Memoirs of Earlier Days in Minnesota, South Dakota, and Saskatchewan,* Iona Private Press, 1981.

(Illustrator) John Rodgers, *Birdwatching for Young Canadians,* Douglas & McIntyre (Toronto, Ontario, Canada), 1982.

The Dreadful Truth: Confederation, illustrated by Graham Pilsworth, Formac (Halifax, Nova Scotia, Canada), 2004.

The Dreadful Truth: Building the Railway, illustrated by Brian Goff, Formac (Halifax, Nova Scotia, Canada), 2005.

Contributor to books, including *Writers on Writing: Guide to Writing and Illustrating Children's Books,* edited by David Booth, Overlea House, 1989; and *Everybody's Favourites: Canadians Talk about Books That Changed Their Lives,* compiled by Arlene Perly Rae, Viking, 1997.

Author's books have been translated into French.

Adaptations

Staunton's works have been adapted as sound recordings.

Sidelights

Ted Staunton's work appeals to children ranging from preschool age to middle graders. Audiences relate to Staunton's stories about familiar childhood experiences that feature action, humor, and authentic dialogue. Through the medium of story he delves into the nature of special relationships and connects with his young audience through authentic dialogue.

Staunton infuses his writing with the uncanny ability to remember what it was like to be a kid. His first book, *Puddleman,* takes readers into the fantasy life of a preschooler named Michael who loves to play in the mud but does not like the real-life problems that result. As Jan Marriott wrote in *Quill & Quire,* "These are all emotions and situations with which most young children can readily identify."

Staunton has also penned a series of stories about the everyday escapades of grade-school friends Maggie and Cyril. *Taking Care of Crumley* reveals the friends' plot to teach a lesson to Cyril's nemesis, the schoolyard bully. Using realistic playground banter, Staunton captures "the terror as well as the pleasure of ultimate social justice," according to Joan Yolleck in *Quill & Quire.* Cyril and Maggie are back at school in *Maggie and Me,* which Nancy Gifford recommended for its "humorous tone . . . dialogue and action" in her review for *School Library Journal.* Gifford described the variety of classmates Staunton includes as "some bossy, some bullies, some leaders (Maggie), and some followers (Cyril)"— someone with whom everyone can identify.

Staunton energizes his "Maggie and Cyril" series by moving the story along at a brisk pace. *Taking the Long Way Home,* the fifth "Maggie and Cyril" book "lays each plot development on top of the previous one to make a precarious structure" designed to keep readers "holding their breath until the last scene," according to *Canadian Review of Materials* contributor Alison Mews. In the end, however, Staunton's popular characters manage to help each other and solve their individual predicaments. Reviewer Andre Gagnon voiced his opinion of the series in *Canadian Review of Materials:* "Staunton's ability to build an episode with quick, funny, unforced dialogue and situations to which children can relate puts this series well above others." *Great Minds Think Alike* chronicles another Maggie and Cyril episode and takes place during summer vacation. This time, Cyril worries about losing his best friend as he searches for adventure. Writing for *Quill & Quire,* Ann Gilmore concluded that this edition to the series is for those who "regard fairy tales as psychologically nurturing and growth-enhancing," and determined it a "wonderful addition to the genre."

Titles such as *Simon's Surprise* introduce readers to new characters with their own set of childhood dilemmas to solve. After being told "when you're bigger" once too often, Simon sets out to prove he's BIG

In Staunton's chapter book, arch enemies Nick and Lindsay are forced to get along when their science teacher assigns them to work together on a team project. (Cover illustration by Roger Lafontaine.)

enough NOW. Early one morning, before his parents awaken, Simon decides to wash the family car by himself. In *Canadian Children's Literature,* reviewer Mary Rubio commented that the text and illustrations work together to capture the parents' "dazed and dumbfounded looks," as well as "proud little Simon standing amid his mess."

Staunton joins illustrator Eric Parker in speeding up the tempo in *Miss Fishley Afloat.* According to *Canadian Review of Materials* reviewer Patricia Butler, in the novel "wacky events . . . take place at such a rapid pace, two readings are necessary to feel that the story has been understood." Sarah Ellis, in her review for *Quill & Quire* described the sea-faring tale as "outrageous, heaping surprise upon coincidence" and the "cartoon-style pictures are energetic and jaunty. The writing is bombastic."

Staunton's "Morgan" series for young readers chronicles the adventures of third-grader Morgan and his classmates, including Aldeen Hummel, who Morgan thinks of as the Godzilla of Grade Three. While the books in the "Morgan" series focus on the title character, the students in the "Kids from Monkey Mountain" series each get a chance to tell a story from their own perspective.

Instead of following the same character from book to book, installments in the "Kids from Monkey Mountain" saga focus on a different student each time, with classmates alternating as minor characters. In the first book in the series, *Two False Moves,* Nick finds out that Lindsey's family might be buying the house his family is renting. Nick immediately targets Lindsey in verbal warfare, and she jibes right back. When their teacher, oblivious to the conflict, pairs Nick and Lindsey together on a project, each learns that there is more to the other than previously realized. Travis is the star, and class-clown, of *Forgive Us Our Travises,* while *Second Banana* stars Ryan, a kid with an annoying laugh and a determination to gain new friends. Reviewing *Second Banana,* Cora Lee wrote in *Resource Links* that "Staunton tells a story that moves like an energetic seven-year-old. . . . His characters are immensely believable, their problems realistic." John Peters, writing in *Booklist,* considered the books in the series "lightweight, comfortably predictable episodes."

The "Kids from Monkey Mountain" series continues with *Princess,* a story about Mary Beth, who strives to be herself even as her mother tries to mold Mary Beth into a princess. "The real-life problems in this novel, combined with the believable characters," make the book "an excellent novel," according to Joanne de Groot in *Resource Links.* Jeff is the star of *Trouble with Girls,* as he and friend Nick—*Two False Moves*—face off against members of EGG, the school's "Evil Girl Group." Janice's loud attitude makes everyone think she is secure in who she is, but in *Stinky,* her contact with a skunk helps her come to terms with her own insecurities and learns to just be herself. The book is "particularly good for students who are struggling with their self-esteem," commented Wendy L. Hogan in *Resource Links.* Laura Reilly, writing for the same journal, wrote of *Trouble with Girls* that "this book and others in the series are highly recommended."

Along with his series books, Staunton is also the author of two longer novels for young adults. *Sounding Off,* a sequel to *Hope Springs a Leak,* focuses on Sam, a too-skinny, too-tall, fourteen-year-old high-school student whose father is also one of his teachers. Just when Sam thinks things cannot get worse in his life, he is drawn into the middle of a controversy about banning a book by a local author. The narrative "veer[s] between slapstick and serious sometimes at dizzying speed," reported Margaret Mackey in *Resource Links. Kliatt* reviewer Joseph DeMarco noted that "Sam is a teen with whom YAs would identify."

Staunton has also written books about Canadian history, including *The Dreadful Truth: Confederation,* the story of how Canada became a country. He describes the living conditions in Canada during the time of confederation and reveals details about the people involved with the country's founding. "Staunton has garnered many

fascinating tidbits of information about these great men that reveal their humanity," wrote Joan Marshall in *Resource Links.*

Readers interested in linking Staunton to his characters do not have to look far. In *Meet Canadian Authors and Illustrators,* Staunton told Allison Gertridge: "The character of Cyril is based on me when I was in grade school. I was a very shy and retiring type like Cyril. But more than the things that happen to Cyril, it's Cyril's outlook or his desires that echo mine." However reminiscent his books may be of his own "normal" and "stable" childhood, Staunton avoids oversimplification and overdoses of sweetness and light. "I'm not interested in writing about nice things or role models, or being cute. I'd rather explore what happens when things go slightly wrong," he told a writer for the *Canadian Children's Book Centre.* "I tend to prefer it when kids can't quite answer their own problems because, after all, who really can?"

At age fourteen, Sam wonders if he will make it to age fifteen; while crushing on a young country singer, his efforts to impress constantly backfire in Staunton's young-adult novel set in Canada. (Cover design by Erin Woodward.)

Biographical and Critical Sources

BOOKS

Canadian Children's Book Centre, 1994.
Gertridge, Allison, *Meet Canadian Authors and Illustrators,* Scholastic Canada (Toronto, Ontario, Canada), 1994.

PERIODICALS

Booklist, February 15, 2001, John Peters, review of *Two False Moves,* p. 1138.
Books for Young People, October, 1988, p. 17.
Books in Canada, March, 2003, review of *Trouble with Girls,* p. 46.
Canadian Book Review Annual, 1998, review of *Morgan and the Money,* p. 522; 2000, reviews of *Morgan's Secret, The Monkey Mountain Monster,* and *Two False Moves,* p. 504; 2002, review of *Trouble with Girls, Stinky,* and *Morgan's Birthday,* p. 518.
Canadian Children's Literature, 1987, Mary Rubio, review of *Simon's Surprise,* p. 105.
Canadian Review of Materials, March, 1989, Andre Gagnon, review of *Mushmouth and the Marvel,* p. 53; November, 1990, Patricia L.M. Butler, review of *Miss Fishley Afloat,* p. 272; November, 1992, Alison Mews, review of *Taking the Long Way Home,* p. 306; November 28, 1997, review of *Morgan Makes Magic;* January 5, 2001, review of *Morgan's Secret.*
Kliatt, May, 2005, Joseph DeMarco, review of *Sounding Off,* p. 31.
Quill & Quire, January, 1984, Jan Marriott, review of *Puddleman,* p. 28; November, 1984, Joan Yolleck, review of *Taking Care of Crumley,* pp. 12-13; August, 1986, p. 38; September, 1989, Anne Gilmore, review of *Great Minds Think Alike,* pp. 23-24; August, 1990, Sarah Ellis, review of *Miss Fishley Afloat,* p. 14; September, 2000, review of *Two False Moves,* p. 63; December, 2001, review of *Princess,* p. 25.
Resource Links June, 1999, review of *Morgan and the Money,* p. 10; June, 2000, review of *Morgan's Secret,* p. 7; October, 2001, Mavis Holder, review of *Great Play, Morgan!,* p. 12; December, 2001, Cora Lee, review of *Second Banana,* and Joanne de Groot, review of *Princess,* p. 21; April, 2003, Wendy L. Hogan, review of *Stinky,* p. 21, and Laura Reilly, review of *Trouble with Girls,* p. 52; December, 2004, Margaret Mackey, review of *Sounding Off,* p. 39; February, 2005, Joan Marshall, review of *The Dreadful Truth: Confederation,* p. 49.
School Library Journal, August, 1985, p. 58; July, 1990, Nancy A. Gifford, review of *Maggie and Me,* p. 79; August, 2001, Linda Beck, review of *Forgive Us Our Travises* and *The Monkey Mountain Monster,* p. 162; January, 2003, review of *Morgan's Birthday,* p. 97; January, 2005, Karyn N. Silverman, review of *Sounding Off,* p. 136.

ONLINE

Canadian Society of Children's Authors, Illustrators, and Performers Web site, http://www.canscaip.org/ (January 20, 2006), "Ted Staunton."
Ted Staunton Home Page, http://tedstauntonbooks.tripod.com (January 20, 2006).
Transatlantic Literary Agency Web site, http://www.tla1.com/ (January 20, 2006), "Ted Staunton."
Writers' Union of Canada Web site, http://www.writersunion.ca/ (January 20, 2006), "Ted Staunton."*

* * *

STEWART, Melissa 1968-

Personal

Born December 9, 1968, in Hartford, CT; daughter of Bruce (a mechanical engineer) and Dorothy (a laboratory supervisor; maiden name, Jayes) Stewart. *Education:* Union College, Schenectady, NY, B.S. (cum laude), 1990; New York University, M.A., 1991.

Addresses

Home and office—Honeybee Productions, 24 Kinsley Rd., Acton, MA 01720.

Career

Healthmark Medical Education Media, New York, NY, associate editor, 1991; Foca Co., New York, NY, project editor, 1992-93, managing editor, 1993-95; Grolier Publishing Co., Danbury, CT, science editor, 1995-97, senior science editor, 1997-2000; freelance writer, 1991—. Member, American Institute of Physics Children's Science Writing Award committee.

Member

American Association for the Advancement of Science, National Association of Science Writers, Foundation for Children's Books, Society of Children's Book Writer and Illustrators (director of New England conference, 2006), Massachusetts Environmental Education Society, Sigma Xi.

Awards, Honors

Recommended Title, National Science Teachers Association; New York Public Library Books for the Teen Age citation, and Best Book of the Year, *Science Books and Films;* nonfiction research grant letter of merit, Society of Children's Book Writers and Illustrators.

Writings

NONFICTION

Life without Light: A Journey to Earth's Dark Ecosystems, F. Watts (Danbury, CT), 1998.
Science in Ancient India, F. Watts (Danbury, CT), 1999.
Rachel Carson: Writer and Biologist, Ferguson (Chicago, IL), 2001.

Tim Berners-Less: Inventor of the World Wide Web, Ferguson (Chicago, IL), 2001.

Seals, Sea Lions, and Walruses, F. Watts (New York, NY), 2001.

Uranus, F. Watts (New York, NY), 2002.

Life in a Lake, Lerner (Minneapolis, MN), 2003.

Small Birds, Benchmark Books (New York, NY), 2003.

Life in a Wetland, photographs by Stephen K. Maka, Lerner (Minneapolis, MN), 2003.

Maggots, Grubs, and More: The Secret Lives of Young Insects, Millbrook (Brookfield, CT), 2003.

Sloths, Carolrhoda (Minneapolis, MN), 2005.

A Place for Butterflies, illustrated by Higgins Bond, Peachtree (Atlanta, GA), 2006.

How Do Birds Fly?, Marshall Cavendish Benchmark (New York, NY), 2006.

Energy in Motion, Children's Press (New York, NY), 2006.

How Do Fish Breathe Underwater?, Marshall Cavendish Benchmark (New York, NY), 2006.

Why Do Seasons Change?, Marshall Cavendish Benchmark (New York, NY), 2006.

How Do Plants Grow?, Marshall Cavendish Benchmark (New York, NY), 2006.

Will It Float or Sink?, Children's Press (Danbury, CT), 2006.

"TRUE BOOKS" SERIES

Mammals, Children's Press (Danbury, CT), 2001.

Amphibians, Children's Press (Danbury, CT), 2001.

Birds, Children's Press (Danbury, CT), 2001.

Fishes, Children's Press (Danbury, CT), 2001.

Reptiles, Children's Press (Danbury, CT), 2001.

Insects, Children's Press (Danbury, CT), 2001.

Hippopotamuses, Children's Press (Danbury, CT), 2002.

Elephants, Children's Press (Danbury, CT), 2002.

Antelope, Children's Press (Danbury, CT), 2002.

Zebras, Children's Press (Danbury, CT), 2002.

Rhinoceroses, Children's Press (Danbury, CT), 2002.

"ROCKS AND MINERALS" SERIES

Minerals, Heinemann Library (Chicago, IL), 2002.

Metamorphic Rocks, Heinemann Library (Chicago, IL), 2002.

Igneous Rocks, Heinemann Library (Chicago, IL), 2002.

Fossils, Heinemann Library (Chicago, IL), 2002.

Crystals, Heinemann Library (Chicago, IL), 2002.

Soil, Heinemann Library (Chicago, IL), 2002.

Sedimentary Rocks, Heinemann Library (Chicago, IL), 2002.

"SIMPLY SCIENCE" SERIES

Atoms, Compass Point (Minneapolis, MN), 2003.

Fossils, Compass Point (Minneapolis, MN), 2003.

Motion, Compass Point (Minneapolis, MN), 2003.

Plants, Compass Point (Minneapolis, MN), 2003.

"RANGER RICK SCIENCE PROGRAM" SERIES

Cells to Systems, Newbridge, 2003.

The Producers, Newbridge, 2003.

Shorebirds, Newbridge, 2003.

"INVESTIGATIVE SCIENCE" SERIES

Animals All Around, Compass Point (Minneapolis, MN), 2004.

Down to Earth, illustrated by Jeffrey Scherer, Compass Point (Minneapolis, MN), 2004.

A Parade of Plants, illustrated by Jeffrey Scherer, Compass Point (Minneapolis, MN), 2004.

Fun with the Sun, Compass Point (Minneapolis, MN), 2004.

Use Your Senses, Compass Point (Minneapolis, MN), 2005.

What's the Weather, Compass Point (Minneapolis, MN), 2005.

Air Is Everywhere, Compass Point (Minneapolis, MN), 2005.

The Wonders of Water, Compass Point (Minneapolis, MN), 2005.

Contributor to books, including *Blueprint for Life, Secrets of the Inner Mind,* Time-Life (Alexandria, VA); *Biology: Visualizing Life,* Holt (New York, NY); and *Biology,* Addison-Wesley (Reading, MA). Contributor of articles and columns to magazines and newspapers, including *American Forests, American Heritage of Invention and Technology, Ask, ChemMatters, Click, Highlights for Children, National Geographic World, Instructor, Math, Science World, Family Planning Perspectives, Her New York, New York Doctor, Washington Square News, Natural New England, North Maine Woods Bulletin, Northern Woodlands, Odyssey, Ranger Rick, Today's Science, Wild Outdoor World, Wildlife Conservation, Writer, ZooGoer,* and *New York Daily News.*

Sidelights

In the "About the Author" section of her first published book, *Life without Light: A Journey to Earth's Dark Ecosystems,* Melissa Stewart related a story about walking in the New England woods with her father. Having been asked if she noticed anything different about the trees in that particular part of the woods, Stewart said she noticed that the trees were smaller. Her father told her that there had been a fire approximately twenty-five years earlier, and that all the trees were new growth. "I was hooked," Stewart later recalled. "Ever since that moment, I have wanted to know everything about the natural world." As an adult she has channeled her boundless curiosity into a career as the author of nature-focused nonfiction for children. On her home page, Stewart wrote: "Now I get paid to learn all about the natural world and share it with other people. What could be better?"

Stewart has written on a wide variety of subjects, from nature to biography to atoms. *Light without Life,* which was honored as the Best Book of the Year by *Science*

Books and Film, describes for teen readers what life is like near the hydrothermal vents far below the surface of the ocean. As Carolyn Phelan wrote in *Booklist.* "the quality of the writing" is superior, and the title is "well-researched." Another of Stewart's titles, *Maggots, Grubs, and More: The Secret Lives of Young Insects,* also presents young readers with descriptions of forms of life they normally would not observe. Insects are shown growing from eggs to young insects until they are fully mature. Karey Wehner, writing in *School Library Journal,* considered the title a "lucid, well-organized introduction" to the young lives of insects.

Moving to much larger creatures, *Animals All Around* introduces readers to techniques scientists use in scientific observation of animal species. In *School Library Journal,* Kathryn Kosiorek complimented the "clear, precise sentences and carefully chosen questions" incorporated in Stewart's text. Like *Animals All Around, Air Is Everywhere* is designed to involve readers in dialogue through questions. "The author poses questions, asks students to make predictions, and suggests simple experiments and observations that will enhance their understanding of basic science concepts," according to Sandra Welzenbach in *School Library Journal.*

Stewart's biographies *Tim Berners-Lee: Inventor of the World Wide Web* and *Rachel Carson: Biologist and Writer* describe the lives of scientists who impacted advances in technology and environmentalism. For the book on Berners-Lee, Stewart combines a limited biography of the inventor, who is still alive and is very private, with advice on getting into the computer science field. "This interesting combination of biography and career guide should have strong appeal for students," wrote Sandra L. Doggett in *School Library Journal.* When Stewart came in contact with the work of Rachel Carson, she "felt a deep affinity toward her life and work," as she told Sue Reichard in an interviewer for *Suite 101 Online,* and this connection inspired the biography. As Stewart explained in her interview, Carson originally thought she had to chose between being a scientist and a writer; then came the moment she realized she could do both. "That's exactly how I felt when one of my college biology professors suggested that I become a writer. It was a great aha moment for me, as it was for Ms. Carson."

Noting that Stewart writes articles for adults as well as penning children's books, *Suite 101 Online* interviewer Reichard asked Stewart about writing for multiple audi-

Stewart delves into a word that is often unseen and misunderstood in **Maggots, Grubs, and More: The Secret Lives of Young Insects.** *(Photograph by M.H. Sharp.)*

Part of the "Investigate Science" series, Stewart's **Air Is Everywhere** *describes air's qualities and importance and includes activities and experiments for hands-on learners. (Photograph by Kevin R. Morris.)*

ences. "I like the variety of writing for many different audiences and the challenges associated with each group," the author replied. "Writing for young children is fun because they are so naturally curious, and I know they will listen intently as a loving adult reads the story to them or pay close attention as they struggle to read it themselves. Middle graders and high school students can understand more sophisticated language and more complex concerns, and they have a broader view of the world. When I write for adults, I can really stretch as a writer, using my vocabulary reserves and including allusions that kids just won't get. I like doing that once in awhile."

Biographical and Critical Sources

BOOKS

Stewart, Melissa, *Life without Light: A Journey to Earth's Dark Ecosystems,* F. Watts (Danbury, CT), 1999.

PERIODICALS

Booklist, July, 1999, Carolyn Phelan, review of *Life without Light,* p. 1945.

School Librarian, spring, 2003, review of *Sedimentary Rocks,* p. 52.

School Library Journal, June, 1999, p. 154; August, 1999, Lynn W. Zimmerman, review of *Life without Light,* p. 180; October, 2001, Sandra L. Doggett, review of *Tim Berners-Lee: Inventor of the World Wide Web,* p. 192; November, 2001, Kathleen Isaacs, review of *Rachel Carson: Biologist and Writer,* p. 186; July, 2003, Kathryn Kosioreki, review of *Fossils,* p. 119; January, 2004, Karey Wehner, review of *Maggots, Grubs, and More: The Secret Lives of Young Insects,* p. 160; October, 2004, Kathryn Kosioreki, review of *Animals All Around,* p. 150, and review of *Maggots, Grubs, and More,* p. S43; March, 2005, Sandra Welzenbach, review of *Air Is Everywhere,* p. 202.

School Science Review, Terry Jennings, review of *Life in a Lake,* pp. 133-134.

Science Books and Films, March, 2003, review of *Crystals,* p. 71; July, 2003, review of *Life in a Wetland,* p. 167; July-August, 2004, Mary Jane Davis, review of *Animals All Around,* p. 180.

ONLINE

Melissa Stewart's Home Page, http://www.melissa-stewart. com (January 20, 2006).
Suite 101 Online, http://www.suite101.com/ (November 1, 2005), Sue Reichard, interview with Stewart.

*   *   *

STEWART, Whitney 1959-

Personal

Born February 3, 1959, in Boston, MA; daughter of a lawyer and a counselor; married Hans C. Andersson, September 17, 1988; children: Christoph Andersson. *Education:* Brown University, graduated, 1983. *Hobbies and other interests:* Traveling, reading, meditation, yoga, running.

Addresses

Home—New Orleans, LA. *Agent*—c/o Author Mail, Lerner Publishing Group, 1251 Washington Ave N., Minneapolis, MN 55401.

Career

Children's book writer and freelance editor. Formerly worked as a travel agent.

Member

Society of Children's Book Writers and Illustrators, Authors' Guild, Author's League.

Writings

BIOGRAPHIES; FOR CHILDREN

To the Lion Throne: The Story of the Fourteenth Dalai Lama, Snow Lion, 1990.
The 14th Dalai Lama: Spiritual Leader of Tibet, Lerner (Minneapolis, MN), 1996.
Edmund Hillary: To Everest and Beyond, Lerner (Minneapolis, MN), 1996.
Aung San Suu Kyi: Fearless Voice of Burma, Lerner (Minneapolis, MN), 1996.
Deng Xiaoping: Leader in a Changing China, Lerner (Minneapolis, MN), 2001.
Becoming Buddha, illustrated by Sally Rippin, Lothian (Melbourne, Victoria, Australia), 2005.
Mao Zedong, Twenty-first Century Books (Minneapolis, MN), 2006.

OTHER

(Editor, with Vicki Lewelling and Paula Conru) *Speaking of Language: An International Guide to Language Service Organizations* (adult linguistics text), Prentice-Hall, 1993.

Jammin' on the Avenue: Going to New Orleans, Four Corners Publishing (New Orleans, LA), 2001.
Blues across the Bay: Going to San Francisco, Four Corners Publishing (New York, NY), 2001.

Contributor of short fiction to *Highlights for Children.*

Stewart's papers are held at the deGrummond Collection, University of Southern Mississippi.

Work in Progress

Beyond: A Writer's Memoir; an early reader set on Nantucket; *Mr. Lincoln's Gift,* for Hildene, forthcoming.

Sidelights

Whitney Stewart is an author of biographies for younger readers that draws on her interest in Eastern history and culture. In *Deng Ziaoping: Leader in a Changing China, Mao Zedong,* and *Aung San Suu Kyi: Fearless Voice of Burma* she profiles influential political leaders while in *The 14th Dalai Lama: Spiritual Leader of Tibet* she outlines the life of Tenzin Gyatso, who as the religious leader of Tibet won the Nobel Peace Prize in 1989. Stewart views the opportunities she has been given to write her biographies as "miracles": she has met with the Dalai Lama four times, has climbed mountains in Nepal with Sir Edmund Hillary (the first person to climb to the summit of Mount Everest), and has interviewed Aung San Suu Kyi, leader of Burma's democracy movement. In an interview with Patricia Austin in *Teaching and Learning Literature,* Stewart said of her books, "I have to choose a subject I can live with for a long time. It's hard and it's involving, so I have to pick people who inspire me."

Stewart began writing in high school through a correspondence course offered by the Children's Literature Institute. While attending Brown University a few years later, she met as many authors and editors as she could. Because Brown offered no formal children's literature program, Stewart designed her own independent major and thesis. When a professor suggested that she focus on children's biographies, Stewart recalled the biographies of her youth: "awful—fictionalized and full of made-up conversation." The historical works of well-known children's author Jean Fritz quickly changed her opinion about biographies, though, and Stewart began a correspondence with Fritz that ultimately helped launch her own career.

After graduating from Brown, Stewart indulged in her love of travel by getting a job at a travel agency, and combined it with her interest in rock climbing by spending a year planning a trip to the Himalaya. She read about Tibetan history and philosophy, then made her first trip there in 1986 with her mother. While there, Stewart was greatly inspired by the story of the Dalai Lama and his philosophy and proposed writing a book about him for Snow Lion Publications. The publisher's acceptance resulted in letters of introduction on her behalf and eventually four interviews with the Tibetan leader.

For her next children's biography, *Edmund Hillary: To Everest and Beyond,* Stewart collaborated with photographer Anne Keiser. Lerner accepted this title, as well as another biography on the Dalai Lama. These two titles became the first in Lerner's "Newsmakers" series. Stewart was impressed by Sir Edmund Hillary, not only for his extraordinary achievements as a mountaineer—with expeditions to the trans-Antarctic in New Zealand, travels up the Ganges River, and a search for the Himalayan yeti—but also for his humanitarian work to help the Sherpa people of the Himalayan region improve their lives and environment.

When Stewart decided to write about a woman for her next book, she bypassed the entertainer-type subjects suggested to her by teachers and librarians, and chose Aung San Suu Kyi, founder of the National League of Democracy in Burma and winner of the 1991 Nobel Peace Prize. The same week Stewart's book proposal was accepted by Lerner, Suu Kyi was released by Burma's military government after spending six years under house arrest.

Using the Internet, Stewart was able in three weeks' time to find Burmese scholars to contact for information on Suu Kyi. However, she soon found that arranging the trip to Burma and an interview with this controversial subject would not be as easy as her trips to Tibet. Since it is a punishable crime to criticize the Burmese government, Stewart had to tell Burmese authorities that she was visiting Burma to meditate at Buddhist temples. In the two weeks she spent in Burma, Stewart felt as if she were being followed. Her one-page letter to Suu Kyi requesting an interview cost Stewart seventy dollars and had to be delivered by courier. The two finally met, but for only thirty-five minutes. When she finished writing the manuscript that would become *Aung San Suu Kyi,* Stewart became concerned about the accuracy of details in her work and asked three Burmese scholars to read over her manuscript. In *Booklist,* Ilene Cooper called Stewart's book "a thorough, well-documented effort."

Writing *Deng Xiaoping* presented Stewart with new challenges. First, as she explained to Peg Kohlepp in the New Orleans *Times-Picayune,* although she found his life inspiring, his alliance with Mao Zedong's communist principles and his role in ordering the massacre of students in Tiananmen Square in June of 1989 made Deng less "ethically or spiritually inspiring" than her other subjects. Deng had also passed away, so no interview was possible; in addition, most information about the Chinese leader's life was published only in Chinese, which Stewart does not read. Ultimately, however, the understanding she gained through her research made Deng fascinating; as she told Kohlepp, for Deng "to work alongside Mao Zedong—that in itself would have been one of the hardest challenges of his life." Her biography, which follows Deng's life from his slow rise to a position of influence within Mao's government, his ability to weather a series of political setbacks, and his

involvement in Communist China's invasion of Tibet in 1950, is framed by the history of China in the twentieth century. While noting that Stewart "has a slight tendency to generalize," Barbara Scotto wrote in a *School Library Journal* review that *Deng Xiaoping* provides middle-grade students with "a good introduction to a complicated and important 20th-century figure."

Discussing her decision to write biographies for younger readers, Stewart once told *SATA:* "I hope to introduce children to people and to ideas that can change my readers' orientation to life. With global understanding comes peace. If I can contribute to that understanding, I am fulfilled.

"In 2005, I published my first picture book. *Becoming Buddha* was a collaboration with my friend, Australian author/illustrator Sally Rippin. Working with Sally was a joy, and I love reaching a younger audience. My second picture book, *Mr. Lincoln's Gift,* a story about Lincoln's portrait artist Frank Carpenter, took three years of research."

Biographical and Critical Sources

BOOKS

Amoss, Berthe, and Eric Suben, *Ten Steps to Publishing Children's Books,* Writer's Digest Books, 1997.

PERIODICALS

Booklist, December 1, 1990, p. 755; April 1, 1997, Ilene Cooper, review of *Aung San Suu Kyi: Fearless Voice of Burma,* p. 1321.
Far Eastern Economic Review, September 11, 1997, Bertil Lintner, review of *Aung San Suu Kyi,* p. 52.
School Library Journal, June, 1996, p. 165; May, 1997, Judy R. Johnston, review of *Aung San Suu Kyi,* p. 150; July, 2001, Barbara Scotto, review of *Deng Xiaoping: Leader in a Changing China,* p. 132.
Teaching and Learning Literature, September-October, 1996, Patricia Austin, "Whitney Stewart, Biographer," pp. 41-48.
Times-Picayune (New Orleans, LA), January 25, 1996; February 25, 1996; May 12, 1996; April 15, 2001, Matt Berman, "'Going to' New Awleens: Whitney Stewart Gives Kids a Primer on Our Good Life"; April 16, 2001, Peg Kohlepp, review of *Deng Xiaoping.*
Voice of Youth Advocates, December, 1997, review of *Aung San Suu Kyi,* p. 338.

ONLINE

Whitney Stewart Home Page, http://www.whitneystewart. com (January 3, 2006).

STRACHAN, Linda

Personal

Born in Edinburgh, Scotland; married; children: three. *Ethnicity:* "Scottish/Italian." *Education:* Attended Kilgraston School (Perthshire, Scotland).

Addresses

Home—Scotland. *Agent*—Fraser Ross Associates, 6 Wellington Place, Edinburgh EH6 7EQ, Scotland.

Career

Author and storyteller. Bacteriology lab technician, 1972-73; fashion model, 1973; retail fashion buyer, 1976-80; co-owner of business, 1986-96. Freelance writer, beginning 1996; writer-in-residence and creative-writing tutor. Member, Literature Forum for Scotland, 2003-06. Kilgraston Association, president, 1996-2001.

Member

British Society of Authors (committee member of Scottish branch, 2003-06).

Awards, Honors

Scottish Arts Council, grant, 1999, and professional development award, 2004.

Writings

FOR CHILDREN

What Colour Is Love?, illustrated by David Wojtowycz, Bloomsbury (New York, NY), 2003.

"HAMISH MCHAGGIS" SERIES; FOR CHILDREN

Hamish McHaggis and the Edinburgh Adventure, illustrated by Sally J. Collins, GW Publishing (Thatcham, Berkshire, England), 2005.
Hamish McHaggis and the Ghost of Glamis, illustrated by Sally J. Collins, GW Publishing (Thatcham, Berkshire, England), 2005.
Hamish McHaggis and the Skye Surprise, illustrated by Sally J. Collins, GW Publishing (Thatcham, Berkshire, England), 2005.
Hamish McHaggis and the Search for the Loch Ness Monster, illustrated by Sally J. Collins, GW Publishing (Thatcham, Berkshire, England), 2005.
Hamish McHaggis and the Wonderful Water Wheel, illustrated by Sally J. Collins, GW Publishing (Thatcham, Berkshire, England), 2005.
Hamish McHaggis and the Skirmish at Stirling, illustrated by Sally J. Collins, GW Publishing (Thatcham, Berkshire, England), 2005.

Linda Strachan

Greyfriars Bobby, illustrated by Sally J. Collins, GW Publishing (Thatcham, Berkshire, England), 2005.

READERS; FOR CHILDREN

The Hut, illustrated by Michael Reid, Rigby Heinemann (London, England), 1998.
The Cat in the Tree, illustrated by Michael Reid, Rigby Heinemann (London, England), 1998.
Coins!, illustrated by Michael Reid, Rigby Heinemann (London, England), 1998.
Fire!, illustrated by Michael Reid, Rigby Heinemann (London, England), 1998.
Popstars, illustrated by Michael Reid, Rigby Heinemann (London, England), 1998.
Jamie the Paranormal Investigator, illustrated by Michael Reid, Rigby Heinemann (London, England), 1999.
Beth Runs Away, illustrated by Michael Reid, Rigby Heinemann (London, England), 1999.
The New Teacher, illustrated by Michael Reid, Rigby Heinemann (London, England), 1999.
Hope's Pizza Party, illustrated by Michael Reid, Rigby Heinemann (London, England), 1999.
Beth's Talk, illustrated by Michael Reid, Rigby Heinemann (London, England), 1999.
(Reteller) *The Trojan Horse and Other Greek Myths,* illustrated by Ross Watton, Pearson-Longman (London, England), 2000.

A Ball Called Sam, illustrated by Shelagh McNicholas, Rigby Educational (Orlando, FL), 2000.

The Giant and the Frippit, illustrated by James Cotton, Rigby Educational (Orlando, FL), 2000.

Korka the Mighty Elf, illustrated by Mike Spoor, Rigby Educational (Orlando, FL), 2000.

Fizzkid the Inventor, illustrated by Woody, Rigby Educational (Orlando, FL), 2000.

Space Station Orion, illustrated by Chris Robson, Rigby Educational (Orlando, FL), 2000.

Rascal, illustrated by James Browne, Rigby Educational (Orlando, FL), 2000.

Computer Error, illustrated by Tony Albers, Rigby Educational (Orlando, FL), 2000.

The Grey Boatman, illustrated by Liz Alger, Rigby Educational (Orlando, FL), 2000.

Flood!, illustrated by Bruce Hogarth, Rigby Educational (Orlando, FL), 2000.

(Reteller) *Tales on a Cold Dark Night,* illustrated by Barbara Vagmozzi, Pearson-Longman (London, England), 2000.

The Galapina Treasures, illustrated by Debbi Mourtzios, Rigby-Heineman (Port Melbourne, Victoria, Australia), 2001.

Who Lives Here? (nonfiction), illustrated by Wayne Ford, Nelson (London, England), 2003.

What's That Sound? (nonfiction), illustrated by Ruth Rivers, Nelson (London, England), 2003.

What Is It? (nonfiction), illustrated by Mike Phillips, Nelson (London, England), 2003.

Walk in the Woods (nonfiction), illustrated by Pricilla Lamont, Nelson (London, England), 2003.

Can You Get Our Ball?, illustrated by David Mostyn, Oxford University Press (Oxford, England), 2004.

Melting Snow, illustrated by Arlene Adams, Oxford University Press (Oxford, England), 2004.

Gordon Gets Even, illustrated by Kelly Waldek, Ginn (Aylesbury, England), 2004.

Tarella, illustrated by Julian Bruére, Educators Publishing Service, 2006.

The Astonishing Book, illustrated by Debbie Mourtzios, Educators Publishing Service, 2006.

Contributor of short fiction to anthologies, including *Other Worlds,* 1999, and *Collections 6* and *Collections 8,* both Rigby-Heinemann, 2001.

"ZOOLA" SERIES; READERS

Zoola, illustrated by Julian Mosedale, Ginn (Aylesbury, England), 1997.

Zoola and the Green Burger, illustrated by Julian Mosedale, Ginn (Aylesbury, England), 1997.

Zoola and the Funfair, illustrated by Julian Mosedale, Ginn (Aylesbury, England), 1997.

Zoola and the Burglar, illustrated by Julian Mosedale, Ginn (Aylesbury, England), 1997.

Zoola and the Plane, illustrated by Julian Mosedale, Ginn (Aylesbury, England), 1997.

Zoola Is Kidnapped, illustrated by Julian Mosedale, Ginn (Aylesbury, England), 1997.

Zoola and the Ghost, illustrated by Julian Mosedale, Ginn (Aylesbury, England), 1997.

Zoola's Box, illustrated by Julian Mosedale, Ginn (Aylesbury, England), 1997.

Sidelights

Linda Strachan told *SATA:* "I always envy those who can say they have 'always wanted to be a writer.' I almost fell into writing by accident and now I wonder how I could ever have done anything else. My only regret is that I didn't start writing years earlier, but perhaps I wasn't ready.

"Looking back I have always loved books and stories. But one rather unfortunate remark, "This child lacks imagination" in a school report when I was very young left me with the firm conviction that I would never have any ideas of my own! I would sometimes like to meet that teacher again and show her my books.

"Some of my books have been for children who are less able, or reluctant readers. I love the idea that they might encourage children to discover the delights of reading. When I go into schools I am always keen to show the students that they each have their own wonderful imagination!

"I am fortunate in that there are so many talented children's writers and illustrators in Scotland, close to where I live. Children's writers are very supportive of each other and I enjoy having the opportunity to work with other writers or even just to meet up and discuss books, publishers, opportunities and ideas. We also have the Edinburgh International Book Festival every August which is two weeks when we can all get together and have the chance to listen to authors from all over the world. Writing is essentially such a solitary occupation that it is great to meet with other writers and illustrators to exchange views and information.

"One of the things I love about writing for children is that it is so varied. I can be writing a picture book one week and doing research for a teenage novel the next. Deadlines for educational books (those written for use in schools) can sometimes be incredibly tight and there is usually a very detailed brief to work from, whereas a trade publication can often have a much longer timescale and is left very much more up to the author. Each is a different challenge.

"When I wrote *What Colour Is Love?* I wanted to explore the juxtaposition of the senses and emotions in a way that we do not normally expect, while still producing a story that parents can read with very young children to introduce them to colour and animals. I find it works well in schools I visit when I can get the children to make animal noises, make faces to show different emotions and also to think about what colours they think different emotions might suggest to them.

"Some of my books have been translated into languages such as French and Portuguese. I love to see how the text has been translated and where the differences are.

When an elephant poses a question, all his jungle friends puzzle over the answer in Strachan's picture book **What Color Is Love?** *(Illustration by David Wojtowycz.)*

"While I am writing an illustrated book I usually think in pictures which can sometimes cause bit of a surprise when my mental images contrast with the illustrator's ideas. But a picture book is a work of two halves and I think the illustrator's ideas bring an essential added dimension to the story.

"Usually I am finished writing before the illustrator starts work. However, working on the "Hamish McHaggis" books has been an exciting time as the illustrator, Sally J. Collins, lives near me and we are able to work very closely on everything from characters to layout. The books have been very well received and Sally and I continue to add to the series."

Biographical and Critical Sources

PERIODICALS

Carousel, summer, 2003, Valerie Bierman, review of *What Color Is Love?*

School Library Journal, May, 2004, Kathleen Whalin, review of *What Color Is Love?,* p. 125.

ONLINE

Linda Strachan Home Page, http://www.lindastrachan.com (January 25, 2006).

*   *   *

SUTHERLAND, Jon 1958-
(Jak Shadow, Jonathan D. Sutherland, Jonathan David Sutherland)

Personal

Born April 24, 1958, in Halesworth, Suffolk, England; son of John Francis (a civil servant) and Vera (a civil servant; maiden name, Stoodley) Sutherland; married Diane Elizabeth Canwell (a writer), October 29, 2003; children: Joshua Alistair, Easter Alexandra. *Education:* Guildhall University, B.S. (politics and sociology; joint honors), 1981. *Hobbies and other interests:* Military history, war-gaming.

Addresses

Home—232 Beccles Rd., Gorleston-on-Sea, Norfolk NR31 8AH, England. *E-mail*—dianejon@btinternet.com.

Career

Writer, editor, and educator. Games Workshop, London, England, editor, 1983-85; College of North-East London, lecturer, 1985-89; Great Yarmouth College, Norfolk, England, lecturer, 1989-2000.

Awards, Honors

Best of Reference designation, New York Libraries, and Editor's Choice designation, *Booklist,* both 2004, both for *African Americans at War.*

Writings

ADVENTURE GAME BOOKS

(With Simon Farrell) *Madame Guillotine: The French Revolution,* illustrated by Brian Williams, Andre Deutsch/Collins (London, England), 1986.

(With Simon Farrell) *The Last Invasion: 1066,* illustrated by Bill Houston, Andre Deutsch/Collins (London, England), 1986.

(With Simon Farrell) *Through the Wire: The Great Escape,* Andre Deutsch/Collins (London, England), 1986.

(With Simon Farrell) *Sword and Flame: The English Civil War,* illustrated by Bill Houston, Andre Deutsch/Collins (London, England), 1986.

(With Simon Farrell) *Redcoats and Minutemen: The American War of Independence,* Andre Deutsch/Collins (London, England), 1987.

(With Simon Farrell) *Bardik the Thief,* illustrated by Paul Bonner, Methuen (London, England), 1987.

(With Simon Farrell) *Issel: Warrior King,* illustrated by John Blanche, Methuen (London, England), 1987.

(With Simon Farrell) *Your Party Needs You: The Election Gamebook,* Andre Deutsch/Collins (London, England), 1987.

Thunder in the Glens: The Jacobite Rebellion, Andre Deutsch/Collins (London, England), 1987.

(With Simon Farrell) *Darian: Master Magician,* illustrated by John Blanche, Methuen (London, England), 1988.

(With Simon Farrell) *Coreus the Prince,* Methuen (London, England), 1988.

(With Simon Farrell) *The Fear Factor: Terrorism in the City,* Andrew Deutsch/Collins (London, England), 1988.

(With Simon Farrell) *Blazing Beacons: The Spanish Armada,* Andrew Deutsch/Collins (London, England), 1988.

Fantom Empires: The Brick Lane Golem, Wizard (Thriplow, England), 2005.

Fantom Empires: The Devil's Chariot, Wizard (Thriplow, England), 2006.

GAME BOOKS; TELEVISION TIE-INS

(With Diane Canwell) *Visionaries,* Marks & Spencer, 1986.

(With Diane Canwell) *Transformers* (based on the television series), Marks & Spencer, 1987.

(With Diane Canwell) *The Interceptor,* Chatsworth Publishing, 1987.

(With Diane Canwell) *Star Trek* (based on the television series), Simon & Schuster, 1990.

(With Nigel Gross) *The Zone Zapper* ("Sonic the Hedgehog" series), Fantail (London, England), 1994.

(With Nigel Gross) *Sonic vs. Zonik* ("Sonic the Hedgehog" series), Fantail (London, England), 1994.

(With Nigel Gross) *Street Fighter II: Yak Attack,* Boxtree (London, England), 1995.

(With Nigel Gross) *Street Fighter II: Dragon's Breath,* Boxtree (London, England), 1995.

(With Nigel Gross) *Genesis Quest* ("Lemmings Adventure Gamebook" series), Penguin (London, England), 1995.

Hypnosis Enigma ("Lemmings Adventure Gamebook" series), Penguin (London, England), 1995.

Lemmings Adventure Gamebook (includes *Genesis Quest* and *Hypnosis Enigman*), Penguin (London, England), 1995.

"FOOTBALL FANTASY" SERIES; INTERACTIVE FICTION; WITH GARY CHALK

Thames United, Wizard (Thriplow, England), 2004.

Mersey City, Wizard (Thriplow, England), 2004.

Bridgewater United, Wizard (Thriplow, England), 2004.

Trent, Wizard (Thriplow, England), 2004.

Medway Athletic, Wizard (Thriplow, England), 2004.

Tyne United, Wizard (Thriplow, England), 2004.

Clyde Rovers, Wizard (Thriplow, England), 2005.

Avon United, Wizard (Thriplow, England), 2005.

Derwent Town, Wizard (Thriplow, England), 2005.

Tame Wanderers, Wizard (Thriplow, England), 2005.

"FEAR" SERIES; UNDER PSEUDONYM JAK SHADOW

The Emerald Pirate, Wizard (Thriplow, England), 2005.

The Spymaster, Wizard (Thriplow, England), 2005.

The Crime Lord, Wizard (Thriplow, England), 2005.

The Space Plague, Wizard (Thriplow, England), 2005.

The Fear Agency, Wizard (Thriplow, England), 2006.

NONFICTION

(With Nigel Gross) *The Unauthorized How-to-Beat-Nintendo Gamebook,* Boxtree (London, England), 1990.

(With Nigel Gross) *Insurance in Action,* Lloyds of London (London, England), 1991.

(With Nigel Gross) *Marketing in Action* (with case studies), Pitman Publishing (London, England), 1991.

David Beckham, Invincible Press (London, England), 1997.

(With others) *Snapshots in Time: 100 Years of Change,* Dempsey Parr (Bristol, England), 1998.

(As Jonathan D. Sutherland) *Speed and Power,* Dempsey Parr (Bristol, England), 1998.

Encyclopedia of World History, Dempsey Parr (Bristol, England), 1999.

Encyclopedia of British History, Dempsey Parr (Bristol, England), 1999.

Encyclopedia of World Facts, Dempsey Parr (Bristol, England), 1999.

Ghosts of Great Britain, Breedon Books (Derby, England), 2001.

British History, Dempsey Parr (Bristol, England), 2001.

World History, Dempsey Parr (Bristol, England), 2001.

Unsolved Victorian Murders, Breedon Books (Derby, England), 2002.

Ghosts of London, Breedon Books (Derby, England), 2002.

Irish History, The Foundry, 2002.

British History, The Foundry, 2002.

World History, The Foundry, 2002.

Tanks and AFV's of World War II, Airlife (Marlborough, Wiltshire, England), 2002.

Commanders and Heroes of the American Civil War, Airlife (Marlborough, Wiltshire, England), 2002.

Battles of the American Civil War, Airlife (Marlborough, Wiltshire, England), 2002.

Elite Forces of World War II, Airlife/Crowood (Marlborough, Wiltshire, England), 2003.

Napoleonic Battles, Airlife/Crowood (Marlborough, Wiltshire, England), 2003.

African Americans at War: An Encyclopedia, 2 volumes, ABC-CLIO (Santa Barbara, CA), 2003.

Europa Militaria: Union Troops, Crowood (Marlborough, Wiltshire, England), 2005.

Europa Militaria: Confederate Troops, Crowood (Marlborough, Wiltshire, England), 2005.

How to Paint Wargame Figures, Crowood (Marlborough, Wiltshire, England), 2006.

How to Make and Paint Wargame Terrain, Crowood (Marlborough, Wiltshire, England), 2006.

Wargaming the American Civil War, Cerberus, 2006.

NONFICTION; WITH DIANE CANWELL

Business: Intermediate GNVQ, Pitman Publishing, 1994, 2nd edition, 1995.

Advanced Business, Hodder Educations (London, England), 1994, 2nd edition, 1995.

Business Organisations and Systems, Hodder Educational (London, England), 1996.

Marketing, Hodder Educational (London, England), 1996.

Human Resources, Hodder Educational (London, England), 1996.

Business in the Economy, Hodder Educational (London, England), 1996.

Production and Employment, Hodder Educational (London, England), 1996.

Financial Forecasting, Hodder Educational (London, England), 1996.

Financial Transactions, Hodder Educational (London, England), 1996.

Business Planning, Hodder Educational (London, England), 1996.

Foundation Business, Hodder Educational (London, England), 1996.

Foundation Business Options, Hodder Educational (London, England), 1996.

Foundation Leisure and Tourism, Hodder Educational (London, England), 1996.

Foundation Leisure and Tourism Options, Hodder Educational (London, England), 1996.

Operating Admin Systems, Hodder Educational (London, England), 1996.

Consumer Protection, Hodder Educational (London, England), 1996.

Organisational Structures and Processes, Pitman Publishing (London, England), 1997.

Planning and Decision Making, Pitman Publishing (London, England), 1997.

Business Administration for Secretarial Certificates, Heinemann (Oxford, England), 1997.

Intermediate IT, Hodder Educational (London, England), 1997.

Communication in Business, Heinemann (Oxford, England), 1997.

World War II: A Source Book, Flame Tree (London, England), 2003.

True Crime, The Foundry, 2003.

RAF Air/Sea Rescue Service 1918-1986, Pen and Sword (Barnsley, South Yorkshire, England), 2005.

Saxons and Normans at War, Cerberus, 2005.

Romans and Carthaginians at War, Cerberus, 2005.

African Americans in the Vietnam War ("American Experience in Vietnam" series), World Almanac Library (Milwaukee, WI), 2005.

American Women in the Vietnam War ("American Experience in Vietnam" series), 2005.

BTEC First Business, Nelson Thornes (Gloucestershire, England), 2005, 2nd edition, 2006.

Norfolk Murders, Fort (Ayre, Scotland), 2006.

Beautiful Gardens, The Foundry, 2006.

Flying Insects, Amber Books (London, England), 2006.

Social Insects, Amber Books (London, England), 2006.

Also co-author of "Hodder GNVQ" unit book series and business texts for Nelson-Thornes and Edexel.

NONFICTION; UNDER NAME JONATHAN SUTHERLAND; WITH DIANE CANWELL

The Zulu Kings and Their Armies, Leo Cooper (Barnsley, South Yorkshire, England), 2004.

Key Concepts in Accounting and Finance, Palgrave Macmillan (New York, NY), 2004.

Key Concepts in Marketing, Palgrave Macmillan (New York, NY), 2004.

Key Concepts in Human Resource Management, Palgrave Macmillan (New York, NY), 2004.

Key Concepts in Operations Management, Palgrave Macmillan (New York, NY), 2004.

Key Concepts in International Business, Palgrave Macmillan (New York, NY), 2004.

Key Concepts in Strategic Management, Palgrave Macmillan (New York, NY), 2004.

Key Concepts in Management, Palgrave Macmillan (New York, NY), 2004.

Key Concepts in Business Practice, Palgrave Macmillan (New York, NY), 2004.

The First Battle of Britain (1917-18), Leo Cooper (Barnsley, South Yorkshire, England), 2006.

The Battle of Jutland, Leo Cooper (Barnsley, South Yorkshire, England), 2007.

The Berlin Airlift, Leo Cooper (Barnsley, South Yorkshire, England), 2007.

TELEVISION SCRIPTS

(With others) *The Crystal Maze* (television game show), Chatsworth TV, 1987.

The Haunted Dungeon (television series), ITV, 1988.

Biographical and Critical Sources

PERIODICALS

Booklist, July, 2004, review of *African Americans at War: An Encyclopedia,* p. 1860; January 1, 2005, review of *African Americans at War,* p. 779.

Choice, September, 2004, S.D. Campbell, review of *African Americans at War,* p. 82.

Journal of Military History, October, 2004, Bernard C. Nalty, review of *African Americans at War,* p. 1302.

Reference Reviews, March, 2004, John Lawrence, review of *African Americans at War;* May, 2004, Blanche Woolls, review of *African Americans at War.*

School Library Journal, June, 2004, Janet Woodward, review of *African Americans at War,* p. 89.

ONLINE

Wizard Publishers Web site, http://www.iconbooks.co.uk/wizard (December 19, 2005).

*   *   *

**SUTHERLAND, Jonathan D.
See SUTHERLAND, Jon**

*   *   *

**SUTHERLAND, Jonathan David
See SUTHERLAND, Jon**

SWANSON, Wayne 1942-

Personal

Born August 1, 1942, in Regina, Saskatchewan, Canada; son of Carl (a contractor) and Violet (Soderberg) Swanson; married Carol Diane Shreeve (an author), July 3, 1965; children: Timothy, Carolyn. *Education:* University of Alberta, B.Ed., 1964; Carleton College, M.A., 1970; University of Victoria, M.B.A., 1994.

Addresses

Home—4387 Torrington Place, Victoria, British Columbia V8N 4T3, Canada. *E-mail*—wswanson@pacific-coast.net.

Career

Environment Canada, Ottawa, Ontario, land-use planner, 1970-74; Ministry of Forests for Province of British Columbia, Victoria, British Columbia, Canada, resource consultant, 1974-84; restaurant owner-manager in Victoria, 1984-87; resource-management consultant, 1987-94; freelance writer. Canadian Cystic Fibrosis Foundation, Victoria Chapter, president, 1995-2000, regional director of Victoria Island Region, 2001-03.

Young Readers' Choice Awards Society of British Columbia, founder and president, 1996-2000.

Awards, Honors

Breath of Life Award, Canadian Cystic Fibrosis Foundation, 2000.

Writings

Why the West Was Wild, Annick Press (Toronto, Ontario, Canada), 2004.

Work in Progress

Two young-adult novels, one an historical novel about a cattle drive and the other a contemporary novel about serious illness in the family.

Sidelights

In *Why the West Was Wild* Canadian-born writer Wayne Swanson creates what *Booklist* contributor Ed Sullivan dubbed an "appealing, abundantly illustrated" introduction to the history of western America that ranges from the California gold rush of the late 1840s through the

Swanson's highly illustrated Why the West Was Wild *includes numerous period images, such as the painting* The Call of the Law, *by artist Charles M. Russell.*

nostalgic Wild West shows that traveled the continent at the end of the nineteenth century. Including period photographs and the art of George Catlin, Charles M. Russell, and Frederic Remington, Swanson also presents biographies of iconic figures such as Buffalo Bill, Jesse James, and Kit Carson.

Although a *Kirkus Reviews* critic commented that the book presents "the Myth of the Wild West at its most romanticized" and distills the history into a mix of brave pioneers, barroom floozies, black-hatted desperados, and bloodthirsty Indians, *School Library Journal* contributor Jerry D. Flack described *Why the West Was Wild* as "an attractive starting point for students studying this colorful era." Wendy Hogan noted in a review for *Resource Links* that Swanson "vividly brings back the romance, adventure and dreams of . . . the heroes who fought to run the bandits and bank robbers out of town."

Swanson told *SATA:* "A casual conversation can change your life. A friend and I were discussing my visit to the Gene Autry Museum of Western Heritage in Los Angeles. We reminisced about how Western stories loomed large in our formative years but rarely grab the attention of today's youth. Still, we agreed that the excitement of the old West could enthrall kids if they had something to pique readers' interest.

"My friend suggested I propose a book to arouse curiosity about the old West—to bring to life some of the colorful characters who became legends. She knew that my writing experience consisted of publishing personal essays in periodicals, producing public information brochures and professional reports, and writing a novel (unpublished). More importantly, she knew that I grew up in Lethbridge, Alberta, Canada, close to the infamous Fort Whoop-Up, site of the last Indian battle, and near the heart of Alberta's ranching country. Western blood coursed through my veins. As they say, the rest is history.

"Interest in this bit of Americana extends well beyond the borders of the United States. On a global scale, the book portrays one of the largest movements of people anywhere, one of the greatest land development eras, and one of the most lawless times. Certainly there are many parallels with Canadian history, such as the gold rushes and railway buildings."

Biographical and Critical Sources

PERIODICALS

Booklist, August, 2004, Ed Sullivan, review of *Why the West Was Wild,* p. 1928.

Kirkus Reviews, June 1, 2004, review of *Why the West Was Wild,* p. 542.

Resource Links, June, 2004, Wendy Hogan, review of *Why the West Was Wild,* p. 31.

School Library Journal, June, 2004, Jerry D. Flack, review of *Why the West Was Wild,* p. 176.

SWEENEY, Joyce 1955-
(Joyce Kay Sweeney)

Personal

Born November 9, 1955, in Dayton, OH; daughter of Paul (an engineer) and Catharine (a bookkeeper; maiden name, Spoon) Hegenbarth; married Jay Sweeney (a marketing director), September 20, 1979. *Education:* Wright State University, B.A. (summa cum laude), 1977; graduate study in creative writing at Ohio University, 1977-78. *Politics:* Democrat. *Religion:* Unity. *Hobbies and other interests:* Native American studies, Florida natural history, professional wrestling.

Addresses

Home—Coral Springs, FL. *Agent*—George Nicholson, Sterling Lord Literistic, Inc., 65 Bleecker St., New York, NY 10012.

Career

Philip Office Associates, Dayton, OH, advertising copywriter, 1978; Rike's Department Store, Dayton, advertising copywriter, 1979-81, legal secretary, 1980-81; freelance advertising copywriter in Dayton, 1981-82; full-time writer, 1982—. Teacher at creative-writing workshops.

Member

Society of Children's Book Writers and Illustrators, Florida Council for Libraries, Mystery Writers of America.

Awards, Honors

Delacorte Press First Young-Adult Novel prize, and Best Books for Young Adults citation, American Library Association (ALA), both 1984, both for *Center Line;* Best Books for Reluctant Readers designation, ALA, 1988, for *The Dream Collector; The Dream Collector* and *Face the Dragon* named New York Public Library Books for the Teen Age, 1991; Best Books for Young Adults designation, ALA, 1994, for *The Tiger Orchard;* Best Books for Young Adults designation, ALA, and named New York Public Library Books for the Teen Age, both 1995, Nevada Young Readers' Award in young-adult category, and Evergreen Young Adult Book Award, Washington Library Association, both 1997, all for *Shadow;* Quick Pick for Reluctant Readers designation, ALA, named New York Public Library Books for the Teen Age, and Nevada Young Readers' Award listee, all 1997, all for *Free Fall;* Best Books designation, ALA, 1999, for *The Spirit Window;* Top-Ten Book for Tweens designation, *Working Mother* magazine, 2000, and *Booklist* Top-Ten Sports Book designation, both for *Players;* ALA Quick Pick for Reluctant Readers, 2004, for *Takedown.*

Writings

YOUNG-ADULT NOVELS

Center Line, Delacorte (New York, NY), 1984.
Right behind the Rain, Delacorte (New York, NY), 1985.
The Dream Collector, Delacorte (New York, NY), 1989.
Face the Dragon, Delacorte (New York, NY), 1990.
Piano Man, Delacorte (New York, NY), 1992.
The Tiger Orchard, Delacorte (New York, NY), 1993.
Shadow, Delacorte (New York, NY), 1994.
Free Fall, Delacorte (New York, NY), 1996.
The Spirit Window, Delacorte (New York, NY), 1998.
Players, Winslow Press (Delray Beach, FL), 2000.
Waiting for June, Marshall Cavendish (New York, NY), 2003.
Takedown, Marshall Cavendish (New York, NY), 2004.
Players, Marshall Cavendish (New York, NY), 2005.
Headlock, Henry Holt (New York, NY), 2006.

OTHER

Contributed book reviews to periodicals; contributor of short stories and articles to periodicals, including *New Writers, Playgirl, Co-Ed, Green's,* and *Writer;* contributor of poetry to *Blue Violin* and *Poetry Motel.* Author of monthly column for Fort Lauderdale *News/Sun-Sentinel.*

Author's works have been translated into Danish, Dutch, Hebrew, and Italian.

Adaptations

Free Fall was adapted for audio cassette by Recorded Books Inc., 1997.

Sidelights

Called a "master at depicting the inner working of families," by *Horn Book* reviewer Patty Campbell, Joyce Sweeney writes realistic fiction for young adults that centers on family issues and friendship. Beginning with her first novel, *Center Line,* Sweeney puts the modern American family under the magnifying lens and probes its structure, its strengths, and its dysfunctions. Her more recent novels deal with teen suicide, divorce, homosexuality, fantasized love, the supernatural, and environmental concerns, all which play out against the backdrop of family relations. "Perhaps it's because I didn't have one in the traditional sense that I am always writing about families," Sweeney told an interviewer for *Authors and Artists for Young Adults* (*AAYA*).

Sweeney's father died when the author was a young child; consequently, "I was an only child, . . . it was just me and Mom," she recalled. Her first five years were spent in a rural town near Dayton, Ohio, where she developed a lifelong love for the outdoors and nature. It was a rude awakening for her to move to Dayton just before beginning school. "I may not have realized it at the time," Sweeney said, "but I missed the country and didn't really like the city. When I went to school I was doubly an outsider—a country kid and one who was already bookish. I just had no idea how to relate to the other kids."

Books were an important part of Sweeney's childhood, especially favorites such as *Heidi, The Wizard of Oz,* and *Peter Pan.* A writer by the fourth grade, she was tackling the novels of John Steinbeck and also attempting to sell her own work—mostly poetry—to magazines. Reaching high school presented a new beginning to the shy writer, and she took advantage of it, inspired in part by the writings of Norman Vincent Peale. As a freshman in high school she met the boy who would later become her husband. She also continued her writing, branching out into fiction and influenced by a teacher who had published several short stories and was able to show Sweeney the ropes of publishing.

During college, Sweeney studied English and creative writing at Wright State University. While a college freshman, she sold her first piece of fiction to *New Writers,* and in her junior year she sold another story, this time to *Playgirl* magazine. "That second sale was an affirmation for me," Sweeney explained in her *AAYA* interview. "It told me that I could actually build a career as a writer." After graduation, she took more creative-writing courses in a master's program at Ohio University. Though she did not complete the degree, the experience was a positive one. "You're not taught how to write fiction in English classes. No one talks about how to stay in point of view, for example. For this you have to take creative writing courses. And I had some great teachers like Daniel Keyes who taught me valuable lessons. Also just being around professional writers was an inspiration. Here is this person who writes books for a living, and he goes to the dentist. He does shopping. He's a human like me. This made it seem possible for me to become a writer, too."

Sweeney married in 1979, began her working life, but her jobs in advertising and as a legal secretary left little time for her writing. Finally, Sweeney's husband convinced her that the only way to become a writer was to do it full time. With his support, a year later she started the long process that led to her first novel. Not long thereafter, the couple relocated to Florida, where they still reside.

That first novel, *Center Line,* was written as an adult novel although it features young protagonists: five brothers who escape an abusive father to learn about family responsibilities on their own. The novel was inspired by something Sweeney read about the Beatles as very young men in Hamburg, Germany. "Here were these irresponsible, overgrown kids in Hamburg," Sweeney explained, "and they had to learn to look out for each other. Something similar was happening with me, too. In my marriage I was having to learn about responsibilities by caring for another human, my husband. I thought this would make a great centerpiece for a story about real coming of age." The writing was the easy part; Sweeney's agent submitted the manuscript to almost thirty publishers before putting it in the pool of first-book contestants for the Delacorte Press First Young-Adult prize. Winning that prize secured the novel's publication as well as a healthy advertising budget.

Center Line tells the story of the Cunnigan brothers: oldest brother Shawn, Steve, Chris, Rick, and Mark. Their mother has been dead for a number of years, and their alcoholic father regularly beats one or the other of the boys. To escape this intolerable situation, Shawn cashes out his college account. The brothers steal their father's car and hit the road, determined to live on their own until they grow up. The skills of each brother soon come into play: Chris proves to be the Romeo of the group and scores so well in that domain that he even shares his surplus with his brothers. Young Mark earns money during difficult times as a "blind" guitarist in a shopping mall. Along the way, Steve "drops out" of the group and marries an older woman, and the remaining four end up in Florida working on a fishing pier. Things are fine for a time until Rick and Shawn get into a fight, and Rick blows the whistle on his brothers. An understanding judge, however, remands the others to Shawn's custody—their father has since disappeared—and all is neatly wrapped into a happy but cautionary ending.

Sue Estes, writing in *Booklist,* concluded that *Center Line* is a "powerful novel for mature teenagers," while a reviewer in the *Bulletin of the Center for Children's Books* commented that "this is a strong first novel . . . with fast-moving adventure, a gritty sense of place, and controlled scenes of comedy, drama, and pathos." Writing in the *Wilson Library Bulletin,* Patty Campbell compared Sweeney's first novel to *The Outsiders* by S.E. Hinton, noting that *Center Line* "has a plot twist that makes it a much more subtle and interesting work than *The Outsiders.*"

Sweeney followed her initial publishing success by re-working a novella she had written before *Center Line.* Again, she did not consciously write a YA novel; rather, she explores a difficult time in her own life through a brother and sister in *Right behind the Rain.* Kevin is twenty-one, handsome, and a talented dancer with a part in an upcoming movie. He goes home to Ohio for the summer, where his younger sister, Carla, is dazzled by his success. However, Carla soon sees that Kevin is deeply unhappy; his success has become a burden, his strive for perfection a prison. While others see only the golden boy, Carla sees possible danger ahead, and when Kevin buys a gun, it becomes her task to talk him out of killing himself.

Right behind the Rain "was inspired by feelings I personally had during college," Sweeney explained. "I felt I had to be perfect: the four-point student. I also took care of our home when mom was working. And I had

to be the perfect girlfriend as well as future great writer. I finally worked things out, but I definitely had suicidal feelings for a time. And it is amazing how many kids respond to this when I visit at schools. Invariably there is at least one student in the crowd who says 'How did you know I was feeling like this?'"

Reviewing *Right behind the Rain,* a *Publishers Weekly* commentator noted that Sweeney's "simple, sensitive writing conveys all the emotions of a memorable summer," while a *Kirkus Reviews* critic emphasized the "close, caring relationship between brother and sister" that "is easy to believe," and concluded that "this relationship [is] the novel's strongest asset and one readers will appreciate." Sweeney commented that "one of the obvious weird things about my life is that I was an only child and have devoted my whole career to writing about sibling relations."

The Dream Collector is a reworking of important lessons Sweeney learned as a teen entering high school. "If you make a wish, you can work it out," Sweeney said in her interview. "It's important kids understand that. It's not so much magic as willing something to happen. But then of course you have to watch out what you wish for. That's what makes the dramatic tension in *The Dream Collector.*" In the novel, fifteen-year-old Becky is faced with a quandary: what to get family members for Christmas when funds are limited and

High schooler Sophie, in the final stage of her pregnancy, refuses to reveal the name of her baby's father yet is haunted by the fact that she has never been told the identity of her own dad. (Cover illustration by Jane Wattenberg.)

wish lists are somewhat extravagant. She opts to buy everyone a self-help book that describes how an individual can make his or her wishes become reality. Like a genie released from the bottle, the gift books unleash conflicts in the family as well as joyful surprises. Brother Tim gets the kitten he wanted; Scott manipulates family finances to get a fancy racing bike; their mother, who wanted lots of money, leaves their father for another man; budding poet Julia finally gets published; and Becky herself goes on a date with the neighbor, only to discover that she likes his friend Tom more. A reviewer in *Publishers Weekly* commented that in *The Dream Collector* "Sweeney ably delineates family relationships as she explores the nature of dreams and the pitfalls of ambition," adding that "her affecting and tender novel presents a perfect blend of humor and dramatic tension."

Challenges to friendship, the agony of teen love, and dreams from the past inform *Face the Dragon, Piano Man,* and *The Tiger Orchard.* In *Face the Dragon* best friends Eric and Paul join four other teens in an accelerated class at high school. *Beowulf* becomes not just the subject-matter for the class, but the theme of the book as well, as each of the characters in Sweeney's story has to confront his or her own personal dragon. Eric has always felt under the shadow cast by the more confident Paul, and determines not only to tackle the demon of public speaking, but also to battle Paul for the attentions of fellow student Melanie. Though Eric has always viewed his friend as supremely confident, Paul is in fact racked by fears that he may be gay. When their teacher exposes these fears, Eric comes to Paul's defense, much like Beowulf's comrade, Wiglaf, does. Barbara Chatton noted in *School Library Journal* that the "frank language of adolescents is aptly depicted and flows naturally," and *Booklist* reviewer Stephanie Zvirin wrote that in the novel "Sweeney says a lot about jealousy, pride, and embarrassment, and about what friendship really is."

Jeff, age twenty-six, is the romantic lead in *Piano Man.* A talented young musician, he lives next to fourteen-year-old Deidre, a budding chef. Crushing on this older man, Deidre decides that the way to Jeff's heart is through his stomach. Unfortunately, Jeff's heart belongs to another, gourmet cooking or no, and Deidre's gourmet-style romantic advances remain ignored. Subplots involve other wrong choices by women: Deidre's widowed mom is dating again, but not happily, and her cousin Suzie is going out with an abused teen who keeps her at arm's length. "This is far from a formula treatment of the not-smooth course of true love," observed Zena Sutherland in *Bulletin of the Center for Children's Books.* "The plots are smoothly integrated, the characters are well-defined and consistent, and the writing has, in both dialogue and exposition, a natural flow." Susan R. Farber commented in *Voice of Youth Advocates* that "Sweeney is expert at portraying the highs and lows, the dreams and expectations of young

When a new player joins the team, his ultra-competitive attitude and the fact that his star teammates are injured in bizarre accidents leaves team captain Corey concerned in Sweeney's 2000 novel.

women in love (lust? like?)," while a *Kirkus Reviews* contributor applauded the "deft dialogue, willing players, and plausible events" that constitute this novel.

Sweeney again turned to her own experiences for inspiration in writing *Shadow.* "When my husband was a kid, his family had no pets . . . ," she explained. "So his dream was to have pets galore. We adopted cats all over the place it seemed, and then feline leukemia struck. Over the course of several years we lost five cats. That loss touched me profoundly. I knew I wanted to use the material somehow in a book, but not a dead-pet story. Something more. Then I decided I wanted to write a supernatural story. I enjoy those tales myself and wanted to try my hand at one. It came to me that this might be the perfect way to use the grief I felt for the loss of those cats."

The eponymous cat in *Shadow* has been dead for a year, but thirteen-year-old Sarah still grieves its passing. Add this to the continual feuding between her older brothers, Brian and Patrick, a father who dotes on Brian and a mother who picks on him, and a girlfriend who nearly cuckolds one brother with the other, and a recipe for

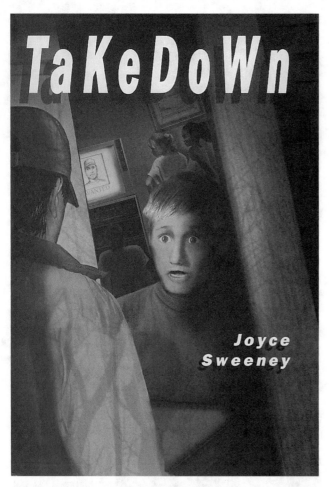

When an escaped convict and murderer holds Joe and his six friends hostage, the teen must decide what price he is willing to pay in order to be a hero. *(Cover illustration by Steve McAfee.)*

domestic disaster is in place. Soon Sarah begins seeing her dead cat, and after confiding this to the housekeeper, Cissy, who has a natural proclivity for things supernatural, she is informed that her cat is probably returning in the spirit to warn her of impending danger. Further complications ensue when Sarah realizes she is in love with her childhood friend, Julian. When she confides her experiences with Shadow to Julian, his skepticism nearly destroys their budding romantic relationship. The impending danger becomes all too real when Brian discovers his girlfriend on the verge of becoming intimate with his brother Patrick. An enraged Brian nearly strangles Patrick; they are stopped only by what appears to be the ghost of Shadow.

"This page-turner is a psychic novel built around realistic feelings, emotions, hates, fears, and love," noted Bonnie Kunzel in *Voice of Youth Advocates.* Kunzel deemed *Shadow* "well-written and bound to be a teen pleaser with its mixture of sibling rivalry, romance, and psychic revelations." Bruce Anne Shook, writing in *School Library Journal,* observed that "characters are realistically drawn, and the plot is riveting," and called the conclusion "nicely done." A *Publishers Weekly* re-

viewer felt that Sweeney "offers believably complex characters" and "challenges conventional views of reality."

Free Fall is the story of four boys—two antagonistic brothers and their friends—who get trapped in an underground cave. Neil and Randy are high school athletes and best friends. Together with Neil's younger brother David and his friend Terry, they explore a cave in Florida's Ocala National Forest. There is tension between the boys from the outset, but it reaches a climax when they realize they are lost. Neil tries to climb out, but falls and breaks a leg. David ultimately comes to the rescue by finding an underwater passage out of the cave, but not before the quartet have shed their macho façades and shared their darkest secrets. *Booklist* reviewer Ann O'Malley commented that "Sweeney mixes excitement with finely crafted characters and credible psychological underpinnings to deliver a powerful punch." A reviewer in *Horn Book* called *Free Fall* a "taut survival story" and noted that "the book features gritty, realistic dialogue and insightful characterizations." Pam Carlson concluded in *Voice of Youth Advocates* that the novel is "a gripping, sometimes scary tale of survival and brotherhood," while a *Publishers Weekly* commentator wrote that, "lean and skillfully wrought," *Free Fall* "hooks the reader and doesn't let go."

Environmental concerns combine with another dysfunctional family in *The Spirit Window,* the story of Miranda and her summer visit to her dying grandmother on a Florida island. Miranda is accompanied by her psychiatrist father, Richard, and his new, young, and spoiled wife, Ariel. Grandmother Lila and her son do not see eye to eye on the real estate she will leave behind at her death: he intends to develop it but she wants it preserved. To this end, she leaves the land to her young, part-Cherokee assistant, Adam, who shares Lila's beliefs in preservation and to whom Miranda is strongly attracted. Miranda soon finds herself torn between loyalty to family and her feelings for Adam in this "gentle story about two adolescents far wiser and more mature than the adults in their lives," according to Beth Anderson, writing in the *Voice of Youth Advocates.* A reviewer in *Bulletin of the Center for Children's Books* noted that "Sweeney has a strong sense of place that contributes to an overall setting of mood that is very effective," while *School Library Journal* contributor Angela J. Reynolds concluded that a "love story, a mystery, and a spiritual journey combine to make this a satisfying read."

Sweeney features another female protagonist in *Waiting for June,* her 2003 YA novel. High-school senior Sophie is pregnant—very pregnant—and receives hostile treatment at school, while at home her mother is plainly upset about her daughter's condition and the fact that Sophie refuses to say who the baby's father is. Haunted by strange dreams in her sleep, Sophie also finds herself haunted in real life when she begins receiving threatening, unsigned notes. Ultimately, the threads of Sweeney's plot resolve themselves, the ending buoyed by Sophie's optimistic nature and the kindness of some special friends. Elizabeth Stolle, reviewing *Waiting for June* in the *Journal of Adolescent and Adult Literature,* wrote that Sweeney "weaves a dream world of myth and legend through a revealing and realistic plot," while in *Kirkus Reviews* a contributor noted that the mystery will "keep readers interested all the way to the happy . . . end." Praising Sweeney's resilient teen protagonist, a *Publishers Weekly* contributor predicted that readers "will admire Sophie's courage and humor," as well as her upbeat personality.

High school sports is the backdrop for *Players,* as senior Corey begins to suspect that Noah, an ambitious new player on the basketball team he captains, is behind some injuries that have befallen the team's top players. Turning detective after a gun is planted in his best friend and fellow starting-squad member's locker, Corey manages to solve the crime, but not before Noah commits one last evil act. In *School Library Journal,* Todd Morning wrote that Sweeney's YA thriller "scores as a fast paced story of the unmasking of a sociopath," while Roger Leslie dubbed it a "real winner" in his *Booklist* review, adding that the author "does a great job of depiction male teenagers" through "authentic dialogue and realistic relationships."

More thrills are served up in *Takedown,* which finds thirteen-year-old Joe Anderson excited about having his friends over to his house while his parents are not home. An innocent party where a televised wrestling match is the planned entertainment turns terrifying, when an escaped murderer breaks into Joe's home and holds the young teens hostage. Noting the novel's appeal for reluctant readers, Ed Sullivan noted in *Booklist* that *Takedown* is a "fast-moving story" in which the "professional-wrestling angle will intrigue fans of the sport." In *School Library Journal,* Jessi Platt praised Sweeney's text for its "simple language," while a *Kirkus Reviews* contributor dubbed the novel a "corker of a hostage drama [that is] laced with humor."

Sweeney continues to dedicate her writing to the YA market. "I used to think that I would somehow graduate to adult fiction from YA, but no longer," she admitted in her *AAYA* interview. "This is where I can make a difference; this is my audience. And the teen years are where the important decisions are made, ones that affect the rest of a lifetime." "I try not to think of my audience a lot," she also commented. "Mostly I try to work through some experiences in my own life, thoroughly disguising myself. . . . I don't think of message. My unconscious knows what the message is, but I don't want to be thinking about that. Instead, I want to put issues out there, to open things up for discussion. I certainly want to be a force for good, but that has to come naturally through the story. It can't be forced and planned."

Biographical and Critical Sources

BOOKS

Authors and Artists for Young Adults, Volume 26, Thomson Gale (Detroit, MI), 1999.

PERIODICALS

Booklist, April 1, 1984, Sue Estes, review of *Center Line,* p. 1110; December 15, 1989, p. 827; September 15, 1990, Stephanie Zvirin, review of *Face the Dragon,* p. 157; July, 1994, p. 1936; April 1, 1995, pp. 1404, 1416; May 27, 1996, review of *Shadow,* p. 81; July, 1996, Ann O'Malley, review of *Free Fall,* p. 1819; April 1, 1997, p. 1310; March 15, 1999, review of *The Spirit Window,* p. 1302; October 1, 2000, Roger Leslie, review of *Players,* p. 337; September 1, 2003, Frances Bradburn, review of *Waiting for June,* p. 115; October 15, 2004, Ed Sullivan, review of *Takedown,* p. 406.

Bulletin of the Center for Children's Books, June, 1984, review of *Center Line,* pp. 194-195; June, 1992, Zena Sutherland, review of *Piano Man,* p. 281; May, 1998, review of *The Spirit Window,* p. 341; February 2004, Elizabeth Bush, review of *Waiting for June,* p. 246.

Horn Book, November-December, 1994, Patty Campbell, "The Sand in the Oyster," pp. 756-759; spring, 1997, review of *Free Fall,* p. 84.

Journal of Adolescent and Adult Literature, April, 2004, Elizabeth Stolle, review of *Waiting for June,* p. 617.

Kirkus Reviews, May 1, 1984, p. 153; May 1, 1987, review of *Right behind the Rain,* p. 726; November 15, 1989, p. 1678; October 1, 1990, p. 1398; May 15, 1992, review of *Piano Man,* p. 676; May 1, 1996, p. 694; October 1, 2003, review of *Waiting for June,* p. 1231; October 1, 2004, review of *Takedown,* p. 970.

Kliatt, March, 1995, Claire Rosser, review of *The Tiger Orchard,* p. 12.

Publishers Weekly, February 10, 1984, review of *Center Line,* p. 194; May 8, 1987, review of *Right behind the Rain,* p. 72; November 24, 1989, review of *The Dream Collector,* p. 72; January 30, 1995, review of *The Tiger Orchard,* p. 101; June 24, 1996, review of *Free Fall,* p. 62; November 6, 2000, review of *Players,* p. 92; November 3, 2003, review of *Waiting for June,* p. 75.

School Library Journal, April, 1984, p. 127; June, 1987, p. 114; November, 1989, p. 129; October, 1990, Barbara Chatton, review of *Face the Dragon,* p. 145; April, 1992, p. 150; September, 1994, Bruce Anne Shook, review of *Shadow,* pp. 242-243; November, 1996, p. 126; March, 1998, Angela J. Reynolds, review of *The Spirit Window,* p. 224; September, 2000, Todd Morning, review of *Players,* p. 238; October, 2003, Catherine Ensley, review of *Waiting for June,* p. 180; January, 2005, Jessi Platt, review of *Takedown,* p. 137.

Times Literary Supplement, August 24, 1984, p. 954.

Voice of Youth Advocates, February, 1990, Susan Rosenko-etter, review of *The Dream Collector,* p. 348; April, 1992, Susan R. Farber, review of *Piano Man,* p. 37; October, 1994, Bonnie Kunzel, review of *Shadow,* pp. 218-219; June, 1996, Pam Carlson, review of *Free Fall,* p. 102; April, 1998, Beth Anderson, review of *The Spirit Window,* pp. 50-51; June, 2005, Cyndi Gueswel, review of *Takedown,* p. 139.

Wilson Library Bulletin, March, 1984, Patty Campbell, "The Young Adult Complex," pp. 502-503; January, 1990, p. 7; September, 1994, p. 127.

ONLINE

Balkin Buddies Web site, http://www.balkinbuddies.com/ (January 1, 2006), "Joyce Sweeney."

*   *   *

SWEENEY, Joyce Kay
See SWEENEY, Joyce

W

WEILL, Cynthia 1959-

Personal

Born December 30, 1959, in New York, NY; daughter of Stephen and Frances Weill. *Education:* University of Pennsylvania, M.S.; Wesleyan University, M.A.; Columbia University Teachers College, M.Ed., doctoral study.

Addresses

Home—697 West End, Apt. 12C, New York, NY 10025. *E-mail*—csw2001@columbia.edu.

Career

Glastonbury High School, Glastonbury, CT, Spanish teacher, 1986-99; Catholic Relief Services, Hanoi, Vietnam, program manager of education, 1999-2002; Aid to Women Artisans (humanitarian concern), founder; writer.

Awards, Honors

Three National Endowment of the Humanities awards; Fullbright award; American Library Association Notable Books for a Global Society designation, 2003, and Best of Children's Books designation, Bank Street College of Education, 2004, both for for *Ten Mice for Tet!*

Writings

(With Pegi Deitz Shea) *Ten Mice for Tet!*, illustrated by To Ngoc Trang and Pham Viet Dinh, Chronicle Books (San Francisco, CA), 2003.

Work in Progress

Dónde está?, a book teaching animal names using Latin-American artisan work; *Guillermina*, a book about the life of Mexican ceramicist Guillermina Aguilar.

Sidelights

Teacher and children's book author Cynthia Weill made her writing debut with *Ten Mice for Tet!*, coauthored with veteran children's writer Pegi Deitz Shea. In this multicultural tale, which features unique, vividly colored art that is based on Vietnamese embroidery, a group of enthusiastic mice prepare for a Vietnamese New Year celebration. Beginning with the cleaning and preparation that goes into the event, the group of mice eventually enjoy the festivities in a story that "will hold the interest of even the youngest readers" according to a *Publishers Weekly* critic. A commentator from *Kirkus Reviews* stated that Weill's book provides young listeners with "an inviting, informative introduction" to a less-familiar holiday celebration.

Weill told *SATA:* "Before co-authoring my first book *Ten Mice for Tet!* I worked as a teacher, an art historian, and in the field of humanitarian assistance. For many years, I also worked with artisans in developing nations, helping them to improve their products and promote their work.

"All of these elements came together when I was living in Vietnam and discovered the village of Quat Dong. Artisans there have practiced the art of embroidery since the sixteenth century. After working with master embroiderer Pham Viet Dinh for about six months, we finally hit upon the perfect showcase for his work: traditional woodblock prints. After seeing the results, the artwork for *Ten Mice for Tet!* was born. Since then, I have continued to work with artisans to use their work as the illustrations in my books. Working with artisans collaboratively to develop their work for educational materials has also become the focus of my doctoral research at the Teacher College of Columbia University."

Biographical and Critical Sources

PERIODICALS

Booklinks, January, 2005, Kay Weisman, review of *Ten Mice for Tet!*, p. 24.

The illustrations for Weill's Ten Mice for Tet! *are designed by Vietnamese artist To Ngoc Trang and then embroidered by Pham Viet Dinh.*

Kirkus Reviews, November 1, 2003, review of *Ten Mice for Tet!,* p. 21.
Publishers Weekly, December 15, 2003, review of *Ten Mice for Tet!,* p. 71.
School Library Journal, December, 2003, Tali Balas, review of *Ten Mice for Tet!,* p. 140; October, 2004, review of *Ten Mice for Tet!,* p. 22.

ONLINE

Chronicle Books Web site, http://www.chroniclebooks.com/ (September 27, 2005), "'Chuc Mung Nam Noi' or Happy New Year!"

*   *   *

WIGGIN, Eric E. 1939-

Personal

Born May 10, 1939, in Albion, ME; son of Eric E. and Pauline Wood (Fuller) Wiggin; married Dorothy Jean Hackney (a cook), June 1, 1963; children: Deborah Elizabeth Wiggin Snyder, Mark Ernest, Andrew Eric, Bradstreet Thomas. *Education:* New Brunswick Bible Institute (Canada), diploma, 1961; Fort Wayne Bible College, B.Re. 1963; St. Francis College (IN), M.S. (education), 1972; also attended University of Maine. *Politics:* Republican. *Religion:* Baptist. *Hobbies and other interests:* Small farming, gardening, poultry raising.

Addresses

Home—3420 Cline Rd., Muskegon, MI 49444.

Career

Minister, educator, and writer. Palermo Baptist Churches, Palermo, ME, pastor, 1965-68; English teacher at schools in Waterville, ME, 1966-68, and Fort Wayne, IN, 1968-73; Faith Christian School, Fruitport, MI, English teacher and librarian, 1973-74; Piedmont Bible College, Winston-Salem, NC, instructor in English, 1974-78; Glen Cove Bible College, Rockport, ME, instructor in English, 1978-79; full-time writer, 1979—. Substitute teacher; adult Sunday school teacher. Member, Bethel Baptist Church.

Awards, Honors

Honorable mention, Maine Press Association, 1981, for investigative reporting.

Writings

"REBECCA" SERIES; BASED ON BOOKS BY KATE DOUGLAS WIGGIN

Rebecca of Sunnybrook Farm: The Child, Wolgemuth & Hyatt (Brentwood, TN), 1989, published as *Rebecca of Sunnybrook Farm,* Bethel, 1994.
Rebecca of Sunnybrook Farm: The Girl, illustrated by Joe Boddy, Wolgemuth & Hyatt (Brentwood, TN), 1990, published as *Rebecca of the Brick House,* Bethel, 1994.
Rebecca of Sunnybrook Farm: The Woman, illustrated by Joe Boddy, Wolgemuth & Hyatt (Brentwood, TN), 1991, published as *Rebecca Returns to Sunnybrook,* Bethel, 1994.

"MAGGIE'S WORLD" NOVEL SERIES

Maggie: Life at the Elms, Harvest House (Eugene, OR), 1993.
Maggie's Homecoming, Harvest House (Eugene, OR), 1994.
Maggie's Secret Longing, Harvest House (Eugene, OR), 1995.

"HANNAH'S ISLAND" NOVEL SERIES; FOR YOUNG READERS

A Hound for Hannah, Emerald Books, 1995.
The Mystery of the Sunken Steamboat, Emerald Books, 1995.
The Mysterious Stranger, Emerald Books, 1995.
The Secret of the Old Well, Emerald Books, 1996.
The Lesson of the Ancient Bones, Emerald Books, 1996.
The Texas Rodeo Showdown, Emerald Books, 1998.

OTHER

The Hills of God, Harvest House (Eugene, OR), 1993.

The Heart of a Grandparent: Investing Yourself in Your Grandchildren's Future, Harold Shaw (Wheaton, IL), 1993.

Blood Moon Rising, Broadman & Holman (Nashville, TN), 2000.

The Gift of Grandparenting: Building Meaningful Relationships with Your Grandchildren, Tyndale House Publishers (Wheaton, IL), 2001.

Freelance reporter for *Bangor Daily News, Confident Living, Maine Paper, Maine Sunday Telegram, Moody Monthly,* and *Rockland Courier-Gazette,* 1979-84. Managing editor, Maine Civic League *Record,* 1982-84.

Work in Progress

Several novels for adults and children.

Sidelights

A former minister and teacher, Eric E. Wiggin is a distant cousin to the husband of Kate Douglas Wiggin, the author of the childhood classic *Rebecca of Sunnybrook Farm,* which was first published in 1903. "Most New England Wiggins are descended from Captain Thomas Wiggin, who came to New Hampshire in 1623," Wiggin once explained to *SATA.* Although he began writing for children in the 1970s, Wiggin has his first work, *Rebecca of Sunnybrook Farm: The Child,* published in 1989. He has gone on to publish two other novels featuring the characters from the "Rebecca" novels, as well as several works of Christian fiction and the nonfiction title *The Gift of Grandparenting: Building Meaningful Relationships with Your Grandchildren.* Also featuring Christian-based themes, Wiggin's "Hannah's Island" novel series for young readers features the adventures of Hannah and Walt Parmenter, two homeschooled siblings who frequently find themselves in more trouble than they bargain for.

Biographical and Critical Sources

PERIODICALS

School Library Journal, May, 1998, Megan McGuire, review of *The Secret of the Old Well,* p. 149.

ONLINE

Evangel Publishing House Web site, http://www.evangel publishing.com/ (December 19, 2005).*

*   *   *

WISE, Lenny
See WISE, Leonard

WISE, Leonard 1940-
(Lenny Wise, Leonard A. Wise, Leonard Allan Wise)

Personal

Born December 10, 1940, in Chatham, Ontario, Canada; son of Sol (a storekeeper) and Sylvia (a homemaker; maiden name Miller) Wise; married November 18, 1970; wife's name Sandra (a consultant); children: Michelle Wise Szecket, Stephen Ari. *Ethnicity:* "Jewish." *Education:* University of Toronto, B.A., LL.B. *Religion:* Jewish. *Hobbies and other interests:* Documentary films.

Addresses

Home—49 Roe Ave., Toronto, Ontario M5M 2H6, Canada. *E-mail*—leonardwise@yahoo.com.

Career

Attorney, writer, and actor. Lawyer in private practice in Toronto, Ontario, Canada, 1970-2000; writer and actor, beginning 1970. Member of board of directors, Canadian Refugee Association; member of North York V.D. and Birth Control Center. Food critic for *Toronto Star,* 1974-76.

Member

Alliance of Canadian Cinema, Television, and Radio Artists.

Writings

Making out in Toronto, NC Press, 1979.

(Under name Lenny Wise) *Toronto Eats: A Guide to over 150 Restaurants,* Can-Do Press (Toronto, Ontario, Canada), 1981.

Leonard Wise

Toronto Eats from A to Z: Apple Pie to Zabaglione: Where to Find the City's Best, Fenn Publishing (Mississauga, Ontario, Canada), 1996.

(Under name Leonard A. Wise; with John W. Chisholm) *Are We Hungry Yet?: A Guide to the Best Budget Restaurants for Florida-bound Drivers,* MayHaven Publishing (Mahomet, IL), 1996.

More Toronto Eats from A to Z, Fenn Publishing (Mississauga, Ontario, Canada), 1997.

(With Allan Gould) *Toronto Street Names: An Illustrated Guide to Their Origins,* Firefly Books (Toronto, Ontario, Canada), 2000.

The Way Cool License Plate Book, illustrated by Christine Gilham and George Walker, Firefly Books (Toronto, Ontario, Canada), 2002.

Sidelights

While working as an attorney, Leonard Wise also built a second career through his talent for writing, working as a food critic as well as an historian in his home-town of Toronto. With *The Way Cool License Plate Book* Wise addresses a younger audience, creating a book designed to engage passengers on long family road trips. Including de-coding games for a variety of skill levels as well as sidebars containing "Plate Facts" and other license-plate trivia, Wise's book "can provide several hours of fun for the whole family," according to *School Library Journal* contributor Eldon Younce.

Wise told *SATA:* "I began writing in 1969 as a student of the University of Toronto when I was asked to contribute comedy sketches to a college show called U.C. Follies. Its director, Lorne Lipovitz, later took me as a writer to the Canadian Broadcasting Corporation for three years and changed his name to Lorne Michaels. I turned down an offer to write for the television programs *Laugh-In* in 1973 and *Saturday Night Live* in 1974, both of which decisions I now regret.

"The *Toronto Star* newspaper hired me as a food critic from 1974 to 1976, though I knew nothing about food (the editor was my camp counselor), which resulted in a number of humorous restaurant guides from 1981 to 1996.

"*Are We Hungry Yet?: A Guide to the Best Budget Restaurants for Florida-bound Drivers* was the result of a family motor trip to Florida trying to find decent diners in which to eat. After being rejected by eighty-one American publishers, a small publishing company in Illinois accepted my idea and sold a copy of my magnum opus to every library in America.

"*Toronto Street Names: An Illustrated Guide to Their Origins* was the result of its publisher begging me to write a history book of Toronto's streets after being turned down by two of Toronto's best historians. Though I failed history in high school, the book sold 30,000 copies and was the biggest seller in Toronto in 2000.

Wise collects a host of games, license-plate lore, and information on vanity-plate coding that combine to entertain both short- and long-haul back-seat travelers in this 2002 book.

"I write in longhand because computers came along too late for me."

Biographical and Critical Sources

PERIODICALS

Canadian Book Review Annual, 2000, review of *Toronto Street Names,* p. 325; 2002, review of *The Way Cool License Plate Book,* p. 561.

Publishers Weekly, November 25, 2002, review of *The Way Cool License Plate Book,* p. 71.

Resource Links, February, 2003, Evette Signarowski, review of *The Way Cool License Plate Book,* p. 45.

School Library Journal, April, 2003, Eldon Younce, review of *The Way Cool License Plate Book,* p. 194.

*   *   *

WISE, Leonard A.
See WISE, Leonard

*   *   *

WISE, Leonard Allan
See WISE, Leonard

WOLFER, Dianne 1961-

Personal

Born October 28, 1961, in Melbourne, Western Australia, Australia; daughter of Donald (a manager) and Audrey (a teacher) Davidson; married Reinhard Wolfer (a systems manager), December 23, 1984 (died, 1995); children: Sophie. *Education:* Melbourne State College, Diploma of Teaching; Western Australian Institute of Technology (now Curtin University), Certificate of Fluency in Japanese; University of Western Australia, M.A. (creative writing). *Hobbies and other interests:* Traveling, reading, swimming, bush-walking, photography, yoga, scuba diving.

Addresses

Home—P.O. Box 421, Denmark 6333, Western Australia, Australia. *E-mail*—dianne@denmarkwa.edu.au.

Career

Teacher, Western Australian Education Department, 1984-87 and 1991-92, Japan International School and American School in Japan, Tokyo, 1987-90. Has taught missionary children in remote western Nepal and intensive Japanese classes for airline employees. Guest speaker, 1993—; Society of Women Writers (Western Australian Branch), editor of *Papermates* magazine, 1996—; guest appearance on radio programs, 1998; runs writing classes and workshops. Denmark Agricultural College, Denmark, Western Australia, Australia, teacher of vocational English.

Member

Society of Women Writers (Western Australia branch), Fellowship of Australian Writers, Children's Book Council, Amnesty International, Australian Conservation Foundation.

Awards, Honors

Society of Women Writer's Bronze Quill Award, 1992; Fellowship of Australian Writers (FAW) Furphy Award for best novel, 1995, and Western Australia Young Readers Book Award (WAYRBA) third-place award, 1996, both for *Dolphin Song;* South-West Literary Award, 1995, for play *Christmas Lunch;* Mary Grant Bruce Short-Story Award, FAW, 1997, for *Donkey Ears;* Wilderness Society Environmental Award shortlist, and WAYRBA shortlist, both 1999, both for *Border Line;* Family Therapists' Award for Children's Literature shortlist, 2001, for *Choices;* WAYRBA shortlist, 2002, for *Border Line,* 2005, for *Choices,* and 2006, for *Horse Mad.*

Writings

FOR CHILDREN AND YOUNG ADULTS

Dolphin Song, Fremantle Arts Centre Press (Fremantle, Western Australia, Australia), 1995.

Border Line, Fremantle Arts Centre Press (Fremantle, Western Australia, Australia), 1998.

Choices, Fremantle Arts Centre Press (Fremantle, Western Australia, Australia), 2001.

Horse-Mad, Fremantle Arts Centre Press (Fremantle, Western Australia, Australia), 2005.

Photographs in the Mud, illustrated by Brian Harrison-Lever, Fremantle Arts Centre Press (Fremantle, Western Australia, Australia), 2005.

The Kid Whose Mum Kept Possums in Her Bra, Fremantle Arts Centre Press (Fremantle, Western Australia, Australia), 2006.

Also author of readers for Thomson Learning, including *Butterfly Notes,* 2002, *Ironkid,* 2003, *Being Billy,* 2003, *Scuba Kid,* and *Jungle Trek.* Author of one-act play *Christmas Lunch,* 1995. Work represented in anthologies, including *Going down South,* 1992, and *Going down South Two,* 1993. Contributor of short stories, poems, and articles to magazines, including *Lucky, Western Word, Nature and Health, Infant Times, Western Review, Let's Travel,* and *In Perspective.*

Wolfer explores two parallel lives for teenager Elizabeth, each of which result from the decision she might make after learning that she is pregnant. (Cover design by Marion Duke.)

Work in Progress

Shadows Walking, a YA novel; *The Shark Callers,* a fantasy novel for middle-grade readers.

Sidelights

A teacher who has worked in Tokyo, Japan as well as in Nepal in addition to schools in her native Australia, Dianne Wolfer pens novels for children and young adults that focus on life in modern Australia and Pacific countries. Geared for older readers, her novel *Choices* finds teen Elisabeth coping with an unwanted pregnancy, while *Dolphin Song* focuses on the intersection between the human and natural world. In this latter book—Wolfer's first published novel—sixteen-year-old Melody forgets about her own adolescent problems when a dolphin that shares the teen's favorite swimming spot becomes injured in a fisherman's net, with tragic results. Noting that Wolfer has "done her dolphin research," Sharon Rawlins noted in a *School Library Journal* review of *Dolphin Song* that the author "clearly sympathizes" with her finned protagonists. On a more humorous note, *Horse-Mad* presents younger readers with an interesting predicament as an eight-year-old horse named Bay wakes up one morning to find that she has been transformed from a sleek, swift, and graceful horse into a gangly, hairless (and tail-less), human child.

"I feel very lucky to be able to live in a beautiful area on the southwest coast of Western Australia," Wolfer once told *SATA*. "My home is surrounded by bushland, and it's a short drive to the dramatic beaches of the Southern Ocean. Parrots, wrens, and lorikeets feed outside my window, and if I'm up early I see kangaroos nibbling on my neighbor's lawn (our lively dog hasn't learned to ignore them yet!). In spring, the bush shows off its wild flowers and whales calve in the bays offshore.

"As you may have guessed, the environment and unique beauty of the corner of Australia in which I live play an important part in my writing. I am interested in the conflicts that occur when humans meet nature, so my books have environmental undercurrents and themes. Friendship and the bonds between characters are also of great importance to me as a writer.

"I love traveling and have lived in several countries (Thailand, Nepal, and Japan). My family and friends are scattered around the world, and I hope that, through my writing, I can foster an interest in other countries and cultures." Wolfer's novel *Border Line* is inspired by this interest in contrasting cultures; its story of a teen uprooted from friends, home, and school due to a parent's job relocation is set in both urban Australia and a remote area of the country called the Nullarbor where people—let alone people her age with whom she can be friends—are rare.

"The things I like most about writing as a profession are that I can work my own hours and that I am able to go to schools and other communities to meet interesting

When her family moves to a remote area of Australia, Cassie thinks her life is over until some new friends and a new attitude turn things around in Wolfer's 1998 novel. (Cover design by Marion Duke.)

people," Wolfer also told *SATA*. In addition to writing, she teaches vocational English at a local agricultural school, where, as Wolfer remarked on her Web site, her students teach her "a lot about cattle, sheep and engines." In 2002 she walked the Kokoda Track through Papua New Guinea, a trip that inspired *Village Trek,* her well-received World War II-based picture book *Photographs in the Mud,* and a young-adult manuscript titled *Shadows Walking.*

Biographical and Critical Sources

PERIODICALS

Australian Book Review, June, 1995, p. 62.
Magpies, July, 2001, review of *Choices,* p. 42; May, 2005, review of *Photographs in the Mud,* p. 38; September, 2005, Russ Merrin, review of *Horse-Mad,* p. 39.

ONLINE

Dianne Wolfer Home Page, http://www.members.wetnet. com.au/dianne (September 27, 2005).

Illustrations Index

(In the following index, the number of the *volume* in which an illustrator's work appears is given *before* the colon, and the *page number* on which it appears is given *after* the colon. For example, a drawing by Adams, Adrienne appears in Volume 2 on page 6, another drawing by her appears in Volume 3 on page 80, another drawing in Volume 8 on page 1, and so on and so on. . . .)

YABC

Index references to *YABC* refer to listings appearing in the two-volume *Yesterday's Authors of Books for Children,* also published by Thomson Gale. *YABC* covers prominent authors and illustrators who died prior to 1960.

M

Author Index

The following index gives the number of the volume in which an author's biographical sketch, Autobiography Feature, Brief Entry, or Obituary appears.

This index includes references to all entries in the following series, which are also published by The Gale Group.

YABC—*Yesterday's Authors of Books for Children: Facts and Pictures about Authors and Illustrators of Books for Young People from Early Times to 1960*

CLR—*Children's Literature Review: Excerpts from Reviews, Criticism, and Commentary on Books for Children*

SAAS—*Something about the Author Autobiography Series*

Author Index